D1200258

The Cost
of Good Intentions

HJ
9289
.N4
M67
1980

The Cost

of Good Intentions

NEW YORK CITY AND

THE LIBERAL EXPERIMENT, 1960–1975

Charles R. Morris

W · W · NORTON & COMPANY

NEW YORK · LONDON

WITHDRAWN

3 l0110

Tennessee Tech. Library
Cookeville, Tenn.

Copyright © 1980 by Charles R. Morris. *All rights reserved*. Published simultaneously in Canada by George J. McLeod Limited, Toronto. Printed in the United States of America.

THE TEXT OF THIS BOOK *is composed in photocomposition Caledonia. Display type is Palatino. Composition and manufacturing by the Maple-Vail Book Manufacturing Group. Book design by Marjorie J. Flock.*

W. W. Norton & Company Inc. 500 Fifth Avenue New York N.Y. 10110
W. W. Norton & Company Ltd. 25 New Street Square London EC4A 3NT

Library of Congress Cataloging in Publication Data
Morris, Charles R
    The cost of good intentions.
    Includes bibliographical references and index.
    1. Finance, Public—New York (City)   2. Default
(Finance)—New York (City)   3. New York (City)—
Politics and government.   I. Title.
HJ9289.N4M67   1980   336.747'1   80–12989

ISBN 0–393–01339–1

2 3 4 5 6 7 8 9 0

TO BEVERLY

Contents

Acknowledgments

I SHOULD DECLARE my interest at the outset. I was employed by New York City from 1969 to 1973, first to expedite capital construction programs, then as an assistant budget director, and finally as director of the city's welfare and Medicaid programs. I was therefore peripherally involved in a number, but by no means most, of the events described in this book and was centrally involved in a few. But the book is in no way a memoir, nor is it intended as an apologia or as an exposé. It is simply my best attempt to reconstruct as objectively as I can what actually happened, and why. All of the factual data can be found in official records or other standard sources, and people who are quoted directly were aware that they were speaking for attribution.

The research and writing was made possible by a grant from the Ford Foundation, and Mike Sviridoff and Lou Winnick at the foundation provided encouragement and advice at every stage of the project. Jon Weiner and Peter Goldmark read all of the manuscript, often in successive drafts, and each provided literally hundreds of suggestions involving every chapter. Mary Schoonmaker gave me the original idea for writing the book, helped formulate the first outline, and provided useful material on finance and labor. Steve Isenberg was a friendly critic throughout. Ray Horton read drafts of several chapters and pointed me toward key research material. Mary McCormick read a late draft and spotted most of the passages where my rhetoric outran my data. Warren Moscow was a valuable source on the Wagner era and provided detailed criticisms of the first half of the book. Joan Leiman shared her research on the city's Medicaid program, and Diana Murray provided a number of insights into city health and antipoverty programs. District Council 37 gave me free run of their research library, and John Guertin and Sol Collangelo of the city's Office of Labor Relations were extremely generous with their time and their files. The municipal reference librarians never failed to impress me with their knowledge of city government source material. All of the many people I interviewed, most of whom are acknowledged in the text, were courteous and patient with my questions. Rosemary Johnston typed the manuscript. My wife Beverly and my three children, Michael, Kathleen, and Matthew, provided the extra measure of affection, tolerance, and support I needed to complete the project. Needless to say, responsibility for errors and misinterpretations is my own.

C.R.M.

Introduction

NEW YORK CITY'S government ran out of money in April of 1975. There was simply not enough cash in the city treasury to pay the bills that were falling due. The immediate source of the problem was the city's practice of borrowing short-term to pay current operating expenses. When the short-term loans fell due, usually in three or six months, the city would borrow again to pay them off. A large number of loans fell due that April, and the banks announced that, for a variety of reasons, they would no longer renew them.

The underlying problems, of course, were more basic than access to financial markets. The loans had been necessary because, over a number of years, the city's current expenses had grown to the point where they far exceeded the revenues the city received from local taxes and federal and state aid. Because city taxes had already been raised to the point where they were higher than almost anyplace else in the country—and there were no immediate prospects for significant increases in outside aid—there seemed little possibility of both paying off the loans and maintaining normal operations. If the crisis had not come in April 1975, it would have come later, and probably not very much later.

New York State eventually came to the aid of the city with loans and advances that enabled operations to continue and creditors to be paid, although for a period holders of some short-term notes were forced to delay collection of their principal. The Municipal Assistance Corporation was created to stretch out the city's short-term loans, which had risen to such levels—more than $6 billion—that there was no reasonable prospect of their being paid off. Later, a state-controlled Emergency Financial Control Board was placed in effective receivership over the city's budget and spending decisions. The city itself undertook major retrenchments, laying off tens of thousands of employees—welfare workers and policemen, teachers and sanitationmen, university professors, nurses, firemen, and building inspectors. After much hesitation the federal government provided loans, and then loan guarantees, and somber officials set about trying to discover how—or whether—the city could be restored to financial health.

The crisis itself was no small event. For a while, when bankruptcy or default appeared likely, experts believed that a financial collapse in New York City would lead to a similar collapse of New York State's credit, whose pattern of borrowing was inextricably linked to that of its leading cities. Two collapses of such magnitude could, plausibly, threaten the stability of United States financial markets and touch off a major credit contraction. Banks with assets heavily tied up in New York securities suddenly appeared to be dangerously extended. Rates on state and local borrowing rose throughout the country, and market access became more difficult even for local authorities in England. Financial analysts began to re-examine the generally easier arrangements for local borrowing that had sprung into existence since the 1950s.

Because the financial crisis was such a spectacular event and received such spectacular coverage in the national media, it tended to obscure to a degree how deep-seated were the problems that had brought the city to such a state of ignominy. City administrators could have avoided their confrontation with the bankers if they had cut back on spending several years earlier instead of borrowing; and the cumulative savings from the cutbacks would have made the reductions somewhat less severe than those imposed from the outside. But the citizens still would have been in very much the same position as they were after the crisis—with less fire and police protection than they probably needed, decaying schools and parks, a university system in decline, and insufficient capacity for rebuilding their arterial streets, rusting bridges, the inadequately maintained subway system, or the ancient water and sewer systems. The decline would have been less cataclysmic, but perhaps no less dispiriting.

Explanations abound for the straits in which the city found itself. Most center on the incompetence of local elected politicians or their recklessness in pursuit of votes, the greed of the municipal unions, and the willingness of the citizenry to vote, year after year, for the officials who promised most resoundingly to turn New York into an island of Swedish-style socialism. Daniel Patrick Moynihan provides perhaps the simplest of all simple explanations: "By 1974, per capita debt in New York City was $1,767, while in Chicago it was $427. Most any working man can pay off $427. Few can swing $1,767. And that is really all there is to say on the subject."

But precepts—avoid debt and evil mayors—are not explanations. What requires untangling is how the long-term trends affecting the city combined with the policies of consecutive city administrations to produce the final debacle. The fifteen years that preceded the fiscal crisis were ones of remarkable upheaval after a long period of relative stability. The city was tossed by forces of such magnitude—racial shifts, an aggressive civil rights movement, a revolution in citizens' expectations, newly muscular unions, a collapse of basic managerial capacity, steep and seemingly permanent economic recession—that to speak of a crisis seems almost anticlimactic. Buffeted by change, local elected officials lost control. The fiscal crisis is in fact more a symptom and a symbol of the loss of control than a separate event requiring separate explanations.

None of the three mayors who served during the period—Robert Wagner, John Lindsay, and Abraham Beame—was by himself responsible for the city's difficulties; but the perceptions and misperceptions of each helped to shape the eventual contours of the crisis. The loss of control was the cumulative result of outside forces and local policies, of the interplay between problem definitions, policymaking, and outcomes in the real world.

This book is an attempt to sort out some of the underlying trends and key policy decisions that influenced the course of events. In particular, to trace how problem perceptions, or what administrators *thought* was happening to the city, affected what actually did happen, and roughly how much effect they had. The period covered is approximately 1960 to 1975, coinciding, that is, with the end of Wagner's three terms as mayor (1954–65), Lindsay's two terms (1966–73), and the beginning of the Beame administration (1974–77). The greater part of the book focuses on the Lindsay administration. He was mayor for more than half of the period in question; more so than Wagner, and in marked contrast with Beame, he attempted to be a spokesman—indeed almost a national rallying point—for new approaches to urban government. It was also during his two terms that the impact of the civil rights movement and the new power of the unions were most forcefully apparent and the city began its ten-year-long slide into economic recession.

I. *Wagner and Lindsay*

N O TWO MEN better symbolize the changes that took place in urban politics during the 1960s than Robert F. Wagner and John V. Lindsay.
Wagner, mayor from 1954 through 1965, thirty years in city politics,
proud of his identification with "the little schnook" who paid the taxes, feature-
less face, rasping accent, bumbling appearance. Lindsay, six-foot-four, blonde,
chiselled good looks, St. Paul's and Yale, precise diction, confident bearing,
and a national reputation as the brightest of a bright group of young Republican
congressmen who were actively struggling to reorient their party toward liberal
and progressive politics.

Urban politics had long been seen as a dull business, vaguely disreputable,
the refuge of small-time politicians and gray bureaucrats, of little interest outside a small circle of aficionados—the good-government reformers, the City
Hall reporters, and the blackbird flock of lawyers, insurance brokers, contractors, and real estate men who survived from the political table. People with a
competitive edge went into advertising or tested their mettle by climbing corporate ladders; truly intelligent people thought about foreign affairs, international development, balances of global military power; idealistic young people
joined the Peace Corps. But the 1960s brought a growing sense of unease
over the sterile suburbs and mounting pollution that accompanied American
success; and when the civil rights movement came North and uncovered the
plight of the black poor in declining cities, the "urban crisis" moved to the fore
of the country's political agenda. Hand-in-hand with the discovery of cities'
problems was a rediscovery of their attractions. Writers like Jane Jacobs taught
that cities were places of variety and excitement, that the polyglot stew of the
Upper West Side or Greenwich Village in New York offered possibilities for
personal expansion and human contact that were missing in the monochromatic
tract developments that were blanketing the megalopolis.

ROBERT WAGNER

If John Lindsay personified the dashing new spirit that was striding to take up the urban challenge, Robert Wagner typified for many New Yorkers just what was wrong. With American politics changing at a dazzling and, to some, alarming pace, Wagner remained firmly entrenched in the old political methods. While massive population movements and a revolution in expectations presented urban government with epochal challenges, Wagner seemed to offer only committees and bromides. In an age when the political style was set by the Kennedys—vigorous, youthful, morally impelled—Wagner looked liver-spotted, like Eisenhower.

For all his lack of excitement, Wagner was certainly among the more competent of New York's mayors. He was no Fiorello La Guardia, to be sure, but he brought a level of ability and personal honesty to the office that had been conspicuously absent during much of the city's history. Son of a famous senator, he was fed on politics from birth. As a small boy he was allowed to stay up on Sunday nights, when Al Smith would drop in to play low-stake poker and talk politics. After finishing Yale Law School, he was awarded a safe state assembly seat in his home district in Manhattan, and after military service he was successively appointed tax commissioner, commissioner of housing and buildings, and chairman of the City Planning Commission. In 1949 he was elected borough president of Manhattan, where he distinguished himself with a scandal-free administration, some imaginative ideas on housing, and good relations with the new Puerto Rican community.

After an unsuccessful try at the nomination for U.S. Senator in 1952, Wagner won the backing of Tammany (Manhattan's Democratic clubhouse) for the mayoral race the following year and easily unseated the somnolent incumbent, Vincent Impellitteri. His first-term record could fairly be termed distinguished. The state's Mitchell-Lama housing program, which produced tens of thousands of middle-income housing units throughout New York, was designed in his office. He had a good record on air and water pollution control, passed a much upgraded housing code, and was an effective national advocate for cities. Wagner won his party's senatorial nomination in 1956 but was defeated by Jacob Javits in the general election. Recovering quickly, he returned home to win a second term as mayor with a 928,000 vote margin, adding the support of most of the city's good-government groups to his organization base.

But by the end of his second term, Wagner and his administration were looking tired. According to *The New York Times*, things had "run badly downhill." There were "long periods of drifting inaction, broken only by occasional bursts of activity." One by one, scandals had bloomed, involving building inspections, fire inspections, purchasing, parking meter contracts, and maintenance and construction in schools. Wagner's attempts to isolate himself from responsibility for the scandals merely underscored his image as a do-nothing mayor. He lost the backing of the organization, and by the early winter of 1961, Tammany boss Carmine DeSapio was taking no pains to conceal his search for a new candidate.

It was both easy and dangerous to underestimate Wagner's resilience. With what a long-time aide called his "delicate sense of self-protection," Wagner had for some time been taking quiet soundings of the reform wing of the party, led by Herbert Lehman and Eleanor Roosevelt, who were anxious to back a strong candidate against the machine. In the summer of 1961, he went on the attack, suddenly accusing DeSapio of trying to dictate to his administration and leading an organized ring of "secret corruption." DeSapio hit back with rumors that Wagner had taken a free trip to Europe and had refused to answer questions before the state commission on investigation. Brooklyn leader John Sharkey scored Wagner's "ineptness, indecision, his total inability to cope with the job as Mayor." Overwhelmingly, all five Democratic borough organizations endorsed Arthur Levitt, the state comptroller, as the next candidate for mayor.

To attack the machine, Wagner, in the space of a few months, created a machine of his own, becoming possibly the first mayor in the country to organize the bureaucracy as a political force. One by one, the civil service association and the major unions—the transit workers, the firemen, Harry Van Arsdale's electrical workers—lined up in support. Paul Screvane, a former garbage truck driver who had risen to become a martinet sanitation commissioner, was Wagner's choice for city council president. Abraham Beame, budget director and assistant budget director since 1946, was chosen to run for comptroller. The fire commissioner, Edward F. Cavanaugh, resigned to manage Wagner's campaign.

In the primary election, Wagner virtually ran the organization out of the city. Sweeping almost every district in every borough, he became the unchallenged leader of the party in New York City. With strong support from the Kennedy White House, who were anxious to modernize the party in New York, he won the general election by a comfortable margin; assured of control over federal patronage, he became the de facto leader of the state Democrats as well. Within a year, the state party chairman and all of the county leaders in New York City, except the redoubtable Charles Buckley in the Bronx, had been replaced by Wagner men.

The solid achievement that attracted the reform groups was Wagner's record in housing, always his major interest as mayor. His dream had been to make New York a "slumless city," and until events caught up with him, he seemed well on the way toward reaching his goal. The years from 1950 to 1965 saw a dramatic improvement in the city's housing stock. There had been virtually no housing construction in the private sector during the Depression, and the war effort had pre-empted private investment until late in the 1940s. The last census before Wagner took office showed that the city had its most severe housing shortage on record. The overall vacancy rate was less than 1 percent, and almost 140,000 poor black and Puerto Rican households were crammed into single-room-occupancy units, many of which were badly deteriorating. By his last year in office, the total stock of housing units had increased by almost 18 percent. The proportion of overcrowded units—more than one person to a room—had been cut in half, the number of blacks and Puerto Ricans in single-room housing had been reduced to less than 100,000, despite the rapid increase of the poor black and Puerto Rican population. Substandard units declined by almost a third, and by 1965 made up only 8 percent of renter-occupied units.

The reduction in substandard housing was to a substantial degree the work of clearance. With Robert Moses chairing the mayor's Slum Clearance Committee, New York consistently encumbered more than half the nation's urban renewal funds. Moses's bulldozer approach was later much criticized, but the aggressive clearing away of ancient tenements was a prerequisite to massive new construction. Overall, his completed projects produced more housing than they destroyed—and, of course, all of it was standard. Public housing, constructed with federal assistance for low-income families, was built at a rate of more than 5,500 units per year during the entire twelve years that Wagner was in office. The state and city Mitchell-Lama program, which provided subsidized mortgage financing to build apartments for middle-income tenants, produced more than 7,700 units a year after it got off the ground in 1958. In all, during Wagner's three terms, the public sector added 130,687 new housing units to the city's stock. From 1958 through 1965 public housing and publicly aided construction accounted for almost 40 percent of new units completed, despite boom years for the private builders. By way of comparison, during John Lindsay's first administration, public housing construction fell to an annual rate less than half of Wagner's average, and publicly aided units were at a consistently lower level until the creation of the state's Urban Development Corporation and the rebuilding of the city's Mitchell-Lama capacity during Lindsay's second term. And the city did more than build housing. Again with Moses serving as city construction coordinator and providing much of the driving force, the record of city construction during Wagner's administration was excellent. He built more than 300 new schools; there were literally hundreds of new playgrounds, libraries, and community facilities; five new hospitals were opened; and thousands of acres were added to the city parks.

Wagner was a shrewd judge of staff men, and he got consistently superior work from high-quality people. Warren Moscow recalls being advised, as he was about to start working for Wagner, "This guy is going to use you and me exactly as he needs us, and he will always be the Mayor." A friend recalled: "He not only knew what a man wanted, but how much he wanted it." He had an excellent record in labor relations, instituting modern labor relations machinery but keeping fairly tight control over labor cost increases. His successful personal intervention in a bitter newspaper strike in 1962–63 demonstrated his skills as a mediator. His social conscience was of a high order, in the direct line of his father and Al Smith and the finest traditions of the state's Democratic party.

But Wagner's virtues had their obverse side, and if his talents loomed large, they were often overshadowed by his defects. The splendidly subtle political instincts could appear merely Machiavellian, the ability to await the precise tactical moment easily turned to indolence, the urge to compromise could become doubletalk.

Wagner's inability to face up to Robert Moses was legendary. Upon taking office as mayor, Wagner had let it be known that he would not reappoint Moses to the City Planning Commission: His positions as construction coordinator and parks commissioner—in addition to all his other jobs—were enough. When swearing-in day arrived, Moses, enraged at any diminution of his powers, stalked into Wagner's office with a filled-out appointment sheet in his hand, and Wagner meekly signed it. Again, during his first campaign Wagner had promised the citizens of East Tremont in the Bronx that he would fight for a route change in Moses's plan for the Cross Bronx Expressway that would spare their homes; yet, faced with Moses's implacable insistence that the route proceed *his* way, Wagner quietly gave in, although a whole neighborhood was destroyed in consequence. When citizen groups opposed to the construction of the Lower Manhattan Expressway deluged City Hall with complaints, Wagner gave them written assurances that the highway would be dropped; but with Moses pushing hard, the highway stayed on the official map, and the weight of the city administration stayed clearly behind the road until John Lindsay finally killed the proposal. The most humiliating episode involved Moses's insistence on forcing Joseph Papp's New York Shakespeare Festival out of Central Park. When Wagner tried to intervene, Moses simply refused to return his telephone calls. Daily, the newspapers headlined the mayor's attempts to talk to his parks commissioner. Moses even talked to the press about his refusal to talk to the mayor. Finally, Wagner had lunch with Moses and agreed that things would be done Moses's way—although the theatre eventually won the right to stay through the courts.

Moses wasn't the only strong commissioner whom Wagner had difficulty in facing down. Stephen Kennedy, police commissioner from 1955 to 1960, was a martinet who, to his credit, went after corruption and inefficiency in the force with a will and flair that was not seen again until Patrick Murphy a dozen years later. On the other hand, Kennedy could sometimes seem paranoid, listening to his men's radios to ensure that they said nothing critical about him, carrying out shakeups of the force—almost capriciously, it sometimes appeared—all of which contributed mightily to the radicalization of the Patrolmen's Benevolent Association (PBA). After Wagner had signed his executive order announcing the right of collective bargaining for all city employees, Kennedy announced that it would not apply to the police and that he would refuse to recognize or treat with an organization that behaved like a union. Wagner squirmed uncomfortably over his commissioner's stance but would not overrule him. Finally, Kennedy resigned, in the wake of a work slowdown engineered by the newly militant PBA, and with visible relief Wagner appointed Michael Murphy who immediately set about bringing the police into the city's normal labor-management procedures.

Although his own honesty was above doubt, his aggressiveness in pursuing scandals was sometimes questioned. When it was revealed that an urban renewal developer on the West Side of Manhattan was systematically milking the project for profits and giving the city nothing in return, Wagner steadfastly refused to take action (in part, because it would have involved dealing with Moses and his Slum Clearance Committee) and finally admitted to an incredulous press that he had been "misled" for five years. Despite highly publicized allegations of corruption in the maintenance of the city's *in rem* buildings (buildings that the city had foreclosed for non-payment of taxes), Wagner took no action for two years until a state investigation led to indictments of the principals. Similarly, his follow-up on corruption in purchasing, parking meter maintenance, and school construction always seemed slow, leaving him open to charges—as often as not with political motivation—that he failed to provide moral leadership.

Then, in his last years in office, Wagner lost the support of an increasingly aggressive black leadership. The attacks on Wagner from the civil rights leadership, and the Congress of Racial Equality (CORE) in particular, were unfair. Wagner had always been interested in the problems of the poor and the minorities. The migration of poor blacks and Puerto Ricans to New York City peaked in the 1950s, and early 1960s, and he tried valiantly to redirect city services. Federal juvenile delinquency money was tapped to provide summer jobs for young people from the slums. Money was found to pay for the Higher Horizons program for disadvantaged pupils—extra teachers, audio-visual aids, and bilingual or Spanish-language instruction. Finally, when Robert Moses relinquished his city posts to build the World's Fair, Wagner reorganized the city's housing programs and attempted to structure major renewal on Manhattan's West Side in the new liberal mode—with emphasis on relocation, rehabilitation, community participation, and small-scale projects. In 1964, anticipating the national government, Wagner created the city's Attack on Poverty, under the direction of a coordinating council headed by Paul Screvane and involving all the city's key department heads. With $15 million in flexible appropriation, its major task was to coordinate the city's welfare, housing, educational, and job programs for the benefit of the poor.

But there was no possible way that Wagner's good intentions could have kept pace with the temper of the new generation of black spokesmen. By 1964 the civil rights movement had reached its zenith in the South and was turning its energies and its anger toward the Northern cities. The new black leaders had been beaten, jailed, and shot at in the Mississippi delta and the hill country of Alabama; they had seen some of their comrades die in the struggle, and they were in no mood for gradual transition. They wanted control over their own programs, and they wanted it right away.

The alternative seemed to be civil disorder. Family structure and traditional authority broke down under the pressures of ghetto life, and a generation of uncontrolled children was spreading predation and terror through the city's streets. Protests slipped easily into riots. Looting and burning broke out in Harlem and Corona in 1963, and the following summer, after a black youth was killed by an off-duty police officer, protest rallies converged on police precincts in black areas throughout the city. When crowds threw Molotov cocktails, the police returned gunfire, and rioting broke out in Bedford-Stuyvesant and central Harlem. One person was killed, hundreds were injured, and after thousands of police had restored an uneasy order, the prospect of imminent violence hung over the city for weeks. Civil rights leaders descended on New York from all over the country—Martin Luther King, James Farmer, Stokely Carmichael. They were quick to draw a moral from the disorders: Without fundamental change in the city's dealing with its poor, there would be more riots.

Police brutality became a rallying issue, and dark rumors circulated of men and women being held incommunicado for hours, of prisoners who had died from police beatings, of increasingly unrestrained violence in containing demonstrations. The police commissioner was dubbed "Bull" Murphy. The anger increased when police internal review procedures found the officer whose shooting had touched off the 1964 rioting innocent of any wrongdoing. In May 1965 a City Council subcommittee called for outside review of police actions, and on the following day Murphy resigned, to the evident jubilation of blacks and Puerto Ricans. Wagner replaced him with Assistant U.S. Attorney Vincent Broderick, who announced a series of measures to improve the department's handling of internal complaints and to upgrade police human relations training but refused to cede on the issue of outside review.

During the same months Wagner's antipoverty programs became almost as controversial. The new Economic Opportunity Act required "maximum feasible participation" by the poor, and when the city applied for federal funds, the director of the Office of Economic Opportunity, Sargent Shriver, said that the poor would have to have a greater role on the city's administrative boards. CORE denounced Wagner's plans as an example of his disregard for the aspirations of blacks. Republican Senator Jacob Javits pronounced the city plan a "travesty," and in the House of Representatives, Adam Clayton Powell, Jr. of Harlem threatened to hold up funding for the entire national program unless Shriver took effective steps to guarantee that New York's poor would share the power (or that their representatives would—which, in Harlem meant Adam Clayton Powell, Jr.). An agreement was finally worked out, but there was no longer any way that Wagner could satisfy the militants. CORE had already announced "open war" against the mayor in his bid for a fourth term. James Farmer, CORE's leader, struck at his "complete apathy . . . and complete disregard for the problems of the Negro and Puerto Rican communities and the major problems of the City."

There seemed to be little doubt that Wagner had lost control of events. Throughout 1965 the *Herald-Tribune* ran an award-winning series, "City in Crisis," documenting the city's sad estate. Despite all Wagner's efforts in public housing, waiting lists were ten years long, with 660,000 people in need of apartments. The schools were "torn by overcrowding and sub-standard teaching," a "political football for the Mayor, the Board of Education, the civil rights leaders and the racists." There were 70,000 young people "roaming the streets, out of work and out of school," while the city's antipoverty effort, according to Bayard Rustin, was "just a cap pistol." As strikes like that of the welfare workers grew more critical every day, the paper charged that the mayor spent his time "wheeling and dealing for political control of a State legislature more than 100 miles away." The mayor's proudest achievements in urban renewal were just a cover, one article maintained, for "Negro or human removal, the shifting of a minority group from one slum to another." Despite spending more than $2 billion on housing and slum clearance, "the slums continue to spread, the ghettos remain, and there is a critical shortage of low- and middle-income housing."

Critics hammered at Wagner's indecisiveness, his inability to inspire action. Kenneth Clark said, "It's not corruption that is killing this City. New York is dying from creeping dry rot, steadily increasing blight, and a total lack of leadership. Time is running out for this City." Dick Schaap, a columnist for the *Herald-Tribune* wrote: " [Wagner is] nothing more than a neighborhood politician . . . His vision ends at the wall of a political clubhouse . . . he is the Mayor of New York City and he belongs in Newark." John Lindsay advised that "New York has lost its willpower." *Fortune* magazine observed: "The truth is that serious-minded voters have given up all hope of having responsive, efficient City government."

The final disgrace came that spring, when Wagner announced that after years of fiscal legerdemain, he couldn't balance the budget. One thousand police had just been added to the Transit Authority to stop a wave of muggings and robberies, and another five hundred had been promised to fight crime in the streets. Welfare rolls were rising by nine thousand persons a month; there was heavy enrollment pressure in the schools; the antipoverty programs were expensive. The city's traditional sources of revenue, heavily dependent on the real estate tax, just weren't growing fast enough to keep up with the demands.

With admirable straightforwardness, Wagner announced that he would borrow to make up the deficit. "A bad loan is better than a good tax," he pronounced, and "human needs are greater than budgetary needs." In the hope that a future referendum would allow the city to increase its ceiling on real estate taxes, he proposed to sell bonds worth $256 million to finance current expenses. The bonds could be paid off after the real estate levy was allowed to rise.

If the poor were unimpressed by Wagner's financial exertions on their behalf, the financial community was shocked. The Citizens' Budget Commission attacked Wagner for "incredible fiscal mismanagement." Abraham Beame, who had broken politically with Wagner, denounced the scheme harshly—particularly when it became clear that the borrowing would cut into the city's capacity to undertake public construction.

Although Wagner's re-election to a fourth term had been deemed a near-certainty only the year before, by the spring of 1965, private polls showed that his support throughout the city was slipping badly and that he would almost certainly lose in an election contest against a strong candidate. In May he announced that he would not seek another term, citing his wife's recent death and his desire to spend more time with his sons.

THE AGENDA CHANGES

As Robert Wagner prepared to leave office, with problems of housing, relocation, poverty, racial polarization, and finance breaking around his head like angry waves, an influential body of opinion within the city was ready to lay the blame for New York's sudden, and all too obvious, decline squarely at his feet. There was a new rationalist style in government, one that imbued the Kennedy White House and suffused Lyndon Johnson's drives against poverty and inequality; it was premised on a confident optimism that the most intractable problems would give way before the resolute assault of intelligent, committed people. If New York's problems were growing worse, the explanation must lie in the mayor's lack of resoluteness and commitment.

What had really happened was that the problems Wagner had been trying to solve had shifted beneath his feet. He was cut in the mold of the best of the 1950s mayors—committed to housing improvement and physical renewal. It was a strategy that started from the assumption of a more or less static population, and it made eminent good sense when he took office. After the city's population stabilized in the 1920s, New York had settled into a pattern of an integrated, predominantly white, working-class city with a high standard of living and generous municipal services supported by its central position in the Northeast's booming industrial base. Because public investment had been choked off by the Great Depression and World War II, the city faced, in the immediate postwar period, a massive deficit in capital facilities. It needed better schools and hospitals, standard housing, libraries, and solutions to the growing problem of traffic congestion. The public housing projects, for all their megalithic weight and lack of architectural amenity, were eminently successful, filling rapidly with upwardly mobile working-class families, anxious to escape the squalid conditions of the ancient tenements. The city's only problem was how to build new units fast enough. No one anticipated that in little more than a decade the high-rise projects would be viewed as the height of urban folly, immense vertical slums, depersonalizing and alienating, seedbeds of crime and pathology. The time was long gone by 1965, when newspapers hailed a project like the Mid-Manhattan Expressway as "big men getting together to make a big decision for the common good." Now when people thought about physical renewal, they worried about relocation—and particularly the relocation of blacks and Puerto Ricans. New school buildings mattered less than integration. More important, there was no longer the confidence that providing schools and teachers ensured a decent education. Virtually all the failures ascribed to the administration by the *Herald-Tribune*'s "City in Crisis" series were failures to achieve personal integration of blacks and Puerto Ricans into the city's life. If welfare rolls were soaring and seventy thousand young people had dropped out of school and were making New York City a dangerous and uncomfortable place, by implication it was the city's fault: If the administration possessed the will and the vision, it would do something about it. These were clearly not the problems that Robert Wagner had been trained to solve, or the problems he had thought he was supposed to be solving when he became mayor. Significantly, by 1965 he seemed prepared to admit that they were the ones he should have been working on but that he didn't quite know what to do.

ENTER LINDSAY

The essence of John Lindsay's promise was that he would bring almost total change. Son of a well-to-do, if not immensely rich, New York banker, he had attended the best private schools, crewed at prep school and college, served as a naval officer in World War II, graduated from Yale Law School, and become a partner in one of the city's prestigious Wall Street law firms. He entered politics against the advice of his father but with the enthusiastic participation of his wife Mary. Their first political experience in New York City was in 1949, campaigning for Wagner's unsuccessful Republican opponent in the election for borough president of Manhattan. In 1952 Lindsay became president of the Manhattan Young Republicans, and he joined its executive board the following year. In 1956 he left his law firm to become executive assistant to U.S. Attorney General Herbert Brownell. He returned home in 1958 to challenge a stodgy Republican incumbent in the 17th Congressional District, called the "silk stocking" district after its fashionable East Side constituency, although it included most of central Manhattan and parts of Greenwich Village and Spanish Harlem.

The regular Republicans came up with an attractive younger candidate to oppose Lindsay, but Lindsay ran a saturation, whirlwind campaign masterminded by another young lawyer, Robert Price, who, like Lindsay, had chafed at the cold hand the party elders kept on Republican affairs in the city. More than five hundred volunteers canvassed house-by-house throughout the summer, and—with almost twice the normal voter turnout—the insurgent Lindsay carried the primary by a comfortable margin. *The New York Times* called him "one of the bright hopes of the Republican Party," and after a victory in the general election, he was labeled a future presidential possibility.

In Congress Lindsay gained national attention, if not the favor of the Republican leaders. As a civil libertarian his record was outstanding; on more than one occasion, his was the only voice in Congress raised against potential legislative encroachments on individual liberties. His maiden speech in Congress was to challenge a venerable Midwestern Republican for attacking the Supreme Court. That same year he testified against, and helped defeat, an Eisenhower administration bill that would have broadened the authority of the State Department to refuse passports. Later, he was the only congressman to speak and vote against a bill widening the post office's powers to seize obscene materials, and he valiantly engaged in a series of battles—usually on the losing side—with the formidable chairman of the House Un-American Activities Committee, Francis Walter. He still managed to pay careful attention to his home constituents and was re-elected with ever-increasing margins: In 1964 he was returned with more than 71 percent of the vote.

The high point of Lindsay's legislative career may have been his role as drafter and floor manager of key sections of the 1964 Civil Rights Act. The praise he received for the bill's passage was deserved, and at least one national magazine that year named him as a probable Republican presidential nominee in the not-too-distant future.

But for all his success, Lindsay was growing increasingly frustrated in Congress. His persistence in voting the Democratic position on spending bills, for example, and his break with the Republican leadership on the crucial issue of expanding the membership of the House Rules Committee, virtually guaranteed that his congressional prospects were limited. Doing battle with the hierarchy won headlines but not the choice committee assignments. By 1964 Lindsay was resigned to the fact that his most cherished congressional goal, appointment to the Foreign Affairs Committee, was not to be his. Outside of the House there were few opportunities for political advancement: Nelson Rockefeller seemed certain to run for New York State governor again when his term expired in 1966; Jacob Javits was a fixture in one Senate seat, and Robert Kennedy had just won the other. The only opportunity, if opportunity it was, would be a race for mayor. Republicans had not seriously challenged a Democrat for the mayoralty since La Guardia, and he was technically a Fusion candidate. But Wagner was looking increasingly vulnerable as 1965 opened. If he ran as expected, there would almost certainly be a split in the Democratic ranks, and the right candidate—a new face and a strong campaigner—might be able to edge in.

From Lindsay's point of view, he had to consider the ominous fact that no mayor of New York had ever gone on to higher office. The job seemed too grinding, too tarnishing, and the sheer weight of detail too inevitably belittling. On the other hand, New York City and other large central cities were being thrust onto centerstage as never before. "The cities are where the action is," said Daniel Patrick Moynihan. The federal government had passed all the bills it could pass; the local scene was where they would have to be implemented. Walter Lippmann agreed: If New York City could not be made to function effectively, there was little hope for the Great Society.

Under pressure from New York's Republican governor, Nelson Rockefeller, Lindsay circled cautiously around the mayoral prospect early in 1965. At first, he withdrew his name after Rockefeller refused to guarantee an uncontested nomination and adequate financing, but he wavered under heavy pressure from the national Republican party. Finally, he agreed to run, announcing that he had been "troubled" by the city's decline since his original decision to withdraw. The Republicans were jubilant. Rockefeller, Javits, and W. N. Thayer, publisher of the *Herald-Tribune*, raised a war chest of $1.25 million, and Lindsay won the official party endorsement by acclamation. Even more crucially, with the strong backing of Liberal Party leader Alec Rose and the president of the International Ladies' Garment Workers Union (ILGWU), David Dubinsky, Lindsay won the Liberals' endorsement, an important source of swing votes with strong ties to the reform wing of the Democrats and a key element in Wagner's 1961 victory.

The campaign was organized by Robert Price, and it was a masterpiece. Self-consciously emulating La Guardia, Lindsay announced he would form a

Fusion ticket, with Timothy Costello, Liberal Party Chairman, as candidate for
city council president and Milton Mollen, a Democrat and Wagner's housing
coordinator, as the candidate for comptroller. Price and his volunteers painfully
constructed computerized voting profiles of each of the city's five thousand
electoral districts, isolating the swing votes and the strategy likely to appeal to
each. Lindsay was indefatigable. With poor name recognition at the start of the
campaign, he campaigned in every assembly district at least once, and in most,
two or three times. Ten thousand volunteers canvassed from more than a
hundred storefronts.

On the Democratic side, Wagner's withdrawal touched off a scramble in the
primary that ended with Abraham Beame eking out a victory over Paul Screvane and inheriting a badly split party. Although he had publicly broken with
Wagner during the previous months, he could neither avoid running on the
mayor's record nor inherit Wagner's popularity. Wagner himself did little to
help out. After having tempered his support of Screvane in the primary, his endorsement of Beame came only late in the campaign, and then it was cold.
Beame's attempt to build on Lyndon Johnson's landslide victory of the previous
year never seemed to get off the ground, and Robert Kennedy's attempts to
help out only drew attention from the colorless candidate. Important segments
of the reform movement—particularly in Greenwich Village—announced that
they would bolt the party in favor of Lindsay. William F. Buckley, the barbed-
tongued, Roman Catholic editor of the *National Review*, entered the race as a
Conservative, with the declared intention of drawing Republicans away from
Lindsay, but his candidacy cut heavily into the working-class Catholic vote, a
natural Beame constituency.

The election itself was one of the closest in the city's history. Lindsay won
by 102,000 votes—less than 44 percent of the electorate. Beame carried all the
traditional Democratic voting blocs—Jews, Irish, Negroes, Puerto Ricans—but
he didn't carry any of them by the necessary majorities. Where Johnson had
carried Harlem by 9:1, Beame took it by only 2:1. The traditional Democratic
majorities of 70 percent and more among Jewish and Irish voters slipped to only
50 to 60 percent. Lindsay's decidedly makeshift combination of traditional
Republicans, Liberals, and reform Democrats was enough to carry the city.

LINDSAY SETS THE TONE

The words used most frequently to describe John Lindsay by the people
who worked closely with him, particularly in his first term in office, are "puritan" and "moralist." There was a combative instinct, a drive to do battle for
right, that had been the consistent thread of his whole congressional career.
Mitchell Ginsberg, his first welfare commissioner, tells how he had been in-
vited to make a speech to the Republican platform committee in 1968:

I had no intention of identifying the presentation with the Mayor, because my views
were known to be somewhat radical. But Bob Sweet [then Deputy Mayor] was urging
me to cancel the presentation. He was afraid it would hurt whatever chances Lindsay
had for the Vice-Presidential nomination. Lindsay came in during the discussion, and

when he found out what it was about, he told me to go ahead and to tell them that I was speaking for him!

A later commissioner says, "I never had any trouble getting him to back me up, or stick his neck out. In fact, the more controversial a position appeared, the more eager he'd seem to support me."

The puritan's vision of the universe as a constant struggle between good and evil infused Lindsay's first months in office. His inaugural address was full of the sounds of combat against "ignorance and bureaucracy," against "the profiteers of poverty," against "greed and prejudice . . . in high places," and most of all, against "the special interests" who flaunted their defiance of the public good. *The New York Times* reported his obvious pleasure in conceiving himself as "a lone figure at war with the power structure." He took particular delight in offending the Wall Street and business interests that had contributed so generously to his campaign. This self-image permeated his early administration. Robert Price seriously considered entitling a speech "Riding Shotgun with John Lindsay on the Urban Frontier." When his programs were in trouble with the legislature, he announced a "fight without compromise." Problems with unions were struggles against "power brokers." Problems involving blacks and Puerto Ricans were framed in moral terms as issues of oppression and exploitation.

If the problems of the city stemmed from a lack of leadership, Lindsay was resolved to lead. He seemed to conceive of the mayor as the personal steward of the city, responsible for every detail of its administration, the one man who carried every burden. He would wake up late in the night and phone police precincts at random to see if there had been any rapes or robberies, taking more than a little pleasure in retelling the shocked reaction of the police operators when they realized that it really was the mayor on the line. He dashed from a dinner party in his evening clothes to be at the scene of a fire—not for publicity he insisted (although there was plenty of that), but to make sure it was being handled correctly. When the first snow fell, he personally helped the sanitation men start shovelling. He picked up litter at Lincoln Center and cleared a lot in the South Bronx. He insisted that top officials take turns manning City Hall at night to deal with any emergencies that might come up. "There are a lot of lonely people in this City," he said, "and this way, they feel someone is watching over them at night."

If Wagner had lacked resoluteness, Lindsay would show that the most difficult problems could be solved by sheer force of will, by physically wrestling them into submission. During the transit strike that started on his first day as Mayor, he insisted on maintaining all-night vigils in his office "to force a settlement." He slept little his entire first month in office, as though the city would slip away from him if he relaxed his control for only a few hours. Particularly during the strike, he delighted in marching the three miles from Gracie Mansion to City Hall, with puffing reporters trailing behind. The physical power of his long strides, the crackling energy, seemed calculated to overawe the flabby bureaucracy that was holding up progress.

As mayor, Wagner had been a mediator among interest groups; Lindsay intended to command. An executive order setting out new hiring procedures, he said, "stands supreme over civil service rules and existing collective bargaining agreements." A complex and politically-sensitive proposal to reorganize trans-portation agencies within the city was sent to the legislature with little advance political preparation. The mayor needed it, he wanted it, it was inconceivable that the legislature wouldn't give it to him. Jay Kriegel, a close aide through both of Lindsay's administrations, said in the first months, "He wants action all the time. If you're in the field, and a decision ought to be made right there, he can get awfully mad if you take the time to check back with City Hall."

One of the most controversial proposals of the administration was for a network of "Little City Halls," storefronts of the variety that had been so suc-cessful in his campaign, where citizens could drop in, make complaints, meet officials, and talk over their concerns, places that would focus on coordinating services, breaking through red tape, and really solving problems. Cynics saw it as a naked ploy to build a political machine by a man who had only weak ties to a formal party structure; but a reasonable judgment is that Lindsay really be-lieved his own rhetoric. He spoke feelingly of the need for communication be-tween the government and the citizens, the need for genuine contact between the mayor and the people at the most personal level: Government was too im-portant to be left to the politicians.

Lindsay's grandiose conception of himself and his powers struck seasoned insiders as fatuous, and certainly arrogant. "There's a lack of humility in the ad-ministration from the top down," said Paul Screvane. Another observer shook his head. "He just doesn't know what he doesn't know." But the role staked out by the mayor was exactly the one that influential segments of the media—par-ticularly, the *Herald-Tribune* and *The New York Times*—had been insisting that he play. The whole thrust of the liberal indictment of Wagner, which was the basis of Lindsay's campaign, was that he was too aware of the limitations of his office. When Wagner adopted the liberal programs, as he did, he seemed not to convey the confidence that they would really work: He didn't seem to share in the rationalist faith that all problems were soluble. Indeed, sometimes the faith felt by the new mayor and his staff was almost pathetic. "If they would only give us time," muttered one aide, after being confronted with an angry crowd of slum-dwellers who wanted jobs and housing now. There was no question that the city would solve the problem, no suspicion that housing and jobs in the slums might be things that the city wasn't very good at providing. It would just take a little time.

Whatever the source of Lindsay's misconceptions, the professionals set out early to cut him down to size. Mike Quill, the leader of the transit workers, was the most openly vitriolic. When Lindsay demanded that transit strikers agree to a settlement and treated Quill as one of the detested "power brokers," Quill mocked him publicly, "He's a pipsqueak! A little boy!" and forced Lindsay to buy a settlement dearly. Robert Moses seemed at first to be genuinely con-cerned when Lindsay announced his plans to reorganize Moses's transportation agencies, but then he met with the mayor. "If you elect a matinee idol mayor, you're going to get a musical comedy administration," he grinned to his staff when he returned from the meeting. Moses made sure that the legislative hearing in Albany on Lindsay's transportation proposal was a careful setup. Lindsay arrived, unprepared for anything but an informal discussion, to find virtually the entire power establishment of the state, including two former governors, the major unions, and the financial powers, all arrayed against him. The proposal was quickly killed.

When Lindsay announced that "summer hours" for city employees would be ended (that is, the long-standing practice of allowing most municipal employees to go home an hour earlier than usual during the summer), Victor Gotbaum, the leader of the city's largest union, announced that they would continue as always, or else the mayor would be faced with a general strike. Lindsay relented and announced that summer hours could be retained for July and August. Gotbaum said they would start on June 20, as usual, and again the mayor was forced to back down.

The most important management program, in Lindsay's eyes, was the reorganization of the city departments into ten so-called superagencies. To create most of the new agencies would require legislation from the City Council, and Lindsay prepared a 150-page omnibus reorganization bill, insisting that the council pass it as submitted. He eventually got most of what he wanted, but only after publicly backing down from his earlier insistences and redrafting the legislation into department-by-department bills, submitting to a full council debate on each proposal and accepting a number of their amendments.

The problems that Lindsay faced, and helped to create, and the progress that he made in his first year in office were illustrated by his efforts to increase the city's tax base in order to fend off an impending fiscal crisis. After the election and upon learning the details of the city's finances, Lindsay announced that he was "a receiver in bankruptcy." The statement was an exaggeration, but it was not very far from the truth. A history of fiscal gimmicks, reliance on one-shot revenues—and particularly, Wagner's borrowing during his last year in office—had left the city treasury depleted and unsound. According to the State Chamber of Commerce, New York's fiscal affairs were "in chaos." With service and wage demands apparently climbing inexorably, there was no possibility that the city could continue its current financial course.

Recognizing the severity of the problems, Wagner had appointed a Temporary Commission on City Finances, which issued a broad-ranging report in 1966 that called for new taxes and thoroughgoing management reform to finance needed expansion and dampen unnecessary spending. Lindsay adopted the commission's tax recommendations in substance, although with a number of changes, and shortly after taking office he prepared a package designed to raise additional net revenues of about $520 million. The key to the proposal was a graduated personal income tax that would apply to commuters and residents alike and would generate $385 million. A change in the method of business taxation would net another $70 million, with the remainder made up of an increase in the stock transfer tax and increased water charges. If enacted, the proposal would allow maintenance of the ten-cent transit fare, permit a balanced budget, for the next several years, and give the city a tax structure that would be much more sensitive to economic growth and general inflation.

The campaign to sell the proposals to the state legislature got off on the wrong foot from the very first day. In a briefing session arranged by Rockefeller with state legislative leaders and finance officials, Lindsay angrily attacked the state commerce commissioner, who questioned the advisability of further business and stock transfer taxation. Then the new administration appeared to be confused as to whether the proposals should be submitted directly to the legislature or would require a formal enactment first—a "home rule message"— from the City Council, as was the custom. By electing to go directly to the legislature, Lindsay irritated the City Council—and particularly David Ross, the majority leader, who was anxious to work with him. In the end the proposals had to come back to be submitted through the Council, anyway. And Lindsay made no secret of his displeasure when Rockefeller—although he proclaimed his sympathy for the proposals—insisted on adopting a position as a benign arbiter instead of coming out wholeheartedly in support of the package.

The proposals ran into heavy weather in the legislature almost immediately. The plan to tax commuters was particularly resisted by suburban representatives, and business lobbied intensively against the new business taxes. The president of the New York Stock Exchange announced that his organization would seriously consider relocating if the levy on stock transfers were increased. Skepticism increased when the legislative staff discovered that the package would generate a surplus for the city of about $130 million. Lindsay conceded that there would be a surplus, but it was necessary, he argued (quite correctly), to replenish the reserve funds that had been depleted under Wagner and to develop a cushion for expected cost increases in subsequent years. The City Council announced that they were in no mood to pass taxes in order to generate a surplus for the mayor and began a quadrille with the legislature to shift the blame when taxes were eventually increased. The council wanted a home rule message asking permission to pass taxes but did not wish actually to commit themselves to do so. After the legislature had granted the taxing authority, the council could then take credit for reducing the proposals. The legislature wanted the council to commit themselves unequivocally to a package so that the political onus would not rest with Albany.

Lindsay watched the jockeying with horror, then proceeded to attack all the parties to the debate. He denounced the "big business" opposition and demanded that his packages be passed intact. Otherwise, he indicated, he would "take to the streets" to remind the voters that "all of Albany is responsible." The threat of political retaliation, with overtones of civil disorder, served only to stiffen opposition. Sensing the drift of events, the City Council leadership refused to accompany Lindsay to an Albany negotiating session, publicly dissociating themselves from the mayor's stance. When Rockefeller intervened to effect a compromise, Lindsay insisted on a "clear statement of support" from the governor and then charged all sides with "political cowardice."

Eventually, to Lindsay's chagrin, Rockefeller stepped forcefully into the situation and took over the negotiations. A $283 million package was hammered out in a series of marathon sessions at the Executive Mansion. It was far from ideal but was arguably enough to meet the city's immediate needs. The key change was the loss of equal treatment for commuters and residents: Commuters would still be subject to the personal income tax, but only at a fraction of the rate imposed on residents. Lindsay feared (again, correctly, judging by later events) that the differential tax burden would only hasten the flight from the city of the financially better off. Even with the changes the package failed its first attempt at passage in the legislature, and Rockefeller had to reach back into his considerable political resources to ram the package home. The City Council then twitted the mayor by making further minor amendments in the taxes before passing them and by ostentatiously cutting some of the mayor's favorite ideas—notably the little City Halls—to make up the shortfalls. Relations between Lindsay and Rockefeller, which had always been correct rather than friendly, were severely strained by the episode, although the two men publicly made peace a few weeks later.

But despite all the bruisings, and all the needles administered with such glee by the insiders, the atmosphere around City Hall remained one of heady excitement. If there was any place in the country where things were going to be done, where bright people would finally get a chance to show what they could do, it was Lindsay's New York City. The *Daily News* ran photographs of out-of-state license plates as a new breed of urban professionals converged on the city, many from the Ivy League business or law schools, with newly minted degrees in city planning, or with experience in one of the major foundations or the national administration's still hopeful War on Poverty.

The consensus that bound them together was that the most daunting problems would respond to enthusiasm and intelligence. Lack of money was an obstacle, but not the major one. Despite the long-term decline of investment in the cities, there were more than enough resources moldering in the cobwebby bureaucratic warrens. Archaic welfare procedures could be streamlined, work could be scheduled more efficiently, and purchasing and construction processes could be simplified—all freeing energies for improving the quality and tone of city living. In any case, the growing federal surplus was being increasingly directed toward urban areas through the Economic Opportunity Act, Model Cities, new Federal programs for schools, and the other bullish new ventures of the Great Society.

Sometimes, all that seemed to be required was the spark of genius. There was a shortage of funds for schools, but the city owned tracts of land that had long since been condemned in anticipation of new construction, and many of them were in prime areas. Why not sell the air rights on the land for private construction, on the condition that the builder construct a school on the first several floors? At a stroke, more efficient land development and school construction could be had at no cost to the city. Resources could be compounded from imagination.*

* The mechanism—the Educational Construction Fund—was actually created and built a number of new schools around the city, combining school construction with commercial air right develop-

Sometimes, the call was for courage to plan on a large scale. The city had agonized over whether to build the Cross Brooklyn Expressway, a colossal elevated structure that would link the Long Island Expressway to lower Manhattan and provide rapid truck access to the ports and central markets. Powerful interests insisted that it would help to reverse the city's declining importance as an industrial center and would divert the traffic that daily choked the more southern routes; but highways are city destroyers, and the price of the economic improvements would be a strip of cancerous blight right across the borough. What if the city seized the opportunity that the new construction provided and built a linear city—or even several linear cities—linking the boroughs through the air and creating new urban land on spidery superstructures? A famous architectural firm provided the plans. The federal government was interested. It could be done.*

Most important, the reformers believed, there was a need for a consciousness of community. Traditional politicians and urban builders didn't understand that neighborhoods were living entities. Municipal "improvements" and urban renewal that cut through invisible lifelines left empty blocks and sightless windows in their wakes. Neighborhood renewal had to be on a scale that people could plan for themselves: Rehabilitation would be stressed over clearance; public housing would be "vest pocket" in size and scattered; community boards would look over the architectural shoulder and plan their own projects the way *they* wanted them.

Perhaps no one caught the spirit of the new administration better than the ebullient Thomas Hoving, Lindsay's new parks and recreation commissioner. There were kite-flying "happenings" in the parks on windy fall days; business donated the funds for rock concerts and travelling theater; and, perhaps best of all, park roads were closed to traffic on weekends and summer days and given over to cyclists, skateboarders, and joggers. Tourists needn't stay away; they were welcome. New York was glittering. It was "Fun City."

Indeed, there was visible progress—particularly, on the fiscal front. Rigid hiring controls allowed Lindsay to close the books on his first fiscal year with a slight surplus, and for the first time in years without borrowing or depleting the city's reserves. The following spring, at the close of Lindsay's first full fiscal year, he was able to announce that there was only a very slight deficit, which, again, could be met without borrowing or reserve depletion. Moreover, the reserves had been restored to health by a payment of $50 million, overall borrowing throughout the year had been sharply reduced, the city had redeemed more debt than it had issued, and a start had been made on discharging Wagner's $256 million loan.

The Citizens' Budget Commission and the editorial writers of the major newspapers hailed the "amazing reversal" of the long downward trend. Comp-

ment. There was probably no saving of funds. The Board of Education insisted on maintaining responsibility for school construction, and there were costly coordination problems between the board and the commercial developers.

* The proposal eventually died.

troller Mario Procaccino reported that the city was in "excellent financial shape" and that it was time for the bond agencies to reconsider the adverse judgments that they had been passing on the city's credit rating. The Temporary Commission on City Finances praised the "concrete steps" that had been taken, and the "hopeful beginnings" of the new administration. "The groundwork had been laid," they went on, "for better personnel practices, improved transportation coordination, larger intergovernmental aid, and more effective municipal management."

Lindsay had taken office promising both rectitude in the administration of the city's financial affairs and responsiveness in its programs. With all the setbacks, after just a year in office, rectitude would seem to have been achieved. Now the job was to make the city responsive.

II. *The Public Sector Expands*

EXPANSION IN THE NATIONAL AND STATE GOVERNMENTS

LINDSAY WAS HARDLY ALONE in his drive toward responsive government. With the federal government leading the way—particularly when Lyndon Johnson was in the White House—the fifteen years from 1960 to 1975 were a time of unprecedented expansion in government domestic spending. Spurred by the plight of the blacks and Puerto Ricans in Northern cities and the deplorable health and education opportunities available to the poor in the South, the national mood turned toward reform. A sufficient number of liberals were elected to Congress to wrest control of crucial committees from conservative Southern and Midwestern congressmen and substantially change a long-standing system of Federal priorities. The country's underlying prosperity made it all possible. In 1964 Johnson was able to sign on successive days the Economic Opportunity Act, which created a national War on Poverty, and legislation directing across-the-board tax cuts for almost everyone. Social conscience was free.

As the barriers to change came down, a stream of legislation poured out of Washington—besides the War on Poverty, there were Model Cities, the Elementary and Secondary Education Act, Medicare and Medicaid, and greatly improved social security benefits. When concern for civil rights and the poor was generalized to problems of pollution and congestion, the federal government responded with subsidies for urban mass transit, tough new air and water quality standards, and sharply increased levels of funding for sewage treatment and air pollution control. By 1967 even cataloguing the immense range of new initiatives was a formidable task; the federal government's own catalogue—a sort of local government shopping list—listed more than $15 billion in aid available, scattered through four hundred separate grant-in-aid programs—although beleaguered local officials insisted that the programs numbered more than a thousand. One count showed, for instance, programs in five separate agencies providing assistance for sewage treatment facilities, three programs in three separate agencies for deaf children, and more than thirty separate agencies involved in teacher training.

With the rush of programs, federal domestic spending increased sharply, as did the involvement of the federal government in local affairs. The federal cost of cash income maintenance programs doubled from 1960 to 1970 and doubled again by 1975. Aid for manpower, education, and social service programs jumped from $1.3 billion in 1960 to $10.3 billion in 1970, and to $18.2 billion in 1975. Programs to purchase medical and other essential services climbed even more drastically— from $1.1 billion in 1960 to $14.2 billion in 1970 and $33.2 billion in 1975. Pollution control and related assistance quadrupled during the same period. While the overall federal budget tripled from 1960 to 1975, the share devoted to domestic programs increased even faster, from $28.5 billion to $173.7 billion—or an increase of 509 percent—and the federal share in local and state budgets increased by 40 percent. Underlining the shift in national priorities, defense spending declined from its traditional dominant position in the budget to less than a third of the total amount, and by 1975 cash income maintenance programs alone were budgeted for a larger amount than national defense.

In many ways the device hit upon by the lawmakers for increasing federal involvement in local affairs—the categorical grant-in-aid—was as important as the absolute volume of the new federal commitments. Funding was allocated for specific purposes, and usually with detailed operating conditions attached, reflecting a prevailing lack of confidence in state and local administrations. In the South local autonomy too often meant racial discrimination; too many state legislatures in the North and West seemed sleepy, rural-dominated, special-interest societies. Just as important, it requires lobbies to push new programs through the legislative process. Detailed program specifications reassured program supporters and enhanced the power of the legislative committee chairmen who worked with them.

The categorical programs were specifically designed to change the emphases of state and local governments, and they were successful in large measure. A common device was to include generous federal funding in the early stages of a program, with the expectation that local funding would pick up the program later. Community mental health programs, for example, receive 90 percent of their funding in the first year from federal sources, but the federal share is phased out entirely over a seven-year period, leaving the local government with an expensive program, a high standard of service, and an organized set of supporters. Public employment programs began the same way: total federal funding for the first year was available to create jobs for people on welfare, but local officials were left to face a financing problem or the pain of reducing a popular program as the federal support was reduced in subsequent years. Programs developed "vertical autocracies" of their own, a chain of officials stretching from the local government through the state and regional federal bureaucracies to Washington and the halls of Congress. Elected officials rarely could afford the time or trouble to master the complex laws and regulations and were increasingly the captives of their program-oriented bureaucracies, who held the secret to the continued expansion of outside funding.

But if any state needed encouragement to expand its undertakings, New York was not among them. The state had a long tradition of helping the less fortunate, dating at least from Al Smith's landmark program to equalize educational funding by transferring resources from wealthier districts (in that era, primarily New York City) to the poorer upstate areas. And in Nelson Rockefeller, governor longer than any other man (from 1958 to 1974), the state had a chief executive who was uniquely able to combine a strong drive for program expansion with the personal capacity to overmaster whatever obstacles stood in his way, be they bureaucratic, legislative, or financial.

The powerful expansionist impulse that Nelson Rockefeller brought to state government was in his family's tradition—they had long tried to live down their legendary wealth with a broad range of philanthropic undertakings—and was consistent with his basic personality. One reporter wrote: "As governor, he had a kind of nineteenth-century optimism, a conviction that any problem must, somewhere, have a solution." It was also good politics. Rockefeller was a perennial presidential candidate, and, at least until 1968, his national aspirations rested on his position as spokesman for the Northeastern liberal wing of the Republican party, which was in competition throughout the decade with the hard-line conservatism of the South and West. Republicans were hopelessly outnumbered nationally, the reasoning went, and the route to victory lay in capturing the center of the national consensus. At least through the first half of the 1960s—or until the bills began to come in—that seemed definitely supportive of the drive toward government initiatives to equalize opportunities between blacks and whites and rich and poor, to put out lifelines for the cities, and to make up for decades of underinvestment in the public sector.

Whatever the source of Rockefeller's sense of the state as the cutting edge for social reform, he was able to carry through his personal vision as no other governor ever had. For at least thirteen of his fifteen years in office, he exercised iron control over the legislature, managing them with an adroit combination of patronage, personal charisma, superior staff work, and financial resources that would be applied unhesitatingly in critical campaigns to punish defectors and support the loyal. He generously supplemented the incomes of his closest personal aides to keep them in the government, and he could assure top people lifetime positions within the family financial and business empires in return for good service rendered. Other governors might have been daunted by the rigid financing constraints imposed by the state constitution and the increasing propensity of voters in the 1960s to reject state bond issues. But Rockefeller could call upon his unparalleled personal connections within the New York financial community, including conspicuously his brother's Chase Manhattan Bank, to underwrite billions of dollars of loans without the technical backing of the state government.

In his fifteen years as governor Rockefeller transformed the state's higher education system from "a few small, scattered colleges" with 38,000 students to a network of 71 campuses with an enrollment in excess of 246,000. He reorganized New York City's mass transit system, brought Robert Moses to heel in a way successive New York mayors must have envied, and made major improvements in the passenger railroads. He built or rebuilt 109 hospitals and nursing homes throughout the state, 23 new mental health facilities, at least 90,000 new housing units, 3 new communities, and a billion-dollar-plus complex of marble office buildings in the state capital. He consistently anticipated federal initiatives in pollution control and transportation construction and explicitly linked his programmatic drive to the needs of the minority disadvantaged. The state's Urban Development Corporation, for example, a construction agency empowered to raise its own funds and override local zoning and building codes so it could build at top speed, was rammed through the legislature on a "message of necessity" following the assassination of Martin Luther King. His narcotics addiction programs were the largest in the nation and the welfare standards the highest in the nation. His first Medicaid program granted free and comprehensive health insurance to 45 percent of the citizens of the state.

It would be a gross overstatement to say that Rockefeller's initiatives lay at the root of New York City's overextension. John Lindsay was only too ready to compete with Rockefeller for that honor. But it is accurate to say that expansion in the state and expansion in the city went hand in hand—as indeed it did in the rest of the state's local governments. (For example, during the period under discussion, short- and long-term debt actually increased at a faster rate in the rest of the state's local governments than it did in New York City.)

But there was more operating than the force of powerful personalities, as important as John Lindsay, Nelson Rockefeller, and Lyndon Johnson were to the final shape of New York City's financial disaster. A basic change was the sense of rationalist omnicompetence that, particularly after World War II, became the quintessential liberal dogma. The position was not as arrogant or as unreasonable as it appears to the jaundiced eye of a later decade: science had won the war; the European economies had been transformed; industry had converted to a peacetime footing without another Depression; the "new economics" was managing an unprecedented increase in living standards; American science would shortly put a man on the moon. John Kennedy betrayed a stunning lack of prescience when he announced that the government problems remaining were merely technical or administrative, but he spoke for most of his generation.

The rationalist error is to impose simple patterns of causation on partial data; and when rationalist logic was wedded to moral conviction, as was the case with programs to cure racial injustice, it is hardly surprising that social scientists so often confused their enthusiasms and their research results. For example, little in Lyndon Johnson's War on Poverty was new—most of the programs had been around for decades. What was new was its grandiose expectations. The conquest of disease, the conquest of ignorance, the technocratic hegemony that New Dealers dared only dream about seemed finally within reach. Men like Johnson, Rockefeller, and Lindsay had little to do with defining the new principles; at best, they were running breathlessly to keep the newest developments in sight.

When John Lindsay took office in 1966, the technocratic expansion was already rampant, although he reinforced it in important ways. The hyper-development of the city's university and hospital systems are good illustrations of the trend, and a brief sketch of the histories of both those institutions will be helpful.

HOSPITALS TRANSFORMED

New York City's municipal hospital system is the oldest in the country, dating from the infirmary that was established in 1736 in an almshouse on the present site of Bellevue Hospital. Bellevue opened as a separate institution for "the sick poor" in 1825; and by 1875, as a response to the mass of immigrants who increasingly threw themselves on the city's resources, five separate hospitals had been established. There is no question that these were minimum-service institutions; for the most part, care was provided by female convicts or convalescing patients.

As the five boroughs consolidated and the population pushed settlement to the city's borders, the hospitals expanded alongside, and by the mid-1920s the city had built, purchased, or taken over from financially strapped charities twenty-one separate hospitals, as well as a number of clinics and outstations, and operated a city-wide emergency service. Some 18,000 beds, a little less than 30 percent of the city's total, were in municipal institutions, and standards of medical indigency were such as to qualify a majority or near-majority of the population for free care.

New York City's generosity and commitment to health care was unique, but it was sustainable because municipal hospitals were not particularly expensive to operate. Nurses and aides worked long hours, usually on split shifts, with no overtime and with low pay. Hospital internship was a relatively recent requirement for qualification as a physician, and interns competed fiercely for the few available placements. There were no paid medical staffs. Local general practitioners provided the patient care: They took care of their own patients and, for the sake of the collegial atmosphere and clinical experience, took turns staffing clinics and participating in rounds. The best of the city institutions were affiliated with medical schools; Bellevue was connected with three. In return for teaching opportunities, the hospitals received additional medical staff and top-level department supervision, again, at no cost to the city.

In reality, with the exception of the one or two outstanding institutions like Bellevue, the level of care provided in most city hospitals was probably never very good. A 1934 report to Mayor La Guardia, for instance, found the hospitals in "deplorable condition"—overcrowded, undermaintained, poorly staffed. Patronage was rife, the standard of professionalism was low, and immense strains were being generated by the steadily increasing numbers of indigent patients. Even in the mid-1950s, when the municipal system was widely recognized to be in serious difficulties, experienced staff recalled that things had been considerably worse twenty or thirty years previously.

From the end of World War II, the system found itself in a state of permanent crisis. The sudden flowering of medical research and technology after the war placed a premium on specialization. Hospital residency training—in effect, postgraduate training for qualified physicians—became virtually mandatory. From 1945 to 1955, residency opportunities tripled, far outpacing the increase in medical school graduates, and most of the new residencies were in the strong private institutions able to win federal research funds. As young doctors gravitated toward the more prestigious centers, the unaffiliated voluntary and municipal hospitals were left at a marked disadvantage in attracting staff. To make matters worse, the drive toward specialization dried up the pool of general practitioners that had always provided the bulk of patient care. All of the non-affiliated hospitals suffered; but the city hospitals most of all, because they tended to be located in the poorer neighborhoods, from which doctors were emigrating at least as rapidly as their more affluent patients.

As medicine grew more complex, nursing standards increased as well. In 1935, a staff of fifteen nurses was considered adequate to provide around-the-clock, seven-day coverage for a hundred general-care patients. By 1955 the standard called for forty-seven nurses and was rising. Split shifts had ended, which meant that three nurses were required to cover a post where two had once been sufficient. By the end of the 1950s there were ten "allied health professionals" for every doctor—occupational therapists, medical technologists, X-ray technicians, dietitians, social workers. Educational and licensing standards rose sharply, and along with them came increased professional consciousness, demands for higher pay, and insistence on better working conditions.

Perversely, the city reinforced the trends. In the enthusiasm to make up for the deprivations of the Depression and the war, the city floated in 1949 a $150-million bond issue to open five new hospitals and rebuild half the remaining plant. The new facilities were much more technically sophisticated and consequently much more expensive to operate. The dilemma was that the city could build hospitals, but it couldn't staff them and couldn't maintain them.

By 1959 the accumulating crises could no longer be ignored, and Mayor Wagner convened a study group chaired by David Heyman, a member of the city hospital board, with Dr. Ray E. Trussel, who was on leave from Columbia University, as staff director. The precipitating incident was the withdrawal of accreditation from Gouverneur Hospital. Unable to attract qualified residents and interns, the city had been increasingly relying upon foreign-trained physicians, many of whom had failed to pass the American Medical Association's screening test for foreign graduates. At Gouverneur, it was revealed, *all* of the residents and interns were foreign graduates who had flunked the screening exam.

The recommendations of the Heyman Commission reflected the then-current mainstream of medical thinking. They argued, in effect, that medicine was a high-technology undertaking, properly practiced in a medical school/science center complex, and preferably in a teaching environment. Left to their own resources, there was no hope of the city's nonaffiliated institutions ever attracting the quality of staff necessary for modern practice or achieving levels of clinical excellence in keeping with their presumably great traditions. The solution was to contract with the outstanding private institutions in the city for the provision of medical staff and clinical supervision. The concept of affiliation, of course, was not new. What was new was that the city would now pay for the affiliation privilege.

There was plenty of precedent for a financial relationship between city hospitals and the non-profit ("voluntary") institutions, although historically they catered to quite different clienteles. Virtually all the municipal beds were in wards, and virtually all the patients were the indigent, who were cared for at city expense, or patients who were eligible under the various welfare programs. The voluntary hospitals had a large percentage of private or semi-private rooms and much higher percentages of paying patients. During the Depression, however, some 60 percent of the city's population qualified under the standard of medical indigency. The city hospitals became seriously overcrowded, and utilization of the voluntary hospitals dropped precipitately. A mutual problem was solved when the city agreed to reimburse the voluntary hospitals for the care of indigents. Political pressure and administrative inertia kept the relationship in force even when the justification for it passed. By the 1960s there was ample bed space in municipal hospitals, but the city continued to pay voluntary hospitals to care for indigent patients. Finally, in 1961 the voluntary hospitals lobbied successfully to get the arrangement codified in state legislation and the responsibility for setting reimbursement rates assigned to the state commissioner of health, who promptly set in train substantial rate increases for city patients.

As third-party health insurance came to be generally available after World War II, the city was further disadvantaged. Because Blue Cross—the dominant medical insurance plan in New York—would pay for semi-private rooms, covered patients gravitated away from the city system of ward care. By 1958 about 23 percent of the patients in voluntary hospitals had Blue Cross coverage, but only 9 percent of the municipal patients. At the same time, because third-party insurance typically did not pay for outpatient care, virtually all of the increase in outpatient traffic, and it was substantial, took place in the municipal hospitals. Even worse, but more difficult to quantify, was the apparently widespread practice among some voluntary hospitals, of transferring patients to municipals when their third-party coverage expired—in particular, "dumping" long-term, chronic-care patients, who were the least interesting medically and almost always losing propositions financially. By the time of the affiliation recommendations, then, a substantial amount of money was already being diverted from the city treasury to the voluntaries—both directly, through reimbursement, and indirectly, through dumping and monopolizing third-party payments. Tying affiliation and financing together would lock in the fiscal fortunes of private and municipal institutions more tightly than ever.

The Heyman-Trussel affiliation recommendations were greeted with wide acclaim, and Wagner moved with alacrity to implement the main provisions of the report—most particularly, by inducing Trussel to extend his leave from Columbia and become commissioner of the Department of Hospitals. The voluntaries were delighted at the prospect of affiliation contracts. Although deterioration had not proceeded at quite the headlong pace as in the city hospitals, about half the voluntaries were running continuing deficits, and one author calculated that about half of the deficit institutions were in serious difficulty. Heyman made clear the financial potential of the new arrangement: "The City has the money," he said, "but not the management." Trussel stipulated that affiliations would not be restricted to medical schools—which might have been the logical conclusion from his analysis of the problem. The director of Catholic Charities, with both Misericordia and Mary Immaculate Hospitals in precarious condition, called Trussel a "genius" and rhapsodized at the possibility of a "jointly financed" hospital system that would strengthen the voluntaries and create municipal hospitals "second to none." Both hospitals were awarded affiliation contracts, although in at least one case the affiliated muncipal was arguably in better condition than the mother institution.

The situation that confronted Trussel when he took office was undoubtedly urgent. The city hospitals needed an infusion of medical staff, and they needed it quickly. But in his haste to arrange affiliations—contracts had been negotiated for all but two of the city's hospitals by 1965—Trussel seriously underestimated the costs of the new program. Although he had estimated to the City Council that the contracts would cost only a "few millions," the contracts ballooned from $3 million in 1961 to $84 million in 1966 and to $127 million in 1967.

Probably more important, being a doctor, and associated with a leading medical school, Trussel apparently assumed that professionals would behave honorably. As it turned out, the voluntary institutions and their professional staffs displayed the kind of avarice usually associated with the Tammany politician of legend. Double-billing and false timesheets by both medical and administrative staff were widespread. Money was diverted from life-saving equipment to buy office furniture and exotic research machinery. Doctors who were being paid to be in attendance refused to appear, leaving nurses to handle delicate lifesaving procedures. One affiliated anesthesiologist justified his absence from municipal surgeries by saying that the patients were "not private patients." Although the contracts provided a 10 percent overhead factor for administrative costs, these costs were typically billed directly, and another 10 percent overhead was collected on top. Maimonides Hospital received a contract to staff and supervise the psychiatric unit at Coney Island Hospital, even though Coney Island had the strongest psychiatric unit in the area and Maimonides had no psychiatric service at all. The money was used to create a new unit at Maimonides and draw off the Coney Island personnel to staff it. New York Medical College was given a contract to provide social services at Coler and Metropolitan Hospitals, although New York Medical had no social services department and the service had been a long-standing one at both the city institutions. New York Medical skimmed off an overhead rate and subcontracted the service to Columbia University. New York was also awarded the anesthesiology contract for Coler and Metropolitan, although its own anesthesiology accreditation had been withdrawn. Although the contracts forbade it, most of the affiliates found ways to pay supplements to the city administrative and medical staff. The practice of dumping was refined to a science. With access to patients' records at the city institutions, paying patients in the municipal wards were routinely transferred to the parent institution and immediately transferred back when their resources expired. Even the desired infusion of medical staff, although it was accomplished on paper—if at great cost—may have been more apparent than real. In the one institution checked in detail, state investigators found that patient care was still almost entirely in the hands of foreign graduates, because the supervising physicians simply never appeared. In short, the voluntaries milked the city for all it was worth.

The emphasis on high-technology medicine implicit in the affiliation contracts resuscitated the city's hospital construction program, which had lagged after the burst of new building following World War II. Capital authorizations for hospitals jumped from $10.4 million in 1960–61 to $85 million in 1965–66. New Harlem Hospital was opened in 1969, and the new Bellevue the following year. In the face of general dissatisfaction with the pace of municipal construction, Governor Rockefeller secured legislation authorizing the state to finance and build up to $700 million of municipal health facilities throughout the state, with heavy emphasis on New York City. State financing secured by long-term city leases avoided encumbering the city debt limit, and construction through a newly created public authority sidestepped the bureaucratic delays endemic in the city's capital construction process. Contracts were quickly let for three lavish $100-million-plus facilities, one of which, Woodhull in Brooklyn, must represent a sort of municipal medical millennium: all three hundred rooms are private, with estimated operating costs in excess of $400 per patient day.

The final step in the transfer of resources from the city to the private medical sector came with the creation of the Medicaid program in 1966. Part of the price of overcoming the long-standing medical resistance to government-financed health insurance was the promise that fees would be at the prevailing rates charged to private patients. The enormous new capacity for medical spending drove prices up sharply. The medical chicaneries that had been revealed in the affiliation contracts were but the palest foreshadowing of the wholesale fraud that beset the new program. "Medicaid mills" popped up in the slums like fungi after a storm, excessive billings by nursing home operators were almost standard procedure, and the last vestiges of charity medicine disappeared from the city. At the same time, the potential of the program for assisting the municipal institutions was blunted by a steady decline in their utilization as Medicaid recipients sought care at the voluntary institutions or with private physicians. Outpatient visits dropped by 18 percent from 1966 until 1969, when stricter levels of eligibility for Medicaid threw large numbers of non-paying patients back on city resources.

By state law about 30 percent of the Medicaid cost was a city responsibility, although with the open-ended nature of the program, there was virtually no control over the total amount of the liability. By 1975 the city was spending $115 million per year of city tax money on Medicaid reimbursements to private hospitals, $136 million to nursing homes, and $30 million to private physicians. The city's tax share of the affiliation program was another $70 million, and an additional $344 million in local taxes went to support the city hospitals. Total city tax funds spent through Medicaid were $550 million, and Medicaid spending from all sources represented 27 percent of total medical expenditures in the city. To put the numbers in perspective, total city tax spending for public assistance grants in all categories during the same year was $436 million.

In short, the hospitals were captured by professionals imbued with the rationalist faith in high-technology solutions to almost anything. Health care was a good thing. In particular, since well-off people appeared to be in better health than poor people, the professionals could glibly identify their drive for a greater share of the city purse with the needs of the new minorities. For its part, the city lurched from crisis to crisis, never comprehending that the service it was trying valiantly to maintain was now something fundamentally different from what it had been just a few decades before and foolishly keeping faith with a tradition that was quite possibly false all along. The massive infusion of capital from the state construction programs and the Medicaid inflation enriched the medical establishment and left the city with a grossly overcapitalized, underused, and fiercely expensive hospital system that it could not possibly hope to maintain and operate properly and which, by all accounts, still provided woefully inadequate service to the poor. Ironically, the same system in 1979 provided employment for almost thirty-five thousand of the most upwardly mobile of the new black and Puerto Rican immigrants to the city. Their dreams of fully sharing in the promise of America have become inextricably intertwined with the city's folly.

Dramatic as it is, the transformation of the hospitals was hardly unique. Much the same account can be given, although more briefly, of the City University of New York.

CITY COLLEGE TRANSFORMED

The New York City educational authorities created the Free Academy for advanced education for city residents in 1847. It was a progressive step, but hardly an epochal one. After all, Massachussetts had founded Harvard College more than two centuries earlier, and it was forty years since Thomas Jefferson had been actively promoting the idea of a national university. Almost from the beginning, pressures for expansion were intense—undoubtedly due in part to the disproportionate immigration into New York of European Jews, who valued advanced education much more highly than other immigrant groups. The Normal School for Women, later called Hunter College, was opened in 1870, and after almost thirty years of agitation, Brooklyn residents obtained evening classes in 1917. Al Smith signed legislation creating the Board of Higher Education and mandating free tuition in 1926, and in the next dozen years, decisions were taken to proceed with Brooklyn College, Queens College, and—on the urging of Mayor La Guardia—the School of Police and Fire Science. Following World War II and the sharp upsurge of interest in engineering and industrial processes, four institutes of applied arts and sciences were opened, later to be incorporated into the curricula of the senior colleges. The first community colleges—at least those designated as such—came in the 1950s, and by 1960 the system comprised four senior colleges, three two-year community colleges, and two divisions of City College soon to be split off as separate colleges in their own right: Lehman College and Baruch College. Total enrollment was ninety-three thousand, or almost two-and-a-half times the enrollment in the state college system. The relative backwardness of the state's higher education system was an impetus to development in the city. In 1960 New York was one of only three states that did not offer publicly supported doctoral training, and although it was one of the wealthiest states in the country, its per capita spending for higher education was barely at the national average and only about a third that of California.

The city system was usually under financial pressure. As with the hospitals, it was easier for successive administrations to open institutions than it was to maintain and operate them. In 1937, for example, faculty voted to accept pay cuts in place of imposing tuition in order to assist the colleges over a difficult financial period. There was temporary relief in the immediate post–World War II period as "paper tuition"—collections from the federal government for eligible GIs—amounted to about 25 percent of the revenue stream. Another period of serious financial strain ensued from about 1955, when the pool of eligible veterans began to dry up, but there was temporary relief in 1960, when the state legislature awarded the first truly substantial aid. That year the state created the State University system and undertook to reimburse the city for all teacher training expenses, one-third the cost of the first two years of college, and one-half of future debt service.

But despite financial strain, the twenty years after World War II were a heady, exhilarating time for higher education. The war and the atom bomb had demonstrated the power of the new technology. There was little doubt that the world was on the threshold of major change and that the professors were the torchbearers of a new dispensation. College teaching had once been a monkish profession; intellectual fare provided a thin subsistence unless one had the good fortune to marry wealthy. The 1950s introduced the jet-age professor, advisor to governments and consultant to corporations. Russia's successful testing of atomic weapons and the launching of the first Sputnik drove home that international success, perhaps even survival, would depend on education. John Kennedy's election was the final vindication. Academics flowed to Washington, elbowing the generals out of the defense department and rescuing social policy from the bureaucrats. Philosophers might not be kings, but they stood right next to the throne.

In New York the surge of interest in higher education translated into a plethora of committees and study groups. The report to Governor Rockefeller of the 1960 Heald Committee rang like a tocsin: "Higher education in America has been propelled into a distinctly new era [as a result of] an explosion of knowledge, a surge of population, an almost unbelievable breakthrough in science and technology, and possibly more important than any other force, a menacing international contest between democracy and communism." Like the doctors, and like Charles Wilson, the professors knew what was good for the country. A City College study group reported: "[There is] manifest need for increased university resources for the country and particularly New York State . . . It is particularly appropriate that the City College of New York should become a great university center."

Unlike other institutions, the colleges were in the peculiarly happy position of needing to expand in order to develop the resources to man their future expansions. The City College group went on: "The number of New York students in college will triple in the next twenty-five years. Only greatly expanded graduate programs can ensure that this rapidly expanding population will receive the proper quality of instruction. Without it, the entire educational fabric of the City, the State, and the country will be weakened."

Of course, much of the puffery was real. The world, and the New York City job market with it, was getting to be a much more technical place. Bookkeepers were being replaced by computer programmers, and higher education was becoming increasingly essential to compete. But the colleges also generated much of their own demand: In 1959 almost 80 percent of nurse training in the city was carried out in hospital nursing schools; by 1967 students enrolled in degree-granting City University nurse training programs had increased more than four times, and by 1972 more than fifteen times—from 364 to 5,465—while the old hospital schools were rapidly phasing out. The availability of degree programs in medical records, inhalation therapy, and radiology, to name just a few, undoubtedly contributed to an improvement of hospital care, but at the same time, it increased professional identities and led to the demands for higher pay and ever-higher licensing requirements.

The breakthrough came in the 1960s. Enrollment growth had been slow throughout the previous decade, largely due to lack of space and facilities. (The percentage of high school graduates finding a place at a senior college declined through the 1950s, and admissions standards were raised at most schools to keep ahead of the demand.) From 1960 to 1970, however, total enrollment more than doubled—from 93,000 to 198,000—and full-time enrollment jumped from 36,000 to 103,000. Personnel grew even faster—from 4,303 to 15,217. The City University Construction Fund was created in 1965, endowed with the power to raise funds outside the city's borrowing limit (but with the security of city leases) and to expedite construction. By the end of the decade, the system boasted a graduate center, ten senior colleges, and eight community colleges.

The Great Society programs for higher education signalled another change in emphasis—from providing educational opportunities for qualified students to qualifying students for higher education. Then, in 1970, with the enthusiastic support of the State Board of Regents and Governor Rockefeller, the city, despite its perennial fiscal crisis, declared Open Enrollment for all of the city's students. Registrations climbed faster than ever, hitting a high point of 271,930 in 1974, while full-time personnel passed the 20,000 mark. Through the fifteen-year period from 1960 to 1975, spending on higher education by the city increased at an annual compounded rate of 20.5 percent—that is, total spending doubled every 3.7 years. The budget at the beginning of the period was $45 million, and $612.4 million at the end—an increase of 1,258 percent, compared to a 393-percent increase for the city as a whole. About half the total was met from city tax receipts.

Just as had happened in health care, the very nature of the enterprise had changed in fundamental ways, but the changes were covered over with old slogans. Despite the constant city budgetary strains, it had once been a plausible undertaking to offer a liberal arts senior college program for top high school graduates. More high school students may have attended college in New York City than elsewhere, and admission standards were liberal, but until recently the enrollment population was still a relatively small elite. Although $21 million may have been a sizable piece of the budget in 1954, for example, it was still only a little more than a third of the budget for the fire department. But once again, the city allowed the professionals to define how the system should grow and trapped itself into offering universal higher education insurance. Even allowing for their self-interest, the reasoning of the educators wasn't necessarily wrong: The arguments for more higher education are probably stronger than the arguments for more medical services. But the capacity of the city to provide such a good was never entered into their equations.

With the professionals at the wheel, the city was already speeding toward the limits of its resources by the time John Lindsay took office in 1966. He was not the man to slow the pace: He came determined to make the antiquated machinery responsive by first making it rational.

RATIONALIZING CITY GOVERNMENT

It would have required more prescience than even the best politicians possess for John Lindsay to have perceived, when he took office, the ultimate excesses of high technology in education and health. If there had been one theme in his campaign that had attracted the support of the reform groups around the city, it was the promise to breathe life into the government with technology and "high-efficiency" business methods. Wagner's Temporary Commission on City Finances had seen better management as one of the major avenues toward long-run improvement in the city's financial situation. Lindsay's view, and there was considerable truth in it, was that the city was a hopelessly bureaucratic morass. Certainly, there was little chance of his genuinely making the government machinery more responsive to the citizenry unless a fresh wind dispelled the miasma.

The centerpiece of his plans for management reform was to reorganize the ninety-odd city departments into ten superagencies. The "absence of planning and coordination had become chronic," he said early in his administration. "It's all scotch-taped together. City departments deal with each other almost by treaty . . . With each [of the new superagencies] taking charge of a definite and integrated field, and with clear lines of control and communication, I could know what's going on all the time. And we can save a lot of money that way, too." The separate departments dealing with rent control, building inspections, urban renewal, and relocation, as one example, were combined into a single

Housing and Development Administration, where a single administrator would be able to organize a unified attack on the problem of improving the city's housing stock. Similarly, welfare, manpower training, and anti-poverty programs would all come together in a Human Resources Administration; the departments dealing with highways, traffic control, and ferries would form a Transportation Administration; sewers, water and air pollution control, and sanitation would be an Environmental Protection Administration, and so on. The ideas were not without merit, but reorganization easily became an intellectual game. Sewers protected the environment, but replacing sewers meant tearing up streets, so a case could be made that highways and sewers should be under the same management, in order to minimize disruption by coordinating street resurfacing and sewer repair. It could be similarly argued that job training would best be handled by the agency that was concerned with economic development and business relations: It all depended on whether the reasoning began with the potential employee or potential employer. Still, reorganization did give a satisfying sense of dealing with big issues. Boxes on paper shifted easily, and as the cluttered bureaucratic map yielded to order and symmetry, there was an illusion of departments advancing in massed ranks upon slums, poverty, and pollution, all arrayed in neat priorities.

Much of the intellectual support for reorganization stemmed from an analytic, scientific approach to government that had demonstrated its power in the hands of Robert McNamara at the Department of Defense. He pioneered the use on a large scale of Program, Planning and Budgeting Systems, or PPBS, which was later ordered by President Johnson to be applied throughout the federal government. The essence of PPBS was to define problems in terms of outputs, and then to trace the outputs back through the functions required to produce them. In education, for example, smaller class sizes or more reading specialists are inputs, not outputs, and are unjustifiable except to the degree that they improve the performance of the children. Ideally, a budget would be developed in terms of the cost of each additional increment of educational improvement one wished to buy for the students. The spending decision would then be translated into a detailed purchasing schedule of the additional teachers or reading materials required to produce the desired improvements.

The education example, of course, makes plain the weaknesses in the approach. There is no certain way to relate educational inputs and outputs; decisions on class sizes have to be made on faith, or by an intuitive sense of how small a class a teacher needs to maintain reasonable order. Nevertheless, PPBS was still a useful tool for analyzing what the city did. In any organization as large and as long-standing as the city government, there were bound to be operations whose reason for being had long since been forgotten.

Lindsay's key recruit to implement new management systems was Frederick O'Reilly Hayes, who became budget director in August 1966. Hayes was a housing expert, a veteran of the Federal Budget Bureau, and a top official in the national War on Poverty. He also turned out to be a top recruiter, and the city's Bureau of the Budget quickly became a cynosure for the young professionals coming into city government from all across the country. Hayes insisted

only that they be "very bright"; Harvard Business School graduates were especially preferred because they had, he said, "that little extra arrogance" it took to
survive in the bureaucratic maze. Peter Goldmark, only twenty-six years old,
was typical of the new recruits: A graduate of Harvard, he had worked with
Hayes in the Office of Economic Opportunity and joined the budget bureau to
head the new division of program analysis. The PPBS effort was headed up by
Carter Bales, a young partner from McKinsey and Co., the management consulting firm.

Bales and a McKinsey team put together an early example of the systems
approach to city government. With the strong support of the administration,
the City Council had passed Local Law 14, a bill mandating specific reductions
in emissions from stationary sources of air pollution, primarily incinerators. The
question was whether the city would be in compliance with its own law. The
project team developed an elegant "issue map" that charted alternative routes
to city compliance. For example, in the Housing Authority, the city agency that
operates public housing, there were more than twenty-six hundred incinerators
dumping 450 tons of particulate matter, mostly fly ash, into the air each year. It
was far from the largest source of pollution in the city but was one of the most
visible, and one that could be pinned embarrassingly on the administration.
The issue map worked backward from the compliance schedules in the law,
analyzed the various types of incinerators, set out the technical feasibility and
cost of the various alternatives—sanitation pickup of the raw trash, compaction
and pickup, or installation of devices to clean the smoke before it was emitted.
The costs varied according to the age, size, and the state of repair of the incinerators, and federal or state aid would be available for some upgrading plans
but not for others. The plan then laid out the most desirable options from the
city's point of view, established a schedule for the actions that would have to be
taken, and identified the appropriate assignment of responsibility for each action throughout the various agencies involved. It even specified detailed reporting forms so that the Mayor could keep advised of progress. It was something new in city government, and exactly what Lindsay had been looking for.

The city's lagging capital construction program was another area where the
budget bureau's new managers were involved early. As many as twelve different agencies were involved in approving the plans for a single project. Harlem and Bellevue Hospitals were carried in the budget for seventeen and fifteen years, respectively, before they were finally completed. Just reviewing
the final plans for a police station took almost a year. In one case, involving a
number of projects, the parks department took seven years from the date that
the projects were authorized before beginning design work. In 1968 more than
two thousand major construction projects and fifty thousand minor ones, involving more than $3 billion, were in various stages of planning, design, or con-
struction. A computerized project tracking system was devised to help manage
the system. As a new project was authorized, a detailed schedule was fed into
the computer, along with the name of the individual responsible for reporting
the completion of each milestone. The computer then reported automatically
on the lagging projects—a technique called "management-by-exception." Re-

ports were kept to a minimum, and top management attention was drawn only to the projects in trouble.

It soon became evident that something more was needed beyond issue analysis and intelligent scheduling. For all the high-quality work that had gone into the air pollution control project, the agencies by and large simply ignored the schedules. Responsibility was fragmented among various departments and bureaus, and when the planned milestones were missed, there was always someone else to blame. To its immense chagrin the city ultimately had to request an extension on compliance with the law. The solution was to move from issue analysis to project management. A new staff of management technicians, working jointly out of the mayor's office and the budget bureau, was organized around sets of high-priority programs—the air pollution project, opening drug treatment centers, expediting the hiring of minority policemen, rehabilitating emergency rooms, building "vest-pocket" swimming pools, commercial development of the Brooklyn Navy Yard, breaking a taxi licensing backlog, starting rat control and cleanup programs in Model Cities neighborhoods. A separate team worked full-time on the ongoing capital construction program. A project manager was assigned to supervise each project—to troubleshoot, to help the agencies stay on target, and to blow the whistle when accomplishments lagged. The approach created supervisory confusion and left its share of bruised feelings, but things began to move. Pools were built right on schedule, and overall construction performance improved. There was progress on the emergency rooms, most observers were impressed with the rat control project, and there was rapid expansion of the police force. The air pollution project was difficult right to the end, and there was little progress on the drug treatment centers—at least during Lindsay's first term—but the achievement as a whole was promising.

Certainly, the city was a fertile field for scientific management or, by the mid-1960s, for management of any kind. The city bureaucracy depended on complex, often elegant manual systems that had been designed and implemented by the so-called "Depression geniuses," a corps of extraordinary men who had been recruited into city government during the La Guardia years, when opportunities in the private sector were nonexistent. They were retiring in large numbers, and the ranks of competent managers below them were dangerously thin. "They were mules," said one observer. "They carry the City on their backs, but they were sterile. There's no generation to follow them." System after system was clanking almost to a halt, wheezing with age and the pressures of new service demands. The superb fire dispatching system, combining roller street address files and plastic chip boards locating equipment, devolved into scrambling chaos as alarms from poorer neighborhoods—most of them false—tripled and quadrupled. Discounts on quantity purchasing had long since been lost because the city could not pay its bills on time. The inability to perform cut right across the most routine business. The city couldn't issue birth certificates on time, pay overtime when it was due, maintain its automotive fleets, deliver asphalt to men filling potholes, submit claims for federal and state aid payments, supply diaper pins to obstetric wards, or hire key staff.

(Capital projects moved slowly, in part, because a third of all authorized architectural and engineering positions were empty.) If employees were late or participated in job actions, the payroll system couldn't dock them; when they were hired they weren't paid; and when they retired they would as likely keep on being paid.

Ironically, just as it was the center of the new management efforts, the budget bureau was also the heart of the problem. Tight central control was the organizing principle of the city's transactional system. The central budget document listed each position in the government and the precise salary allotted to each. After a budget was officially adopted, it was filed with the comptroller, the authorized paymaster. Agency salary vouchers would be paid only if they were accompanied by an authorization from Budget "freeing" the line. The bureau often issued blanket authorizations for routine, high-turnover hiring, but these could be, and often were, withdrawn. Lindsay himself complicated the process by establishing new hiring controls to meet the fiscal crisis in his first year in office: His freeze required mayoral authorization for the hiring of new employees, which, in practice, meant a second piece of paper from the budget bureau. Supplies and equipment were handled in a similar manner. There was less detail in the budget, but a comprehensive and finely detailed purchasing schedule would be filed with the comptroller by each department's budget examiner, and deviations from the schedule would not be honored. The actual buying was handled by the department of purchase, which ran on a complex manual system of its own and was in some cases years behind on its purchasing schedules.

It was not a system that dealt kindly with change. Any variation in a budget line from the original filing with the comptroller required a formal modification from the budget bureau. Collective bargaining settlements would take thousands of modifications and months to implement, and if a new commissioner wanted to bring on staff in slightly different positions and at different salary rates than those originally scheduled, he would have to wait his turn in the queue. Invariably, the wait would be a long one. One result was that agencies routinely, and illegally, shifted lines from program to program to match salaries with people and simply listed employees under the wrong titles. In one of the largest city agencies, more than half the staff was working out of title and out of location: An accounting firm that was called in to restore some semblance of bookkeeping integrity finally reconstructed a current organization chart from the addresses on the paychecks. Getting authorization for new types of employees—for an economist, for example, in an agency that hadn't previously employed one—required action by both the budget bureau and the central department of personnel. The operating rule was that Budget would not process a modification until Personnel had approved the new title, but—Catch-22—Personnel would not act on the title request until the budget bureau had processed the line modification. The procedures were enough to reduce commissioners to tears—particularly the new, younger men who had been attracted to city government by the opportunity to create movement, the doers Lindsay was so proud of.

The conflict between the overhead control system and Lindsay's urge toward responsiveness burst into the open in 1966 during one of the recurrent hospitals crises. In the spring *The New York Times* ran a series of articles exposing outrageous conditions in city hospitals. There were operating rooms without sepsis controls, wards without nurses, emergency rooms that violated elementary provisions of the health codes, broken plaster and leaking pipes throughout entire institutions, and millions of dollars of new equipment standing uncrated because of the lack of staff to use it. The new health administrator, Howard Brown, made a tour of the worst institutions and pronounced conditions "heartrending, disgraceful." One physician quite seriously calculated that a patient's chances for survival would improve if he simply stayed home. The case was taken up by a state senator from Queens, Seymour Thaler, a sharp-featured lawyer with a reputation for investigative crusades who was sometimes bruited as a potential mayoral candidate. Thaler began a drumfire of speeches denouncing the city hospitals. Midnight surprise visits disclosed even more shocking conditions than before.

Amid a welter of investigations, the budget bureau gradually emerged as a prime villain of the piece. The hiring controls had left one hospital with only seventeen nurses for eighteen hundred patients, another had four for eleven hundred, and a third had five for seven hundred. Joseph Terenzio, the hospitals commissioner, defended himself by pointing to staffing requests that had been unanswered—in one case for a year, and in other cases even longer. Long-promised rehabilitations of scandalous emergency room conditions in Bellevue and Greenpoint hospitals had been blocked, because the budget bureau found the plans too costly. In Bellevue test tubes were being sterilized in pots on a gas stove; X-rays at Metropolitan were delayed more than two months for lack of proper equipment. Repairing a wheelchair took a year. It took 9½ months to buy a $10 urinary catheter. Thaler alleged that Budget had diverted $100 million in new Medicare and Medicaid funds to the general fund in order to defray overall city operating expenses. Conditions were intolerable, and the pressures on Lindsay to relax the controls mounted. Hayes defended his staff and grumbled that the problem was not so much money as poor management—that there were adequate resources, if they were only used efficiently—but he eventually had to back down.

The immediate crisis passed when the hiring controls were lifted and the project management teams began to expedite the rehabilitations, but the chronic problems persisted. "We were just awash in a sea of paper," Hayes recalls. More than forty thousand individual requests had to be processed by the budget bureau each year, and at least a third of them involved hospitals. Three years later, a frustrated Hayes revived a proposal to place the hospitals under the management of a separate public entity, the Health and Hospitals Corporation, so that the city could be shut of the processing, once and for all.

The complex overhead controls may have been indefensible, but they weren't necessarily irrational. Their primary purpose was simply to stop people from spending money. The civil servants had little confidence in commissioners: They thought of them as vandals, ground scorchers passing by. When decentralizing spending authority was recommended to Harry Bronstein, the budget bureau's chief examiner—who ruled on all the countless requests that flowed through the bureau—he could pull out a thick file on commissioner behavior: Give commissioners authority, and they would buy personal cars, hire chauffeurs for themselves and their staffs, buy expensive telephone equipment, furnish their offices. To the civil servants, commissioners were just politicians. Commissioners didn't care about budget balances, they insisted, because they would be gone when the bills came in. Commissioners' commitments were to their own constituencies, their own egos, and whatever fad was the order of the day. The processing systems may have been incredibly complex and unworkable, but a certain amount of judicious incompetence served a homeostatic purpose. What commissioner ever had the courage to turn down a request for a salary increase from a politically connected staff member, the civil servants would ask. It was understood that some approval processes were literally unworkable, but that meant that if a commissioner really needed something, he would come himself to the budget bureau and fight for it. Then the civil servants could judge whether the request was self-serving or truly in the interests of the city.

From the standpoint of the traditionalists, there was good reason to view many of the new management efforts with concern. The new initiatives—more policemen, better staffing and supplies for the hospitals, drug treatment centers, more playgrounds, and better park maintenance—almost always involved spending more money, and in some cases a lot more money. Granted that the red tape was costly and inefficient, but sometimes so was progress. The new state construction agencies performed prodigies in expediting hospital and university construction, but the expensive new plant, particularly in hospitals, came on line just as the enthusiasm for operating expensive new establishments had begun to erode, along with the city's financial capacity.

The construction of the North River Water Treatment Plant is a classic illustration of the point. Planned for some fifteen years to provide primary treatment for the last outflow of raw human waste to the Hudson, it had almost completed its stately course through the review processes in 1968, just as the environmental movement became a major political force. The state and federal governments applied heavy pressure for the highest feasible treatment standards. "Ninety-percent removal" at the North River plant was a slogan of the first Earth Day celebration and received powerful support from Senator Robert Kennedy. A federal enforcement conference was held on the issue; large-scale federal aid was planned in the Congress. The city engineers finally collapsed under the pressure and agreed to redesign the plant.

The treatment upgrading probably never made much technical sense. Pollution in the lower Hudson is largely industrial and chemical. Secondary treatment of human sewage removes the coliform bacteria that can cause gastrointestinal and other infections among swimmers, who are about as common as dolphins in that part of the river. But the expansion enormously increased the land area required and prompted protests from the neighboring Harlem community. A series of intense neighborhood meetings were held to hammer out a compromise: A park would be built on top of the plant to convert it to an amenity. Costs escalated to a billion dollars, more than three times the original estimate; but a concerted project management effort accomplished the entire redesign, including the park, and a start on construction in less than two years from the date of the original decision. By the time the fiscal crisis hit in full force, construction contracts for the new plant had already been let. In 1975 the partially finished structure was abandoned.

Even the effort to improve program analysis was suspect. A budget bureau veteran counseled the newcomers: "Once you start learning about the departments, you'll just end up spending money." Again, there was truth in the warning. The purpose of systems analysis is to bring resources to bear on objectives. With the inflation of government objectives in the 1960s, a proper mustering of resources almost inevitably meant increased spending commitments. Health care provides a case in point. The budget bureau looked at the problem of supplying reasonably priced medical care in the ghettoes and conceived of health centers modeled after pilot programs of the federal Office of Economic Opportunity. Lindsay described the plan:

[It] means bringing small, immediately accessible health-service centers into the neighborhoods, thereby relieving the burden on the outpatient clinics in the big hospitals, where the jam-ups take place now. The large hospital complexes, with full laboratory facilities and beds for people who need extended hospitalization, will be the hub of the health-service wheel, and the neighborhood centers all over the City will be the spokes.

The budget bureau had reasoned that Medicaid would finance the program, but, unfortunately, Medicaid was cut back just as the program got off the ground. At the first center about 40 percent of the patients had no coverage at all and became additional charges to the city. In the meantime, the state health construction agency was already proceeding on four new centers and the city agencies on another three. The analysis of the problem was probably correct, and there was little doubt that the poor needed better medical services, but, as in so many cases, improved understanding meant increased spending.

A common problem, despite all the PPBS jargon, was that insufficient attention was often paid to the content of the program that was being expedited. The most glaring example is probably the early attempt to start up a network of residential drug treatment centers. Drug addiction was clearly a major problem in New York. There were at least a hundred thousand heroin addicts, and the cost in terms of crime and social disorganization was substantial. Lindsay had promised to do something about the problem, and early in his administration he hired Dr. Efraim Ramirez, from Puerto Rico, who had apparently had success treating addicts in a closed residential setting with group therapy techniques. Ramirez was an effective propagandist and quickly acquired his own agency and a sizable budget, but he did not have the organizational skills to mount a program of the size and complexity required. The project management staff was assigned a target of getting two thousand addicts into residential treatment. After a year they conceded failure. The politics of the drug bureaucracies were too byzantine and the hair-splitting controversies surrounding the dif-

ferent treatment methods too abstract and bitter for the management technicians to blast through. As it turned out, the failure was a happy one: It soon
emerged that almost all types of drug treatment were ineffective, and that residential treatment was both ineffective and dreadfully expensive. The point is
that the drive to quantify, although a healthy trend in many aspects of the city's
operation, could obscure deeper realities. Opening five new drug treatment
centers looked like measurable progress in the war against drug addiction, but
in reality drug treatment centers and the levels of addiction had very little to do
with each other.

A common problem was the confusion between reduced unit costs and actual savings. A private business can improve its profits if it expands production
to reduce unit costs, provided it can still sell its product. But in the city, more
efficient production often meant increased spending. Neighborhood family care
centers could deliver health services more efficiently, but if they were delivering new services, they were simply increasing outlays. Specially designed
neighborhood swimming pools were cheaper than conventional installations,
but installing them meant spending more money, even though the cost per
user was dropping. In fact, most of the "savings" generated by government (not
just in the city) are really measures of effectiveness improvement and are not
savings at all. More efficient garbage collection is no saving, if the city would
have otherwise merely left the garbage on the street. The fallacy was a particularly dangerous one in New York, where demands for new service were so
intense and the apparent political benefits of improved effectiveness were so
high.

In the final analysis, however, the troubling aspects of the new management
initiatives were not a sufficient argument for the maintenance of the old systems. The overhead controls had outlived their time, their usefulness, and
their creators. The very paralysis they generated created much of the pressure
for quick-fix solutions and helped to place such a premium on proving that the
city could actually *do* something—anything. Routine performance had come to
require heroic effort, and civil servants are not often the stuff of heroes. The
city was suffused with laxity. Dedicated executives were defeated, and the
nonperformers always had an excuse ready at hand. Hayes reflects:

Good management could have meant so much. It's not that you could save enormous
amounts of money, but it's that the lack of tautness was reflected in so many ways. You
were always starved for data, for instance, and got used to making decisions on the back
of an envelope. I'm sure we made a lot of bad decisions that way. But you could never
lay your hands on the information you needed. And it was very difficult to find out if any
of the new programs were actually working. You could never really tell whether it was a
bad idea to begin with, or whether people had just not bothered to do it right.

The problem was that genuine management reform was such a formidable
undertaking, requiring years of slogging work, political resources, money, and
energy. It could not be addressed easily by an elected management whose time
horizons extended only to the next election. Three successive budget directors—Hayes, Edward Hamilton, and David Grossman—tried seriously, for ex-

ample, to address the problem of adequate accounting systems, but the task was too daunting. It meant too many awkward changes over too long a time and with apparently little immediate benefit. An elected executive wasn't obviously better off with a good accounting system than with a poor one: The bad system could even be more convenient. It wasn't until the fiscal crisis itself that there was a sufficient commitment to do what was necessary about an obvious, long-standing, and serious problem, and then the pressure came almost entirely from the outside. In a similar vein, Hayes reflected on his experience trying to improve the management of the sanitation department:

We'd done some analytical work that showed where they could make some savings, but they wouldn't seem to listen. So, finally, in exasperation, I cut their budget by that amount. They still refused to make any changes and appealed to the Mayor that the streets were getting dirtier, but he didn't intervene. Then we did some more analysis and I cut their budget again. We did this every year. Until they finally just beat me. It was an oriental defense in depth. It was like dealing in a foreign market. You know you're being overcharged, but they just stand there smiling inscrutably, until finally you pay the rupees or whatever. The election was coming around. The streets were getting dirtier and dirtier, and I finally gave them back their men.

With basic reform so difficult—although in later years there would be some important progress—it was inevitable that the first management improvement efforts focused on discrete tasks that could be readily broken off from the ongoing operations of the city. As such they would tend to be new projects, things that the city hadn't done before, something more to undertake and eventually to pay for.

The rationalizing efforts, then, were another expansionary force. Improved management and more rational managers might save money in the long run, but for the immediate present, in John Lindsay's first term, they were a powerful reinforcement to the pressures operating elsewhere in the government to broaden the scope and extend the reach of the public sector.

III ▪ *Blacks and Puerto Ricans*

JOHN LINDSAY took office determined to deal with the urban crisis; and the crisis in New York City was inextricably bound up with race. Crime and violence in the streets were overwhelmingly black. Most drug addicts were Puerto Rican and black. The slums that were scarring the city, outpacing efforts at renewal and new construction, were black and Puerto Rican slums. Blacks demanded integrated schools, remedial programming, more sensitive teachers; Puerto Ricans needed special language training. If public housing projects were increasingly unlivable and crime-ridden, it was because of their new black and Puerto Rican tenants. As the incidence of arson and building abandonment soared in the black and Puerto Rican slums, firemen wasted their resources chasing false alarms set by black and Puerto Rican children. Black and Puerto Rican youngsters vandalized park and playground equipment; their parents "airmailed" garbage from tenement windows. The illegitimacy, venereal disease, child abuse, broken families, and juvenile delinquency that swamped the city social agencies were concentrated in black and Puerto Rican families. Poverty and welfare in the City, or at least the visible portions of it, were black and Puerto Rican problems. "Community control" meant black or Puerto Rican control.

Clearly, the future of the city hinged on its new minorities. If they could not be absorbed into the taxpaying middle classes, there was nothing ahead but disruption and decline. Although Lindsay would not have claimed to know precisely how to solve the problem, the general task seemed clear. The position of blacks reflected centuries of white discrimination and mistreatment. The civil rights movement was confirming the black claim to full legal equality with whites, but equality in fact would require massive investment in compensatory programming by the government. The strains on government were likely to be immense, but the consequences of inaction seemed to outweigh by far the dangers of undertaking the enterprise.

LINDSAY, RACISM, AND CIVIL RIGHTS

The civil rights movement was central to John Lindsay's career. It was one of the great political movements in American history, and it is almost impossible to overestimate its impact on American government, North and South. The driving force of the movement was a sense of moral outrage at the racist character of American society, an outrage fed by the brutal response of Southern authorities to early civil rights organizing and gradual exposure of the subtle, more hypocritical, white resistance to black progress in the North.

The practical effect of the official racist doctrine in the South after the Civil War was to deny to blacks the normal routes of social and economic advancement open to other ethnic groups. Lynchings, arson, and brutal intimidation stamped out the small class of black entrepeneurs and cast blacks outside the pale of the political process. In 1865 virtually all skilled craftsmen in the South were black; by 1900 they had been almost totally displaced by white labor. After the boll weevil decimated cotton crops in the 1920s, discriminatory enforcement of federal farm legislation, combined with sheer force, dispossessed the black sharecropper and small landowner to permit white aggregations of large holdings. Whites suffered as well, but the burden fell with fierce disproportion upon blacks. Disgraceful schools, contaminated water supplies, shanty housing and mud streets led to rampant ignorance and disease—the result of conscious policy enacted by the white power structure.

Life in the North was sporadically better, but only sporadically. In New York, for instance, schools and public accommodations were largely integrated by the end of the nineteenth century; black realtors played an important role in the opening of Harlem to blacks; some black businessmen moved easily in white circles; and by the 1920s, there was at least a handful of ranking black public officials. But for the great mass of blacks, opportunities were severely limited by the European immigrations, which produced a seemingly endless stream of white proletariat that poured into the Northern cities. The job competition between the blacks and the Irish engendered one of the "harshest intergroup hatreds in history." New York saw bloody race riots in 1863 and 1900—the latter with the active support of the white police force.

The color lines in the North tightened with the acceleration of black migration after 1900—two hundred thousand blacks moved Northward from 1900 to 1910, five hundred thousand in the following decade, and nine hundred thousand during the twenties. The intense job competition led to another outbreak of race rioting after World War I, the most serious of which was in Chicago in 1919. Blacks suffered cruelly from the Depression, and racism excluded them from sharing in the recovery. Almost all locomotive firemen, for example, had been black until the 1930s, when white unions, resorting to physical intimidation and murder, made the jobs a white preserve in the space of a few years. Even during World War II, munitions factories were stopped by hate strikes protesting the presence of black workers. The use of blacks as strike-breakers in prewar Detroit created lasting hostilities, and Detroit was the scene of the worst of the major race riots that swept the country in 1943.

That blacks continued to migrate to the North in the face of rampant discrimination is testimony to the semi-feudal economic and social character of the South. The attractions of war work swelled the migration to 1.7 million in the 1940s, and it remained at high levels for the next twenty years—1.5 million in the 1950s and 1.4 million in the 1960s. After the social conditions in the South were transformed by the civil rights revolution and the South's economic renaissance, the migration abruptly reversed. In the first half of the 1970s, the net black migration was from North to South for the first time, and most large Northern cities lost black population. New York City was virtually unique in the 1970s in experiencing a net immigration of blacks, because there was a substantial influx of West Indians that began in the late 1960s and continued strongly through the next decade.

Puerto Ricans were never the victims of racism to the same degree as American blacks; but their color difference from white Americans and the fact that the peak of the Puerto Rican migrations was roughly contemporaneous with the black movement North after World War II served to link Puerto Rican and black problems—even though relations between the two groups have tended to be hostile. Ambitious Puerto Ricans have long been attracted to the mainland, but it was the introduction of cheap air transport that opened the door to migration on a large scale. The mainland Puerto Rican population rose from seventy thousand in 1940 to nine hundred thousand in 1960 and 1.4 million in 1970, although most of the growth since 1960 resulted from the high Puerto Rican birth rate instead of migration. The Puerto Rican migration, in contrast to that of the blacks, concentrated almost exclusively on New York City in its early phases, although there has been more dispersion in recent years. Like the blacks, the Puerto Ricans reversed their migration in the 1970s, with the improvement in the island's economy: forty thousand Puerto Ricans, net, returned to the island from the mainland in 1972.*

To the degree that poverty is evidence of discrimination, Puerto Ricans had as great a claim on the civil rights movement as blacks. By every available measure—family poverty, welfare enrollment, employment, labor force participation, female-headed families—Puerto Ricans in New York were considerably worse off than blacks; and throughout the 1960s, as black incomes improved relative to whites', the gap between blacks and Puerto Ricans actually widened.

In 1966, when Lindsay took office, the civil rights movement was at its zenith but was at the same time entering a state of deep crisis. The legal barriers against equal voting rights, equal employment, and equal housing were coming down, at great cost of blood and bitterness, but victory was turning to ashes as the mass of blacks and Puerto Ricans in Northern cities sank ever deeper into squalor and despair. Lyndon Johnson sounded the theme at Howard University, six months before Lindsay assumed his mayoralty, when he announced

---

* In the 1970s the city's Hispanic population began to receive large infusions from Latin America—Brazilians, Colombians, Venezuelans, Panamanians. A 1979 estimate put the city's non–Puerto Rican Hispanic population at 450,000, but the estimates are extremely imprecise, and there is relatively little good information on the economic performance of the various groups.

"the next and more profound stage in the battle for civil rights": moving the fight from the South to the Northern ghettos. For the majority of blacks trapped in the urban slums, said the president, "the walls are rising and the gulf is widening." It was a call to a crusade, and there was more than a streak of the crusader in John Lindsay's character.

Lindsay's commitment to social progress for blacks was both deeply felt and abstract—very much in the tradition of the brahmin abolitionists of a century before. "He didn't really know that many blacks," says Mitchell Ginsberg, "particularly not poor ones. I don't think he ever felt very comfortable with welfare, for instance. His commitment was more to equal rights than to the poor." Abstraction is not the same as detachment: The puritan instinct is often a fierce one. "One thing I always admired about John," says another aide, "was that he could really get angry when he saw some poor black guy stuck in a lousy ghetto. He never got hardened to it."

The blurring of abstract conceptions with daily realities is not only a brahmin failing, for it infected much of the later civil rights movement. Just as the abolitionists had expected blacks to achieve self-sufficiency immediately upon emancipation, the civil rights leadership seemed to expect economic parity with whites, or something approaching it, to follow closely upon the achievement of full legal equality. When no such decisive change was immediately apparent, the failure was taken as evidence that racism was more deeply rooted than anyone had suspected, and the movement quickly radicalized. The Watts riot of 1965, for example, was termed a "manifesto" in quite respectable circles. Charles Silberman, an editor of *Fortune*, recommended in his influential *Crisis in Black and White* the Saul Alinsky technique of "rubbing raw the sores of discontent." Change would almost certainly be accompanied by violence, Silberman wrote, and right action would require "heroic decisions" from the country's leadership. Just as plantation owners after the Civil War had used their economic power to maintain blacks in serfdom, the modern enemy in the North was "welfare colonialism," a subtle admixture of economic supports and invisible restrictions that maintained the black in permanent dependence. Dignity and self-respect could be attained only by revolt against the system.

White support for radicalization of the blacks was not limited to an intellectual elite. The welfare protest movement in New York City drew its early main support from the Catholic Diocese of Brooklyn. Hubert Humphrey announced that if he had to put up with conditions in the slums he "would lead a mighty good revolt." Lyndon Johnson was only one of many politicians to justify new programs—almost any new programs—by the need to forestall riots, which by 1967 seemed to be viewed almost as a reasonable mode of expression. At its worst the revolutionary impulse became radical chic. Protestant audiences in New York applauded the castigations of James Forman and debated seriously his demands for billions in reparations. Black Panthers starred at fashionable cocktail parties. Suburbanites in slacks descended upon Harlem, five thousand strong, to clean and paint for the residents. Businessmen solemnly sported black and white "Give a damn" buttons.

Lindsay was by nature a controversialist, and although the exigencies of of-

60 *The Cost of Good Intentions*

fice gradually pushed him toward more conservative attitudes, his initial instincts were toward the radical positions—massive government interventions to solve ghetto problems, participatory democracy for blacks and Puerto Ricans, community control of antipoverty programs and schools, and a view that civil disorders were more a reflection of white failings than of black indiscipline. He made no secret of this in his campaign. Wagner's failings, in the eyes of the reformers, had not been unwillingness to ameliorate slum conditions or insincerity in proposing new programs: It was his tepid commitment to change, his insistence on working through traditional mechanisms.

Lindsay's early view was crystallized by his work as vice chairman of the National Advisory Commission on Civil Disorders—the Kerner Commission—which published its report in March 1968. He was the most forceful advocate of a strong report and played a key role in bringing the other commission members to the same stance. The introduction of the report states the position eloquently:

Our nation is moving toward two societies, one black, one white—separate and unequal. . . .
Discrimination and segregation have long permeated much of American life; they threaten the future of every American. . . .
To pursue our present course will involve the continuing polarization of the American community and, ultimately, the destruction of democratic values. . . .
The alternative will require a commitment to national action—compassionate, massive, and sustained, backed by the resources of the most powerful nation on earth. From every American, it will require new attitudes, new understanding, and, above all, new will. . . .
Segregation and poverty have created in the racial ghetto a destructive environment totally unknown to most white Americans. . . .
What white Americans have never fully understood—but what the Negro can never forget—is that white society is deeply implicated in the ghetto. White institutions created it, white institutions maintain it, and white society condones it. . . .
[Our recommendations] will require unprecedented levels of funding and performance, but they neither probe deeper nor demand more than the problems which call them forth. There can be no higher priority for national action and no higher claim on the nation's conscience.

Lindsay was making no demands upon the nation that he was not prepared to make upon the citizens of New York, and the Kerner report was required reading for all of his commissioners. The highest priority for all the agencies of city government—parks, sanitation, housing programs, schools—would be the attempt to engineer the rapid uplift of the urban minorities. The centerpiece of the administration's strategy would be the new antipoverty programs, reform of welfare, and a drastic change in police dealings with the ghetto. The War on Poverty would attempt to enlist militant anger in the service of the new federal social programs. The very real perception that welfare meant whites exercising power over black and Puerto Rican clients spotlighted welfare reform as a key civil rights issue. Finally, the police response to ghetto disturbances reflected the emerging view of the legitimacy of protest—even violent protest—that was developing during the later stages of the long struggle for equality.

ANTIPOVERTY PROGRAMS

In the antipoverty programs the Great Society's tendency toward a priori rationalism blended with the moral impulse that inspirited the drive for civil rights and equal opportunity. The original conceptions about poverty in America were in fact heavily influenced by conditions in rural white communities: After all, most poor people were white, and most urban blacks were not poor. But the frustration of civil rights leaders at the increasing concentration of blacks in the lowest socioeconomic stratum of Northern central cities coincided with the frustration of the cities' political leadership at the deteriorating schools, increasing crime rates, failed public housing projects, and blighted urban renewal programs in the neighborhoods experiencing the greatest influx of black and Hispanic immigrants. The various threads of concern combined to weave a syllogism of classic elegance: Lack of opportunity and discrimination confined blacks and Puerto Ricans to a condition of powerlessness and hopelessness in urban ghettoes; powerlessness and despair fostered a sense of alienation and irresponsibility that threatened the stability of the cities; granting economic opportunity and political power would therefore make blacks and Puerto Ricans self-sufficient and responsible citizens and at the same time ward off the impending urban crisis.

Formulated in the abstract, the syllogism is quite probably correct; but it gives no clue to the time frame required for a change in attitude to take hold, nor is it of much help in deciding which government programs will best achieve the hoped-for results or, indeed, whether compensatory programming is even very relevant to the problem. The consensus around the objectives of the antipoverty programs concealed a wide range of inconsistent strategies and tactics, some of them sensible, some of them probably harmless, and some of them just silly. But, for the time being, the formidable combination of rationalist logic and moralist fervor swept away the doubts and inconsistencies.* The chance to eradicate poverty was a heady challenge to a new breed of thinkers and managers who had cut their professional teeth on problems of defense analysis and urban planning, while the opportunity actually to deliver the promise of the civil rights movement commanded the idealism and energy of the political activists who were reshaping the outlines of American government.

The Economic Opportunity Act itself was an awkward amalgam of conflicting theories—aggressive community action, trade union liberalism, traditional settlement house social work—and a pastiche of new programs that reflected more the bargaining power of the interested federal agencies than any coherent

---

* Kenneth Clark's book *Dark Ghetto* which was based on his original program plan for the Harlem antipoverty program, is an excellent example. The book is infused with a genuine passion that obscures an extraordinarily simplistic faith in Dr. Clark's own discipline—psychology—and social science generally to transform whole communities of people.

strategy. There were job programs for youth, employment programs for welfare fathers (the "happy pappy" program), rural development loans and grants, incentives and loans for minority businessmen, aid to impoverished college students, and—presumably binding together the whole—local community action programs (CAPs in the acronymic fashion of the day). CAPs were expected to mobilize local resources in a "comprehensive" program, to "provide services, assistance, and other activities of sufficient variety, scope, and magnitude" to start eliminating poverty, and to conduct their affairs with "maximum feasible participation" of the poor themselves.

Most of the flexible funds in the program flowed through the community action title, and a struggle for control of New York's programs developed during Mayor Wagner's last year in office. Wagner's problems in exercising control were complicated by the presence of two of the early prototypes for the national program: Harlem Youth Opportunities Unlimited (HARYOU) and Mobilization for Youth (MFY) on the lower East Side. Both programs had been established outside the control of City Hall, predominantly with federal funding, and both were exponents of the "rubbing raw" model of community programming.

HARYOU ran into serious political problems before its programs ever got off the ground. Harlem youth may have been powerless, as the program's planners argued, but Harlem politicians assuredly were not. Adam Clayton Powell, Jr. was chairman of the House Subcommittee on Education and Labor and had no intention of seeing the first major opportunities for black patronage dissipated on radical theoreticians. Wagner's own antipoverty programs were held up in Washington until Powell worked out control of the Harlem programs on his own terms. A merger was effected between HARYOU and Powell's own Associated Community Teams (ACT), and the HARYOU planners were forced out of a remodelled HARYOU-ACT. The struggle for control, enervating and disillusioning, was spread through the daily press for months and was a harbinger of the turbulence to come.

MFY had no strong local presences to contend with and was able to mount programs on its own terms—which inclined toward spectacular militance. Dead rats were dumped on Wagner's doorstep to protest housing conditions, mothers marched on local schools to demand better textbooks, top young lawyers were vigilant around the clock to organize rent strikes or investigate police brutality. It was too much, too soon, and the program was cut off at the knees in 1964. Paul Screvane, Wagner's poverty coordinator, denounced the agitation and accused the program of harboring Communists. An investigation disclosed a handful of radicals and enough fiscal irregularities to justify a reorganization and pave the way for a quiet phasing out of the controversial activities.

Radical community organization was alien to Wagner's concept of government, and community control was antithetical to his instinct for controlling patronage. Although he was committed to better service programs for the poor, he expected them to be city programs run out of city agencies. He announced that the city's antipoverty war would be operated by an Antipoverty Operations Board, with policy oversight by a Council against Poverty, both of which would consist entirely of city officials. The plan drew strong protests from the city's voluntary social agencies, and after six months Wagner added them to the Council. Then, to satisfy Powell, Wagner created a private Economic Opportunity Corporation to run the programs—assuring Powell's input—and suitably modified the roles of the Council against Poverty and the Antipoverty Operations Board. That plan in turn was rejected by OEO, which had decided to take seriously the mandate for "maximum feasible participation" of the poor—whatever had been originally intended by that elusive phrase. Wagner compromised by agreeing to create six Community Progress Centers to expand the possibilities for involving local residents in policymaking. To everyone's amazement, Nelson Rockefeller vetoed the compromise—for reasons that were never totally clear—but dropped his objections when Wagner replaced the private corporation with a committee that would be eligible to receive the funds.

The result was a mess. Each of the three different arms of the program began to approve grant requests without checking with the others; commitments were made far beyond the funds available, creating chaos when the shortfalls became apparent the following year. Moreover, because of the slow startup of the City's own programs, half of the funds that *were* allocated weren't spent and had to be returned to OEO. The program submissions themselves were "a lot of garbage," according to one OEO official. In the local communities the situation was even more confusing. The city's Antipoverty Operations Board had awarded seed money to start local programs in eight of the poor neighborhoods; but the following year, the Council Against Poverty created sixteen antipoverty areas that overlapped the first eight, and then the six Community Progress Centers were superimposed on ten of the sixteen areas. The war against poverty rapidly degenerated into internecine warfare among the poor.

Lindsay decided that he would have to start completely over. He appointed a study team headed by Mitchell Sviridoff, a gravelly-voiced former Connecticut AFL-CIO president who had gained a national reputation as director of a pioneering community action program in New Haven, where he had whipped the city's educational and social agencies into line behind a coordinated training and development program for the poor. It was the model of the rationalist intervention strategy—compassion and sensitivity constrained within a tightly managed, smoothly functioning, goal-oriented program machinery.

Sviridoff's team recommended that the programs be drastically streamlined and that the city reorganize all its human service efforts to permit unified programming. Programs for the poor would be centralized in a Human Resources Administration, a giant agency that would meld the new poverty war battalions and the traditional Department of Social Services—with its army of twenty-five thousand caseworkers and welfare clerks. A Community Development Agency would coordinate anti-poverty programs; a Manpower and Career Development Agency, would run job training and placement programs; and an Office of Educational Affairs would provide a formal link between the mayor and the Board of Education and attempt to influence the board in matters affecting the poor.

The political wisdom of concentrating so many potentially controversial programs in a single agency might have been questioned, but it was in the mainstream of the rationalizing impulse of the time. Almost a third of the reorganization report was devoted to a discussion of PPBS and the planning advantages that would accrue from concentrating resources under unified leadership.

To illustrate the problem [the report says] if the head of a family has completed a training course, there must be followup to get him a job. If family problems jeopardize his performance, social services must be brought into play to relieve the pressure. If one of his children needs daycare, it must be provided. A school-age child must get the kind of education that fits his talents and prepares him for a career of opportunity.

Manpower programming was conceived as:

"a chain that links all the pieces so that progress from testing through work experience and skill training to a job can be managed more systematically and sensibly throughout the City."

PPBS would lead to better resource allocation in the schools:

"PPBS might, for instance, show that improved reading levels can be more economically achieved by in-service training of regular classroom teachers than by adding more specialized reading staff."

Far from being daunted by the massiveness of poverty in New York, the report fairly crackled with excitement:

To recognize [the size and gravity of the problem] is to sense a challenge unmatched in America. As the problems are more staggering, the rewards of progress can be greater. And if New York moves forward, other cities facing similar problems may well feel encouraged on the just ground that what is possible in New York is possible elsewhere. What happens here has significance even beyond the borders of the United States.

Enthusiasms aside, it can be doubted whether the newly established agency ever had much of a chance. It was proposing to provide individually tailored social programming for literally millions of people, the great majority of whom were probably less than willing to be programmed for—a classic case of overreaching. Moreover, a difficult undertaking was made impossible by the requirement—absolutely in keeping with Lindsay's campaign promises—that the programs would operate as models of participatory democracy; McNamara-style management would be wedded to Alinsky-Silberman self-determination.

The key agency linking with the poor, and the successor to the various tentacles of the Wagner antipoverty program, was the Community Development Agency. Its staff was controlled by HRA, but its policy board, the Council Against Poverty, was composed entirely of community representatives. Says Sviridoff, who became HRA's first administrator:

I lost on that one. I was never really in favor of participation as an end in itself. But there was a lot of pressure from the mayor's young aides to go all the way. And Washington insisted on the need for more participation. I can't fault them entirely. It was the spirit of the times. There may not have been any choice.

The council would pass on funding proposals from local community corporations, which would be completely independent of the city, except as they were bound by contracted financial and management requirements. In turn, the community corporations would subcontract to a host of local organizations in the target areas, most of which were just being organized to operate programs since funds had become available.

The original hope was that the central staff—largely white—would be able to maintain sufficient control over the council to assure some level of professionalism. It was a wistful hope. There were riots around the country in 1967, and the tight management umbrella planned by Sviridoff and his coterie of experts was almost immediately swamped by the rising tide of black radicalism swirling throughout the ghettos. Field staff—predominantly black and Puerto Rican and predominantly militant—quickly split with the central HRA staff and organized picket lines and sit-ins at headquarters. When blacks came to dominate the community boards, bitter clashes ensued between local blacks and Puerto Ricans—both sniffing the scent of money and patronage. Then Congress began to cut back and earmark the flexible funds, so that council itself became the target of community organizations who felt they weren't getting their fair share. Federal funds were held up for months at a time in 1966 and 1967, adding to the management chaos. A disappointed delegate agency in East Harlem wrecked the offices of the local community corporation. The federal agencies watched helplessly from the sidelines and demanded that the city take control. But the doctrine of community control was by now a sacred rubric: The white administrators could do little but peer into the dark ghettos, vainly trying to distinguish indigenous leadership from mere demagoguery.

Sviridoff and most of the top white staff left at the end of the first year. CDA was taken over by the most canny and capable of the community corporation directors—Major R. Owens from Brownsville—and the strategy explicitly shifted from services to politicization in the black neighborhoods. Lindsay remained a steadfast supporter of the program in public, but his initial enthusiasm had markedly waned. When the Model Cities programs started in 1968, he was careful to keep community participants in a purely advisory capacity.

It is easy to criticize the antipoverty programs, but some of the accomplishments were substantial. Sviridoff was able to channel funds to the Bedford-Stuyvesant Renewal Corporation, an agency that has concentrated with some success on hard economic development issues instead of racial politics, and he provided a helpful boost to a program that broke the color line in the skilled construction unions. The Opportunities Industrialization Center, a manpower program imported from Philadelphia, was among the most successful of the city's training programs. OEO funds set up hundreds of Head Start centers throughout the city, eleven separate family planning programs, twenty-five neighborhood law offices, seven comprehensive health centers, twenty day-care centers and supported literally hundreds of other activities—many of them wasteful, but some of them undoubtedly helpful in limited ways. No one questioned that hiring tens of thousands of ghetto teenagers for summer projects was a worthwhile investment in averting disorders.

The program could be further defended on the grounds that it was provid-

ing valuable training for black leadership,* which was essential if there was
ever to be an orderly transition of political power from the white to the black
working classes. Moreover, although the antipoverty programs are associated
in the public mind with the city's fiscal profligacy, the actual costs to the city
were not very high. For all the rhetoric, Lindsay spent less city tax money each
year on antipoverty programs than Wagner had. Lindsay's antipoverty local tax
spending peaked at about $37 million in 1968–69—or about 1.2 percent of the
local funds in the budget. Manpower training costs reached $50 million a year
at their peak, but the financing was through long-term bonds. It was not the
type of financing that impressed bankers, but the annual debt service on $50
million of thirty-year bonds is only about $3.6 million a year—not a trivial sum,
but only a tiny fraction of the city's annual debt service costs.

Some major costs were intangible. When five thousand youngsters, led by
an HRA employee, descended on the City Council and attempted to overturn
councilmen's cars to protest the expiration of summer programs, the excesses
were inevitably laid directly on Lindsay's doorstep. Lindsay suspended the employee involved, but it was lost on no one that he hesitated considerably before
doing so, for fear of further disorders. And antipoverty salaries were high:
Most white workers earned a good deal less than newly minted middle-
level black poverty executives, and the comparisons did not predispose to racial
harmony. Even though the money spent was mostly federal money, a taxpayer
could argue that tax dollars were tax dollars, no matter whose account they
came from. Finally, some indirect costs were substantial. One of the major
targets of the community corporations was the city welfare program—the other
side of HRA. Organization efforts were intense, and the city welfare rolls grew
dramatically—not incidentally reinforcing the stereotype that welfare is a program that whites finance for blacks.

In terms of the vaulting goals they had set for themselves, of course, the
programs were doomed to failure. Although it is true that antipoverty programs
were never sufficiently funded, the funds that were available, while far short of
what was required for their ostensible purposes, were still more than the city
could manage effectively. Probably the most important contribution was simply
the provision of jobs—middle-class, civil service, white-collar jobs—for large
numbers of blacks and Puerto Ricans, a service not at all unlike that performed
for the Irish by an even crasser system of patronage a couple of generations earlier. It is an accomplishment easily subject to facile denigration, but the rapid
progress of the black middle classes since the mid-1960s owes a substantial debt
to the broadening of employment opportunities in state and local government,
particularly in human service occupations.

A substantial number of the poor, however, either did not or could not
work. For them the new employment opportunities offered by the antipoverty

* There is not universal agreement on this point. Leaders of the poor were not usually elected, but
were merely recognized by the whites, putting a premium on attention-getting displays instead of
hard political work. Most putative leaders, it would later turn out, could not really mobilize fol-
lowers in a crunch. A black political scientist suggests that the process could actually have retarded
black political development.

programs were of small relevance. Although welfare programs seem to have figured little in the original planning of the antipoverty programs, they were of far
greater importance in providing resources to the poor. Moreover, because welfare was a program administered by whites for an overwhelmingly black and
Puerto Rican clientele, it was also emerging as a key area of controversy in an
increasingly militant civil rights movement.

WELFARE

Lindsay's choice as commissioner of social services, which included the
city's welfare and social work programs, was Mitchell Ginsberg, a professor of
social work at Columbia University. Ginsberg made no secret of his views on
welfare: He came from the same faculty as Richard Cloward, an original or-
ganizer of MFY who was providing the intellectual underpinnings for a national
radical movement for welfare rights, and he believed with a passionate intensity that the system was inequitable, degrading, and corrupt. Clearly, Lindsay
felt the same way. "I had made a speech before the Citizens' Union," says
Ginsberg, "where I called for national reform of the program. The mayor called
me the next day and said he had read my speech and wanted me to do the City
job. He said he was looking for someone who could give the problem the level
of attention it deserved." Significantly, both men conceived of the assignment
in a national context: New York City's was the largest local program in the
nation, and Lindsay wanted changes in New York to be a bellwether for national policy.

There was little dispute that the system was in need of reform. First of all, it
was incredibly complex. There were separate programs for the permanently
disabled, the aged poor, and the blind, for one-parent families with dependent
children, for two-parent families with children (provided one of the parents had
satisfied certain detailed employment and unemployment requirements), and a
catch-all program of "home relief" for people who fell through the net of the
other programs but could meet detailed requirements of temporary disability
or unemployability. Grant levels varied from program to program, and in Aid to
Dependent Children (ADC), the single biggest program, grants were built up
from detailed tables that accounted separately for rents, heating requirements,
the food requirements of children of different sexes at different ages, clothing
needs at various times of the year, school expenses, and myriad other details of
daily living. Each of the special elements in the grant was to some extent
discretionary on the part of the caseworker—similarly situated families often
received quite different amounts of money, and caseworkers could bargain with
families to accept their advice on other matters in order to qualify for a more
generous grant. Welfare eligibility also conferred eligibility for health care
programs, food stamps, surplus food, free school lunches, public housing, daycare, and other benefits, so the final package could contain a complex and often
substantial array of benefits. The situation was further complicated by the introduction of "earned income disregards": That is, in the hope of encouraging
recipients to work, a specified percentage of earned income would not be

counted against the basic grant, in order to avoid a dollar-for-dollar grant reduction (to avoid, in effect, a 100% tax rate on earnings). The various programs
were governed by thick volumes of regulations, which had been issued separately by the federal government, the state, and the city over some thirty years.
They were duplicative, overlapping, and inconsistent, both internally and one
with the other, and, to say the least, desperately confusing to client and
caseworker alike.

Just as important, the program was expensive. There were more than five
hundred thousand people on welfare when Lindsay took office. The welfare
budget was $563 million, $192 million of which was charged against city tax
receipts, while the state and federal governments shared the remainder. Ominously, after a period of long stability during the 1950s, the rolls had begun to
grow rapidly during Wagner's third term, and since 1962 had been rising at an
annual rate of about 12 percent, sufficient to double the caseload every six
years.

The high and rising cost of welfare was a favorite theme of Lindsay's campaign, but he was attacking welfare as a symptom of a declining economy rather
than criticizing welfare spending itself. For his part Ginsberg did not consider
welfare spending his direct concern—in the sense of its being something he
could control. "I always viewed the cost of welfare to be whatever it is," he
says. "If people are eligible and apply, you have to put them on. Certainly, I
never wanted to assist ineligibles, but all the evidence, at least in the early
days, was that ineligibility levels were low." National policy at the time was
consistent with the Ginsberg view. Both HEW and OEO exhorted States to
increase welfare spending. The logic was that as economic recovery and antipoverty programs reduced the need for welfare among people who could work,
welfare grants would be made sufficiently generous to allow those unable to
compete—the aged, the disabled, or children and their mothers—to live in
minimum dignity and comfort.

It was precisely the concern for costs on the part of previous administrations
that was the target of the burgeoning radical attack on welfare that was gather-
ing strength just about the time Ginsberg assumed his new position. The at-
tackers charged that welfare administrations kept costs down by manipulating
the rules. MFY, HARYOU-ACT, and the hosts of storefront agencies that were
popping up around the city found that unfair welfare administration was the
most frequent complaint of people coming to them for help. The problem
linked directly with civil rights. Cloward and his colleague, Frances Fox Piven,
showed that welfare rolls had failed to expand during the 1950s, even though
the black poor were streaming into the cities; only administrative repres-
sion seemed to account for the fact. Even moderates felt revulsion at the detailed inquiries into a single mother's sex life. Caseworkers defended their
delving into personal matters—boy friends might be a source of child support—
but critics saw it as white prurience about black sexuality. Ginsberg's predecessor, James Dumpson, a black himself, had been a liberal on most issues, but
Ginsberg wanted to go further. His first act in office, to establish his credentials

as a reformer, was to outlaw "midnight raids"—surprise night visits by case-workers to see if a woman was cohabiting with a man while receiving payment as a single mother. When he announced the new policy, he specifically asked the welfare rights organizations to bring to his attention any instances of staff members who violated the new order.

The birth of the welfare rights movement in the city can be pinpointed to 1964, when Frank Espada, later the director of community organization under Lindsay, began organizing clients in the East New York section of Brooklyn, closely followed by MFY on the lower East Side. Carefully reading the manuals, Espada and the MFY staff discovered that most clients were eligible for higher grants than they actually received. The regulations stipulated living conditions in such detail—for instance, a kitchen should have a fruit reamer—that almost everyone could qualify for additional special grants to reach standards. Their first organized efforts were only sporadically successful. MFY sponsored a winter clothing campaign in 1965, and while they managed to secure a number of special grants, the effort bogged down in the complicated welfare procedures. The following winter they linked with Espada's group to coordinate a minimum-standards campaign that was more successful but still of limited impact. By this point, however, welfare rights were becoming something of a national issue. George Wiley had left CORE to become the first director of the National Welfare Rights Organization; a nationwide rights conference was held in Syracuse at which New York contingents were the dominating influence.

A turning point came with the publication of an article by Cloward and Piven in the *Nation* on May 2, 1966, which set out for the first time a coherent strategy for the movement. They argued that the existing system survived only by intimidating and underpaying clients. A massive campign to enroll eligible clients and to get full benefits for those already on the rolls would cause the system's financial collapse and ensure its replacement by an equitable, federally administered program of guaranteed income maintenance. The tactics should include a mass educational campaign and public disruption of local welfare offices. The disruption, it was argued, was necessary to enhance the clients' sense of power in dealing with the system and to increase the pressure on state and local governments to pass the burden to the federal government. The article generated immense excitement among radical antipoverty workers and was a blueprint for the organizing drive in New York. The Catholic diocese of Brooklyn, spurred by militant young priests who had been doing storefront duty, provided full-time organizing staff the following year, and Catholic Charities financed training sessions. The city caseworkers' union provided financial assistance and moral support. It became something of a badge of honor for caseworkers to manipulate the regulations to build the largest possible grant for a client, and the union included welfare liberalization as part of its bargaining demands. The HRA community corporations that were being set up around the city under the direction of Frank Espada, who now worked for the city, placed welfare rights organization high on their agenda. Even Ginsberg gave the

movement an initial boost: During his first year in office he lectured caseworkers over closed circuit television that there were more persons in the city
eligible for welfare and not receiving it than were on the rolls.

The peak years for the movement were 1967 and 1968. Half the National
Welfare Rights membership in the country was in New York City. A fair hearings campaign insisted on a rarely used due process procedure before closing a
case. After swamping the centers with fair hearings requests, the groups won
standardized fair hearings procedures, including Spanish translators, babysit-
ters during the hearings, carfare, and night hearings for working mothers. A
special grants drive generated $5 million in increased grants in just a month's
time in 1967. The caseworkers' union brought additional pressure on the city.
As applications began to rise rapidly, contractual limits on caseloads were regularly exceeded, and the caseworkers insisted that the city drop detailed investigations and complicated paperwork procedures in order to make it even easier
to accept new cases.

In mid-1968 Ginsberg estimated that the special grants drive was costing
the city from $10 to 12 million per month in additional outlays. In April the
campaign focused on spring clothing; in June, on school graduation expenses;
during the summer, on camp clothing and camp expenses; in August on telephones. The campaign of disruption was in full swing. There was a three-day
sit-in at the commissioner's office, and unruly demonstrators closed centers
throughout the city. One sit-in reportedly netted $135,000 in new grants. A
second insisted on demands averaging $300 to $400 each for some 270 families.
Mounted police were required to clear demonstrations from HRA headquarters. Workers often boycotted the centers where clients were demonstrating,
partly from sympathy, but increasingly from fear. In August, the *New York
Times* wrote: "The demonstrators have jammed the centers, sometimes camp-
ing out in them overnight, broken down administrative procedures, played
havoc with the mountains of paperwork, and have . . . thrown the City's Welfare program into a state of crisis and chaos."

The state and the city finessed the movement in the fall of 1968 by replacing
the special grants with a simplified basic grant that would be uniform for all
clients, removing at a stroke one of the most effective client organizing issues.
The movement's frustration spilled over into violence. There were new disrup-
tions throughout the city, demonstrations at City Hall, and injuries to both
police and demonstrators. At one center the protesters ripped telephones from
the center walls, scattered papers, and threw desks into piles in the middle of
the intake rooms. The centers counted more than two hundred incidents a
month as the demonstrations reached a pitch. Frightened workers stayed home
when the demonstrators were joined by militant local CORE groups and contingents of Black Panthers.

The protests died out through the winter, and the welfare rights movement
steadily declined in importance thereafter, but it would be years before the system would dig out from under the confusion and chaos in the centers. With
paperwork hopelessly snarled and applications still building, waiting times

stretched from hours to days and even weeks. Clients were by now thoroughly hostile, while workers who were once sympathetic were intimidated and resentful. Partly from conviction, and partly to ease the workload, Ginsberg instituted a declaration application system that did away with time-consuming home investigation. The move drew plaudits from HEW and *The New York Times* but the sobriquet "Come-and-Get It" Ginsberg from *The Daily News*.

The overall costs to the city were enormous. During Lindsay's first term the welfare caseload more than doubled and spending jumped from $400 million to $1 billion, with about a third of the total coming from city resources; and because welfare clients were also eligible for the new Medicaid program, total welfare and welfare-related health costs rose to more than $2 billion.

The radicals failed in their quest for national reform. Although they nearly succeeded in bankrupting local governments, as they had intended, the response was not a more generous national system, but cutbacks in grant levels—in 1971—and eventually, much more stringent welfare administration at all levels of government. With the economy heading rapidly into recession, welfare reform had threatened to become something rather new in American politics: instead of merely granting the poor a continued share of a growing economy, the massive expansion of the rolls began to approach actual redistribution of income from the middle class to the poor. It was not a policy that most Americans—or even John Lindsay—were prepared to support. By his second term Lindsay himself was at least as disenchanted with welfare as he had been with the more radical concepts of community participation in the antipoverty programs. His hopes for reform from that point concentrated almost solely on ideas to transfer a greater share of the costs to the state and federal government.

To liberal reformers the sharpest disappointment was the sudden upsurge in dependency. The original strategists of the antipoverty program seemed sincerely to believe that the increased opportunities for minorities from Great Society programs and civil rights victories would actually reduce the welfare rolls. Instead, something like the opposite happened: Black male unemployment declined sharply through the first half of the 1960s to its lowest level in many years, but black ADC rolls went up anyway. To many whites, particularly middle-class taxpayers who, however begrudgingly, had come to accept the new requirements for equal rights and opportunities for the poor, the spectacle of blacks demanding more welfare seemed to confirm the stereotype of black shiftlessness. (Blacks were far more prominent in the welfare rights movement than Hispanics, even though Hispanics derived much greater proportional benefit from welfare liberalization.) Granted, perhaps, that women with large numbers of children could not be expected to work, but as Edward Banfield pointed out, *somebody* was fathering all those children and not contributing to their support. And if the souring of the welfare rights movement dashed the hopes of the more optimistic social planners, the violence of the movement was frightening. The driving energy behind the campaign for civil equality was transmuting into incendiary destruction.

RIOTS

In 1963, whites and blacks clashed in Savannah, Georgia, and Cambridge, Maryland, and there were serious incidents in Harlem, Chicago, and Philadelphia. In Birmingham, Alabama, police used dogs, cattle prods, and fire hoses against civil rights marchers; blacks were shot at and their houses burned; and white businesses were burned in retaliation. The following year civil rights demonstrations turned to violence in Jacksonville, Florida. A black woman was shot from a passing car, and for the first time black youths threw Molotov cocktails. A demonstration against school segregation in Cleveland, Ohio, turned to violence when a bulldozer killed a white minister.

In Harlem, after months of increasingly militant picketing by blacks against police brutality and job discrimination, a black youth was killed by a white policeman. Angry protests led to bitter fighting between blacks and policemen and finally to firesetting and looting. A week later National Guardsmen were called to Rochester, New York, when two days of violence followed an attempt by police to arrest a drunken teenager at a dance. There were disorders throughout northern New Jersey, and crowds burned buildings in Chicago. Two policemen, one black and one white, attempted to move a stalled car in a Philadelphia slum and touched off two nights of rioting.

The level of violence escalated spectacularly with the Watts riot in 1965. A crowd gathered when police tried to arrest a drunken driver. Youths began to throw rocks, and when police reacted hesitantly the area exploded into an orgy of burning and looting. Police and National Guardsmen responded to apparent incidents of sniping with heavy use of firepower. When the riot subsided on the fourth day, thirty-six people were dead, hundreds injured, and four thousand arrested. Property damage was estimated at $35 million. The following summer saw incidents in almost every major city in the country. Four thousand guardsmen were required to restore order in Chicago, and three blacks were killed. Four blacks were killed in Cleveland amid reports that black extremists were trying to precipitate paramilitary action against the police.

In 1967 a white policeman was stomped to death in Plainfield, New Jersey, after shooting a black man. Widespread looting and burning broke out in Newark, New Jersey, and when police and National Guardsmen encountered snipers, they responded with wild barrages of gunfire. Twenty-three persons were shot to death, twenty-one of them black, including six women and two children. Serious outbreaks also occurred in fourteen other New Jersey cities, in Tampa, Florida, Cincinnati, Ohio, and Atlanta, Georgia. Forty-three people died in Detroit, Michigan (ten of them white), when police and National Guardsmen resorted to tanks and machine guns to control outbreaks of rioting; army paratroopers finally restored an uneasy peace after hundreds of people had been burned out of their homes and property damage had mounted to $45 million—the worst riot in modern United States history. When Martin Luther King was assassinated the following spring, cities were set to the torch throughout the country. Flames crackled within three blocks of the White House.

The riots are still not completely understood. They were not race riots, in the sense of whites and blacks pitted against each other, as in Chicago in 1919 or Detroit in 1943. There was, however, a definite interracial element underlying most of the outbreaks, although in only a few instances was there so clearly a precipitating white-black issue as the shooting of the black youth that touched off the 1964 disturbances in New York. More often, there was simply a state of generalized tension. In Newark, for example, the riot was preceded by weeks of growing anger over a proposal to raze a large area in the black section of the city for a state medical school; in Detroit, black-police relations were tense for several weeks preceding the outbreak.

Even if the riots were intended to express interracial grievances, they were a most bizarre way of doing so. The disturbances were almost totally confined to black neighborhoods, and the vast majority of people killed, injured, or burnt out of their homes were black. Blacks throwing rocks in Watts threw them into crowds of blacks. A black bus driver in Harlem making a wide detour around a disturbed area told a white reporter, "These crazy kids don't care who their brick hits." In the early riots there was some attempt to distinguish between black- and white-owned businesses, but later riots seem to have been color-blind—although police and guardsmen were frequently blamed for destroying black businesses spared by rioters.

The protean character even of single incidents makes generalization extremely difficult. A disturbance could begin as a serious protest but easily transform into a rampage: A crowd would gather; someone would throw a rock through a window; more windows would be broken; some teenagers would start to loot; when there were no reprisals, adults would gradually join in; and the next morning would see old ladies with shopping carts scavenging through the debris.* Still, there was no typical pattern. Whites joined in the looting in Detroit, and some looters were reportedly robbed of their loot. A student of the riots wrote:

Within a one-hour period of time, a person might walk from a bar or a residence to the scene of a street arrest; chat with friends and acquaintances; curse the police; make a pass at a girl; throw a rock at a departing police car; light someone's cigarette; run down the street and join others in rocking and overturning a car; watch someone set the car on fire; drink a can of looted beer; assist firemen in extinguishing a fire as it spreads to an apartment house; and so on.

One riot was described as "a carnival . . . a collective contest similar to that between two athletic teams, with supporters cheering and egging on the contestants." Reporters were especially struck by the holiday atmosphere that suffused looting crowds after King's death. One rioter shouted that it was "early Easter shopping." A youth, asked why he was rioting, said, "Because what's-his-name was killed."

The press and television contributed to the expectation of outbreaks in most cities. Youths watching riots on television felt their manhood challenged. With

---

* This sequence of events may explain the surprisingly respectable character of many of the looters. Arrests would come in the later stages of a riot, after police had been reinforced and were reasserting control; and of course, adults are easier to catch than teenagers.

the constant stress by black and white leaders on the riot as protest, even rock-throwing took on an ennobling dimension. The intense media interest in the riots converted minor incidents into events of the first magnitude and played to the theatrical instincts of community leaders and politicians. The gross over-reactions by police and National Guardsmen that led to so many pointless killings stemmed partly from the pervasive notion that some sort of apocalypse was at hand. Police forces bought halftrack tanks, machine guns, and riot shields; militia laid out elaborate military plans. Black extremists and white students gloried in the coming "revolution." As summers approached, mayors and industrial state governors thought of little else but how to "keep the cities cool." One mayor recalled, "Rumors were coming in from all sides. . . . Ne-groes were calling to warn of possible disturbances; whites were calling; shop-keepers were calling. Most of the people were concerned about a possible bloodbath. . . . We are talking ourselves into it."

Indeed, for a brief while the country seemed to go insane.* Serious antiwar protests degenerated into "Yippie" exhibitionism. When students "occupied" Columbia University, normally sensible politicians like Manhattan Borough President Percy Sutton and Congressman Charles Rangel rushed to declare their solidarity, "whatever the outcome." Police and protesters fought running battles on national television outside the 1968 Democratic national convention in Chicago. Construction workers attacked antiwar demonstrators in lower Manhattan. College students, embittered by their inability to affect events, turned to terrorism.

THE NEW YORK RESPONSE

The riots were John Lindsay's finest hour. His instinct—like LaGuardia's, and in conspicuous contrast to Wagner's—was to be at the scene of trouble. The first disturbance came in East New York in 1966. "We just rushed out there," Jay Kriegel recalls. "It just seemed that if there was trouble, we should be there." They found angry crowds in the street and rockthrowing. Across the no-man's land that separated the black and white neighborhoods came curses from picketing members of a group called SPONGE (Society for the Prevention of Niggers Getting Everything); there was apparently a sniper. Police did not use their weapons, but a shot from a small-caliber rifle killed an eleven-year-old black child named Ernest Galloway. The body and the child's family was re-moved quietly, so the crowd was never aware of the incident. After a strong police presence brought the incident under control, the mayor, Kriegel, and two of his other assistants, Barry Gottehrer and Sid Davidoff, organized a series of meetings throughout the neighborhood. They secured a burial plot for Er-nest Galloway and arranged a funeral outside the neighborhood to avoid an

* On the other hand, insanity may be a normal condition. Banfield notes that in the space of a few years, there were riots in Amsterdam, Tel Aviv, Brussels, Montreal, Calabria in Italy, Jerusalem, and Tokyo. Virtually the whole of France was paralyzed by students; and student terrorism in America is but a pallid shadow of the savage nihilism of the terrorist groups that have plagued West-ern Europe in recent years.

occasion for further violence. The episode ended with a marathon shouting match between whites and blacks at the Blue Room in City Hall. The mayor promised to open a little City Hall in the area (two, if necessary—one for the whites and one for the blacks—a promise that he finally redeemed with funds raised from friends). In return he got a flashbulb-popping handshake between the white and black leaders.

In order to be prepared for future incidents, Lindsay created a Summer Action Task Force under Gottehrer's direction that was later made a permanent part of his office as the Urban Action Task Force. The task force concept, which was emulated in a number of cities, was designed to inform the mayor of developments in the ghetto and provide the ad hoc responses that would hopefully keep the city cool. Summer jobs were allocated to some of the city's worst potential troublemakers. Private industry was canvassed for donations to support bus trips and lunches to get kids out of the city: When youngsters started to stir ominously in a slum neighborhood, Gottehrer's buses would appear and cart everyone off for a day at the beach. Key city officials were assigned to a task force in each neighborhood, to keep City Hall informed and to cut through breakdowns in services—playground equipment lying unrepaired, infrequent sanitation pickups, and, especially, interdepartmental breakdowns. "A neighborhood might have cleaned out a vacant lot with the help of a community corporation," recalls an aide, "but if the sanitation trucks didn't come and cart away the debris, it would start getting strewn all over and things would be worse than ever." Lindsay backed the operation all the way. Gottehrer recalls one incident: Garbage had accumulated in a neighborhood, and people were setting huge piles on fire. Gottehrer called the sanitation commissioner on a weekend evening, finally tracking him down at a party. The commissioner was irritated by the call and said he'd take care of it on Monday. A few minutes later, Lindsay himself called the commissioner, and the problem was taken care of. After that incident, says Gottehrer, people took his calls.

Gottehrer gradually picked up a bizarre set of acquaintances and traveling companions. Mobster Joey Gallo helped to ease tensions among Italian teenagers. James Lawson, a Harlem hustler with a long police record, acted as a guide to the intricacies of the black lower-class community. Two fierce militants became his good friends: Charles 13X Smith, head of the Five-Percenters (85 percent of the people are sheep; 10 percent are just frontmen for the whites; 5 percent will lead the revolution) and Charles 39X Kenyatta, leader of the Mau-Maus (who later metamorphosed into a moderate minister). Kenyatta was impressed with Lindsay: "Lindsay helps. He'll leave Gracie Mansion on five minutes' notice, and he'll talk to the bottom of the barrel."

Gottehrer's style, his casual dress, and his questionable friends raised eyebrows throughout the city, even among the Mayor's other aides, but it could not be demonstrated that his methods didn't work. Detroit blew that summer, and the flames from Newark could be seen across the Hudson, but New York City was spared the riots that afflicted the rest of the country. Tensions rose in East New York and in the Bronx; there was a window-breaking rampage one night in Bedford-Stuyvesant; a gang of youths invaded midtown one July afternoon. A mugger was shot in Brownsville, and a nasty confrontation ensued, but police restraint and good crowd work defused the situation. The mayor was everywhere, walking through the worst slums, shaking hands, talking to people on their stoops, bantering with teenagers. The city held.

A key element was the transformation of the police response. With Lindsay's strong backing Police Commissioner Howard Leary and Police Chief Sanford Garelik devised a wholly new set of tactics for dealing with civil disorders. Sidney Cooper, a long-time commander, says, "The old response was based on hardware—the Tactical Patrol Force model. You'd come out dripping to your ankles with metal to overawe people. It's the Los Angeles approach. But this was an entirely new era. Confrontation politics was something we'd never encountered before. These people were *hoping* for a confrontation."

"The plan we evolved," says Garelik,

was to use the police who were familiar with the area as the frontline. Cops used to say that the Tactical Patrol Force breaks the glass, but who picks up the pieces? Then we would back up the frontline by flooding the area with blue uniforms. In the old days we were always very conservative about manpower. "Don't use too many men' was the motto. We changed that. We said if nothing happened the men weren't wasted. It meant the response worked. In East New York I was able to clear the street myself, walking down the middle of the street with nine men. But everybody could see there were 600 men at the end of the block. We could get 1,000 men anyplace in the City in an hour or so.

"I was very impressed with the logistics," says Kriegel. "Some nights they seemed to be busing hundreds of cops back and forth across the city all night long. And they managed to give their men truly good briefings, to bring them into hostile territory late at night, and keep them cool, keep them from overreacting."

"It was hard on the men sometimes," admits Garelik, "but we'd appeal to their pride. We'd ask, 'Are you going to let the lowest common denominator in a community dictate your response? We're professionals. We'll react and control things on our terms.' "

Command presence was of vital importance.* In tense situations a sergeant or lieutenant would be allocated for every five patrolmen, to keep reminding them of their role and to make the hard decisions. Cooper says:

The really new thing was that you weren't out on your own. Things almost blew in Brownsville, for instance. I was on the scene with my men, but Garelik was there, too, and so was Leary and the Mayor. They knew what I was doing, and we could talk over the next move. I didn't have to worry about being second-guessed or crucified the next day if things had gone badly.

* The most serious loss of command control probably occurred during the "occupation" of Columbia in 1968. There were special factors that made the police job extremely difficult. The protracted deliberations by the faculty before requesting police assistance allowed the situation to polarize and gave the radicals time to plan a resistance. And somehow insults to the police from largely white and middle-class students were more difficult to bear than those from a black teenager. Still, one of the potentially most explosive buildings was cleared virtually without incident by men in squads of five, each with a superior officer. Later, when the action broke into fighting knots, the commanders lost contact with the men and a virtual police riot ensued.

"Intelligence was crucial," says Garelik.

Remember, everything was happening at once—outbreaks in the slums, war protests, welfare demonstrations, the hardhats, Columbia. Ninety-five percent of the time, people didn't want trouble, so our problem was to separate out the crazies. Most of the time, I would meet with groups planning protests ahead of time to convince them that the police was not the enemy. An anti-war group or a welfare group was usually interested in the television cameras, so we'd make things easy for them—find out who wanted to be arrested and arrange the arrests at the right time. Some of them would insist on resisting arrest, so we'd explain how they could resist without getting hurt by simply lying down. Then we'd carry them out in front of the cameras. Obviously, we couldn't do that kind of thing with the ghetto disturbances, but we had good intelligence there, including some of Gottehrer's contacts.

It came very close a couple of times. When we had things going in two or three boroughs at once, our logistics were stretched very thin. We had to recognize when we couldn't control a situation. We'd lose a skirmish to avoid losing a war. If there were a handful of cops on the scene and a couple of hundred kids broke out in looting, we didn't want to go in shooting and then have things get really out of hand. I'd trade glass for lives any day. We'd try to establish a perimeter, keep things from spreading until more men got there and we could control by sheer weight. For instance, immediately after the King assassination, 125th Street went so fast there was no way we could get there on time. That night, things almost blew clear across the City. We had serious incidents all at the same time in Harlem, Brownsville, Bedford-Stuyvesant, the Bronx, and Coney Island.

The King riots were the most serious ghetto incidents during the entire administration and demonstrated the Lindsay containment tactics at their best. As looting and fires broke out throughout the city, police worked through the night to cordon off incidents. Sanitation trucks were on the streets at 3:00 A.M., and as incidents were brought under control, glass and fire debris were swept up. When morning came, an area would look almost normal. Incidents were muted in the press and on television. Sporadic disorders continued for several days but never linked into a chain reaction. New York may not, in fact, have gotten off as lightly as it first appeared. The police counted no less than six hundred separate incidents, and the fire damage throughout the poorer neighborhoods was extensive. On the whole, however, Lindsay's tactics were almost certainly right. There was no more looting and burning in New York than anywhere else and probably a good deal less than in most other major cities. Massive confrontations between slumdwellers and police were avoided, as were the war-zone death tolls that were seen in Los Angeles, Newark, and Detroit. The tough stance of mayors like Richard Daley may have been widely admired by conservatives and police spokesmen, but most cities across the country seem to have adopted the New York tactics sooner or later. Just for one example, in Kansas City, during the disturbances following King's death, police at first tried to overpower rioters but were quickly forced to revert to New York's containment style: Meeting the disturbances with force and firepower merely caused events to escalate out of control.

There were a number of questions that could have been raised about the Lindsay riot control tactics: At what point did cooperation with underworld characters, for example, amount to extortion? Were the police *too* restrained during major incidents, as some merchants and insurance companies later charged? For the most part, however, the city's performance was widely praised. In the fall of 1967, for example, Harlem businessmen hosted a luncheon for Lindsay and Leary—quite simply to thank them for saving their businesses. As other cities turned to New York for guidance on managing civil disturbances, their most pressing problem at the time, Lindsay emerged as the undisputed spokesman for urban problems (one columnist dubbed him the "Mayor of America"), a position merely confirmed by his prominence on the Kerner panel. With the public mind concentrated on the problems of keeping peace in the cities throughout most of 1967 and 1968, rising welfare costs and the emerging management failures in the antipoverty programs could be overlooked, and John Lindsay was viewed, with some justice, as the most successful big-city mayor in the country.

PERCEPTIONS OF RACE

If Lindsay's sensitive handling of urban disorders earned him national prominence by the spring of 1968, his handling of the racially charged school strikes that occurred only a half-year later (and which will be discussed in Chapter V) nearly ended his political career; yet the principles which seemed to serve him so poorly in the school strikes were consistent with his first-term approach to racial issues and had been spelled out in some detail in the much-praised Kerner report.* The fact is that by 1968, public perceptions of racial issues were changing rapidly. In many respects, the change in attitudes was nothing more than a backlash of prejudice against the aggressiveness with which blacks had been pressing their demands; but in other ways, the growing uneasiness with the concept of racial problems espoused by Lindsay, the civil rights leadership, and most liberal spokesmen reflected an intuitive awareness that black development was a more complex problem than was often admitted, and not one that would be solved only by removing discriminatory barriers and providing compensatory programs. There were alternative explanations and prognoses for the pattern of black socio-economic advancement. None of them, it can be certain, was or is completely correct; but different ways of conceptualizing problems lead to different policies and strategies, and some are more useful at certain times and in certain situations than others.

One important alternative view of Northern blacks—as modern immigrants—casts black problems in quite a different perspective than the paradigm that underlay, for instance, the original conceptions of the antipoverty program. Measured against the rate of progress of other immigrant groups, it could be argued that blacks were progressing about as fast as could be expected. Moreover, viewing blacks as urban immigrants is not at all unreasonable. The most massive black migrations Northward occurred only after World

*For example, the report took pains to emphasize the critical importance of community participation and community control of institutions that serve the ghetto.

War II, and while it is not possible to allocate birth rates precisely among native and immigrant blacks, it is entirely plausible that the majority of blacks in New York City are post-1940 immigrants or their children. The black migrations were driven by the same economic impulses that motivated most other new arrivals. To civil rights leaders the Northern slums may have been the failure of a dream, but to blacks emigrating from the shantytowns of the South, they represented substantial advancement. A man who earned the median Southern black income in 1960 and emigrated North to earn the median Northern black income in 1970 would have seen his income more than triple.

Different ethnic groups have assimilated at different speeds, although most seem to require about two or three generations in the cities before moving substantially into the stable working classes, and some, like the Irish, seem to have taken even longer. Jews and Japanese, two cultures that emphasize urban living and close family ties, have been the most successful ethnic groups economically, even though both were subjected to serious discrimination and persecution. The Italians arrived a generation later than the Irish, but by the pre–World War I era, they were far less likely than the Irish to be on public relief rolls, and by about 1950 Italian family income seems to have surpassed that of the Irish—even though the Irish were generally better educated than Italians. Reports from pre–World War I Irish slums put current black and Puerto Rican problems in perspective: Fatherless families were common; the wife was typically the regular wage earner—usually as a domestic or a seamstress—while the father drifted from one spell of unemployment to another or became besotted with drink. One social worker was horrified at the precocious sexual amorality of the children and reported that sodomy was common even among boys of seven or eight. Irish riots were "massive, recurrent, and violent," and the crime rate seems to have been appalling.* Moreover, despite the variety of ethnic achievements and shortfalls, *no* group ever made the leap from urban immigrant to the middle class in so short a space as the fifteen years or so that separated the peak of black Northward migrations from the zenith of the civil rights initiatives in the mid-1960s.

Whether or not the immigration perspective, with its focus on intergenerational improvement, is a more useful way of conceptualizing black problems, it is clear that explanations that concentrate exclusively, or even primarily, on patterns of white discrimination as the controlling factor in recent black development, cannot account for the varieties of black performance. It has long been documented, for example, that West Indians, with their intense devotion to hard work, thrift, and economic self-improvement, fare much better on the mainland than do American blacks, although both are presumably subject to

---

* It is open to question whether the Irish crime rate ever reached the level of that in the modern black slums, and it is unfortunate that precise comparisons are impossible. The level of black criminal violence may well be unique. Black youths commit violent crime about two to five times more frequently than comparable populations of Puerto Ricans or Chicanos, and leaving aside blacks, the American crime rate drops to levels not much higher than those in most West European countries. Silberman argues powerfully that black crime is rooted in slavery and white mistreatment. If the plague of black crime is in fact the price of racism, the nation is paying in kind and paying dearly.

the same discriminatory barriers, both were enslaved about the same time from the same parts of Africa, and the West Indian system of slavery was, if anything, even more degrading than that in America. Furthermore, black families who have made the move into the middle class have been forging ahead rapidly since 1960: The income of black two-parent families, for example, was 77 percent of white two-parent families in 1977, compared to 67 percent in 1967; the income of intact black families with a head of household under 35 is, for all practical purposes, equal to that of comparable white families; and the income of black families earning more than $20,000 per year is actually improving faster than that of white families in the same income bracket.*

On broader measures blacks have also fared relatively well: Educational levels among blacks were about equivalent to white educational levels by the 1970s, and from the mid-1960s blacks penetrated broadly into white-collar, craftsman, and operative job categories—the industrial classifications one and two status levels above their traditional concentration in the "service and other" category. The traditional measures of social disorganization also recede dramatically as blacks achieve middle-class status. When blacks are matched with whites on such factors as age, home ownership, and education, for instance, the blacks are slightly less likely than whites to be single-parent households.

More recent concerns have focused on the degree to which the rapid improvements enjoyed by segments of the black population have not been shared by the great mass. Female-headed families have continued to increase rapidly among blacks, and black teenage unemployment persists at appallingly high levels. The sharp divergence in black economic trends has caused many observers to worry about the emergence of a permanent "underclass" of blacks—unintegrated, crime-prone, and dependent, a sort of permanently mocking legacy of slavery and racism.

But speculations about permanent underclasses still seem premature. The rise in female-headed families is worrisome, but the same trends, if not so dramatic, are evident among white and Hispanic families. Black teenage unemployment—almost 40 percent in 1976—is far too high, but examination of the numbers places them in calmer perspective: About a fourth of unemployed black teenagers are in school and looking only for part-time work, and much of the remaining unemployment is accounted for by the tendency of teenagers to skip from job to job, with frequent short spells of unemployment in between. Teenagers are some twelve to twenty times more likely than adults to leave a job voluntarily and, interestingly, unemployed black males are only about a fourth as likely to be unemployed long-term (fifteen weeks or more) as unem-

* Part of the improvement stems from the higher incidence of multiple earners in black families. Blacks still lag behind whites when measured individually. While incomes of two-parent black households moved ahead strongly in 1967–77, the income of black female-headed families also improved slightly, relative to whites during the same period, probably reflecting improvements in transfer payments. However, interestingly, the black-white income ratios for *all* black families slipped slightly during the same period. The apparent contradiction probably reflects the large number of younger, unattached blacks who set up households during the period, which would tend to depress statistical comparisons with whites.

ployed white males. The unemployment figures, on the other hand, do not reflect the high rate of black teenage withdrawal from the labor force. Some part of the withdrawal probably represents discouragement from encountering discrimination or, possibly, the effects of past discrimination—depressed expectations and poor labor market connections. But some part of the tendency toward labor force withdrawal must reflect the easy availability to the competent slum hustler of illegal opportunities that are much more rewarding, financially and socially, than low-wage employment. Somewhat ironically, by the late 1970s concern about the high levels of black teenage unemployment in New York managed to coexist with concern over the allegedly hundreds of thousands of illegal immigrants arriving in the city to take unskilled employment.

Finally, however well-founded the concern about dichotomized economic development among blacks, if they are at all like other immigrant groups, there is no reason to expect progress across the entire population at a uniform rate, and there is every reason to expect the advancements of the last decade to continue and become more broadly based, particularly as the teenage population stabilizes and begins to decline over the next dozen years or so. The blacks, after all, are not the first group to be assigned to the "permanent underclass." In 1914 a social welfare report pondered the fact that many of the most troubled families in New York's West Side slums were third-generation Americans and lamented: "In each generation the bolder spirits moved away to more prosperous parts of the City. This left behind the less ambitious and the weaker of the population. Hence may be seen not the readjustment and amalgamation of sturdy immigrant groups, but the discouragement and deterioration of an indigenous American community."

Whatever the "right" view of black problems, it is clear that Lindsay's formulation of the issue during his first term—although very much in the mainstream of the time—was inadequate and one-sided, as he himself seems to have recognized by his gradual retreat from the more radical positions. The view that the low socio-economic status of blacks was a consequence of past discrimination was undoubtedly correct; but the assumption that continued slow progress represented either continued oppression or insufficient compensatory programs, while containing elements of truth, was seriously misleading.

The mainstream formulation did not lead to much difficulty during the very early stages of Lindsay's administration. The Kerner Commission, for example, was probably wrong in its view that urban riots were primarily a form of civil rights protest,* but the major consequence of that view was the insistence on

* The commission, for example, misread—and miscalculated—its own data to demonstrate that propensity to riot rose with educational levels, a contention that lent powerful support to the "frustration" theory of the riots—i.e., that they were outbreaks by upwardly mobile but persistently stymied people. Recalculations of the commission's data show, in fact, that the opposite was the case: The rioters were overwhelmingly unattached, poorly educated young males; the tendency to riot *decreased* with education. The recalculations, of course, do not disprove the commission's hypothesis, but they lend greater support to the supposition of Banfield and others that rioters were more interested in "fun and profit" than serious protest and were taking advantage of the black-white tensions to go on a spree.

police restraint—which was almost certainly the right policy, no matter what its premises. Lindsay was more receptive to welfare liberalization than many other public officials, but welfare growth in New York City was of about the same magnitude as elsewhere, although the growth spurt in New York occurred earlier than in the rest of the country. And no mayor could have stayed aloof from the antipoverty programs, although one less ideologically committed than Lindsay might have been more skeptical of the programs' grander promises and less prepared to compromise management issues in the name of community participation.

But there were important consequences of a simplistic view of race problems—both for relations with blacks and relations with whites. Formulation of black issues in polar black-white terms obscured the class divisions in the black community. The administration was shocked in 1967, for instance, when a plan to build public housing near a middle-class black community in Queens met with fierce opposition. The community feared that lower-class blacks would bring the lower-class lifestyles, the crime and vandalism, that they had been working so hard to escape. Most important, by stressing that black and Puerto Rican problems were primarily ones for whites and the government to solve, Lindsay was implicitly committing the city to massive new tasks that it seemed poorly equipped to undertake and that he would in fact have been hard-pressed to specify except in the most general terms. Not surprisingly, there was a steadily growing resentment on the part of the city's white taxpayers and, equally important, a dangerously wide gulf between the administration and the rank-and-file of city employees.

IV. *Employees*

THE TRANSIT STRIKE: 1966

JOHN LINDSAY'S INTRODUCTION to city labor relations was a cruel one. Five hours after he took the oath of office, the city's transit system—the lifeline of its commerce and industry—was shut down by the Transit Workers' Union. The strike came with all the inevitability of the climax in a medieval morality play—only the costumes were missing.

Throughout the campaign Lindsay had attacked Wagner for conducting labor relations behind the closed door of his City Hall office. A vote for Lindsay would be a vote against backroom bargaining; a reformed labor relations system would substitute formalized and impartial mechanisms for the intimate feasts of the power brokers. No one personified the old methods better than Mike Quill, leader of the transit union—a leprechaun of a man, round-faced, pink-cheeked, with owlish horn-rimmed glasses, a blackthorn cane, and a musical brogue. He had founded his union in 1934 and fought hard for many years for recognition. Truculent, vituperative, and intensely theatrical, he was a decided exponent of a rough-and-ready school of labor relations and highly suspicious of Lindsay and his reforming ideas.

Quill entered the stage two days after the November elections. Speaking softly, with a slight smile, he presented "not demands, but modest requests": a 30 percent raise in pay, a four-day, thirty-two–hour week, six weeks of vacation after one year, half-pay retirement after twenty-five years—the list went on and on. The new mayor-elect (Quill insisted on pronouncing his name "Lindsley") was welcome to sit at the table; in fact, Quill recommended it. Wagner was not so sure. At first he suggested that Lindsay should just stay in touch, then later agreed with Quill. Lindsay, wary of being drawn into a scenario he couldn't control, agreed only to keep informed and, much to Quill's irritation, left on a planned vacation.

Over the years transit negotiations had taken on a rhythm and a ritual of their own. Two months or so before the biennial New Year's deadline, Quill would present a package of demands so extreme that a strike would appear inevitable. Then, as tensions mounted, Wagner and Quill would retire to the fastnesses of City Hall to find out what Quill could really live with. At the eleventh hour Wagner would miraculously come up with just enough money to avert disaster for another two years.

The last settlement, in 1964, had been in keeping with all the traditions. Quill needed a sizeable settlement to fend off restiveness in his union, one of the lowest paid in the city, and the Transit Authority was running a deficit. Harry Van Arsdale, president of the Central Labor Council, entered the talks to help, and Theodore Kheel was called upon to mediate. Kheel had been Wagner's labor adviser and was trusted by the unions. Van Arsdale, Wagner, and Quill had been friends for years. Wagner had helped Quill break a craftsmen's strike in 1958 to win sole bargaining rights for his union, and Quill had been the first labor leader to back Wagner in his 1961 fight against the organization Democrats. Between them, they developed an acceptable package just at the strike deadline, and Wagner, by various subterfuges, worked the extra money into the Transit Authority's budget in order to preserve the fifteen-cent fare—although technically, the city wasn't supposed to subsidize the Authority's operating expenses.

As the drama unfolded in 1965, the strike seemed written into the script just as surely as the settlements had been in previous years. The Transit Authority was running a deficit of at least $13 million, and, as usual, the politicians said there could be no increase in the fare. This time, however, Wagner was in no position to come up with the extra money: he would be gone by January 1, and he couldn't commit Lindsay. Kheel entered the negotiations as a mediator, at Quill's insistence, but he had no direct access to the mayor-elect. Lindsay's labor advisers were Alec Rose and David Dubinsky of the Liberal Party, who came from a different union tradition than Quill and Van Arsdale and were cool to both men. Furthermore, Lindsay was reluctant to make private deals regarding his budget to save Quill's face. If there was genuine controversy, an impartial fact-finding panel, agreed to by the union and city, was the way to resolve it and ensure at the same time that the public interest was upheld.

When Lindsay finally did come to the table at the end of December, it seemed to Quill that the mayor-elect couldn't understand his cues. Instead of coming up with money, Lindsay lectured both sides and instructed them to reach a settlement that was equitable to the union but fair to the public. He suggested that if the union was patient, the Transit Authority's deficit could be taken care of: he was planning to ask for state legislation that would allow highway bridge and tunnel toll surpluses to subsidize the subways and buses. Quill was outraged. Lindsay seemed like a "babe in the woods" he told the press; he acted like a "pipsqueak;" he "didn't seem to know what it was all about." As the last week before the strike ground down, Quill cursed at Lindsay to his face. "You wanted this job," he stormed, "And you're here for the duration. You have to cease acting like a juvenile." More than one observer saw it as a clash of cultures. "Quill looks at Lindsay," Jimmy Breslin wrote, "and sees the

Church of England." An aide said, "All Quill can think of is, 'Down with Protestantism, up the Irish!' "

Finally, on December 31, amid his inaugural preparations, Lindsay agreed to provide extra funds so that the Transit Authority could make an offer. The actual proffer was smaller, in fact, than the settlement reached two years before. At midnight Quill said mellifluously that it was "a peanut package, but we don't reject it." However, because it would take time to consider the proposal, the strike would proceed as planned.

The strike was illegal under the state's public employees law, and the city immediately secured an injunction against it. Quill tore up the injunction before the television cameras, shouting "Let the judge drop dead in his black robes," and was carted off to prison, where he suffered a dramatic heart attack. A delegation of labor leaders got Lindsay's agreement to transfer Quill out of the prison hospital but were told by a Quill aide to mind their own business. Quill preferred his martyr's shrine (in fact, he died a few weeks after the strike was ended).

Lindsay, trying to organize his new administration during the day, sat through bargaining sessions all night. He surveyed traffic jams in a police helicopter, walked from Gracie Mansion to City Hall, gave pedestrians lifts in his city car, and when his patience finally broke, bitterly assailed the union: "The government of this city will not capitulate before the lawless demands of a single interest group. It will not allow the power brokers in our city or any special interest to dictate to this city the terms under which it will exist in New York."

But for twelve days the city slowly strangled on its traffic until Lindsay agreed to pay tribute. The final package included an average 15 percent wage package over two years (as opposed to presidential wage and price guidelines of 3.2 percent per year); a restoration of differentials for skilled workers (who had not done well under Quill's union); free uniforms; guaranteed health and welfare benefits; a $500-per-year pension bonus; and an end to the pension "death gamble" (under the new contract pensions were guaranteed to widows of workers who died eligible but unretired). Rockefeller promised $100 million in additional aid, about half of which was new money and half advances of money already due. The legislative leadership agreed to cooperate in exempting the strikers from the state antistrike penalties, which, among other things, made strikers ineligible to receive wage increases for three years. Quill began calling Lindsay by his right name.

Lindsay put the best face possible on the contract and defended himself against criticisms from Robert Kennedy and Lyndon Johnson that the settlement was inflationary. He estimated that the agreement would cost $43.4 million for the subway workers and possibly $9 million more for the bus workers, as against a $33.6 million settlement two years previously. The mediation panel that came up with the settlement recommendations thought that the cost would be more like $60 to 65 million, while Quill trumpeted a $70 million figure.

The costs of the strike were unquestionably high. Business sources es-

timated that the strike cost the city $100 million a day in lost business and that
for some businesses the loss may have been irreparable: spokesmen for the garment district claimed that because the strike hit them in the middle of the
springwear season, fearful buyers had switched to out-of-state suppliers. One
columnist wrote of the strike as an "insult," one of a series that was making the
city an ever more difficult and wearying place to live and work. Worst of all, if
the strike had elements of a morality play, the moral was all too clear for the
city's other unions. John DeLury, leader of the sanitationmen, said that the
transit workers had "opened up a new ceiling. The least we can expect is what
they got. The City is far from broke." John Cassesse, president of the patrolmen's union, weighed in with similar sentiments. A *New York Times* labor reporter summed it up:

First, the strikers proved that public employees could leave their jobs without danger of
being dismissed under the state's strict but unenforceable Condon-Wadlin law which
prohibits such strikes. Second, the transit settlement was so high—the workers received
twice as much money as they ever got from Mr. Wagner—that other unions want big
settlements. Finally, and perhaps most important, many labor leaders began muttering
that the Republican Mayor was "antilabor."

There is no question that Lindsay mishandled the strike. His late entrance
into the talks, his preachments, and his unwillingness to find money for a real-
istic settlement before the strike deadline all contributed to the hardening of
positions. The famous "power broker" speech during the second week of the
strike was self-indulgent posturing. His performance at the bargaining table,
and that of his top aides, was inept. One reporter writes that the $500 pension
bonus—an item the union had vainly been seeking for years and didn't expect
to get—was thrown almost casually on the table by Deputy Mayor Robert
Price, to be snapped up by an amazed union.

But to lay the blame entirely on Lindsay is to shoot at too easy a target. The
strike hit before he had even assembled his administration. Wagner did little to
help, while Quill's delight in humiliating the tall Yalie was all too palpable.
More important, a strike may have been inevitable. Anthony Russo, a top city
labor official under four mayors, says: "I watched the 1965 election returns with
[a transit union official]. When they announced Lindsay as the winner, [the
union official] turned to me and said, 'Now we have to have a strike. This guy's
going to be tough, and we need a big settlement this year. I don't see how we
can get it without striking.' "

A. H. Raskin, the veteran labor reporter writes, "In hindsight, most observers were convinced that Quill needed so big a wage increase in 1966 that no
mayor could have given it to him without a strike." Quill's Irish leadership was
under pressure from an increasingly black and Puerto Rican—and increasingly
militant—membership. His cozy relationship with Wagner had not been translated into generous settlements, and to maintain control he had to deliver big.

The situation was the same throughout the work force. As one union official
admitted candidly, "Lindsay has walked into a hornet's nest." For years,
Wagner had been building a record as a labor statesman and handing out the

absolute minimum in settlements. His success was very much a personal one. An old-shoe style, lots of "schmooze," friendly personal relations with the union leaders, an ability to outsit anyone at a bargaining table, were all elements in the formula, but union militancy was rising, and the issues and the leadership were changing. Whether Wagner, or anyone, could have maintained control much longer is very much open to doubt; in fact, by Wagner's last months in office, control was already slipping from his fingers.

CITY UNIONS BEFORE 1966

Unions are still a relatively new phenomenon in city government. Mike Quill's transit workers were strong enough to block a plan by Mayor William O'Dwyer in 1945 to sell off the Transit Authority power stations, but for the most part municipal unions did not come of age until late in Robert Wagner's tenure as mayor. Unionism and public employment were not concepts that mixed easily. Wagner's police commissioner, Stephen Kennedy, viewed a police union as unthinkable; until well into the 1960s, many teachers considered unions incompatible with their status as professionals; and a top executive in the Department of Hospitals said in 1962 that unions had no place in an agency devoted to public service. Even George Meany, as late as 1955, said: "It is impossible to bargain collectively with the government."

Associations of civil servants and uniformed employees had existed for many years and had occasionally wielded respectable amounts of political power. The civil service associations secured state constitutional protection for pension benefits in 1938, the same year that New York City's firemen managed to write into the constitution a provision guaranteeing them equal shifts—a protection that police had secured in 1911 in a state statute. John DeLury's Uniformed Sanitationmen's Association was for many years a potent local political force. ("Only God can guarantee 100 percent delivery," said DeLury. "We are sure of 99 percent based on past performance.") But although associations were occasionally effective pressure groups, there were no organizations with the right to represent employees against the government until Wagner established the city's labor relations machinery during his first and second terms in office.

Wagner was under no particular pressure to endorse unionization. He had bid for employee votes during this first election campaign, but civil service support was not a decisive factor in his victory. His majority in the 1957 election was the largest in the city's history, and he enjoyed solid backing from organized labor without making special concessions. The extreme disarray of the city's personnel system when he took office, however, demanded a major overhaul, and Wagner's strong family ties to organized labor predisposed him to include a formalized labor relations process as part of the overall reorganization. By executive order in 1954, he granted employees the right to organize, established grievance procedures—in which employees could be assisted by a union representative—and created labor-management committees to discuss working conditions and to foster cooperation between management and workers. The city's Department of Labor was created to certify unions, approve rep-

resentation units, and assist in resolving disputes. Employee titles were simplified and rationalized into broad classes that were roughly consistent across
departments, and a Career and Salaries Appeals Board that included union
members was created to hear disputes over pay and classifications. The city
agreed to collect union dues through payroll deduction in 1957, putting union
income on a reliable footing, and union representatives were allowed released
time from their city jobs for union business. The final breakthrough came in
1958, when Wagner issued his Executive Order No. 49—hailed by organized
labor as the "little Wagner Act" or labor's "Magna Carta"—granting unions the
right to bargain collectively for their members and making New York City one
of the very first jurisdictions in the country to adopt essentially private-sector
forms for its labor relations.

Despite the sweep of Wagner's reforms, there was little immediate difference in the conduct of labor-management relations.* The unions were still very
weak and much more absorbed in organization and survival issues than bread-
and-butter problems of pay and working conditions. With the notable exception of Quill's transit workers, Wagner did what he could to keep them that
way. Instead of having the city labor department establish broad bargaining
units as the basis for certification contests, the initiative was left to the employees to petition for recognition. The inevitable result was small, highly fragmented units, a multiplicity of competitive unions, and a maximum of raiding.
Wagner also kept a firm political hand on the certification process so when
leaders did win recognition, they were likely to feel some personal debt to the
mayor. Finally, the rules governing collective bargaining specified that a union
had to represent a majority of city employees in a class before it could bargain
for them. As long as the unions stayed small and divided, the rule made the
right to bargain a dead letter for the majority of city employees, who were in
titles that cut across departments—clerk, motor vehicle operator, or laborer,
for example.

The collective bargaining rules themselves were delayed for two years before being issued, and when they were finally produced, they construed the executive order in the narrowest possible terms. The order had stipulated that
unions had the right to bargain over "terms and conditions" of employment,
but the rules defined "terms and conditions" to include only pay, fringe benefits, promotions, and time and leave rules. In fact, at first everything except
salaries was effectively excluded from the table; even fringe benefits were
seriously negotiated only in 1962. "There was no real bargaining at all," says
Russo.

---

* At least the differences were not immediately visible. A veteran civil servant suggests that the
new grievance procedures had a devastating effect on city supervisory practices. The city provided
no training for its managers in coping with the new procedures, and supervisors were shocked to
find themselves being cross-examined before grievance tribunals to justify actions that had previously been considered routine. Because grievance representation was usually the only service
that unions could provide their members, they concentrated on it with a vengeance.

It was really more of a joke. Harry [Bronstein, the budget bureau's chief examiner, who bargained for the city] would schedule eight meetings a day in his office and turn up the heat so it was unbearable. Each union leader would get fifteen minutes. They would make their pitch, Harry would listen, then say, 'OK, we'll let you know.' Wagner got away with it because the union guys worshipped him. They just kissed his ass.

Wagner maintained his position by what Raskin calls a sustained exercise in "palmanship" with labor's top leaders, and particularly, Quill and Van Arsdale. Any union leader with a problem, no matter how detailed—a favor for a member, a job for a relative, a problem with a department head—could get to Wagner through Van Arsdale. The leaders' egos were pampered like tender garden shoots. The mayor always turned out for union dinners, conventions, testimonials, weddings of officers, or bar mitzvahs for grandchildren. And he would back his friends to the hilt. When Quill's control over the transit workers was shaken by an eight-day strike by dissident motormen and craftsmen, Wagner pulled out all the stops. The Transit Authority paid bonuses to nonstrikers and threatened mass reprisals against the strikers. The strike leaders were jailed, spies were planted in the strike headquarters, and strike meetings were bugged. When the bugs were discovered, Wagner thundered: "Whoever is responsible for the bugging is going to regret it, mark my words. I'm mad as hell." Raskin says, "The evidence was unmistakable that the Transit Authority and the police were up to their eardrums in the electronic eavesdroppers," but disciplinary action never materialized.

Wagner's methods were undeniably effective, but he was rapidly losing control by the end of his third term. For one thing, public employee unionism was no longer such an exotic concept. John Kennedy had granted the right of collective bargaining to federal employees in 1962, and national public employee union membership had doubled in a decade. As the unions grew there was pressure from the ranks to stop "collective begging" and start genuine bargaining. A crucial shift in the power balance was signaled in 1965, when District Council 37 of the American Federation of State, County, and Municipal Employees (DC 37, AFSCME), led by Victor Gotbaum, won a representation election in the Department of Hospitals. The victory gave DC 37 a sufficient majority of employees across the city to qualify it as the bargaining agent for the major citywide titles. With its bargaining credentials established, the pressure was on the melange of little local unions to consolidate under the DC 37 umbrella. The era of the balkanized unions was ending.

Then, also in 1965, Wagner suffered a major defeat at the hands of the welfare caseworkers and supervisors. Welfare caseloads had been growing rapidly, and the caseworkers and supervisors wanted a contractual limit placed on their workload. When the city stuck to its position that workload was a managerial prerogative that could not be bargained away, the workers struck. Wagner had weathered brief strikes before, but this time the workers dug in for a long siege, sustained in part by ideology: heavy workloads prevented them from handling cases effectively, they argued, so the strike was for the benefit of clients as much as for themselves. Five thousand workers were discharged, and nineteen union leaders went to jail, but the strike dragged on. Management kept about a third of the welfare centers open to dispense emergency assistance, but as clients grew increasingly restive and angry, Wagner was forced to yield. The compromise was that the issues of wages and working conditions would be submitted to a fact-finding panel headed by an independent expert, Professor Donald Schottland from Brandeis University; Wagner would agree to be morally bound by the panel's findings; and the city would not seek Condon-Wadlin penalties. (The striking caseworkers and supervisors were eventually excused from penalties under the same legislation that exempted the striking transit workers in 1966.)

The findings of the panel sounded the death knell for Wagner's bargaining methods. It recommended generous wage settlements and upheld the unions' claim that workload was a bargainable item. From that point, the city would have to bargain on "salaries and salary grades, fringe benefits and other perquisites, promotions, Time and Leave rules and Pay Plan rules and regulations, workload, working conditions, changes of title, and personnel practices pertaining to the titles in the Contract."

In other words, almost anything the unions wanted to talk about was potentially bargainable. Driving its point home, the panel instructed Wagner to set up another panel comprising representatives from the city government, the unions, and members of the outside community to recommend revisions in the city's entire labor relations apparatus. Wagner, not wishing to touch off another strike, meekly complied. A tripartite panel was appointed and developed recommendations that were eventually the centerpiece of the Lindsay reform program.

The welfare strike, in its own way, was as devastating a defeat for Wagner as the transit strike was to be for Lindsay the following year—although it was not nearly so public. The unmistakable lesson from the entire episode was that a determined union that was willing to strike a sensitive service could outface even the most skillful mayor. The transit strike merely reconfirmed the lesson. Most important, as Raymond Horton points out, the welfare strike settlement signaled an irrevocable shift in the balance of labor relations power away from City Hall. Wagner had opened the door to the expansion of union influence among municipal employees; by skillful maneuvering throughout his last term, he had kept the opening to the width of a crack; but in his last year in office, he was shoved aside, and the unions came bursting through, brimming with the discontents and frustrations that had accumulated through the long years in the darkness.

Any mayor coming into office in 1966 would have had a difficult time dealing with the unions. In Lindsay's case there were special factors operating to make the relationship about as bad as it could possibly be.

LINDSAY AND EMPLOYEES

Lindsay did not win the 1965 election with the help of civil service votes, and he made no secret of his feeling that the city's bureaucracy was badly in need of a thorough shaking up; but as the dust clouds from his new broom came puffing up from agency after agency, they were just as often damped down by the unions. Parks department employees sabotaged his first City Hall Christmas tree celebration after his parks commissioner tried to violate time-honored seniority and geographic assignment rules. An attempt to put buildings inspectors in uniforms and increase their workloads led to a protest at the Board of Estimate and an administration backdown. John DeLury hinted darkly at a job action if the administration went through with its plans to put intensive cleanup crews into the city's ghetto neighborhoods. Firemen broke off contract talks in protest against a city plan to reduce the manning on trucks and use firemen as inspectors during off-peak hours. Police did the same when the city announced a plan for one-man patrol cars in low-crime areas. The city agreed to arbitrate the issue and won, but the PBA finally stopped the plan by "simple ultimatum."

Lindsay was most often right on the substance. Every other large city in the country, for example, used one-man patrol cars. Performance in the building department was notoriously poor. A good case could be made that fire department trucks were overmanned.* But the Lindsay style set employees' teeth on edge. His public pronouncements and the attitudes of his young aides seemed to convey disdain. Civil servants bridled at the persistent attacks on "the bureaucracy." "We resented the Chinese error," says one, "the notion that we were all part of a faceless, obstructionist mass." The PBA protested publicly when City Hall assistants sent policemen to fetch sandwiches and routinely commandeered police cars when they were in a hurry. "It might not have been so bad if they'd asked for a favor," says Edward Kiernan, a PBA leader, "but it was more like, 'Here's five bucks. Get some sandwiches and be back in fifteen minutes.' " DeLury fulminated against "these young and immature people coming in the administration." Victor Gotbaum, who established the best working relationship with Lindsay of any union leader, said, "Lindsay is an upper-middle-class guy who doesn't really understand unions. But he's got to realize that this is an area of slow change."

The problem was vastly complicated by race. Lindsay was putting on pressure for improved performance at the same time that blacks and Puerto Ricans were making the daily job much more difficult. Parks maintenance was slipping, partly because of rising vandalism. Building inspectors were afraid to go

---

* This issue is a complex one, however. Reduced manning on pumpers was related to hose size. The required hose capacity was related to building size and density, and manning requirements were affected by such factors as the likelihood of having to drag a hose up tenement stairs. Only a small percentage of fires, however, ever required the full hose capacity available. The union opposed reductions in hose sizes, and hence in manning, on safety grounds. In 1968 technicians from the Rand Corporation came up with the idea of treating the water with a polymer that increased its velocity through the hose—"slippery water"—so that hose diameters could be reduced with out losing spraying capacity. The union complained, however, that the slippery water made for unsafe footing. When slippery water was made widely available, the city reduced manning on pumpers in about half the companies—generally those in the least dense areas. Under the spur of the fiscal crisis, there was a second reduction in 1975. The union grieved the reductions, but the issue was eventually settled in the city's favor in 1978.

into the poorer neighborhoods and insisted on travelling in pairs. Sanitationmen resented having to sweep up slumdwellers' garbage and still take the
blame when the streets were filthy the following day. Moreover, Lindsay appeared to leave no doubt whose side he was on: As he increased the pressure
for performance by the whites, he seemed to be enthusiastically handing out
higher and higher welfare payments, opening up no-show jobs in the antipoverty agencies, and turning a blind eye when police and firemen were assaulted
in the slums. Raskin writes that the standard complaint of the union leaders
"freighted with all the fears of the middle class about the Negro's clamor for a
bigger stake in society, is: 'Lindsay had forgotten that a Mayor is supposed to be
for all the people, not just turn everything over to one group.' "

The complex interplay of race, style, the new militancy of the unions, and
the general turmoil of the times is illustrated by Lindsay's relationship with the
police force. Jay Kriegel says:

The 1965 campaign in a real sense was run against the police force. Not that we thought
they were racists, but that the department was old and tired, and badly in need of mod-
ernization. But institutionalized racism *was* an important issue—the problem of brutality and the lack of minorities on the force. The cop on the street took it all as a criticism
of himself.

The first important police issue that hit Lindsay was explicitly racial. Relations between the police and the minority community had been poor for at least
a decade, and a long list of grievances had distilled into a demand for a civilian
review board to receive complaints of police brutality from citizens. As one
scholar put it, police would be punished "swiftly, cruelly, and publicly" for taking a bribe, but when the offense charged involved violence, the traditional
police attitude was "to deplore brutality, but to insist that a certain amount of
force is necessary to protect the public." With a police force that was overwhelmingly white (in fact, Irish, which made matters worse) and arrests that
disproportionately involved blacks and Puerto Ricans, use of force by the police
became a key civil rights complaint.

Proposals for various forms of review boards surfaced in the City Council as
early as 1962, and the demands reached a crescendo with the shooting of a
black youth that touched off riots in 1964. Lindsay was an early advocate of effective review over police actions and took a strong position during his campaign. He came into office determined to live up to his promises, although his
holdover police commissioner resigned over the issue. After city councilmen
begged Lindsay not to force a vote on a bill, he instituted a civilianized review
board by executive order in April 1966. The new board was hardly a radical
departure. Instead of creating a completely independent civilian review
agency, as several council bills had proposed, he simply added four civilians to
the police commissioner's own three-man board. If a complaint came before the
board, they could elect to hold a hearing; if the results of the hearing seemed to
justify disciplinary action, they could make a recommendation to the police
commissioner. The commissioner was free to ignore the recommendation, but
if he was disposed to accept it, he could take no action until the offending po-

liceman had been convicted at a departmental trial conducted entirely before superior officers. To the police the board seemed like a calculated insult, for all the insubstantiality of its procedures. "I'm sick and tried of giving into minority groups, with their whims, their shouting, and their gripes," said Cassesse. A successful PBA signature drive put the question to a referendum the following November and touched off a campaign that featured a television short of a little girl being attacked by a mugger, a poster showing a policeman with one hand tied behind his back, and a slogan "Don't handcuff the police." Lindsay, Robert Kennedy, Jacob Javits, and virtually all the civil rights and church groups in the city organized against the referendum but were crushed two-to-one at the polls. "We were simply mauled," says Kriegel. "It was one of the worst political defeats we could have taken. It was early, it was racial, and it was overwhelming."

The police sense of grievance against the administration was compounded in the next two summers by Lindsay's policy of restraint during ghetto and antiwar disturbances. Passively watching looting was galling to men who had been trained for action, and the close involvement of Gottehrer and Davidoff at the scenes of the disturbances led to charges of "political interference" with the police job, an impression that was strengthened by the peremptory style of the mayor's aides. The easy relations that Gottehrer and Davidoff seemed to enjoy with many of the militants sometimes made it hard to tell whose side they were on. When Neighborhood Youth Corps enrollees stormed City Hall, Gottehrer and Davidoff were moving through the crowd, talking to the leaders, then coming back to confer with the police supervisors, while the ranks were held in restraint. During antiwar demonstrations in lower Manhattan, the mayor's aides walked at the head of the march in casual clothes. Gottehrer insisted that he was trying to direct the march into the right streets, but it looked to the police as though he had joined it. At Columbia University the police were held back for several days while Gottehrer and the mayor attempted to negotiate a settlement. The intense pressure the confrontations imposed on the average policeman sharpened the resentment. "Nobody should have to go through what the men had to put up with at Columbia," says Kiernan. "It was just absolute filth. Students were throwing bags of urine and crap at us out the windows—and bricks. But the City wasn't even going to give us nightsticks and helmets until the PBA demanded it."

The racial animosities deepened when ghetto riots gave way to a pattern of murderous ambushes. Four policemen were killed by blacks in just two months in 1968. White off-duty policemen attacked Black Panthers outside a trial in Brooklyn, and the PBA stepped up its criticism of the administration. Gottehrer and Davidoff were called "hippies"; a union official said, "I think today we are suffering from the Police Department virtually being an arm of City Hall"; off-duty policemen picketed the mayor and chanted, "We want Daley." Finally, Cassesse, pushed hard by his own militant factions, announced he would issue "guidelines" for police conduct during disturbances. The mayor— at least, publicly—wisely bowed out of the controversy while Leary forced Cassesse to back down with a strong statement against insubordination.

In the rancorous atmosphere, virtually every attempt at management change degenerated into a public relations battle between the city and the PBA. Hayes's analysts calculated that they could generate substantial savings and increase efficiency by consolidating police precincts and realigning districts to accord more with crime patterns. The PBA fought the idea by organizing residents in the neighborhoods where precincts were slated to be closed. There was a virtual uprising of alarmed citizens, and the administration beat a retreat, although the new larger precinct houses were in some cases already under construction.

Lindsay won a round on the so-called fourth platoon. Under a state law, manning on each police shift had to be equal, although crime was heavily concentrated in the hours between 6 P.M. and 2 A.M. The union declared war when the city asked the state legislature to repeal the statute. Repeal, said Cassesse, "would give Lindsay the uncontrolled right to play field marshal with New York's law enforcement officers. Vesting such arbitrary power when no emergency exists is unthinkable." But the legislature went along with the city after the PBA's position was undercut by a newspaper exposé of widespread sleeping on the job—"cooping"—during the third shift. (The PBA charged that the mayor planted the stories.)

Thoughtlessly, the administration's pension and recruitment programs added to the volatility of the force. A liberal improvement in the retirement program in 1966* encouraged the departure of older officers, while lower recruiting standards (to expand the force and attract minorities) meant a less reliable core of patrolmen, more willing to listen to extremists and take irresponsible positions. Some fifteen thousand new patrolmen were brought into the force during the 1960s, and they were generally less educated, less intelligent, and came from poorer backgrounds than the generation they were replacing. The percentage of recruits whose fathers had unskilled jobs rose from 10 percent in 1959 to 50 percent in 1963; the percentage with a high school diploma began to drop in 1966; the average IQ of recruits dipped below 100 in 1968 and stayed there. One veteran said: "These new guys are just like the guys on the campuses. You do anything they don't like and they holler. They're always willing to protest about anything. They're really concerned about getting more money, but they're not afraid to talk politics either."

Harold Melnick, president of the Sergeant's Benevolent Association, summed up the situation:

The men saw the minorities getting all kinds of benefits from a liberal administration while cops were treated like fifth class citizens—protecting people who were vilifying them. Police work had always been a family job. Now fathers were talking their sons out of joining the force. That had a lot to do with the dropping standards. And, although you can't force people to move back into the City, we lost something when so many men started to live in the suburbs. Some men even avoid making an arrest if it means missing their car pool.

* Article I pensioners—men who had joined the force before 1940—received the right to retire at full pay after thirty-five years. Post-1940 recruits do not enjoy the same privilege but have more substantially guaranteed benefits at lower cost earlier in their careers.

Russo says: "Hell, it's simple. These guys don't live in the city any more and don't care what happens to it. And a lot of them hate the blacks and Puerto Ricans."

Whatever the causes—the arrogance of Lindsay's aides, the unwillingness to consult before making managerial changes, the PBA's resistance to any change, the strident demands of the minorities, the self-indulgence of antiwar and campus demonstrators, the bigotry and lack of discipline of the new police recruits, the lowered standards, the loss of identification with the city—the situation was deplorable. But to the cop on the beat, Lindsay symbolized everything that was wrong and was roundly hated for it. Kiernan says:

I honestly have to say that we made out better in every material respect with Lindsay than we ever had done with anyone else, but as far as the men were concerned it made no difference at all. In fact, at one negotiating session, the Mayor asked me if it would help sell the contract if he laid in the street and had his picture taken with my foot on his throat. I said "Hell, no, the men would scalp me for not killing you."

Relations between the administration and the police were probably the most publicly and consistently vituperative, but the problems with the firemen were hardly less serious. Threats of job actions stymied a series of management changes—lower manning ratios, consolidation of stations, adjustment of shifts to comport with the frequency of fires—and racial conflicts were every bit as much in evidence. Firemen fought off a Lindsay proposal to lower height standards to help recruit more Puerto Ricans and complained bitterly that Lindsay and his black fire commissioner, Robert Lowery, ignored or downplayed harassment and assaults on firemen by ghetto residents. The mindless arson in large sections of the ghetto required firemen in high-risk districts to chance their lives daily for the sake of people who didn't seem to care, who set fires on purpose. Frederick Hayes recalled:

We had done an analysis of the fire stations that were the most severely taxed. Some had been getting more than 12,000 calls a year. We worked with the Fire Dept. and redistributed the load so no house got more than 6000 a year. Then I went out on a tour, and half-expected the men in the affected houses to be appreciative. But they were incredibly surly and sullen. They didn't care about management, and the redistribution didn't affect their attitudes at all. They just wanted those people out there to get their act together and fly straight. They were sick and tired of it all.

The disaffection pervaded even the top echelons of the civil service. Martin Lang, a career civil servant who rose to become successively commissioner of water resources, sanitation, and parks, and who speaks warmly of Lindsay himself, says: "All these very bright young people coming into the administration had instant solutions to almost everything. The attitude of the professionals, almost to a man, was to lie back and let them fall on their faces."

The flamboyant iconoclasm of Lindsay's new recruits inevitably clashed with the mandarin tradition in the agencies. A civil servant with forty years in the same department says:

For years, administrations would come and go, and new faces would appear at headquarters. We would know they were there to receive their reward, and as a practical matter, they would barely impinge on our lives. But when Lindsay brought in his people, things were suddenly different. They were combing all through the agency, trying to find out how we did things, giving orders to change procedures. And they didn't really understand how the agency worked. It was very unsettling.

Problems in the welfare department showed a striking parallel to the problems in the police and fire departments. The same crippling alienation ran from the front lines to the very top ranks. Intense, and often violent, demands by the client groups put the agency under enormous pressure that coincided with sharply rising, and at times truly fierce, union militancy.* Not only did the workers frequently side with the radical client groups in their campaign of disruption, but—particularly after the 1965 strike—they made important inroads into management prerogatives that had long been taken for granted. The career managers rapidly lost their sense of control over the agency. A top career official says:

A typical management task for a welfare center director was allocating staff between intake and casework. When intake would build up a backlog, the good directors would get out into the client areas, organize the lines, and bring workers down from the casework sections to work off the backlog. But sometime in the middle 1960's, the union got a rule established that only intake workers could do intake, and the caseworkers upstairs could do only casework. But if a director couldn't move around his people, it did little good for him to be out in front on the bad days. He just looked foolish. More and more, directors simply stayed in their offices.

Lindsay's first welfare commissioner, Mitchell Ginsberg, had devoted an important part of his career to a radical critique of the welfare system and communicated a profound mistrust of the career staff. Among his first actions was to remove the long-time director of the key operating bureau in the department and call upon the welfare rights groups to monitor the performance of the centers. It appeared to the careerists that although he was intensely interested in the details of the welfare system, he cared more about his program for national reform than the intricacies of the ongoing operation. The same observer says:

Over the years the "pending file" had been an absolutely sacrosanct control on center performance. If certain casework wasn't completed within an allotted time, the file went into a pending file. If there were more than four or five cases in the pending file at the end of a month, the center director was personally called on the carpet before [the director of the bureau]. Perhaps we were silly, but it was an experience we all dreaded. And you went to great lengths and rode very close herd on your staff to make absolutely sure your casework was completed at the end of each month. But after the shake-up [i.e., when Ginsberg had replaced the top staff] nobody ever asked for pendings anymore, and it appeared that no one really was interested in that level of detail. The attention to work gradually began to slip.

---

*During the strike of caseworkers in 1967, a union official is reported to have tried to throw a strike-breaking worker in front of a subway train. The story may be apocryphal, but the fact that it was recounted and believed by another union official illustrates the intensity of feelings that were generated in union-management conflicts.

The same political tilt toward the militant groups that had so angered the uniformed forces also had its effect on welfare:

The welfare rights groups were permitted to set up tables in the center, and we were subtly given to understand that it was preferred that problems be handled through welfare rights to strengthen them in the eyes of the clients. The attitude of supervisors became, "Well, if there's a problem, the rights groups will tell us about it." The attitude toward work grew very lax. It was infecting everything in the centers.

But it would be quite unfair to lay all the blame on Ginsberg. His campaign for national reform almost succeeded, and a federalized welfare program would have been of profound importance to the city. Equally to the point, his low opinion of the career staff was in many cases amply justified. Over four decades, the agency had become intensely ingrown and resistant to change. The best of the career staff admit that many of the center directors were "woefully inadequate" or even "dreadful." From the front-line worker's perspective, the problem began with middle management. Bart Cohen, a former leader of the caseworkers, says that middle management in the agency conveyed "utter disdain" for the workers, long before Ginsberg was on the scene. Cohen is also the first to admit that the militant breed of workers who were being hired by the thousands, fresh from the campuses, reacted almost reflexively against the least exercise of management authority.

Again, whatever the causes, the downward spiral of capacity was tragic. Under extreme pressure an agency that had long been characterized by rigidity and defensiveness became ever more rigid and defensive. The disruptive tactics of the union leaders were often completely irresponsible, and at times literally destructive. For the senior staff there was a loss of old anchors, a pervasive feeling of disorientation. Work in which they had long taken great pride was condemned as evil and prurient by all sides, even by their superiors. The radical new workers looked hairy and unkempt, seemed to take no pride in their work, and resisted discipline and normal supervision. Top management seemed to be on the side of the most outrageously demanding clients, who were destroying the program and threatened—or even assaulted—staff who tried to stand up to them. At the height of the welfare rights drive, Lindsay was infuriated when he discovered that several center directors had stood by and refused to call in police as clients repeatedly vandalized their centers. But the directors were almost certainly not acting in bad faith to embarrass the administration: allowing the clients to run amok seemed consistent with all that had been going on.

UNIONS AT THE CREST

Following the transit strike Lindsay reeled from one confrontation with the unions to another. Nurses struck in the spring for higher wages.* The nurses' strike was followed by a strike of doctors in more than two hundred city health

---

*They won, and they should have: The city wage scale was so low that 60 percent of the registered nurse positions in the municipal hospitals were vacant.

stations and clinics. They stayed out until the City agreed to raise their pay from $23.50 an hour to $43 an hour—the same as the Board of Education paid them.

The intense competition between the major unions caught the city in a whipsaw. In the fall of 1966, Herbert Haber, Lindsay's new director of labor relations, settled with the policemen and firemen on a two-year package with a basic wage increase of $900 and benefits totalling $465. The police ratified the contract, but the firemen rejected it, so the negotiations had to start over. In the meantime the sanitationmen announced the terms of *their* settlement with the city, and the police were outraged. They insisted that Haber had promised them that the sanitationmen's one-year contract would be worth less than the first year of the PBA's contract. "The police were panicked by the sanitationmen," says Haber. "The sanitationmen were so politically powerful, the police were in dread that they would be overtaken by them. That's all they cared about—keeping ahead of the sanitationmen."

After a new package had been worked out, reallocating the money between salary and fringe benefits, it was rejected again—first by the PBA and then three successive times by the firemen. The firemen began a work slowdown, and the police picketed City Hall. Lindsay complicated matters by insisting publicly that the city would not change its offer. A face-saving formula was worked out by extending the contract period and loading more benefits into the back end of the contract, in order to depress the overall costs. The total package worked out to $642 for a policeman in the contract's first year, compared to the sanitationman's $545, so a cherished rule of 90 percent parity between police and sanitation was preserved.

But the sanitation contract was a breakthrough on another front. Haber followed through on a Wagner promise to give DeLury's men the same twenty-year, half-pay retirement that police and firemen enjoyed. It was a portentous concession, for it was almost certain to produce ripple-effect demands from the other unions, and it reinforced a growing tendency to trade off future benefits to sweeten current contracts.

Generous pensions were nothing new in municipal government: Pensions before World War I were at least as generous as they were in the 1970s.* The

---

*Pension plans were created unsystematically through the nineteenth and early twentieth centuries. Police received pension coverage in 1857, firemen in 1866, teachers in 1894, and citywide employees in 1911. The plans were typically established as a result of employee lobbying, and improvements in benefits, eligibility periods, and other aspects of the plans were legislated almost yearly. The plans provided half-pay retirement after a term of service, with the benefit based on the pay as of the date of retirement in most plans. Firemen, health department employees, and City College employees could retire after twenty years of service with no minimum age, court employees, after twenty-five years, and teachers after thirty. Street cleaners retired after twenty years, but at a minimum age of sixty, police after twenty-five years and a minimum age of fifty-five. Most plans provided that service credits could be earned by employment outside the city, and college employees could earn almost all their service credits elsewhere. The minimum service provisions either did not apply or were sharply reduced in cases of disability, with more generous allowances for disabilities suffered in the line of duty. The disability provisions were extremely vague and were usually administered at the discretion of the department head: For example, some

plans were gradually reorganized and placed on an actuarial footing—that is, annual contributions were set so that future benefits claims could always be met from the assets of the funds. Benefits were restricted to those granted state employees, unless the legislature approved exceptions. In return for the restrictions, the state constitution was amended to provide that, once granted, benefits could never be rescinded.

Under the reorganized plans, police and firemen retained twenty-year, no-minimum-age pensions, while the basic patterns for other employees were twenty-five or thirty-year plans and minimum ages of fifty-five or sixty. Contributions were approximately evenly split between employees and the city and were designed to produce half-pay benefits, with increments for service beyond the minimum period. Average pay over the last five years of employment was the normal base for computing the retirement benefit. The amount of the retirement benefit was not guaranteed, however. Although the employee contribution was designed to produce a half-pay benefit when added to the city contribution, if the actuarial assumptions turned out to be wrong, the employee received only the benefit he had paid for. In fact, the guaranteed city payment plus the annuity earned from employee contributions usually produced something less than the targeted half-pay benefit.

As with so much else, the first steps toward the broad liberalization of pension benefits during the Lindsay years were taken early in the 1960s. First of all, in 1960 Wagner introduced Increased Take-Home Pay for most employees, a device whereby the city paid a specified share of the employee's contributions. The gimmick of ITHP is that it has the effect of a wage increase but is cheaper for the city, because it doesn't affect the base on which pensions, overtime, or social security are calculated. In addition, because it was not, strictly speaking, a pension plan improvement, it could be rescinded (and actually was, in part, during the fiscal crisis). Then Wagner, with the legislature's compliance, guaranteed the half-pay pension target for the sanitationmen, in return for the firm support they had shown him in the 1961 election. When the police failed to extract the same guarantee, Rockefeller, over Wagner's strong objections, put a bill through the legislature that required the city to make up the shortfall between earned benefits and the half-pay promise. A taxpayer's suit based on home-rule principles attacked the bill, but despite his earlier objec-

---

employees were considered to be "constructively" on duty at all times, and only the barest medical certificate was required as proof of disability. By 1914 more than half of all retirees had left under disability provisions. The citywide plan was the most stringent and provided retirement on disability grounds only (which could include old age) but required the certification of an independent board of physicians. The citywide plan, and the plans for firemen, college employees, and certain court employees, required no employee contributions; teachers, health, and certain other court employees contributed 1 percent of their salaries; police 2 percent, and the street cleaners 3 percent. The City paid about 85 percent of total costs, with the bulk of the city contribution met by direct appropriation or the sale of bonds. By 1914 both the city share and overall costs were rising rapidly. In the police department, for example, pension payments exceeded 16 percent of payrolls. Finally, retired employees could, and often did, secure employment in other city departments without prejudice to their pensions.

tions Wagner quietly engineered a bill through the City Council to protect the benefit. Teachers received their guarantee in 1964.

In 1963 the base for calculating police and fire pensions was changed to the compensation earned on the date of retirement, and in the same year sanitationmen won a separate retirement system with a twenty-five-year, no-minimum-age retirement. During the same period the twenty-year, no-minimum-age plan was extended to corrections officers; teachers won an age-fifty-five, twenty-five-year plan, and the service increments that could be earned by police and firemen were increased. In 1965 pension contributions for sanitationmen were changed from a 50-50 city-employee share to 75-25, a benefit already won by the police and firemen, and a sanitationman's maximum contribution was set at 7½ percent of base pay. Also in 1965 the "death gamble" was eliminated for most employees: If an eligible employee died before retiring, his benefits would be paid to his dependents.

The problem with negotiating over pension benefits is that, in contrast to all other forms of remuneration, it is extremely difficult to estimate their costs with any certainty.* The future cost of a pension benefit will depend on the rate at which salaries increase, the rate of interest earned by the pension fund, the rate of the city's contribution, and the retirement behavior of employees—none of which can be predicted with any certainty. Even more uncertainty was introduced when negotiators manipulated the factors on which a pension was based—from the average salary over the last three years before retirement, to the last year's salary, or worse, to the last year's pay—including shift differentials and overtime (or, as was eventually the case with uniformed employees, to the last *day's* pay). Costs were thrown even more out of joint in 1968 when Rockefeller mandated supplements for people who had already retired. Russo admits:

We never should have been allowed to bargain over pensions. You'd sit there with actuaries from both sides arguing over the assumptions of the plan, and the unions could always show that the annual costs would be trivial, but you'd be talking about potentially enormous future costs. It was very hard to compare a pension benefit with a salary increase.

Confrontations did not always involve money and pensions. Welfare workers struck briefly in January 1967 but went back to work when the economic issues were submitted to arbitration. They struck several months later, however, when the city refused to negotiate on non-money issues—lower workloads, streamlined case processing, and better grants for clients. The tactic was a "work-in": Caseworkers would report to their centers but refuse to perform any duties; centers were broken into and flooded; records were torn and scat-

*The sanitationmen's twenty-year pension award in 1966 is a good example of the problem. As the bargaining wound down, there was still a considerable discrepancy between the city's and the union's cost estimates for the new plan. Naively, the city wrote into the agreement that the pension improvement would be granted only if the union's cost estimates turned out to be right, upon further analysis. However, once the benefit had been announced, there was no possibility of its being rescinded, even though the costs were probably substantially higher than the union claim. Worse, the city could not even take credit for its full cost in future bargaining.

tered; locks were jammed; and there were sit-ins at headquarters, telephone threats against Ginsberg, and scuffles with the police. The city held its ground for six weeks and broke the strike. The city's firm stand was made easier because it was supported by DC 37, which represented the welfare center supervisors and considered the caseworkers a runaway union.

Non-monetary issues also figured prominently in a three-week teachers' strike in September 1967. Albert Shanker, president of the United Federation of Teachers (UFT), insists that the strike was unnecessary and that the city's—and particularly Lindsay's—awkward handling of the negotiations made the final settlement much more costly than it need have been. "I really didn't want a strike in 1967," he says. "The union concept was new, and a lot of teachers were still uncomfortable with us. I was anxious to put together a smooth, professional negotiation to demonstrate our responsibility, but the city made it almost impossible."

There was the usual problem of Lindsay's insensitivity to the union leaders' feelings. Lindsay insisted on an early fact-finding, so Haber asked the union for a list of acceptable fact-finders. Shanker recalls:

We provided fifteen names, all of them nationally known. Then one Sunday, I was driving to a television station to appear on a question and answer show and I heard on the car radio that Lindsay had appointed a panel but hadn't used a single one of our names. I blasted him as soon as I got on television. I couldn't quarrel with the selections—at least two of the three—but the process was so irritating. It seemed to convey that he didn't care about our opinions.

The key non-monetary item among the union's demands was the More Effective Schools program, a union-sponsored intensification of services in problem schools. Opinions differ as to whether the program was of substantial benefit to the youngsters, but it clearly eased the pressure on the teachers, which was of great importance to the union. The union viewed the MES program as a trade-off for an agreement with the Board of Education to reduce transfer opportunities from slum schools in order to ensure a stable teaching corps. (Shanker boasts, with justification, that New York's ghetto schools have a higher proportion of licensed teachers than schools anywhere else in the country.) Moreover, Shanker had other problems:

I sat down with the Mayor and explained to him that I had 106 different organizations among the union members—librarians, special education teachers, vocational educational teachers, you name it. To keep the union together, I needed to get special little things for some of these groups. Not for all of them, but for a few each year. Some of the requests were trivial. But the Mayor didn't seem to comprehend what I was talking about. He seemed to have this idea that unions only wanted money. I feel sure he influenced the factfinders in that direction.

As it turned out, the fact-finders came in with the largest money award by far that had been granted in any of the city settlements to that date—20 percent in salary and fringe benefits over two years—and not a single one of the non-monetary demands. In fact, they recommended taking back privileges that the union had won in previous years. When the city announced that it would stick by the fact-finders' recommendations, the teachers struck. In the end, says Shanker, with a touch of smugness, "We got seventeen out of twenty non-monetary demands, and of course we kept the money."

The teachers' settlement and the sanitation breakthrough on pensions were targets for all the other unions to shoot at. As soon as the teachers' strike was settled, negotiations had to begin on the next transit contract, which was due to expire on New Year's Day, 1968. The union leaders set their sights on the sanitationmen's pension and coupled it with wage demands pegged to the teachers' settlements. This time Lindsay handled the politics with a much surer hand. He was involved in the negotiations from the very start but kept a low profile, eschewed public statements, and let the parties bargain. His previous tendency, consistent with reformist doctrine, had been to insist on impartial fact-finding early, announce the recommendations, and try to stick with them; but this time the negotiators reached a settlement minutes before the strike deadline without fact-finding. Theodore Kheel, one of the mediators, said: "The transit negotiations were a great triumph for John Lindsay. He handled himself right throughout. He made all the right moves. The difference between this Lindsay and the Lindsay of the 1966 dispute is like the difference between night and day." The wage settlement was not excessive—5 percent and 6 percent over two years—but the pensions bandwagon kept rolling. Transit workers got their twenty-year pensions, but with a minimum retirement age of fifty.*

DC 37, negotiating a citywide contract (essentially for everyone other than teachers, transit, and the uniformed services), won its own major pension improvements in the same month. Retirement was kept at age fifty-five, but with a guaranteed 55 percent of final salary and more sharply rising benefits thereafter. The city's contribution vested after twenty years, and the employee's share (before the calculation of ITHP) was reduced from one-half to one-third. The agreement also demonstrated the costs of the city's fragmented bargaining structure, because the city and DC 37 were ready to sign off on a much more modest package when the transit settlement was announced. (The Transit Authority and the Board of Education, among others, negotiated independently of the Office of Labor Relations.) "Gotbaum came screaming into my office," says Russo. "He says, 'You're forcing me into the street.' " The negotiations were reopened to bring the citywide pensions more into line with the transit settlement.

For all the turmoil, Lindsay's first two years of labor relations were not without accomplishment. Following through on the recommendations of Wagner's tripartite panel, he created the Office of Labor Relations to provide professional full-time attention to the bargaining process and established the Office of Collective Bargaining—consisting of a seven-man board and associated staff—to provide evenhanded certification for bargaining units and bargaining

*The city hoped that the minimum age would deter an exodus of the most skilled workers, on the theory that men aged fifty would have more difficulty finding alternative employment. How much impact the minimum age had is unclear, but there was certainly the exodus that the Transit Authority feared. Several hundred skilled men retired almost immediately, putting pressure on an already slipping standard of service.

agents and to manage impartial impasse procedures—primarily, expert fact-finding and arbitration.

Considerable progress was made toward consolidating Wagner's legacy of fragmented bargaining units into a more streamlined and coherent system. Keeping the unions divided and competitive was probably a good tactic when most of the unions were weak, but as the major unions gained strength, the competition pushed them toward more militant positions than they would otherwise have felt obliged to take.

The welter of time-honored practices and procedures throughout the city was gradually reduced to writing, setting out the responsibilities of both management and labor. Summer hours, which had existed from time immemorial, were finally put into the DC 37 contract, for instance, but there was also spelled out the responsibility of each employee to participate on a skeleton staff rotation so the city offices could stay open until 5 P.M. A continuing series of arbitrations finally resolved a long-standing list of work rule disputes in the fire department and allowed the city and the firemen to enter into their first written contract ever, in 1968. The first citywide written contract, covering most of the city's white-collar and clerical titles and setting out management and union rights, time and leave rules, and grievance procedures, was negotiated only in 1967.

A number of commentators have drawn adverse comparisons between the performance of the Office of Labor Relations and the Office of Collective Bargaining and the old system of budget bureau and political control, and there is certainly much to criticize. But it was too late to turn back the clock; the old back-of-the-envelope arrangements that had prevailed under Wagner were almost certainly no longer suitable. More budget bureau and political control would hardly be a panacea. One of the most costly settlements of all, for instance—the teachers' pension of 1969—was approved by the budget bureau without OLR participation: The bureau simply missed the significance of the numbers. Furthermore, in 1974, when Abraham Beame reasserted a strong mayoral role in collective bargaining, the city negotiators were told to settle at the highest figures ever.

The problem in Lindsay's first years went far beyond structure and organization. In fact, the structural system he created has become a permanent part of the city machinery and has been widely imitated around the country. Lindsay's problem, in the face of newly powerful unions, was how to make the structure begin to work for him.

THE SANITATION STRIKE: 1968

After the 1968 transit settlement, Lindsay seemed on the point of achieving good relations with the unions. Swallowing his "power broker" rhetoric, he had come increasingly to rely on Van Arsdale and Kheel in difficult negotiations and seemed willing to engage in genuine bargaining instead of reaching immediately for formalistic third-party mechanisms. However, the accommodation was expensive: Since the wave of me-tooism touched off by the 1966 transit settlement and the sanitation pension breakthrough, the city's commitments to its employees had begun to rise very sharply, and there was clearly a limit to how much longer the city could continue to buy labor peace.* In February 1968 the limit seemed to be reached.

The city's contract with the sanitationmen expired on June 30, 1967, but negotiations dragged into 1968. Two mediators appointed by the mayor (DeLury had never agreed to participate in OCB mechanisms) finally recommended a basic wage package of $400, a 2.5 percent increase in ITHP—worth $275 per year— and double-time for Sunday work. It was arguably a more generous package than the police and firemen had won for the second year of their contract, and DeLury was pleased to accept it, although Haber indicated it might be too high for the city to pay; but when DeLury attempted to present the package to his men at a meeting in the City Hall park, he was hooted off the platform, pelted with eggs, and required police assistance to get out of the crowd. For all his legendary iron control, DeLury had underestimated the temper of his men. Like the police and the firemen, they were angry at the city, angry at the changes in working conditions, angry at the apparent preference shown the minorities; they felt like second-class citizens ("garbagemen") and wanted to strike almost for catharsis. At first DeLury tried to conciliate, but seeing his own position threatened, he suddenly raised his bargaining demands, sprinted to the head of the strike vanguard, and led his men out of the garages.

Ten thousand tons of garbage a day began to spill into the city's streets, but Lindsay refused to negotiate until the union returned to work. If a line had to be drawn somewhere, he was willing to draw it in the garbage. Fires began to break out in the piles of trash; rats were increasingly in evidence; and the health commissioner declared a health emergency, warning of possible outbreaks of hepatitis, typhoid, and other infectious diseases. The assault on the senses by the growing mounds of swill was indescribable. The city secured an injunction against the strike, and DeLury went to jail as a band played "When Johnny Comes Marching Home Again." Lindsay's order to other municipal unions to man the sanitation trucks was ignored. The home of a non-striking foreman was shotgunned, and the sanitationmen made it clear that there would be violence if anyone tried to interfere with their strike. Lindsay stalked the garbage-duned streets like a zombie, hollow-eyed from lack of sleep and the anguish of watching the city slip into anarchy.

On the sixth day of the strike, Lindsay asked Rockefeller for help. It wasn't easy. Two days previously, Rockefeller had said that Lindsay would "have to say he's lost control" before he would intervene. Lindsay asked for the National Guard to pick up the garbage and break the strike. To Rockefeller, who was as close to Van Arsdale and the state's major union leaders as Wagner had been,

*From 1966 to 1969 average labor costs per employee rose by about 15 percent per year, compounded. Not all of this can be attributed to union demands. Essentially on their own motion, Lindsay and Haber had initiated a program of bringing pay levels throughout the city to levels comparable with those prevailing in private industry—necessitating raises of 8–11 percent per year in many of the white-collar titles.

the suggestion was preposterous and dangerous. Calling in troops to break a strike conjured up images of the great labor wars earlier in the century. A top labor official called the suggestion "union-busting of the worst sort. It would be catastrophic in the long range for both the city and the unions. Negotiations, not troops, are the answer to this dispute." Van Arsdale threatened a general strike in the city if troops were used.

Rockefeller secured DeLury's release from jail and started the city and the union negotiating again. Five mediators were added to the original two-member city team, and at 2 A.M. on the morning of the seventh day, they announced that the union was willing to settle for just $25 in pay above the original recommendations. Rockefeller called the recommendations "fair and reasonable," but Lindsay refused to accept them. He declared: "I said yesterday the City would not pay blackmail in order to end this strike. The proposed settlement, in my view, asks the City to pay a little blackmail." The strike could continue.

The governor's view of the practicalities of the situation was undoubtedly sound. To bring in the militia would almost certainly have sparked serious violence between the sanitationmen and the guardsmen, and quite probably would have led to a general strike. Moreover, it wasn't at all clear that the troops could operate the equipment and actually clean up the mess. But the mayor had the better grasp of principle. One of the authors of the state's newly revised labor relations law said Rockefeller's insistence on a higher settlement was "the crassest kind of political move . . . The Governor said 'If you've got enough muscle, the community will knuckle under.' "

Outraged that Lindsay had rejected his mediation package, Rockefeller announced that he would ask the legislature to mandate a state takeover of the city sanitation department and would pay the men at the rate his mediators had recommended. At the governor's promise the sanitationmen, who were beginning to feel the pinch of the strike, went back to work and started cleaning up the garbage. Rockefeller delayed the takeover for three days, in the hope that Lindsay would relent, but the mayor stood firm. To Rockefeller's shock the legislature decided to stand with Lindsay. Albany was swamped with mail condemning Rockefeller's sellout and backing the mayor's position. The public had had enough of illegal strikes, and the legislative leadership told Rockefeller there was no chance of passing a sanitation takeover bill. He could stay out on his limb by himself. Lindsay turned the screws by announcing that the returning sanitationmen would get paid at the same rate that they had gotten before the strike.

It was a clear victory for Lindsay. The sanitationmen found themselves back at work with no settlement at all, and public opinion was running so powerfully against them that they didn't dare go out on strike again. As Raskin wrote: "Suddenly the Mayor didn't look like a stiff-necked petulant bumbler any more. The people overwhelmingly sided with him in his not-one-penny-for-tribute stand. "Cool Hand Luke," as one union wag labelled him, had snatched the initiative away from the men who thought he had exposed himself as a hopelessly outclassed amateur."

The contract dispute itself was resolved when the city and the union agreed to submit the dispute to binding arbitration. Vincent McDonnell, chairman of the State Mediation Board, came up with a decision that split neatly down the hairline separating the positions of the two sides. The union got $400, effective July 1, 1967, and $425, effective Jan. 1, 1968, the 2.5 percent ITHP, and a fif-teen-month contract. They did not get the double-time Sunday overtime origi-nally recommended, and the longer time period diluted the impact of the $425 increase in the latter part of the contract. The mayor was able to accept the award without clearly sacrificing his principles, while DeLury could argue he hadn't been totally backed down.

Raskin saw the whole episode as a milestone in municipal labor relations:

It was the first time in many decades that outraged public opinion had ever materially af-fected the outcome of a strike. . . . The landslide of popular revulsion that sent the Al-bany legislature into pellmell retreat and that kept the garbagemen from walking out again . . . may be the tocsin of a fundamental shift in the public's willingness to tolerate tieups in which it is the chief victim.

For Rockefeller, it was a bitterly galling defeat, and many political ob-servers concluded that the bad press he received around the country substan-tially reduced his chances of winning the Republican presidential nomination that summer. Lindsay's popularity in the city soared just as he was receiving nationwide accolades for his handling of ghetto disorders. If he could bring order to municipal labor relations as he seemed to be controlling strife in the city's slums there was hope for the city yet.

V. *The End of the Liberal Experiment*

LINDSAY AT THE CREST

THE SPRING AND SUMMER OF 1968 was the high point of John Lindsay's two terms as mayor. Just as John Kennedy had set the tone for a generation of national politicians, Lindsay was defining a style for big-city mayors. Jerome Cavanaugh in Detroit, Ivan Allen in Atlanta, and Kevin White in Boston consciously fashioned administrations in the Lindsay mold, contrasting sharply with the old-fashioned machines and rasping working-class accents of James H. J. Tate in Philadelphia and Richard Daley in Chicago. No one would pretend that New York City did not have myriad serious problems, but Lindsay seemed at least as well positioned to deal with them as anyone else. It appeared that if he should decide to run for a second term the following year, as everyone expected, he would be unbeatable.

Indeed, the most apparent obstacle to a second term was the very real possibility that Lindsay would move on to higher office. Looking toward the 1968 Republican national convention, the *Nation* entitled an editorial "Why Not Lindsay?":

(He has) a superb record on two key domestic issues—the racial situation and the crisis in the cities. [He was] a key figure in the President's Commission on Civil Disorders, and had a lot to do with the tone and tenor of that report and the fact that it was submitted unanimously in the end. . . . He is the spokesman nationally, and is recognized as such, for the cities [and has] exceptional poise and courage. . . . While Chicago's Mayor Daley [views riots] from his helicopter, Lindsay walks the streets.

Harper's magazine listed among Lindsay's accomplishments: bringing fiscal order to the city; reorganizing the government; breaking up the "Irish Mafia" in the police department; expanding and modernizing the patrol force; bringing five hundred bright new managers into the city bureaucracy; towing forty thousand abandoned or illegally parked cars to ease traffic congestion; opening six new little City Halls; improving the parks; installing tough new standards on air pollution; rebuilding the "housing pipeline"; and being "the only metropolitan mayor credited with singlehandedly cooling the black ghetto." The magazine considered that "despite the grumbles of cabdrivers, jealous politicians, and suburban bigots, John V. Lindsay is generally a popular Mayor" and concluded: "[Because Wagner] had convinced the world that New York is an ungovernable, unmanageable mess, and in view of the fact that New York may indeed *be* an ungovernable, unmanageable mess, then John Lindsay (forty-six years old, handsome, presidential ambitions) may be said to have performed well enough to deserve higher honors."

At the Republican national convention itself, in August 1968, Lindsay was prominently mentioned as the vice-presidential candidate who could build bridges between the party and the nation's cities, and his endorsement of the actual nominee, Spiro Agnew, was assiduously courted by the party leadership. "At that point, John was suddenly Mr. Everything," recalls an aide. "We were on top of the world."

THE TEACHERS' STRIKES: 1968

The administration's bubble burst in the fall of 1968. Except for brief respites, three successive teachers' strikes closed the city schools from opening day until November 19. The strikes were marked by almost unbearable racial tensions. Lindsay appeared vacillating and ineffective throughout, and his stock among the city's voters, both black and white, dropped to probably its lowest point. An analysis of the impact of the strikes on the administration requires a brief chronology of the key events.

The strikes grew out of the movement in the city to decentralize the school system and make its operations subject to greater community control. "Decentralization" and "community control" are obviously related concepts, but they had different histories in the city and came to bear quite different connotations. "Community control" was a euphemism for black control of schools in black neighborhoods. Militant black leaders had begun to demand control over black schools after successive campaigns to achieve integration had failed—because of ineffective implementation of the various plans by the Board of Education and because of the ultimate impossibility of the task. (Seventy-five percent of the public school children in Manhattan, for instance, were black or Puerto Rican.) The theory of the militants was that white administrators and white teachers reinforced a black child's feelings of cultural inferiority—"educational genocide." The movement crystallized when the board attempted to open a new intermediate school, IS 201, in Harlem in the fall of 1966. Militant picketing and a boycott of classes forced the replacement of the white leadership of the school, even though the principal and staff had been chosen for their sensitivity to racial issues and ability to work with black cultural materials. In the wake of defeat at IS 201, the board announced that it would consider undertaking demonstrations in selected school districts to see whether greater community involvement would make a contribution toward solving the dreadful problems in slum schools.

Although the word "decentralization" was often used interchangeably with "community control," it more accurately represented the hope, of rather long and respectable lineage, of devolving the extremely centralized powers of the Board of Education upon local units. Although there were thirty local boards of education, their powers were advisory only, and the local superintendents were little more than conduits to the professional staff of the central board. A system organized around central processing of virtually all matters of supplies, maintenance, repair, curriculum, personnel—no matter how detailed—was inevitably rigid and unresponsive, choking on its own paperwork.

Decentralization got an unexpected push in 1967, when the city's Bureau of the Budget discovered that the city qualified for additional state educational aid if the state formula were applied separately to each of the five city boroughs instead of the city as a whole. The legislature agreed to countenance the city's ploy and provide the additional aid, but only on the condition that the city submit the following year a plan for genuine decentralization.* To assist him in carrying out the legislative mandate, Lindsay appointed a five-member panel, chaired by McGeorge Bundy, president of the Ford Foundation, to make recommendations. The only representative of the schools or teachers on the panel was Alfred Giardino, president of the Board of Education.

Regardless of its political or racial implications, any change in the administrative structure of the educational system was of profound interest to the teachers' union, the UFT. Hard-won rights to tenure, transfer, seniority and work rules could all be affected by the various decentralization-cum-community control proposals that were in the air. But the union was not opposed to experiment. Teachers, after all, considered themselves the primary victims of an overly bureaucratized board, and the union had excellent civil rights credentials and numerous contacts with the militant, change-oriented groups stirring in the ghetto. Opportunistically, the unions also viewed the parents' groups as a possible additional source of pressure on the board for expansion of the More Effective Schools program.

One of the groups the union made contact with was a "People's Board of Education" in Ocean Hill–Brownsville, a drearily impoverished, predominantly black neighborhood squeezed unhappily between the slums of Bedford-Stuyvesant and Brownsville. By all measures—achievement, attendance, disorder—its schools were in dire straits. A group of parents loosely affiliated with

*The additional aid involved was substantial—about $51 million. The state aid formula was skewed toward districts with lower real estate tax bases but with a minimum guarantee for the wealthier areas. By computing the aid separately for each borough, the high Manhattan real estate values were not averaged into the other boroughs, so each qualified for greater assistance, while Manhattan retained its minimum guarantee. Rockefeller was interested in providing more assistance to the city and so was sympathetic to the plan, but the legislature was reluctant to go along unless the Board of Education was actually replaced by genuinely independent boards in the boroughs. They feared, among other things, that every big-city district would qualify for more aid by paper redistricting. State Education Commissioner James Allen seized on the opportunity to advance his long-standing hopes to decentralize the city system, which led to the compromise in the final bill.

Brooklyn CORE and local antipoverty agencies and led by a militant worker-priest, Fr. John Powis, had set out to see what they could do about it. Eventually, the union's leader, Albert Shanker, suggested to Bernard Donovan, the superintendent of schools, that he include Ocean Hill–Brownsville in his list of possible decentralization demonstration programs.

When the Board announced three demonstration districts in the summer of 1967, Ocean Hill–Brownsville was among them, and the People's Board, now a planning council, became the recipient of a $44,000 Ford Foundation planning grant funnelled through Fr. Powis's church. The council hired a district administrator, Rhody McCoy, a black with eighteen years' experience in the system, who was an acting principal of a school for disturbed boys. Then, to the consternation of the central board, which had not yet decided which powers to devolve, the council moved almost immediately to hold an election for a local governing board for the district. By a variety of devices, including a house-to-house canvass, votes were secured from about 25 percent of the parents in the area, and a board was chosen, duly convened and opened for business.

Instead of making a decision on the powers that it would grant to the new board, the central board chose to procrastinate: It would not officially recognize the newly minted local board but would deal with it anyway. Donovan was helpful in securing a partial exemption from civil service rules so that Ocean Hill could hire principals to its taste, but otherwise, the central staff was singularly unforthcoming. McCoy had to wait for weeks for a telephone, and until well into the winter the only office space that could be found for him was in an unheated storefront. During the same period the union withdrew its active participation in the demonstration, both because Donovan had made it clear that there would be no expansion of the MES program and because the union representatives were being made to feel increasingly uncomfortable by the militants on the local board.

The teachers' strike at the start of the 1967 school year was deeply resented by the local board, who saw it as a direct attack on their efforts to make some headway against the educational deprivation of their children. McCoy was one of very few local administrators who tried to keep his schools open during the dispute, and probably the only one to engage actively in strike-breaking activities—recruiting substitutes or volunteers into the classrooms and reporting individual male striking teachers to their draft boards. The antipathies continued to smolder even after the strike's conclusion.

Meanwhile, in November, the Bundy panel made its report to Mayor Lindsay, recommending total decentralization (with up to sixty districts) and a maximum of community involvement. Under the recommendations the central board would have been relegated to the purely ministerial functions of raising and distributing money, while the local boards would have exercised virtually all the other powers of independent school districts. The concerns of the black militant groups clearly weighed heavily on the minds of the drafters. Mario Fantini, the staff director for the Bundy committee and the author of the report, stated that he saw community control as an important step toward achieving the sense of "potency" in the black community that would be a prerequisite to meaningful integration.

Lindsay modified the report somewhat by recommending that high schools and hiring standards remain under central control but otherwise transmitted the plan to the legislature substantially as it emerged from the Bundy committee, despite the strong dissent of Shanker and Giardino. The State Board of Regents, urged on by Kenneth Clark (a member of the board and the author of the first program guide for HARYOU), made further revisions in the Lindsay recommendations (the number of districts was changed to fifty, for instance) but maintained the basic thrust of the recommendations toward thoroughgoing decentralization. After some negotiations, Lindsay agreed to accept the Regents' plan so the city and the state could approach the legislature with a unified position. Despite frantic lobbying by the UFT, virtually none of whose concerns were dealt with in any of the plans, it appeared very likely that the legislature would pass a version of the Regents' plan.

At that point, in May 1968, the local governing board in Ocean Hill–Brownsville voted to transfer out involuntarily—in effect, to dismiss—thirteen teachers and six assistant principals. Included among them were two UFT chapter chairmen—one of whom, at least, had an impeccable reputation—and several others who were generally highly regarded. The process of selection seems to have been one of combustion instead of reasoning. Compounded resentment against a perceived lack of cooperation from the teachers had brought the board to the flash point; the final list was compiled in a rush, largely on the basis of hearsay, and with little analysis of the charges against individuals.

Donovan had no choice but to order the board to reinstate the teachers. The board refused, and parents blocked the entrances when the suspended staff tried to enter their schools. Three hundred and fifty union teachers walked out of the Ocean Hill–Brownsville schools in protest and were dismissed by McCoy for their action. The conflict between the board and the union was not lost on Albany. The year ended with the schools closed in Ocean Hill and the Regents' decentralization bill dead in the legislature.

The legislature finally enacted a bill that essentially postponed the decentralization problem for another year. The central board was authorized to make temporary delegations of its powers to local boards, in order to experiment with the various decentralization modes and allow the demonstration districts to function legally. The central Board of Education was expanded—the new positions would allow Lindsay to appoint a majority of the members—and was instructed to present a detailed decentralization plan the following year. Lindsay appointed seven new board members, at least five of whom were prominently identified with civil rights or antipoverty activities: John Doar, a former justice department civil rights enforcer and president of the Bedford-Stuyvesant Renewal Corporation; Milton Galamison, a militant black minister and a veteran of the school integration battles; William Haddad, a former investigative newspaperman and OEO official; Hector Vasquez, director of the Puerto Rican Forum;

and Ana Conigliaro, a Puerto Rican activist who later marched on Shanker's headquarters. The board set about developing the temporary decentralization plan permitted by the legislature, while Galamison and Haddad worked to reconcile the opposing factions in Ocean Hill.

Throughout the summer, Galamison and Haddad reported optimistically to the mayor's office on the progress of their mediation in Ocean Hill. Their optimism did not flag even when a judge threw out all the charges against all the suspended teachers, virtually ruling out a face-saving compromise. (The failure to make *any* of the charges stick may have stemmed from poor presentation of the charges by McCoy. McCoy claims that he was "set up" by Donovan and Shanker and led to believe that the hearing would be merely a formality.) However, although the transfer controversy was still unresolved, sufficient cooperation was restored between Ocean Hill and the central board to permit McCoy to undertake an aggressive recruiting and licensing campaign for young and idealistic teachers willing to work in the district.

When the board announced its citywide decentralization plans in August, most decentralization advocates saw it as a disappointingly cautious step—it consisted of little more than a modest upgrading of the district boards and superintendents—but the union was still alarmed. Time-and-leave rules existed in the form of board regulations and had never been reduced to contractual status. The new plan seemed to rescind the existing rules and leave it to the discretion of the local boards to promulgate new ones. Nor did the plan, in the union's view, provide sufficient safeguards against repetitions of the spring firings in Ocean Hill–Brownsville.

As the school year approached, the union and the board made little headway on resolving the union's decentralization concerns, and despite the continued optimism of Galamison and Haddad, there was no progress in the negotiations over the Ocean Hill teachers. Finally, on August 30 the union took a strike vote, and for the second year in a row, the schools failed to open as scheduled. Donovan capitulated almost immediately. He revised the decentralization regulations to meet the union demands and assured Shanker that the Ocean Hill teachers would be reinstated—both the original transferees and those who had been fired by McCoy for walking out in the spring. The teachers called off the strike, and the schools opened only two days late.

But when the suspended teachers reported for work at Ocean Hill (some 83 of the 350 dismissed by McCoy the previous spring were still in the district, the rest having transferred out or left the system), they were told to report to a training session where, in McCoy's presence, they were terrorized. They were surrounded by militants, some apparently armed, shouting threats and curses. Lights were flashed on and off, and the teachers were given to understand that their lives would be in danger if they returned to the district. The UFT resumed its strike.

Lindsay tried to maintain a position at the edges of the controversy, not sure that he wanted to be a central figure but unable to dissociate himself from what was going on. He was ideologically committed to the kind of decentralization that was being attempted at Ocean Hill; his antipoverty program—and indeed, some of his own aides—had lent moral and material support to the local board; and the incident had arisen after he had finally been given the opportunity to appoint his own controlling majority to the central board. Inevitably, he found himself in the position of defending the most indefensible actions of the militant blacks. When asked at a parents' meeting in a white neighborhood whether he thought the local board had complied with the order to take back the suspended teachers, Lindsay waffled—"More or less," he replied—and was roundly booed.

The second strike dragged on until September 30. After a depressing series of orders, threats, counterthreats, and posturings by the various parties, the UFT agreed to return, on the condition that the suspended teachers would be guaranteed teaching assignments and that there would be central board observers and police on hand to assure compliance. Despite orders from the central board, the local board insisted that the teachers could not be reinstated. McCoy announced that the teachers could not go into classrooms until they had special sensitivity training. The teachers were heckled by crowds of angry parents and other militants, and there was a riot at the district junior high school. Donovan closed the school, but when he announced his intention to reopen it the following week, the UFT walked out again.

The third strike suffused the city with hatred. White parents were enraged that their children were being denied an education by the irresponsible actions of a handful of blacks in a remote Brooklyn slum. Striking teachers bullied nonstriking teachers. Black militants threatened the picket lines. Anti-semitic literature was produced by blacks and widely distributed by the UFT. Ugly marches and demonstrations were organized around City Hall and throughout the city. Lindsay assailed Shanker, and Shanker assailed Lindsay.

Through it all, the Ocean Hill schools continued to operate. McCoy's summer recruiting had provided him with a corps of non-union teachers who were willing to work during the strike. For many it was the only alternative to the draft: It was Ocean Hill or Viet Nam. Realizing that if Ocean Hill stayed open, Shanker's only leverage was to close the rest of the city's schools, and casting desperately about for solutions, Lindsay decided to close the junior high school by main force. An army of police closed the school—although the action provoked a dangerous confrontation with the black militants—but the strike went on; indeed, it seemed to be taking on a momentum of its own. Martin Mayer writes: "[It] was no longer directed against Ocean Hill. It had become nihilist, an expression of the teachers' distrust of the Board [and] the Mayor."

In the end a settlement was reached. The state and the city agreed unequivocally to enforce the law and the teachers' contract, because they had hardly any alternative. The local board was suspended and replaced by a state trustee. McCoy's principals were removed. The suspended teachers were reinstated, with classroom assignments distributed in writing before their return. McCoy could continue in office at the discretion of the state trustee, as long as he behaved cooperatively. Most important, an occupying army of police was supplied to enforce the agreement. Some weeks of turmoil followed in Ocean Hill, and two trustees were exhausted in as many weeks, but the district gradually settled down. It was a total defeat for the local board. It was also a near-total defeat for the proponents of decentralization. A final bill did pass the legislature the following spring, but it was an extremely weak one. The current thirty boards were retained, permitted to hire the local superintendent, and given some policy voice over curriculum. The demonstration districts were eliminated. The experiment was over.

THE TEACHERS' STRIKES: PERCEPTIONS OF RACE

The 1968 teachers' strikes were fundamentally racial conflicts. The sides were drawn along racial lines, and the invective that flew back and forth across the picket lines was unmistakably racial. Indeed, the strikes almost succeeded in splitting the city labor movement along racial lines. Van Arsdale and the Central Labor Council gave solid support to the strike and were shocked when Victor Gotbaum informed them that DC37, with its heavily black and Puerto Rican membership, would break with the leadership if a settlement was not reached. Matthew Guinan of the Transit Workers' Union (TWU) and Leon Davis, leader of the unions in the voluntary hospitals, lined up with Gotbaum. Bayard Rustin, although he staunchly supported the union's position in public, put heavy pressure on Van Arsdale to expedite a settlement before the split between the black and white working classes became irrevocable.

There is no question that on the technical issues of law and contract, the UFT was in the right throughout. From the point of view of the local board and its partisans, however, the dispute far transcended narrow white legalisms. To them, the issue was whether the white power structure would snuff out a spontaneous expression of blacks' aspiration to control their own destiny. A scholarly account of the local board's refusal to abide by regular transfer procedures says:

If one accepts the rules as defined by the antagonist, then the game is half over. If Ocean Hill had agreed to the rules as defined by a central staff opposed to everything Ocean Hill supposedly stood for, then what chance would the local board have had for survival? McCoy . . . mocked the rules, and thus committed the cardinal sin—[he] asked the bureaucracy to reexamine its first principles. Much as Martin Luther King had asked white society in general to search its conscience, so some people in Brooklyn asked 110 Livingston St. [the central headquarters] to study what it was doing to black children. The reaction was similar in both cases.

The problem with the vaulting rhetoric of the reformers was that it often slipped over the line, in Mayer's phrase, "from meaning well to meaning nothing at all." There was never a practical definition of what would be accomplished by community control, or by a "reconnection" of parents with the system, or how either would lead to better education. The actual mechanics of the plans could hardly be squared with the notions of participatory democracy that inspirited the discussions. For instance, the Bundy panel's thirty to sixty districts would have had average populations of 275,000 to 130,000 people— bigger than almost all the other school districts in the state. Under such circumstances, it is simply nonsense to insist, as one academic advocate of decentralization did, that: "Community control, even a limited decentralization, would have made staff accountable for their actions. Once machinery was smaller and more exposed, the anonymity behind which incompetence, stupidity, and prejudice could hide would be gone."

It was never clear how much the black community at large aligned itself with the radicals. There is some evidence that the second strike enjoyed considerable support among blacks who deplored the outrageous treatment administered to the suspended teachers by the local board's hoodlums. Shanker claims widespread spontaneous support among blacks even late into the third strike; and it is significant that the following spring it was the predominantly black and Puerto Rican paraprofessionals from Ocean Hill–Brownsville who swung a deadlocked representation election to the UFT against DC37. On the other hand, as the third strike wore on, the increasing pressure on leaders of unions with predominantly black memberships is telling evidence that the racial ranks were closing.

If the stance of the mass of blacks was uncertain, Lindsay himself was irrevocably positioned among the white sloganeers. Even late in the third strike, after he had closed the junior high school by force and had offered virtually to delegate his school-closing authority to Shanker, he was still perceived as a leading spokesman for drastic decentralization and for the most thoroughgoing community control. The view was not unfair, despite his lack of control over the major participants, for he was inextricably implicated in the unfolding of events at Ocean Hill. Lindsay saw black control in black schools as a moral issue, a categorical imperative. The pressures from his office and his aides were of critical importance in legitimizing the more radical effusions. Most important, in the summer of 1968, when the definition of the problem was still wobbling uncertainly between the radical demand for "community control" and the more conservative hope for administrative "decentralization," it was Lindsay who finally fixed the terms of the confrontation by a set of board appointments drawn overwhelmingly from the ranks of civil rights and antipoverty activists. Once the dispute was officially clothed in the rhetoric of civil rights and racial reform, there could no longer be effective boundaries around the behavior of the local board.

There have been accusations that Lindsay used the occasion to play black electoral politics; but to read political cynicism into Lindsay's actions is almost certainly wrong. A more conventional politician would have attempted to control the outcome of the Bundy panel report, or at least to stage-manage the prestrike maneuverings of Shanker and McCoy. Lindsay apparently gave no thought to spreading some demonstration districts around educationally sophisticated neighborhoods, in order to build sure success stories for the legislature, and he never seemed to worry about the dangers of splitting blacks and Jews, his two most natural political constituencies. Lewis Feldstein, the mayor's chief educational aide, recalls being at Gracie Mansion during the height of the strikes and listening to the Mayor and his wife engage in an impassioned colloquy on the need for community control. "It wasn't a matter of politics," says Feldstein, "it was whether right could finally prevail."

Lindsay had just reached the pinnacle of his political career by taking precisely that kind of principled stand on matters of race and labor. Certainly, his success in cooling the ghettos conditioned his calm reaction to the excesses of the local board militants, for the essence of his ghetto policy was resilience and restraint. But except for a few unfortunate merchants, ghetto disturbances had relatively little effect on the larger society. Tolerance of militant behavior in Ocean Hill, on the other hand, meant that all the city's children were denied an education. The situation called for clearheaded balancing of the interests of the entire city, not controversialist posturing.

In the final analysis the strikes were not about race so much as they were about perceptions of race. The view of race that Lindsay had made the keynote of his administration was put to an empirical test and was found to relate only distantly to reality. That view, oversimplified and somewhat caricatured, held that blacks were an oppressed people in New York City; that they could assume a rightful place in American society only when they had gained power and control over their own destinies; that the transition to black independence would be traumatic and possibly revolutionary; that the key task of a public official was to facilitate the transition as nonviolently as possible in the interest of white and black society alike; and that in the process inexplicable, outrageous, or even criminal behavior by blacks could be ignored for the sake of the larger goals. As argued in Chapter III, it was a view that was not entirely devoid of truth, nor without substantial support in the intellectual and religious communities, but it was fatally flawed. It perpetuated the mind-fogging confusion of problems of race and discrimination with problems of class. By allowing radicals to speak for the mass of blacks, it ignored the rapid assimilation of blacks that was taking place in the city and disenfranchised the respectable black community. It overweighted the problems of minority progress against the majority's right to aspirations of its own. It proposed a double standard of appraisal and performance, which can never be the basis for an equitable society. Worst of all, it was dangerously polarizing. The mindset of Lindsay's city planning staff, who blamed the problems of the city's blacks on "the callous disinterest of the white middle-class," betrayed a kind of simplistic self-righteousness that was inadequate as a premise for government.

When reality was finally tested, Albert Shanker, the veteran union leader, won the testing hands down. Shanker summed up the differences in world views: "The Mayor simply ignored middle-class blacks. He seemed to think all blacks were violent and would rise up if they weren't placated. He was wrong. The radicals didn't have that much support, and when it came to the crunch, we were the ones who were tough."

MANAGEMENT COLLAPSE

With his aura of success broken by the teachers' strikes, attacks on Lindsay developed across a broad front. Persistent questioning of his ability to achieve genuine management reform had begun as early as 1967, despite the rhetoric about high-technology business methods. Now, as the administration's hopes for racial reconciliation lay in ruins, the doubts about its managerial accomplishments turned into a flood of criticism and complaints.

A newspaper series in January 1969 laid bare the almost total chaos that existed in the Human Resources Administration. In the haste to set up summer programs and to cool the ghetto, there had been little attention to the most rudimentary aspects of recordkeeping, financial controls, or operating procedures. Preference was shown to black applicants for sensitive jobs, almost regardless of qualification, and administrators in key positions were desperately over their heads. The administrator of the multimillion-dollar Neighborhood Youth Corps program was twenty-nine years old, a charismatic divinity student with strong civil rights credentials who had never previously held an administrative job. A young black whose only previous experience was as a low-level accountant was proposed as the controller of the city's sprawling manpower agency until the federal government forced the appointment to be withdrawn. No-show jobs and patronage were rife. Program funds were hopelessly commingled; procedures to pay monies through the city comptroller were regularly circumvented; and millions of dollars were held in private checking accounts to pay for wages, overtime, and expenses without making the required deductions and with no offsetting entries on the city's books. Accounts were unbalanced for months at a time, and payments were made to work-program recipients without any effort to determine if they were actually on the job. In one spot-check, only six out of twenty-nine youth job enrollees assigned to a work site could be found, while the site supervisors (usually city employees with other duties) neither knew nor cared where the others were, nor would they have known what to do with them had they turned up. The superagency structure of which Lindsay was so proud only made matters worse. Decision-making lines were hopelessly confused, and the overhead layer, instead of integrating and streamlining, tended only to overlap and duplicate. The internal procedures were tortuous: An agency planner needed his commissioner's approval in order to communicate with the HRA planning section, which had to cycle its own reply back through the agency commissioner again. One investigator concluded, "It's so bad it will take ten years to find out what's really going on inside."

If some of the new staff were unqualified as administrators, they turned out to be ingenious thieves. A million dollars in HRA checks turned up in a numbered Swiss bank account. A man attempted to use a $52,000 HRA check to buy a house in Los Angeles. Four enterprising young men from Durham, North Carolina—the "Durham mob"—quietly looted almost $1.75 million from the summer work projects by programming a computer to produce checks for phantom enrollees. The scheme was uncovered only when a patrolman noticed a case of HRA checks in the back of an illegally parked car. The staff assigned to develop fiscal controls for the troubled summer work programs pillaged tens of thousands of dollars for themselves. A man indicted for embezzlement from one community corporation was promptly hired in a sensitive position by another. Middle-level staff cynically assumed everybody was stealing.

To federal officials the agency was hopeless. An audit by the OEO declared that the city manpower programs were a "monstrosity." Another official declared flatly that almost all the present HRA staff "were unqualified." The OEO began to reroute its funding directly to delegate agencies when it had the opportunity. Stanley Ruttenberg, the federal manpower administrator, proposed that the city programs be placed under a trustee as early as May 1968 but was quietly dissuaded by the mayor and Ginsberg, who feared it would be "the last blow" for the troubled agency. Afraid of provoking a crisis for liberals in a federal election year, Ruttenberg agreed on a "six-month last chance"—in effect, postponing a decision until his own term of office had expired.

The public was still digesting the HRA scandals when the city was buried under a freak nineteen-inch snowfall that caught the sanitation department monumentally unprepared. The commissioner was in the country for the weekend and could not be reached to order an overtime response, and no one else in the long chain of command through the superagency to City Hall thought he had the authority; so a full day was lost, allowing the snow to pack and freeze. When a snow emergency response was finally ordered, it was discovered that 40 percent of the city's snow removal equipment was in such a state of disrepair as to be unusable, while the private contractor the city usually relied on to do extra plowing had been blacklisted for bidding irregularities—but no one had bothered to arrange for an alternative emergency backup. Continued subfreezing weather made removal of the packed snow even more difficult and added to the rate of vehicle breakdown. The anger in the outlying residential areas mounted as the streets went unplowed, day after day. Lindsay was greeted with jeers and catcalls when he tried to tour the most seriously affected areas. Queens Councilman Matthew Troy called upon Rockefeller to "suspend Lindsay and bring in the National Guard to run the snow removal equipment." A comparison with the city's response in 1961, when a fifteen-inch storm hit, showed up the Lindsay administration badly. Wagner and Screvane had twice as many men and twice as much equipment on the streets almost immediately and cleared the snow in less than half the time. DeLury charged Lindsay with "the systematic destruction" of the sanitation department. According to DeLury, budget cuts, the shifting of lines to the superagency and lack of attention to equipment requirements had left the city "drowning in garbage," but, he declared, the problem was ignored until the snow hit.

There were other adverse comparisons that could be drawn with the Wagner administration. The city's housing program, for instance, had come to a virtual standstill. Lindsay had tried to shift strategy from large multiple-dwelling units to small scattered-site developments that would improve the city's patterns of racial integration. His planners produced a bold master design that utilized vacant sites located in stable middle-class neighborhoods already supplied with schools and other community amenities. In the heady atmosphere of the new administration, the planners naively reasoned that the entire plan could be put through the Board of Estimate in a single session, in order to minimize controversies over individual sites. (Borough presidents must approve site selections.) Instead, the board insisted on site-by-site review and slowly picked the plan to death.

The threat of placing low-income families in middle-class neighborhoods touched off heated protests; including objections from middle-class blacks. In the Forest Hills section of Queens the protests eventually degenerated into a particularly nasty racial confrontation on the pattern that was becoming depressingly routine—opposing white and black picket lines, curses and racial slurs, injured policemen and demonstrators. The sites almost all turned out to be unsuitable, anyway. They had been left vacant for good reason. Furthermore, the planned small developments could not be built economically. The confrontation in Forest Hills in fact began when the city tried to expand a project to bring down unit costs after a liberal Jewish community had agreed to accept a much smaller program.

All of the housing statistics were down. In his third term Wagner had produced 6,034 public housing units per year, while Lindsay in his first term could manage only 3,137. The total of 1,439 units produced in 1968 was the lowest output since the inception of the program. Mitchell-Lama statistics told the same story: Wagner's production had averaged 11,393 units during his third term, more than double Lindsay's first-term annual output of 5,528. The failure of state housing bond issues in 1964 and 1965 partially explained the decline, but under the federal program alone, the city was eligible for 7,500 units per year, if it could only take advantage of the money. The same was true in urban renewal: A large portion of the federal assistance earmarked for the city was returned each year to the national treasury because the city was unable to spend it. Rockefeller took no little pleasure in justifying his proposed state Urban Development Corporation by the city's patent incapacity to deliver. And as the city construction capability deteriorated, the private sector commenced a headlong abandonment: Between 1965 and 1968, 100,000 dwelling units, mostly in slum neighborhoods, were abandoned by their owners and stood hollow-eyed and charred, shelters to winos and junkies, and victims of the vandals and arsonists that picked among the city's skeleton.

Agency after agency told the same dismal story of management failure. The new Medicaid program was at least six months behind in paying its bills, and medical providers had begun to sell their claims to factors or simply to drop out of the program. The constant dollar volume of capital construction was still dropping, while Lindsay's insistence on community participation in design was lengthening the design cycle and increasing costs. Parks maintenance seemed to have slipped even from the depressingly low state it had reached in Wagner's last years. City Council President Frank O'Connor attacked Lindsay's claim that the superagencies were saving money. There were twenty-nine thousand more employees than there had been in 1966, and salaries were higher than ever.

Along with the superagencies, Lindsay had been proudest of the caliber of men he had attracted to city government; yet his new appointees had deserted him en masse: Sviridoff of the HRA, Howard Brown of Health Services, Samuel Kearing from Sanitation, Charles Moerdler from Buildings, George Nicolau from the Community Development Agency, and Deputy Mayor Robert Price. Press Secretary Woody Klein resigned and wrote a book subtitled *The Dream that Failed*. Kearing charged that "nothing works better than two years ago."

The City Club held a conference on whether the city was ungovernable. The city wasn't ungovernable, sneered Wagner. Some people just had more trouble governing it than others.

It is of course unfair to pin all the blame on Lindsay; as Martin Lang says, "He didn't invent the disease." The breakdown in the sanitation department, for example, had been a long time in coming. About 1960, according to Julius Edelstein, Wagner's top adviser during his third term, "DeLury decided that part of his job was protecting his men from doing any work." From that point the department steadily deteriorated. Medical certificates for disability were routinely bought and sold. Part of the scandalous level of equipment downtime was reportedly caused by men vandalizing their own trucks to avoid going out on the street. Bribes were extorted from residents in return for normal service. Lang reports that he visited supervisors in the hospital who had been "brutally beaten" for trying to make their men work. Both Lang and Herbert Elish, another subsequent sanitation commissioner, agree that the Hayes budget cuts so bitterly assailed by DeLury were about right under any reasonable sort of performance standard.

But tracing the roots of a problem was not a sufficient response, even if the explanations were accurate. It was precisely the inherited problems from the Wagner administration that Lindsay had promised to do something about. Four years into the administration, explaining the lag in housing construction by "Wagner's empty pipeline" was becoming repetitive and unconvincing. And Wagner could hardly be blamed for the fiasco in HRA, the exodus of top staff, the crisis of morale in the superagencies, the spiralling welfare rolls, the snarled Medicaid payments, the lag in construction starts. Lindsay had promised substantial and rapid progress in solving the city's management problems and had hired top urban experts from around the country to help him. As Lindsay's first term wound down, the harsh, but just, public judgment was that he had not delivered.

POLICE PARITY: A LABOR RELATIONS DEBACLE

At about the same time that Lindsay's management failures were being trumpeted in the newspaper headlines, the new labor relations machinery championed by the liberal community was being used by the uniformed forces to inflict a resounding defeat on the city bargainers, although the full cost of the debacle—at least $200 million—did not become apparent until 1971.

The city's uniformed forces jealously guarded their status relationships with each other. Police and firemen traditionally had the same pay and pensions and—as far as possible, given the different shift schedules—the same benefits structures. Occasional attempts by one or the other to break the parity arrangement were always bitterly resisted by the other service. In turn, the police and firemen were solidly united against the sanitationmen. Under DeLury's shrewd political guidance, New York's sanitationmen were the highest paid in the country, and they had steadily closed the gap with the other services. By January of 1968 sanitationmen received a base pay equal to 86 percent of the base pay for patrolmen and firemen, had the same pension, and, unlike police and firemen, enjoyed an annuity program, shift differentials, and holiday pay. Depending on how his schedule broke, a sanitationman might well take home a greater package of wages and benefits than the policeman or fireman.

The final element in the complicated equation was the supervisors, particularly the police and fire officers. From 1939 to 1953 police and fire department pay increases were awarded in flat dollar amounts, with the same increase to all ranks. As a result, differentials between supervisors and the front ranks were steadily eroded. A second continuing grievance was the higher rate of pay for first-line supervisors in the fire department—the lieutenants—compared to that for police sergeants, the equivalent police rank. The successful efforts of the supervisors to restore the 1939 differentials and of the police sergeants to win parity with the fire lieutenants were at the root of the parity dispute that cost the city so dearly in 1971.

The police sergeants and fire lieutenants won the restoration of the 1939 differentials in separate arbitrations in 1963. The differentials were fixed by the 1939 base pay rates—$3,000 per year for a patrolman and fireman, $3,500 for a police sergeant, and $3,900 for a fire lieutenant. The arbitration granted, in effect, a pay increase for the sergeants and lieutenants that brought their base pay to ratios of 3.5:3 and 3.9:3, respectively, with the men they supervised. Commensurate increases were awarded up through the command structures of the two departments.

With the differentials restored, Harold Melnick, the canny president of the Sergeant's Benevolent Association, began a quiet but all-out campaign to gain pay parity with the fire lieutenants. It was a classic demonstration of how a dedicated and resourceful union leader could outgun the city bargainers. "I approached it like a war," says Melnick. "I decided it was the most important issue we had, so I committed myself to work fulltime on it and spend whatever was necessary to win."

Melnick began by retaining Frederick Livingston of New York City, one of the top—and most expensive—labor lawyers in the country. With Livingston's help, two years were devoted to preparing a case: A detailed content analysis of the two jobs was carried out, both in New York City and around the country; a compendium of comparative pay practices was developed for jurisdictions throughout the world; the hazard rates for the two jobs were finely calculated. Wagner agreed to arbitrate the issue in 1964, says Melnick, then reneged on the agreement. Haber, new on his job, agreed to submit the issue to fact-finding after settling the 1966 contract.

A three-man fact-finding board chaired by David Cole, a nationally-known arbitrator, was empanelled in late 1966 to hear the case. Melnick had researched each person on the list of fact-finders submitted by the city to veto any "fire buffs." "We killed them in the fact-finding," says Melnick.

We had thirteen lawyers working on the case and four filing cabinets of data, all filed and cross-indexed so it was at our fingertips. The fire officers joined to oppose us and had one lawyer with two manila envelopes, while the city had a kid from the corporation counsel's office with some pieces of yellow paper. They just had no idea we were coming in like that, and were totally unprepared for us. It went so well that on the last day we had Patrick Murphy [a nationally-known police expert and later New York City commissioner] waiting downstairs to testify and didn't even use him. There was nothing left to prove.

The panel reported in early 1967 and found for the sergeants. Because of the city's fiscal problems, however, they recommended that the sergeants receive an increase bringing their pay ratio to patrolmen to 3.7:3, with the rest of the differential to be provided later. Haber thought it was a "bad fact-finding" but felt he had no choice but to accept it. The administration was in the midst of passing its new labor relations program through the legislature and the City Council; a fundamental premise of the program was that in return for a union pledge not to strike, the city would consider itself morally bound by the results of fact-finding and arbitration.

A year and a half later, on September 30, 1968, the contracts for police, firemen, and sanitation workers all expired at the same time. The city saw it as a golden opportunity to fix parities once and for all between the services and avoid the whipsawing that had been so costly the previous two years. The rank and file—particularly the firemen—were in a surly mood. The firemen's union president, Michael Maye, had began talking strike in August and ordered his men to bring home their personal equipment in late September in preparation for a work slowdown. The slowdown was called off when the city and the three unions agreed on a mediating panel chaired by Arthur Goldberg, the former secretary of labor and Supreme Court justice. To everyone's relief, an agreement was reached quickly. DeLury had no interest in another strike after the debacle of the previous February and sat still for a readjustment in the parities. He still had richer fringe benefits than the other two unions but accepted a smaller pay increment, so the ratio of sanitation to police and fire base pay was reduced to 82 percent. DeLury still got a hefty 7.4 percent immediate jump in pay for his men, but the policemen and the firemen got 13 percent. It was an expensive settlement, but if it would provide the basis for orderly future labor relations with the uniformed forces, it seemed worth it.

The sanitationmen accepted the settlement, as did the executive boards of the police and fire unions, but then the rank-and-file police and firemen rejected it.* Both services commenced work slowdowns in late October—right in the middle of the bitterest stages of the teachers' strikes. The city went ritualistically to court to obtain an antistrike injunction and was delighted to find the police union take the high road. Cassesse announced that police had to obey the law and called off his work action for as long as talks proceeded in good faith; under pressure of public opinion, the firemen followed suit.

When the bargaining reopened, it gradually emerged that the real bone in

---

* Haber believes that the sanitationmen, deciding that they may have settled too easily, sabotaged the agreement. Leaflets, apparently from the sanitation union, were circulated among police and firemen on the eve of the contract vote, overstating the sanitation settlement and swinging police and fire department sentiment against the contract. Haber's theory may be true or merely paranoid, but the fact that it could be seriously entertained supplies an insight into the byzantine character of city labor relations.

the throat of the PBA was the new pay ratio for sergeants. In the complicated checks-and-balances world of the uniformed service parities, a gain by one party was a loss for the others. The patrolmen wanted the old 3.5:3 ratio with the sergeants restored. As Haber tells it, Goldberg increasingly focused the mediation on the sergeants' ratio, although they were not a party to the discussions. Finally, in January 1969, with Lindsay facing an election, the patrolmen and the firemen getting increasingly restive, and Goldberg strongly recommending a settlement, Lindsay told Haber to give the patrolmen back their old parities—which he did by an initialled memorandum stating that it was the city's "intent" to restore the old 3.5:3 ratio. The memorandum was not published as part of the contract, but the police settled immediately, and the firemen, now isolated, quickly followed suit.

The memorandum of intent did not necessarily contradict the contract with the sergeants that stated the 3.7:3 ratio—the only contract that actually stated a specific ratio. Haber argues that the sergeants' fact-finding obliged him only to treat fire lieutenants and police sergeants as equals, not to pay them at a specific ratio to their men.* The memorandum of intent, together with the sergeants' fact-finding, would have obligated him to bring patrolmen, and presumably firemen as well, up to a 3.5:3 ratio with their first-line supervisors at the *next* contract. The losers in the parity game, then, would be the sergeants and lieutenants; but they were represented by small and responsible unions, and he thought he could force them to sit still for the adjustments.

The plot thickened when Melnick, who had heard only rumors that his ratio was in jeopardy, decided to press for another fact-finding on the full 3.9:3 ratio. Haber and Melnick agreed on a panel chaired by Theodore Kheel. "I was delighted with Kheel," says Melnick. "He worships Cole and would never overturn a Cole finding." Kheel found for the sergeants again in November 1969, and the city agreed to pay the full differential. Again, on Haber's theory of his agreement with the PBA, there was still no contradiction. The fact-finding merely reinforced the obligation to pay the sergeants and lieutenants equally.

Haber's theory came apart in January 1970. There was a change of leadership in the PBA, and the union decided to resurrect the memorandum of intent, contending that it required the city to pay the patrolmen at a 3.5:3 ratio with sergeants immediately. Haber and Lindsay insisted that the "intent" applied only to the next round of negotiations, that they had an oral agreement with the old PBA leadership to make the ratio readjustments only as part of a comprehensive renegotiation of the parity issues. The union and the city agreed to contest the issue in court. The PBA won a summary judgment, which was upheld in the appellate division but overturned by the court of appeals, who remanded the case for a finding on the existence of the claimed oral agree-

---

* He is probably right. The fact-finding recommended the 3.7:3 ratio, but the course of its opinion makes clear that it is the equivalence of the jobs, not the precise differential, that is at issue. The higher rate of pay for the lieutenants was apparently a hangover from 1937, when fire lieutenants worked longer hours than police sergeants. The panel explicitly noted that, in the absence of special treatment for the lieutenants, the sergeants' 3.5:3 ratio would have been perfectly adequate.

ment. The city lost again before a jury in early 1971. When the city announced that it would appeal again, 85 percent of the patrolmen walked out on a six-day wildcat strike. Miraculously, the city held together with strong street presence by police supervisors and unusually cold weather; the crime rate even dropped slightly. The men came back when Lindsay, Haber, and the union agreed to work out a settlement.

The PBA interpretation of the agreement put the city in a literally impossible position. If police were raised to the 3.5:3 ratio, firemen would demand the same increase, and would almost certainly strike to get it. But the sergeants had a contractual right to the 3.9:3 ratio. If the patrolmen got a raise, the sergeants said they would insist on their rights—which would then entitle the patrolmen to another round, and so on *ad infinitum*. The final settlement was that everyone would take a round, with the sergeants ending up back at their 3.9:3 ratio. The lump-sum back payment to the police alone totaled $83 million, and the entire cost ran into the hundreds of millions when the higher base pay was projected forward onto pensions and future settlements. The rancor surrounding the negotiations meant that the city did not even earn any good will with the windfall payments—about $3,000 per man—and the unions entered the next round of negotiations hard upon the parity settlement, as though the payments had never existed.*

DEFEAT AND RE-ELECTION

In June 1969 Lindsay was defeated by State Senator John Marchi of Staten Island in the Republican primary for mayor. It was his first defeat ever and made his chances for re-election appear bleak indeed. The decision was quickly made to run as an independent to supplement the Liberal line (delivered by Alex Rose in April), but actually to win the election in overwhelmingly Democratic New York City would require a total reversal of fortune. The "arithmetic," as the pros said, just wouldn't work; an enormous crossover of Democratic voters would be necessary for Lindsay to pull off the upset.

The Democrats, divided as always, did their best to help. There was a sharply contested primary with three major candidates: Herman Badillo, representing the more liberal wing of the party; Robert Wagner, seemingly seeking a

---

* For what it is worth, it is the author's view that Haber's interpretation of the episode and the memorandum of intent is the correct one. The memorandum of intent represented an expensive election-year agreement (the sergeants and the lieutenants would have undoubtedly exacted compensation for the reduction in their ratios, so the next settlement with the rank-and-file would need to be high in order to restore the 3.5:3); but it was not the utterly reckless undertaking, literally impossible of performance, that the lower courts and some writers—for example, Raymond Horton—have interpreted it to be. The memorandum of intent was never made part of the PBA contract in a physical sense, and the contract section setting out the wage schedules stipulated that there could be no further wage increases until 1971. If the memorandum of intent had been intended to take immediate effect, there is no satisfactory explanation for why it was not pressed by the old leadership. Once again, however, the city was outgunned in the legal arena—this time it was an assistant corporation counsel against Louis Nizer—and Lindsay was not willing to sustain another strike by the police. Rape was made painless, in the short run, by the provision in the local finance law that allowed the city to sell long-term bonds to finance the settlement.

vindication of his record after the years of attacks by Lindsay; and the rotund, blustering, city comptroller, Mario Procaccino, cut in the classical mold of the Brooklyn clubhouse pol. Wagner bitterly assailed Badillo's perseverance in the campaign, charging that he would split the liberal vote and provide an opening for Procaccino. In fact, the liberal vote did split, and Procaccino won relatively handily. Lindsay's hopes rose.

The first prerequisite was to move away from confrontation with the politically powerful unions. The AFSCME was awarded agency-shop privileges early in the year. A generous contract settlement was quickly reached with the UFT, and a conservative decentralization bill was passed in the legislature, with Lindsay playing a distinctly muted role in the debate. The settlement was reached with the UFA and the PBA that embodied the parity memorandum of intent. One by one, the union leaders announced their support of Lindsay. Victor Gotbaum was the first. Then came John DeLury, convinced that "the Mayor now really understands sanitation problems." Matthew Guinan, successor to the late Mike Quill at the TWU, proclaimed the new warmth between Lindsay and the transit workers. Even Albert Shanker was willing to let bygones be bygones.

Nineteen-sixty-nine was to be the "Year of Delivery," according to the mayor, and delivery this time meant for the ordinary citizen. The police department was strengthened and particularly targeted toward still stable but threatened neighborhoods. Hayes's sanitation cuts were restored and a drive commenced to improve the cleanliness of the city streets. After two years of concerted work, the city finally broke its capital construction bottleneck. With a new computerized management information system in place in the budget bureau that could track every step through the approval maze for every project, Lindsay announced that the city would effectively double its rate of capital construction, from some 250 new starts in the previous year to almost 500. There was something for everyone—massive new water treatment plants, a new police headquarters, five new high schools, thousands of new elementary and preschool seats, crash renovations in the hospitals, safety surfacing in the parks, and new fire stations and libraries scattered throughout Queens and Brooklyn. The system delivered almost exactly on target. It was a classic demonstration of the power of the new management techniques to cut through red tape. Skeptical reporters visited sites to assure themselves that contractors were actually at work.

Then, during the summer, the rate of growth in welfare rolls began suddenly to fall off, easing cash pressures on the city. Critics pointed to a suddenly declining acceptance rate and charged political manipulation. Ginsberg insisted—and still insists—that there was none.

Procaccino was proving an ideal opponent. Despite a few telling sallies at Lindsay's "limousine liberals," his campaign was bumbling and uncoordinated. Inadequately informed on the details of city administration, despite his tenure as comptroller, and easily confused on his feet, he began more and more to appear as the one-issue candidate, the candidate of the white backlash. Herman Badillo was among the first of a train of liberal democrats who announced that,

all things considered, they would have to vote for Lindsay. Even Robert
Wagner refused to disclose which lever he would pull.

Lindsay ran a masterful campaign. Privately, his pollsters built computerized profiles of every voting precinct, looking for the strategy with the precise appeal. Publicly, the candidate was humble, acknowledged his mistakes,
admitted that he might not have fully understood "the pressures on working
whites from the newly aggressive minorities." His bumper stickers and posters
bore the simple logo "Mayor Lindsay," emphasizing his experience and maturity. By contrast, Procaccino seemed faintly comical, hardly a mayor.

When the New York Mets, for ten years the doormats of the National
League, won the World Series, a miasma seemed to lift from the city. Anything
was possible, even civil harmony. By October Lindsay was twenty-one points
ahead in one major poll, fifteen points in another.

As it turned out, it was closer than expected. Lindsay's winning plurality of
42 percent was smaller than it was when he won in 1965 and confirmed his
status as a minority mayor. Post-election analyses showed a disquieting corre-
spondence between districts that voted for Lindsay in 1969 and those that
voted for the Civilian Review Board in 1966. In general, Lindsay won with
votes of minorities and upper-class Jews; the remaining white voters split between Procaccino and Marchi. He had still a considerable distance to go before
he could be mayor of most of New York City.

Lindsay had no illusions about his victory. The events of the previous year
had profoundly changed his concept of the mayoralty: The difficult problems
had proved more intractable than he had ever suspected, the brilliant solutions
less practicable than he had supposed. Although Lindsay never renounced his
liberal beliefs, there was a distinct paring down of objectives in the second administration. The great days of the experiment were over.

VI. *Finance*

JOHN LINDSAY took office promising both financial rectitude and government responsiveness. In his first years in office, with the help of substantial revenue increases, he made significant progress toward restoring the city's financial integrity; but by the beginning of his second term, rapid increases in spending had swallowed up all the new revenues from tax increases and external aid. Responsiveness and rectitude looked more and more like conflicting objectives. Throughout the second term the annual budget battles with the legislature and the relentless search for new revenues and budget-balancing devices dominated the day-to-day workings of the administration.

BACKGROUND: THE CITY BUDGET

The New York City budget is unique. In the first place, it is enormous, by far the biggest municipal budget in the country. It is also one of the only comprehensive local budgets. In Chicago and Philadelphia, for example, and in most other municipalities, the local board of education is a legal entity with independent budgeting and taxing powers entirely separate from the city government. New York City is one of only a few municipalities to operate the local welfare system; no other bears so heavy a share of the costs. Furthermore, New York's long public service tradition has involved the city in undertakings of a breadth and scale found in no other city in the world—the City University, the municipal hospitals, the massive network of water treatment plants, the libraries, the vast transit system. Even the sanitation service is scheduled at a pickup frequency rarely found elsewhere.

The budget is an administration's annual spending plan, the final crystallizing of the countless policy decisions and program tradeoffs among competing interests and constituencies, the most concrete specification of what an administration actually plans to do. A mayor may promise enriched education programs, better police protection, or improved sanitation services, but if the money for the improvements does not finally appear in his budget, the interest groups know that he was just talking.

The budget is really two budgets: an *expense* budget for the day-to-day operations of the city, financed from current revenues, and a *capital* budget, which is the capital improvements spending plan for new city facilities or major equipment purchases and is financed from borrowings. The city's fiscal year runs from July 1 to June 30. Budget preparation usually begins early in the fall preceding the start of the new fiscal year—that is, at least eight months before the start of the fiscal year being planned for and a full twenty months before its end. Creating the budget is an executive function resting primarily with the mayor's Office of Management and Budget (formerly called the Bureau of the Budget). The budget must be approved by the City Council and Board of Estimate* before it is officially adopted.

The expense budget is adopted in the form of units of appropriation, which are large lump-sum spending items, most often corresponding to an entire city agency. Appropriation requests, however, are supported by exquisitely detailed line-item schedules, which are central to the overhead controls that still plague city executives. The budget bureau was originally an agency of the Board of Estimate, or, effectively, of the comptroller, and the day-to-day mechanics of running the city were reduced to a bargaining process between the mayor and board over changes in the budget schedules. La Guardia's 1938 charter reform transferred the budget bureau to the mayor's office, but changes in the schedules still had to be approved by the board. The 1963 charter reform, in the hope of reducing overhead paperwork, introduced the units of appropriation and eliminated the board's authority over schedule changes. But the budget bureau, in a quiet bureaucratic coup, seized upon the charter requirement for maintaining information copies of the line schedules as justification for clinging to the old system of line item controls, so there was no practical difference in the overhead processing requirements. The 1975 charter reforms eased the overhead administrative requirements even further, but the old habits of detailed controls persist, now reinforced by the fiscal crisis.

The snapshots on the next page of city budgets at three different intervals illustrate the major spending claims on the city's resources. Rather more than half of the expense budget is accounted for by labor costs. An analysis of the trends in city spending appears later in this and subsequent chapters.

FINANCING THE BUDGET

The Expense Budget

The financing for the expense budget is built up through a series of steps. First, there is a calculation of all revenues from intergovernmental aid, fees, rentals and from the variety of local taxes that the city is authorized to impose.

---

* The City Council is the city legislature. The Board of Estimate comprises the mayor, the comptroller, the City Council president, and the five borough presidents. Besides its budgetary responsibilities, it exercises important powers over land transactions and public contracts. The three citywide officers have two votes each, while each borough president has one, so the three

	FY 1960–61 $ (millions)[2]	1965–66 $ (millions)	1965–66 % CHANGE	1970–71 $ (millions)	1970–71 % CHANGE
Education	587.5	893.2	52.0	1,839.0	105.9
Welfare and social services[1]	350.5	718.4	105.0	2,309.9	221.5
Higher Education	53.2	92.8	74.4	332.7	258.5
Health and hospitals	229.9	372.9	62.2	679.5	82.2
Police	236.1	308.9	30.8	602.1	94.9
Fire	122.0	160.7	31.7	267.0	66.1
Environmental protection	131.5	186.8	42.1	321.7	72.2
Total expense budget	2,365.2	3,595.7	52.0	7,808.9	117.2
Capital expenditures	315.8	465.8	47.5	1,107.4	137.7

1. 1970 includes Medicaid program.   2. Including funds from all sources.

All of these revenues are credited to an account called the general fund. Estimated general fund revenues are then compared to projected operating expenditures, and the difference must be charged to the real estate tax. Then the city's debt service is computed, and the amount not reimbursable from outside funding sources is also chargeable to the real estate tax. The sum of the two real estate tax computations fixes the real estate tax levy and determines the tax rate against the assessed values of taxable property in the city.

The state local finance law establishes a ceiling on the amount of money that can be raised through real estate taxes, and thus indirectly on the total amount of the budget. The real estate tax levy for operating purposes may not exceed 2.5 percent of a five-year average of the market value of taxable real property in the city. Taxes to pay debt service on funded (i.e. long-term) debt are not subject to the ceiling. The total tax rate on market value in 1969–70, for instance, was $3.39 per $100, of which about $2.50 was allocated for operating purposes and $0.89 for debt service. The published tax rate, however, is based on *assessed* value, which is always lower than market value. The 1970 effective tax rate of $3.39 on market value translated into $5.52 per $100 of assessed value. While the city assessors determine assessed values, the state Board of Equalization determines market values from an ongoing sample of real estate transactions.

Historically, by far the greatest part of the city's revenues was derived from the real estate tax. But particularly in the 1960s and 1970s, the sharp increases in state and federal aid and the city's increasing reliance on a broader range of taxes and fees—personal and business income taxes, sales taxes, the stock transfer tax, and some twenty-odd others—gradually reduced the importance of the real estate tax levy in the overall city financial picture. For example, from 1960–61 to 1970–71 real estate taxes declined from about 42 percent of city revenues to only about 28 percent and in the latter year real estate tax revenue was exceeded by state aid receipts.

---

citywide officers can outvote the other five. Since 1975 the mayor has been barred from voting on his own budget. In practice, the center of power in the board has rested with the comptroller, who is institutionally positioned to oppose the mayor consistently and in detail on spending matters.

Because it is impossible to foresee all eventualities, the local finance law and the City Charter provide means for financing deficits. If a deficit is caused by insufficient appropriations to deal with a public emergency, the city can float loans—sell "budget notes"—generally not to exceed 1 percent of the year's real estate levy. The notes can be issued for a maximum of one year, are not renewable, and are a first-priority claim on the following year's budget. If the problem is a revenue shortfall, the city can draw from its own tax appropriation and general fund stabilization reserve fund, the "rainy day fund." In theory, the city is supposed to maintain the rainy day fund at a level equivalent to 30 percent of the year's real estate tax levy and appropriate up to 2 percent of each year's real estate tax levy for that purpose. If revenue shortfalls are met by drawing on the fund, the withdrawals have to be repaid over a six-year period. In practice, the city has never maintained the rainy day fund at the required level, rarely made the required appropriations, and even more rarely paid back borrowings. Although the two financing methods were designed to meet different contingencies, they are in fact interchangeable, because the city can always adjust its revenue and appropriation estimates to convert a revenue shortfall into an appropriation problem, and vice-versa.

Finally, the city can finance cash flow problems in the administration of the expense budget through a variety of short-term borrowing instruments, the most important of which are tax anticipation notes (TANs) and revenue anticipation notes (RANs). Revenue and tax anticipation borrowing became increasingly important in the 1970s and were the major factor in the city's final financing crisis. It was a loosening of the local finance law's constraints on the issuance of RANs in 1965 that opened the door to creative RAN financing. Prior to 1965 RANs could be issued only against revenue receipts due to be received in the current year, and total receipts estimated for borrowing purposes could not exceed the previous year's actual receipts. The new rules lifted the previous-year ceiling and permitted RANs to be issued against federal and state revenues that were *earned* in the last quarter of a fiscal year but were not scheduled to be received until the next fiscal year. Because RANs did not have to be identified to any specific source of income, the new rules operated as practically no constraint at all. The rules were tightened again after the fiscal crisis.

The Capital Budget

The capital budget, unlike the expense budget, represents less a specific spending plan than a set of borrowing authorizations for individual capital projects. Because of the normally slow pace of city construction and because projects often appear in the capital budget before they have been carefully thought through, there is typically a sizable gap between authorizations in the budget and actual expenditures on construction or purchasing. The gulf between authorizations and obligations makes it difficult for the city to maintain discipline over the budgeting process—after all, it appears to cost nothing to put a project in the budget—and new authorization capacity can almost always be created merely by rescinding old projects that have withered on the vine.

The capital budget is financed by issuing long-term, or funded, debt. Traditionally, city debt was funded by the creation of sinking funds, with the city undertaking to pay into the funds a sufficient annual payment to pay interest and to build up the sum necessary to retire the principal when the bonds matured. More recently, the preferred funding method is through the issuance of serial bonds, which provide for the retirement of principal in more or less equal annual amounts through the life of the instruments. The requirement for annual discharge of principal is less vulnerable to manipulation than the calculation of sinking fund reserves required against a distant bond redemption date.

The local finance law limits outstanding debt to finance capital projects to 10 percent of the five-year average of the market value of taxable real estate. A second category of debt to finance housing through the city Mitchell–Lama program cannot exceed 2 percent of the five-year average of *assessed* values. The difference between debt outstanding and the total debt permissible under the two ceilings is the "unencumbered debt margin" and is the amount available for authorization in the budget. Although the city has only rarely been constrained by its debt limit, the legislature has frequently exempted large projects from the debt limit in order to encourage their construction. Water pollution and sewage projects are the most outstanding recent examples.

The types of construction or purchases that qualify as capital projects are set out in great detail in the local finance law, and each allowable project is assigned a "period of probable usefulness" that limits the permissible funding period for the project. At least until the 1960s, allowable funding times tended to be on the conservative, or short, side and reinforced a general bias in the city toward a foreshortened debt structure. The financing of the IND subway, as an egregious example, was originally planned with four-year bonds, although economic conditions eventually forced a lengthening of the maturities.

In order to meet the cash flow requirements of an ongoing capital program, the city can issue bond anticipation notes (BANs) redeemable from the receipts of bonds issued when a project is actually funded. Similarly, urban renewal notes (URNs) can be issued against future drawdowns of urban renewal authorizations to finance site acquisition, clearance, and development.

The table on the next page is a rundown of the financing components of the city budget at three different intervals. More detailed analyses of trends in budget finance appear in this and subsequent chapters.

BUDGET GIMMICKS

Although state law requires the budget to be in balance when adopted, political pressures invariably tend to push revenue estimates upward and spending estimates down. Underestimating spending requirements and overstating revenues means that the administration can defer tax increases and still have money—at least in the sense of appropriation authority—left over for popular programs. But the accumulated mis-estimates quickly aggregate into a deficit

	1960–61 $ (millions)	1965–66 $ (millions)	1965–66 % CHANGE	1970–71 $ (millions)	1970–71 % CHANGE
Real estate tax base; five-year average actual value: (taxable only)	30,300.0	46,400.0	53.1	61,300.0	32.1
Real estate tax base; five-year average assessed value: (taxable only)	24,900.0	30,900.0	24.1	35,300.0	14.2
Ratio assessed value/actual value	82.2%	66.6%		57.6%	
Real estate levy	1,028.3	1,409.4	37.1	2,080.4	47.6
Ratio R.E. levy/actual value	3.39%	3.04%		3.39%	
Ratio R.E. levy/assessed value	4.13%	4.56%		5.89%	
Federal aid	110.3	307.9	179.1	1,286.6	317.9
State aid	454.9	1,010.1	122.0	2,360.6	133.7
Personal income tax	—	—	—	199.4	—
Business taxes	205.2	316.0	54.0	440.0	39.2
Sales tax	303.0	382.1	26.1	493.6	29.1
All other taxes, fees, etc.	351.3	274.2	21.9	576.4	110.2
Other expense budget financing:					
Budget notes issued	5.3	—	—	360.8	—
RANs, TANs outstanding 6/30	42.9	145.3	238.7	1,302.3	796.3
Funded debt outstanding 6/30	4,176.1	5,018.9	20.2	5,635.3	12.3
BANs, URNs outstanding 6/30	52.2	300.3	472.0	607.8	102.4

problem too big to be ignored. Then the administration has to cut spending or increase revenues—or possibly fall back on a variety of budgetary gimmicks to defer the problem just a while longer. The ingenuity and sophistication with which successive New York City administrations cultivated the arcane arts of budget juggling were the despair of watchdog groups, although just as often the delight of bankers, who reaped considerable profits from the process. Some of the more frequently used gimmicks follow.

Skipping Required Payments

The legislature regularly exempted the city from the requirement of making payments to the rainy day fund, although the city's reserves were almost always maintained at too low a level. A similar result could be accomplished by overestimating earnings from sinking fund or pension fund assets in order to reduce required payments or even generate a surplus for the general fund. Or the bases on which payments were calculated could be changed. The period of funding for the city's pension funds were increased from fifteen to thirty-five years in 1968, substantially reducing the required annual payments. (Fifteen years was probably too short a funding period, but thirty-five years was almost certainly too long.) In 1972 payments to the teachers' pension funds were lagged two years—all other pension funds had been lagged two years from their inception—so the city could skip two successive years' payments.

Rollovers and Rollbacks

Expenses could be reduced or revenues increased by shifting payments or receipts from one fiscal year to the next. In 1973 the date for the semiannual payment of water charges was shifted from July to June, (that is, from the first month of the new fiscal year to the last month of the old one), effectively crediting the city with eighteen months of receipts in a single fiscal year. As long as the same payment schedule is maintained, subsequent fiscal years will still be credited with a full twelve months' receipts—unless the water system ever stops operating; in that case consumers would have a six-month credit during the system's last fiscal year. The 1965 proviso that RANs could be sold against revenues payable in the next fiscal year was, in effect, a rollback of revenues, because it allowed the city to credit up to fifteen months of federal and state aid to the 1964–65 fiscal year.

A more subtle variation of the rollover and rollback technique was the city's practice of using different accounting methods for revenues and expenditures. Traditionally, the city had maintained its books on a cash basis—that is, a revenue was recognized when it was received, and an expenditure was recognized when it was paid. It is equally acceptable to keep the books on an accrual basis—that is, both revenues and expenses are recognized when they become payable, irrespective of when the cash transactions take place. The requirement is only that an accounting system be employed consistently. But the city increasingly began to accrue only revenues, recognizing them at the earliest possible time, while the recognition of expenses was delayed until the actual cash outlay was made. The effect was to roll back to the current year revenues actually received in subsequent years and to roll forward expenses. As the budget pressures increased, rules were sometimes changed in the middle of the year in the relentless drive to squeeze the last dollar of spending authority from the seemingly inexhaustibly resilient city accounts.

The Magic Window

The most sophisticated system of interlocking rollovers and rollbacks is built into the transfers of state aid to its local governments. The state fiscal year ends on March 31, while those of municipalities end on June 30. In order to ease the state through a series of difficult fiscal years in the 1960s, Rockefeller skewed state aid payments to the April 1 to June 30 "magic window." By delaying payment dates until the window period, the state could skip a year's appropriation, (the payment didn't fall due until the state had begun a new fiscal year), but the aid would still get to localities before *their* fiscal years expired, so local budgets were not affected. The system was reversed to assist Abraham Beame cope with looming default in 1975. Aid payments scheduled to be paid in the following city fiscal year were advanced into the window period so that Beame could roll them back into the current year—getting a one-shot slug of new aid without increasing total state spending.

The Pendulum

The fatal attraction of rollbacks and rollovers is that they appear to be costless. The 1973 water-receipt rollback, for example, entailed no reduction of subsequent years' receipts so long as the new collection schedule was maintained. But nothing is free. What had changed was the *timing* of collections. Prior to the rollbacks, water receipts were collected in July and January, or the first and seventh months of the fiscal year. After the rollback the collections were in January and June, the seventh and twelfth months. The change in collection schedules does not affect receipt totals, but it has drastic effects on cash flows. As cash receipts become out of phase with expenditure patterns, the city's only recourse is to borrow short-term; and as there was increased resort to gimmicks and rollovers, there had to be increased resort to borrowing.

The workings of the magic window involved both the state and its localities in huge amounts of short-term borrowing. The localities would borrow through the fall and winter, in anticipation of the state aid arriving after April 1, and would retire the loans as the aid came in. But the state would have to borrow roughly equivalent amounts to finance such large cash outlays at the start of a fiscal year and would retire its borrowings as revenues were collected. The result was a debt pendulum—a gradual build-up of short-term borrowings by localities reaching a peak in the spring, to be replaced in the market by state debt, which was retired over the fall and winter as the local debt was building up again. The debt swinging back and forth between the state and local books was quite substantial—about $3.3 billion by 1975, with interest costs in the range of $100 million. The elegance of the pendulum device lay in the fact that the debt incurred by each level of government would be discharged before the end of its fiscal year by shifting it to the other level. The debt therefore never appeared in end-of-year statements, so the operations of the gimmick were invisible even to close readers of government accounts.

Phantom Revenues

Because the city was allowed to borrow against receivables to balance cash flows, borrowing against uncollectible receivables was a convenient way to raise cash to finance deficits. Like most budgetary gimmicks, the technique was not invented all at once, but evolved over an extended period. In simpler times revenues were quite predictable and did not present significant accounting or auditing problems. Accounts were manually maintained, for the most part, so the city's bookkeeping system bought transactional simplicity at the expense of accounting detail; revenues were accumulated under a very few fund classes, and the bulk of expenditures were made from a single fund class, the "Expense Budget Account." The system was probably archaic and overburdened even in the 1950s but was wholly inadequate to deal with the explosion of intergovernmental aid programs and the seemingly endless invention of new city taxes in the 1960s. Successive comptrollers—Beame, Procaccino, and again Beame—

either didn't understand the problem or were unable to deal with it,* with the result that external aid receipts were hopelessly commingled, aid claims were issued late, or sometimes not at all, the debt accounts were disorderly, and there was only poor current information on the proceeds from the various taxes. Statements of federal and state aid receivables were simply not audited at all until after the 1975 fiscal crisis, when large sums were written off.

But however disorderly the accounts, a receivable on the books was a ready source of cash—whether or not the receivable was ever paid—so long as the city was willing to borrow against it and the banks were willing to renew the loans. Because nobody audited the aid estimates, the city could budget aid claims as optimistically as it pleased and convert the optimism to cash. RANs outstanding jumped twentyfold between 1969 and 1975—to almost $3 billion— although outside aid remained relatively constant. A substantial portion of the increase, possibly $1 billion, was against phantom revenues. One of the advantages of the system as a gimmick was that it could function effectively without anyone's ever deciding explicitly to cheat. As long as the budget bureau didn't carefully monitor its aid estimates, the comptroller didn't audit the receivables, and the banks refrained from asking embarrassing questions, the city could keep on borrowing. There was no cleverness required: Slovenliness all around produced all the money the city needed.

Uncollectible real estate taxes supported a smaller but growing pyramid of TANs. As housing abandonment accelerated, the rate of tax delinquencies increased sharply, but the city continued to treat the total real estate levy as a receivable for borrowing purposes. Even substantial amounts of housing that had come into city ownership through tax delinquency foreclosure were retained on the tax rolls and inflated the putative receivable. "It was the ultimate gimmick," said a wag, "Self-taxation."

Capitalizing Expenses

The 2.5 percent real estate tax limit on operating expenses tended always to be fully utilized, while there was typically ample room within the 10 percent limit on issuance of funded debt. Budget pressures could be eased, therefore, by shifting items of operating expense to the capital budget, so long as the city's legal ingenuity could stretch the definitions of capital projects in the local finance law or the legislature agreed to expand the definitions. Over the years planning and design fees for capital project consultants, the costs of city capital budget staff, automobile purchases, street and park maintenance, the leasing of computer equipment, textbook purchases, manpower training, vocational education in the schools, and lease payments for city buildings all came to be

---

* Sometimes, in attempting to deal with it, they made it worse. Manual accounts were partially computerized in the early 1960s. The manual books carried three accounts for outside aid—one related aid receipts to budgeted aid; a second tracked borrowings against budgeted aid; and the third matched actual receipts against borrowings. The third account was dropped, on the theory that the computer could produce the detail automatically. Of course, it never did, and the link between receipts and borrowings was completely lost.

defined as capital projects. Expense items in the capital budget rose from $26 million in 1964–65 to $722 million in 1974–75. The city may not even have been the state's worst offender in this regard, because most localities used the same technique. Upstate counties, for example, lobbied through the redefinition of textbooks.

Of all the gimmicks, shifting expenses to the capital budget was in some ways the most defensible, but it was the most frequently criticized because it could be easily understood by newspaper reporters. In contrast to some other gimmicks, it was legal and did not involve any falsification of costs. It was simply a device to allow the city to raise real estate taxes outside the 2.5 percent limit. The maturities of the loans were usually short, and the interest costs were low. Particularly with the sharp increases in inflation in the late 1960s, the city probably saved money by amortizing costs in inflated dollars. It was not until the mid-1970s that city interest rates began to include a substantial penalty and the borrowing began actually to limit the city's capacity to undertake capital construction.

MANAGING CITY EXPENDITURES

The Budget: 1945–65

Balancing the city budget has always been a struggle. From 1945 to 1965 returns from the real estate tax levy tripled, but expenses increased fivefold. The shortfalls were made up by steady increases in the sales tax (from 1 percent in 1945 to 4 percent in 1963*), a general business tax, and a host of nuisance taxes—on hotel rooms, race track admissions, amusements, jukeboxes, commercial motor vehicles, bank vaults, and commercial occupancies. State aid increased somewhat faster than the budget, and federal aid almost three times as fast, although the amounts involved were relatively small until the 1960s. Personnel costs were the driving force. For twenty years the number of employees grew at an annual rate of 2.7 percent a year—about a 70 percent total increase—while labor costs grew about 8.6 percent a year, a rate slightly faster than the growth in the budget overall.

Wagner maintained better-than-average spending control during most of his first two terms, but as he moved to deal with the city's pressing social problems in the 1960s, costs began to move up sharply faster than the long-term trend. The increases came across a broad front: Five thousand men were added to the police force during Wagner's last term; educational personnel rose from 55,600 to 87,400, although the number of students increased by only 7 percent; employment in the university system and in the welfare department almost doubled, while the welfare caseload grew by more than 50 percent and costs increased even faster—by more than 80 percent. Overall labor costs per employee moved up three and a half times faster than the rate of inflation.

With his back to the wall, Wagner resorted increasingly to expedients. Cur-

* The sales tax was reduced to 3 percent in 1965, when the state introduced its own 2 percent sales tax. The lost revenues were more than made up by shifting the proceeds of the state's stock transfer tax to the city.

rent expenditures, including claims for back wage settlements, were transferred to the capital budget. Proceeds from the sale of foreclosed real estate were used for operating expenses, instead of going to a capital account. Increased take-home pay (that is, reduced employee pension contributions) substituted for wage settlements. Budget notes were sold every year, and the reserves, particularly the rainy day fund, were run down to the vanishing point—only $155,000 in cash was in the rainy day fund by 1965. Wagner made an attempt at major tax reform in 1963 but was immediately attacked by Comptroller Beame, who suggested that the budgetary problems could be solved by some small spending reductions, beefing up the revenue estimates, and moving the next year's state aid into the magic window. Wagner finally agreed to inflate the revenues and got an extra cent on the sales tax. It wasn't nearly enough to close the gap, and when the city finished the year $115 million in the red, he was excoriated by Beame for mismanagement.

The budget unraveled in 1965–66, the fiscal year that overlapped into John Lindsay's first term. Welfare was still rising fast, as were educational expenditures. Wagner had promised to strengthen the police force, and he could not ignore his commitments to the new antipoverty programs, particularly after two difficult summers in 1963 and 1964. In the end, he resolutely temporized. The legislature agreed to begin the process for a constitutional amendment to lift the real estate tax levy limit from 2.5 percent to 3 percent,* and in the meantime Wagner borrowed to make up the difference. The new real estate levy was a wan hope at best: Two successive legislatures had to pass the measure, and then it had to be approved by referendum. The earliest referendum ballot would be in November 1966, and the voters had proved themselves hostile to voting spending increases. The year closed with a deficit of $312 million. Five-year serial bonds were sold to cover $256 million, and the following year's federal and state aid receipts were anticipated by selling RANs worth $56 million. With an even larger current deficit looming for the next fiscal year, and the limit apparently reached for plundering reserves and one-shot gimmicks, it was clear that strong medicine would be required to restore the books to a semblance of health.

The Budget: 1966–69

Despite all the rancor surrounding Lindsay's first encounter with the Albany legislature, the tax package that he won in 1966 allowed him to plan his first budget on a much improved revenue base. The personal income tax produced an additional $130.4 million in revenue, an increase in the stock transfer tax added $50 million, increased water charges were worth $41.8 million, and the new gross receipts tax on utilities raised $40.8 million. General business taxes were shifted from a gross-receipts basis to an income tax. Its initial impact

* A reasonable case could be made for raising the limit. The 2.5 percent limit was the highest in the state, but no other jurisdiction had so comprehensive a budget as New York City. Elsewhere, the municipality, the county, the school district, and possibly other special districts each enjoyed separate taxing authority, so the cumulative limit could rise as high as 4 percent. On the other hand, no other jurisdiction had so broad a range of general fund taxes as New York City.

was to lower receipts slightly, but the new tax was designed to be more sensitive to economic growth. Overall, the revenue increment from the new taxes was worth more than the rise in the real estate tax limit on which Wagner had pinned his hopes. In addition to the new taxes, Rockefeller's transit strike aid package to save the subway fare got caught in a legal snarl that gave the city a windfall of $84.3 million. When a court declared the subsidy illegal, the fare had to be raised, anyway; but the city had already received the cash and was able to divert it to support general operating expenses. At the same time, the new Medicaid program, also passed in 1966, meant a net savings in health expenditures. With the help of the assorted windfalls and new revenues, Lindsay was able to close the 1966–67 fiscal year without budget notes or deficit borrowing for the first time in almost forty years, while a substantial payment to the rainy day fund put the city on the road toward restoring its financial integrity.

But the sense of fiscal security was short-lived. Total city spending rose 47 percent in Lindsay's first two fiscal years, although inflation was still relatively negligible. It was the fastest two-year spending increase in the city's history. Total city hiring was not the problem—the work force grew 2.7 percent per year, almost precisely the twenty-year average—but labor costs rose faster than normal, about 8 percent per employee each year, probably half of which could be related to Wagner's last round of labor settlements. Lindsay's 1967 teachers' settlement, however, was particularly expensive, with a two-year, 40 percent jump in costs. Social welfare spending was even more important than labor costs. Welfare caseloads increased by more than 50 percent during Lindsay's first two fiscal years, and with liberal grant increases spending doubled. Medicaid spending quadrupled in just two years.

The city's solvency was increasingly dependent on outside funding sources. Welfare and Medicaid carried about 70 percent state and federal shares, and Lindsay's new human resources programs were almost wholly underwritten with federal money. Out of a total two-year budget increase of about $1.6 billion, almost $900 million was met by outside aid—the increase in federal assistance was particularly sharp (87 percent in 1966–67 alone).

The runaway budget growth moderated in fiscal year 1968–69. The new welfare flat grant halted the onslaught of the welfare rights movement on the city treasury; welfare spending grew only 7.6 percent compared to the wild 52 percent growth the previous year. The city's share in Medicaid costs actually dropped $10 million after the legislature temporarily capped the program with a broad range of eligibility cuts. The cuts rebounded on the city hospitals, because the newly ineligible patients were no longer welcome in private institutions, but the net result was probably still a saving. Overall city employment grew rather faster than normal, but the increase in average labor costs slowed. The biggest single employment increase was in the Board of Education and consisted almost entirely of "New Career" paraprofessional aides who were hired for low-wage jobs that were wholly funded by the federal government. The second largest employment increase was in the welfare department, but the hiring came in the latter part of the fiscal year and was concentrated in clerical titles designed to replace higher-paid caseworkers in the bulk of the welfare job titles. On the revenue side, additional school aid and a revised state revenue-sharing program were a significant relief, federal aid continued to grow faster than the overall budget, and a healthy city economy increased personal income tax receipts by 18.3 percent.

The year 1968–69 closed with the city in the black and with little reliance on gimmicks, save for the extension of the pension funding period. Again, there was no drawing on the reserves and no sale of budget notes. A total of $80 million had been repaid to the rainy day fund since the start of the administration. The definition of expense budget items chargeable to the capital budget had been broadened somewhat, but the total had increased only $27 million since 1965–66. Short-term debt outstanding had increased, but the largest increase represented the legitimate sale of BANs as the capital construction program began to move. Long-term debt had increased hardly at all over three years, and RANs had risen only modestly—from $118.6 million in 1964–65 to $128.8 million in 1968–69—although federal and state aid had increased by more than $2 billion during the same period.

THE CITY ECONOMY

Despite the rapid growth in city spending, Lindsay could still plausibly claim during his re-election campaign that he had restored the city to financial health. A buoyant national and local economy had been able to supply sufficient revenues and intergovernmental aid not only to support new spending, but to pay off the accumulated debts of the Wagner administration. Indeed, by most measures New York's was possibly the strongest big-city economy in the country. Unemployment in the city in 1968 was only 3.1 percent—well below the national average of 3.6 percent. Dallas was the only major city with a lower rate. Black unemployment—about double the white rate in the rest of the country—was only 4 percent in New York City, a rate probably equivalent to full employment when account is taken of the higher proportion of teenagers and females in the black labor force. Almost two hundred thousand new jobs were created in the city between 1965 and 1970, a growth rate more than four times that in the previous five years. The annual rate of new office construction was up by 70 percent, with more than 5 million new square feet of usable space being added each year. The real estate tax base was growing at about twice the rate of inflation. Even the long-term slide in manufacturing employment that had been a fixture of the city economy since World War II had slowed to only about two-thirds its normal rate.

The strength of the New York City economy was based in part on its manufacturing concentration on light consumer goods, which tend to be more immune from cyclical swings than the durable goods manufacturing economies of most older industrial cities. Even more important was the premier position of the Manhattan office district as a world business and financial capital. The new breed of corporate gunslingers who were engineering multinational mergers and driving the stock market to dizzying heights naturally converged on Manhattan. The go-go years in business and finance translated into tens of thousands of new jobs in banks, insurance companies, and the back rooms of the stock exchanges, while the new money gilding the city spurred service employment in hotels, restaurants, and theaters.

But a disaster was lurking just beneath the shiny surface of the boom, although few people seemed to recognize it at the time. For all its apparent strength, the surge in employment was built on a peculiarly fragile base. The shift in the city's employment mix was undercutting business tax receipts, while decades of housing mismanagement and population change was undermining the real growth of the property tax base. The sharply elastic new taxes that Lindsay had installed in 1966 would prove just as responsive to a downturn as they had been to the boom. The city was thus dangerously exposed to a recession, and when the first of the post–Viet Nam "stagflations" hit in 1969, the impact in New York was worse than almost anywhere else in the country.

Shifts in Employment

The number of people employed in the city in 1970—3.75 million—was the highest ever. Only 766,000 persons were employed in manufacturing, reinforcing the city's headlong conversion to a service-oriented economy. Manufacturing employment had declined by 181,000 since 1960, but the job losses had been overbalanced by the gain of 387,000 non-manufacturing jobs. New jobs in service employment alone—178,000—kept pace with the losses in manufacturing. Wholesale and retail trade employment had slipped since 1960, but not drastically, while the finance, insurance, and real estate (FIRE) sectors had posted an increase of 74,000 jobs—a healthy 29.3 percent growth rate. Ominously, the biggest gainer after service employment was government, with the addition of 155,000 jobs—a jump of 37.9 percent, in local government.

Viewed with hindsight, New York's enviable position, compared to that of other major cities, reflected temporary phenomena more than underlying strengths. When recession hit in 1969, the bottom fell out of the FIRE sector as a deep plunge in the stock market closed brokerage houses up and down Wall Street. Computerization of the back rooms of the exchanges added to the precipitate loss of jobs—35,000 in the securities exchanges alone from 1969 to 1974. The loss of manufacturing jobs accelerated to an annual pace of almost 44,000: More manufacturing jobs were lost in the five years after 1969 than in the previous decade. Service employment flattened out after decades of growth, and wholesale and retail trade employment took a sharp downturn. Only state and local government employment continued to grow, but not nearly fast enough to make up the declines in other sectors. The total jobs lost in five years was 340,000, wiping out all the gains of the previous decade. New York City's unemployed increased by 83.6 percent from 1968 to 1973, a rate of increase substantially greater than that in the rest of the country or in any other large city.

The loss in jobs was catastrophic enough, but the implications for the city's tax base were even worse than they first appeared. Different types of employment produce different levels of tax receipts for the city. Manufacturing employment, for example, tends to use relatively large amounts of low-priced space per employee, in contrast to the sales and FIRE sectors, which use smaller amounts of space but with much higher assessed values. The low wages in the service sector produce lower personal income tax returns than high-wage FIRE employment, even with the high level of commuting in the financial district. Nonprofit enterprise is heavily represented in services, so business income tax receipts from service employment tend to be poor. Government employment, of course, returns the least in taxes, because it is exempt from both the property tax and the business income taxes. If the tax yield from a single government job is assigned a value of 1, a new job in the services sector can be expected to have an average tax return value of 1.44, a manufacturing job a value of 1.60, a job in the wholesale or retail trades 2.26, and a FIRE job 2.66. In other words, it takes 2.66 new government jobs to replace the lost tax receipts from one FIRE job.

The wholesale rate of job loss after 1969 was in the most tax-productive sectors of the city's economy and was nothing short of a financial disaster. The five-year gain of 33,500 jobs in government and 10,500 jobs in services had to be stacked against job losses of 219,000, 83,000, and 36,500 in manufacturing, sales, and the FIRE sectors, respectively. Each job lost produced on the average almost double the taxes as each one gained. From the perspective of city revenues, the downspin of the economy was twice as bad as a bare reading of the unemployment statistics would indicate, dreadful as they may have appeared to be.

The Real Estate Tax Base

Although it was decreasing in relative importance as a source of revenue, the real property base was still central to the city's financial health. Through the 1960s and 1970s, it was gradually being destroyed by a combination of bad public policymaking, demographic changes, and secular economic trends.

The most damaging of the public policies was the politically expedient continuation of rent control. Rent control had been imposed by the federal government during a nationwide housing shortage during World War II and was continued by the state when federal controls lapsed in 1950, although buildings constructed after 1947 were exempted. The state's avowed policy of moving rents as rapidly as possible to market levels was a political issue in Wagner's third-term campaign—almost all voters were renters—and in 1962 he succeeded in having rent control administration delegated to the city. The city administered the controls far more stringently than the state had done, and rents rose at a rate only about 75 percent as fast as in the previous decade. The result was wide disparity between rents in the controlled and uncontrolled sectors, a continuing "crisis" lack of vacancies in controlled apartments as renters clung to their bargains, and increasingly insufficient cash flows for proper building maintenance. Although most people in rent-controlled units had only modest incomes, almost a hundred thousand controlled households were paying less than 10 percent of their income in rents in 1968, and another seventy thousand paid less than 13 percent. Frank Kristof, the leading authority on rent control, estimates the control subsidy to middle- and upper-income families to have been $220 million a year. Only about half the controlled units were paying sufficient income to sustain even minimum profits, and by 1970 the annual shortfall of investment in the city's existing housing stock was running into the hundreds of millions of dollars annually.

The slowly deteriorating housing stock in controlled neighborhoods was a natural first line of expansion for the new immigrants from the South and Puerto Rico. Not only were rents low, but the lack of an adequate return gave landlords an incentive to induce neighborhood racial change to take advantage of the turnover rent increases and to cut up apartments into smaller units in order to escape the law altogether.* The blight cannot be blamed only on the rent laws, but a generation of underinvestment left many neighborhoods especially vulnerable to the forest-fire spread of deterioration that scarred the city in the 1960s and 1970s.

One result of the spreading blight was a severe housing shortage that peaked in 1967 and 1968. Whites fleeing racial change in older neighborhoods were bidding up prices in newer buildings, at the same time that the boom downtown put a premium on space in Manhattan. Moreover, a restrictive residential zoning ordinance passed in 1961 had virtually choked off new construction by limiting available land areas and halving permissible densities. Privately financed apartment completions in 1968 and 1969 were only a tenth of their 1963 peak, a falling-off that was even sharper than the decline in publicly financed housing. At the same time that vacancies in desirable neighborhoods were trending down toward zero, twenty thousand housing units were being abandoned elsewhere in the city each year. The shortage, in other words, was almost entirely pathological.

The political response made matters worse. With rents rising rapidly, the city passed in 1969 a "rent stabilization" law that brought most of the post-1947 housing under city regulation as well, although of a milder form than the older law. To the industry it seemed like outright betrayal, and it dashed their hope that rent control would gradually disappear as the prewar stock was replaced. Rent stabilization was followed by the passage of a "maximum base rent system" in 1970, which was an elegantly designed attempt to move controlled rents rapidly up to market levels. The problem was that the system was *too* elegantly designed, and the complex computer programs it required could never be made to work. The state intervened with a sweeping vacancy decontrol law in 1971, which, under heavy political pressure, was replaced by another form of rent stabilization in 1974. Only 1,536 private apartments were completed in 1972, a postwar low—private industry had taken a walk.

But, even the worst policies may not have been as damaging as secular economic trends. For example, housing abandonment in the South Bronx, prob-

---

* An owner was entitled to a 15 percent increase when an apartment was vacated—almost five times more than the annual increase for controlled units generally. Further, if he removed his building from the market and "converted" it to new units, it could qualify as a post-1947 building and thus would be exempt from the rent control laws.

ably the most devastated area in the entire city, can be plausibly related to the economics of an obsolete housing stock. The area was one of the most densely populated in the country in the 1940s and 1950s, and the housing stock consists almost entirely of five- and six-story walkups. As population density decreased, fifth- and sixth-story walkup apartments became unrentable at prices sufficient for sound building maintenance, irrespective of rent controls. Arson eventually became the owners' only financially rewarding alternative. One housing expert, pressed to make gross estimates, suggests that rent control was only a minor contributor to abandonment in the South Bronx, although it may have been the predominant factor in areas like Brooklyn's Ocean Parkway.

The combined effects of policy, demography, and economics were that two hundred thousand housing units were abandoned between 1965 and 1974 and the city's housing stock actually shrank for the first time in decades. The annual rate of tax delinquencies rose from $115 million in 1964–65 to $502 million in 1974–75.* At the same time, the rental population was increasingly impoverished. White families who had enjoyed the protection of rent control over the years were moving from the city, leaving black and Puerto Rican families to pay for the increases under the decontrol and stabilization systems. Rent-to-income ratios for all apartments rose from 19.1 percent in 1970 to 24.7 percent in 1975—the highest level since World War II, and rents increased in controlled or stabilized units more than three times as fast as residents' incomes. Because private financing for renovation or purchase could not be found at any price, the value of controlled housing units dropped precipitately—frequently, from five or six times rent rolls to just the value of the annual rent roll itself.

From 1969 to 1974 the property base continued to grow, but only about two percentage points faster than inflation, and an important part of the increase stemmed from revised equalization procedures. Assessed values declined in the Bronx, and were virtually static in Brooklyn.† Dependence on the Manhattan office base was increased, with Manhattan accounting for 70 percent of the assessment gains during Lindsay's second term. When the bottom fell out of the Manhattan office market in 1974, the city's real property tax base simply stopped growing altogether.

* It was for years an article of faith among liberals that increasing tax delinquencies measured landlords' greed better than their profits. The four-year-long city foreclosure procedures allowed the landlord to avoid payment with impunity—"the cheapest loan in town," according to one tract. The theory did not stand up to events. The city moved to a one-year foreclosure proceeding in 1976 and by 1979 had taken over more than thirty thousand housing units, overwhelming its administrative capacities. Landlords, by and large, weren't paying taxes because they didn't have the money or the buildings weren't worth it.

† Part of the flattening of assessments in residential areas is accounted for by the different assessment policies that the city applies to different classes of property. One- and two- family dwellings were assessed at only about 30–40% of market value by 1974, while the ratio for other classes of property ran from about 70% for multiple-dwelling units to almost 100% for downtown office space. As the ratio of assessments to market value dropped over time, the proportionate tax share of one- and two-family residential properties dropped even faster. In fact, taxes for most homeowners declined as a percentage of market value in the decade 1965–75, while the tax rate to market value increased only modestly for most other classes of property holders.

THE BUDGET: 1969–71

As the economy began to sour, both statewide and in the city, Rockefeller opened the 1969 legislative session by announcing sweeping cutbacks in state spending. In part, the state was overextended as a result of its massive new spending initiatives over the past decade; and in part, Rockefeller was acting in time-honored New York political tradition—cutting back on spending in the year before a campaign, in order to build a healthy surplus for a spending splurge during the election year. After a bitter struggle in the legislature—the state actually had to operate for several weeks in the new fiscal year without a budget—suburban legislators managed to retain the school aid formula untouched; but the Medicaid program was cut back again, restrictions were placed on welfare grants, and the state revenue-sharing program was effectively capped. To make matters worse, the stock transfer tax was cut, under industry pressure, so that total city receipts from the state were virtually static from year to year—$1,192.7 million in 1969–70, compared to $1,191.3 million in 1968–69. In constant dollars it was equivalent to a 6.8 percent reduction. The fact that Lindsay was running for re-election in 1969 could hardly be expected to evoke much sympathy from the governor, who was officially supporting Marchi.

In the city, welfare growth stayed on the moderate side, and the state Medicaid cutbacks kept the city share of Medicaid spending relatively flat. But election pressures dictated an expansion of the police and sanitation forces, and the addition of $95 million for an expensive new teachers' contract, negotiated just as the budget was being finalized, was simply buried to avoid political embarrassment after the bloodletting of the previous year. On the revenue side, the real estate tax base continued to move up in advance of inflation, but constant-dollar personal income tax receipts slipped, and total business taxes went down by $15.6 million.

As it turned out, the city scraped through. Budget director Hayes "sweated every last cent" from the comptroller's reserves and sinking funds, retroactive labor agreements were shifted to the capital budget, and $35 million was borrowed from the rainy day fund. Significantly, although Hayes insists he was not even aware of it at the time, short-term RANs outstanding at the end of the year went up sharply, from $128.3 million to $536.7 million. With total state and federal revenues in excess of $3 billion, the borrowing was still within a reasonable range: Plausibly, one-sixth or so of annual aid receipts were earned but not collected in the final quarter. But the borrowings marked the first substantial increase in short-term loans in four years and signalled an ominous shift in the city's fiscal fortunes.

By the next year, 1970–71, the city's ability to scrape through had run out. It was a state election year, and the previous year's cutbacks had generated a state surplus, so Rockefeller could help; but with a growing political feud between himself and Lindsay, he was not about to overextend the state to bridge the city's yawning billion-dollar budget gap. The major new assistance was a sharp improvement in the state revenue-sharing program (to $324 million, about a 60 percent hike) after two years of indefatigable campaigning by Lindsay. The rest of the gap was pasted over with new taxes, gimmicks, and wishful thinking. During the negotiations with the state, all of the city's revenue estimates were revised upwards. Offtrack betting was approved for the city, with a revenue estimate of $50 million. A share in a revised state lottery was calculated at $25 million. More stringent enforcement of parking tickets was supposed to bring in $20 million. An increase in water rates was put down for $80 million. The commercial occupancy tax was increased, new taxes were imposed on parking garages and hotel occupancy, and the state Board of Equalization raised the real property tax base by accelerating its calculations of market values. "It was a bad budget," Hayes recalls. "I figured there was a hard-rock deficit built in of $100 million. But I thought we had a chance to get through by controlling spending very tightly."

The deficit turned out to be much worse than Hayes feared. The city clamped down on hiring, so personnel costs rose only 6 percent, even with the new City University open enrollment program—the lowest increase since Lindsay had taken office. But Medicaid costs skyrocketed—particularly in hospitals and nursing homes—and the city share of welfare costs went up by more than 20 percent. The city tax share for welfare and Medicaid was $696 million—more than all the revenue gains combined since 1966 from improvements in unrestricted state aid programs and from all the new and increased city taxes.

As the spending pressures surged upwards, revenues collapsed. The new lottery, offtrack betting, and parking ticket programs produced only $1.3 million among them, as against $95 million in the budget. Receipts from the new water rates were $25 million less than expected, because the city couldn't revise its billing system in time to take advantage of the rates for the entire year. Receipts from the newly elastic income tax system turned down with the economy: Personal income tax receipts dropped from $205.4 million to $199.4 million. The business income tax falloff was even worse—from $205.1 million to $183.3 million. Total income tax receipts were $117 million less than budgeted. Troubles on Wall Street meant a 10.8 percent fall in the gross receipts tax on financial corporations. Tax returns from real property conveyances fell 15.8 percent. Even the new state revenue-sharing program produced $40 million less than expected, because it was tied to the state's own income tax receipts.

When the year ended the books were officially $361 million out of balance. The legislature authorized the sale of budget notes to cover the gap and allowed three years to pay them back. But on top of the budget notes, RANs outstanding doubled, rising to more than $1 billion, becoming, in effect, a permanently floating deficit.* New Yorkers had become inured to annual budget hysterics,

---

* Assigning a deficit to one set of accounts or another is a matter of taste as much as a science. The reasoning here: By doubling the RANs, the city refinanced the $500 million in RANs outstanding from the end of the previous year and issued another $500 million for the current year. The stream of revenues that should have paid off the old RANs, in other words, was used to meet new expenses, so the old RANs now became a permanently rolling over unsecured debt that could be redeemed, if at all, only by cutting into the city's general operating revenues. The city, of course,

but the city was now in a serious financial crisis. Its revenue base was shattered by the recession. Relations between Lindsay and Rockefeller were openly hostile. Richard Nixon in the White House was dismantling the federal programs that had produced so much new assistance since 1964. There was no relief in sight.

---

could contend that it had paid off the old RANs when the anticipated revenues arrived and then anticipated $1 billion in new revenues due in the last quarter of the fiscal year. However, the volumes of outside aid were not big enough to support that much anticipation. Neither the law nor the city's accounting system required that RANs be identified to specific receivables, so the matter could simply be fudged—so long, that is, as there was a market for the city's paper.

VII. *The Second Lindsay Administration*

HUMILITY AND NATIONAL ADVENTURE

LINDSAY BEGAN his second administration in a mood of humility and conciliation. His inaugural address reflected the new tone. The flash and swagger of his first inaugural was replaced by an implied apology for the excesses of his first term and an attitude of worried concern for the ordinary citizen.

If the Bay Ridge homeowner is uncertain of his neighborhood's future, if the Harlem mother does not know if her child is learning at school, if the Forest Hills family fears to walk the streets at night, if the Morrisania office worker cannot travel home at night in comfort or even decency, then the city is not working for its citizens. . . .

If we do all we hope to do in the next four years, there will still be too much of crime and poverty, too much of slums and pollution. . . .

We are all human, we are all fallible. The test is whether we have learned from the mistakes we have made.

The first round of new appointments reinforced the sense of limited objectives. There was no search for national experts on the urban crisis, no nationwide dragnet for "urbanologists." Two New York City assemblymen, Jerome Kretchmer and Benjamin Altman, were appointed to top posts—heading the Environmental Protection Administration and the Department of Rent and Housing Maintenance, respectively. Gordon Chase, who had been leading a management cleanup in the Human Resources Administration, became health services administrator, braving the medical establishment as the first non-doctor in the city's top health post. Milton Musicus, the state health construction chief, was placed in charge of the Municipal Services Administration. Albert Walsh, the chairman of the Housing Authority, was appointed to the Housing and Development Administration, and Jule Sugarman, who had developed a reputation as a manager in the federal Department of Health, Ed-

ucation, and Welfare, replaced Mitchell Ginsberg at HRA. The emphasis was
to be on running the city better, not breaking new programmatic ground. As
one aide put it, "John's not as certain he's God anymore, and we're not so sure
either."

Lindsay set out consciously trying to build bridges to the disaffected white
working class. The pattern of highly publicized neighborhood walking tours
that had been a hallmark of his first administration gave way to a series of meetings with a much lower profile in Bay Ridge, Canarsie, Flatbush, Bayside,
and other white communities—as often as not held in someone's living room
and without advance notice to the press. There was no question that the attempt to achieve a broader political base would be an uphill struggle. Lindsay's
consistent opposition to the war in Viet Nam had made him a target of criticism
from Vice President Agnew and other spokesmen for the "silent majority"; and
when construction workers rampaged in lower Manhattan following peace
demonstrations in April 1970, they called for Lindsay's impeachment and
shouted curses at the "Red Mayor." On the other hand, a poll of voter attitudes
taken in late 1970 showed there had been a marked shift toward a more favorable opinion of Lindsay's performance in office.

Then Lindsay decided to run for president. From the point of view of national politics, the decision to run was barely plausible: The Democratic party
seemed ripe for a reform candidate, and McGovern seemed too weak to hold
up in a national primary campaign. From the standpoint of city management,
the decision to run was a disaster.

Lindsay had begun to nibble around the edges of the decision in late 1970.
His decision to support Arthur Goldberg for governor against Nelson Rockefeller in 1970 was dictated in part by his need to position himself as an independent, in case he later decided to make a run as a Democrat. By mid-1971,
campaign fever had taken over the administration. JVL associations were
formed around the city, young aides took leave to scout the early primary states,
and Deputy Mayor Richard Aurelio resigned "to take national soundings." The
official party switch came in April 1971, and the steadily accelerating pace of
Lindsay's fundraising forays around the country became a full-time campaign
schedule. By the time the decision to run was formally announced in February
1972 and top officials began resigning for campaign duty, Lindsay was an absen-
tee mayor.

The race was mercifully short. There was a hopeful showing in the Arizona
delegate poll, but in the crucial Florida primary, Lindsay finished a poor fifth.
After virtually identical results in Wisconsin, and without consulting his aides,
Lindsay put an end to the embarrassment. As the local politicians hooted,
"Come back, little Sheba," a thoroughly chastened Lindsay, possessed of a
wrenching new self-perspective, returned from his national adventure.

The price of the campaign for New Yorkers was high. Not only was management attention diverted from the city, but the sudden race for highest office, so
soon after the disarming humility of the mayoral campaign, dissipated whatever
good will Lindsay had succeeded in creating with the white working classes.
The police and fire unions became ever more demanding and ever more unre-

strained in imposing their demands. PBA chief Edward Kiernan convinced his men to end the wildcat parity strike in 1971 by exhorting, "Don't give this man what he wants. Don't make this man president." There were violent white demonstrations against the proposed public housing project in Forest Hills. Delegations from Queens dogged the mayor's footsteps in the Florida primary. Guests at a Lindsay fundraising dinner in Queens had to run a gauntlet of cursing, shoving, and kicking local white residents. A tone of almost unrelieved nastiness settled over civic affairs.

After being strained for years, relations with the state became poisonous. Rockefeller and Lindsay had never liked each other, but the bonds of party fraternity required cordiality, or at least restraint, in public. With Lindsay's support of Goldberg and his break with the Republican party, the personal enmity between the two spilled into the open. Shortly after his re-election Rockefeller announced that a major priority during his new term would be reasserting state control over the city because of Lindsay's "incompetence," particularly in police administration and garbage collection. During the 1971–72 city budget crisis, Rockefeller condemned Lindsay's "inept and extravagant administration" of the city and his "apparent inability to take effective corrective action." In his State of the State message in 1972, Rockefeller indulged in a personal tirade against Lindsay, characterizing New York City as the place "where housing can't be found, streets are unsafe, corruption undermines public trust, traffic is unbearable, garbage can't be picked up often enough . . . and there is no actual control over the City government despite the almost total centralization of power in City Hall." Lindsay struck back with a scathing denunciation of the Rockefeller record: the Attica riots, the breakdown of the state narcotics program, Rockefeller's budget crisis, the deteriorating state-administered subways and commuter railroads.

Lindsay and his staff could hold their own in verbal duels with the state, but Rockefeller had a massive advantage in real power. The city needed state aid in order to survive, and the annual pilgrimage to Albany to balance the budget became an exercise in humiliation. In 1971 Rockefeller introduced legislation to empower the state comptroller to audit the city's operating programs, created a state welfare inspector-general, and established a temporary commission, the Scott Commission, to investigate governmental operations in New York. The vacancy decontrol law passed that year was a calculated slam at the city's inability to manage its rent control program. In 1972 Rockefeller ruminated publicly about breaking up the mayor's powers and decentralizing the city government. The Scott Commission undertook a decentralization study as a first priority, and later Rockefeller created a New York City Charter Commission to restructure the city's operations.

The state welfare inspector-general was George Berlinger, a retired businessman, a conservative, and a former member of the State Board of Social Welfare. He set up his offices in New York City and hired a staff of eighty to comb through case files for errors, which were legion in the beleaguered New York City system. Disaffected welfare employees were only too happy to send examples of mishandled cases to Berlinger's investigators and to feed a daily stream of press releases. Berlinger did not hesitate to generalize from handfuls of cases, and his broadside attacks that "forty percent of the caseload" was ineligible could not be credited; but neither could the figures from the city spokesmen, who stuck resolutely with an outdated and highly suspect federal survey that placed the ineligibility rate at about 3 percent. Under the glare of daily publicity, relations between HRA Administrator Sugarman and Berlinger quickly deteriorated into a barrage of acrimonious letters, accusations, and counter-accusations and, on Berlinger's part, an almost vindictive pleasure in city problems. When a top HRA computer specialist resigned, Berlinger announced gleefully to the press that the city's management program "was crumbling." Even when the city caseload began to decline, Berlinger was convinced that the city was manipulating the caseloads for political purposes or was simply lying about the numbers.

The members of the Scott Commission, with possibly one or two exceptions, were more anxious to appear nonpartisan and genuinely to investigate the operations and structure of the city government. But to Lindsay, and probably to most observers, the commission was merely another weapon in Rockefeller's running feud with the mayor, and Lindsay insisted on treating the commission members as political hatchetmen. Tedious court battles ensued over the commission's powers to call witnesses and compel evidence, and, somewhat forlornly, Lindsay set up a counter-commission to investigate the operations of the state. In the end the delays, the state budgetary problems, and the growing unwillingness of legislators to fund the vendetta led to a curtailing of the commission's original brief. The final product included a damning survey of management in the city's housing and social services programs, rather more superficial studies of health programs and political decentralization, and one excellent and thoroughly detailed study of the city's economic base and fiscal capacity.

Mere harassment could be endured—a thick skin is basic equipment for a politician—but the split with the state had important practical consequences, for the city's fiscal situation grew grimmer year by year.

THE BUDGET: 1971–72

By early 1971, when the shaping of the 1971–72 budget was nearing the stage of final decisions, it was already clear that the current year's deficit would be on the order of $300 million, a shortfall that could not be closed by making cuts. Although $300 million was only about 4 percent of the total budget, it was more than 7 percent of the city tax share in the budget, and it was from city-financed items that the cuts would have to come. But the mayor had direct control over only about $2 billion worth of city-financed spending—primarily in parks, police, fire, and sanitation services and in the expenses of the general government. He had no power to reduce welfare and Medicaid payments, no real ability in the short term to affect the size of the caseload, and no unilateral power to order cuts in the independent agencies—the schools, the university system, and the new hospitals corporation. Three hundred million dollars was about 15 percent of the city tax share in the mayoral agencies, and because the fiscal year was already half over, the cuts would have to be about 30 percent in order to make up the deficit.

Even assuming that the current deficit could be financed with budget notes, the deficit built into the next year's budget would necessarily be even bigger. Inflation would drive up prices, wages were going up, and welfare and Medicaid caseloads were rising inexorably. Some combination of increased taxes and increased aid was obviously necessary, but it was a peculiarly inopportune time to go to Albany for help. Not only were relations between Lindsay and Rockefeller deteriorating rapidly, but the state was in serious financial trouble itself. The combined effects of the recession and election-year spending had left the state with a $200 million deficit, and for the first time in twelve years, Rockefeller had lost control of the legislature. He was forced to retract his own proposal for $1.2 billion in tax increases and watched a conservative legislature chop his budget by $700 million. There were deep slashes in welfare and Medicaid, and the new revenue-sharing program was cut back from 21 percent of state income tax revenues to 18 percent, adding another $50 million to the city's problem.

The city strategists, Lindsay, Aurelio, and Edward Hamilton—who had succeeded Hayes as Budget Director—decided that an all-out assault was the only way to make a dent in Albany's resistance to new taxes or spending. Early in the year Lindsay made public four "option" budgets to dramatize the city's plight—ranging from an "Option One" budget, which assumed no increases in local taxes or state aid and no restoration of the cuts just enacted by the legislature, to an "Option Four," the preferred option, which assumed restoration of the cuts, $880 million in new taxes, and $115 million in new state aid. The new tax package that accompanied Option Four was hardly one designed to win the hearts and minds of conservative suburban legislators. The key element in the proposal was a rise in the personal income tax that would increase its progressivity and equalize the tax burden on residents and commuters. A second proposal was to shift sales tax liability from point of delivery to point of sale—that is, suburbanites shopping in the city would pay the sales tax to the city, at the higher city rate, instead of to their own municipalities. The rest of the package contained an extension of business taxes to self-employed professionals; extension of the sales tax to personal services, movie admissions, restaurant sales under $1.00 (the "hot dog tax"), drug sales, and advertisers; a string of sumptuary taxes on high-tar-and-nicotine cigarettes, leaded gasoline, and nonrecyclable containers; the usual nuisance taxes on autos, bank vaults, beer, and liquor; and an increase in the hallowed nickel fare on the Staten Island ferry.

The consequences of inaction in Albany were painted in apocalyptic terms. The Option One budget meant massive amputations of city services and the elimination of ninety thousand jobs. Half the police department's civilian work force and more than eight thousand uniformed policemen would be laid off; six thousand positions would be eliminated in the fire department; garbage collections would be reduced to once per week throughout the city, and street cleaning would be completely eliminated; average class sizes in the schools would be increased to almost forty, more than sixteen thousand teachers would be let go, and all special school services would be drastically cut; city health services would be virtually gutted, eight municipal hospitals would be closed, and all nonemergency ambulatory clinic care would be eliminated. The list went on and on. The consequences of Option Two were only slightly less dire, and even Option Three, which assumed the mayor's full tax package, implied almost a full hiring freeze and the loss of six thousand jobs through attrition.

Rockefeller's response was cold. The loss of ninety thousand jobs, he observed, would bring the level of city employment back to about where it had been when Lindsay took office. The state itself was planning to lay off more than eight thousand employees and it was time, he suggested, for the city, to "exercise a comparable discipline in the light of the present fiscal crisis."

Lindsay kept up the pressure. Ten thousand city employees marched on Albany. DeLury threatened a general strike. Lindsay fulminated against Albany's "arrogance and contempt" and used the struggle to draw national publicity to America's urban crisis. Demonstrations against the budget cuts in Brownsville degenerated into three days of looting and burning. The level of rancor rose to the point where the bitter 1966 battle over increased city taxes looked like a friendly tête-à-tête. In private, however, state officials acknowledged that they were impressed with Hamilton's presentations of the options and the care and detail that had gone into the preparation of the figures.

In the end Rockefeller yielded. He sat down with the city leadership to work out an acceptable package but was infuriated when the city refused to reduce its estimates of the budget gap. In exasperation, Rockefeller announced that he would work out a package with the legislative leadership himself, pointedly excluding the city from the discussions. The state budget staff decided that the city had overstated its needs by $400 million, and Comptroller Beame chimed in with an announcement that he had discovered $277 million in new revenues—$184 million from raising Lindsay's tax receipt estimates, $67 million through various rollovers and rollbacks of state aid, and $26 million from accumulated surpluses in the teachers' pension funds. Rockefeller finally patched together a $450 million revenue package with the Republican leadership but could not raise enough votes from the Republican rank and file to pass it on the floor. Stymied by his own party, he was forced to seek an alliance with the Democrats, who were insisting on a package of at least $700 million. Lindsay said even that much would cause from thirty to fifty thousand layoffs.

Eventually, the city was brought back into the negotiations, and an agreement was reached on enough taxes and gimmicks to raise $861 million. The new taxes totaled $525 million, including a $190 million increase in the personal income tax that preserved the old 8:1 ratio between residents and commuters. There were $55 million worth of new taxes on business, some rescindments of property tax exemptions, extension of service charges to tax-exempt property, new taxes on property transfers, and new taxes on commercial vehicles and garages. Most of the city sales tax and nuisance tax proposals were retained, except for the tax on drugs and advertisers and the imposition of city sales taxes on suburban purchasers. To make up the balance, the city was authorized to borrow $100 million in anticipation of the passage of a federal revenue-sharing bill; payments to the teachers' pension fund were lagged two years, saving $87 million each year; an $81 million payment to the rainy day fund was dropped; and the schedules of state welfare and Medicaid payments were advanced to produce $68 million. The $100 million installment due on the previous year's budget notes was simply ignored. The city's part of the bargain was to agree not to lay off any employees, so the onus for service cuts could not be laid to legislative stinginess. Rockefeller got in the last lick by appointing the Scott Commission, issuing his statement on city extravagance, and writing a cold letter to Lindsay vowing that there would never be a repetition of the exercise. Although he had actually done much better than reasonably could have been anticipated, Lindsay's summation was that he could not recall a legislative session "more chillingly anti-City . . . as blindly partisan. . . . I cannot recall any leadership of this great State so opposed to progressive change, so ready to punish the poor . . . and so determined to extract the last pound of flesh from its opponents."

Lindsay still had to shepherd the new taxes through the Board of Estimate and City Council, both of which bodies were anxious to take credit for reducing the taxes authorized by the legislature. Beame insisted that there was still $330 million worth of play in the budget because of a combination of revenue underestimates and expenditure overestimates. Lindsay finally agreed to reduce his nominal budget request from $9.1 billion to $8.75 billion, but the council and board cut another $127 million from the tax package by manipulating revenue and welfare spending estimates. The final budget of $8.56 billion looked remarkably close to the Option Two budget that Lindsay had said would require some sixty thousand layoffs. When Lindsay announced that he could live with the budget that came out of the council and board and that there would be no layoffs, the cynics said derisively that it had all been histrionics.

In fact, the city's original estimates, although inflated somewhat for rhetorical effect, weren't that far off. By the end of the fiscal year, although the city's books appeared to be more or less in balance, the gimmicks and questionable borrowings that went to achieve the balance totaled about $700 million,* or enough to finance thirty-five to forty-five thousand city employees. When added to the $400 million tax package finally passed by the City Council, the total came to $1.1 billion, or about what the city said the budget gap was to begin with.

Viewed strictly as an exercise in short-term political tactics, the "option

* The final total included $100 million of new budget notes in anticipation of federal revenue-sharing, $95 million in deferred collective bargaining payments, $68 million advanced welfare payments, $87 million skipped pension payments, $81 million skipped rainy day fund payments, $110 million in sinking fund borrowings, and $155 million skipped budget note repayments ($103 million first installment on the three-year notes issued in 1970–71, and $52 million welfare notes also issued in 1970–71.) The total in this list is $696 million, and, of course, it is exclusive of more subtle techniques such as shifts between cash and accural accounting methods, running down the various appropriation reserve funds, and the like. RAN borrowing outstanding, however, remained more or less constant, as did the level of expense budget items financed from the capital budget.

budget" assault on Albany was a resounding success. In terms of extracting concessions from a recalcitrant legislature, the city fared better than even Rockefeller himself with his own budget. But from a longer view it was a critical turning point for the worse. For one thing, the city seemed finally to renounce
spending cutbacks—as opposed to slower spending growth—as a feasible
budget balancing alternative.

Secondly, the enormous size of the gap, and the apparently magical way it
was made to disappear, seemed to break, once and for all, any hard-and-fast
relationship between the city's ability to raise revenues and its ability to spend.
Wagner had used his share of budget gimmicks, but the Wagner deficits had
been relatively open and aboveboard. The borrowing in 1965–66, for instance,
was openly announced and much debated and criticized. But when hundreds of
millions of dollars were made to materialize by methods that most newspaper
reporters, much less ordinary citizens, simply didn't understand, the common
conclusion was that the budget gaps hadn't existed in the first place. Mere lack
of money would no longer be a very convincing argument against spending.

Finally, the thoroughness with which the Albany legislative leadership and
city budget officials began to mine the seemingly endless store of new budget-
balancing devices was a whole new departure in itself. Over the next several
years, budget gimmicking was raised from the level of haphazard expedient to
an arcane art form, and the practical limits of irresponsibility were pushed further and further out on the horizon.

Both the city and state officials could rationalize and defend their behavior.
Obviously, a liberal Democratic presidential candidacy could not be launched
from a platform of lower spending in the cities, but there were more substantial
reasons as well. The urban crisis was a national phenomenon and it was con-
fidently expected that sooner or later massive federal aid would be available to
make good the deficits. In 1971, for instance, it appeared that new federal funding for social services could net the city as much as $2 billion a year on top of the
expected new federal revenue-sharing bill. The United States Congress still
seemed serious about welfare reform and national health insurance, which
might remove the most crushing burdens of all from the city treasury.
Moreover, the recession was expected to be a short-lived phenomenon, a temporary adjustment to the Viet Nam disequilibriums. If revenues and aid would
soon recover, it made little sense to impose deep cuts on vital services when
other alternatives were readily available. Had all or even some of the possibilities for improved revenues and economic performance actually happened,
the city's gamble might have seemed in retrospect to have been a smart decision. In fact, in fiscal year 1972–73, when both the economy and federal aid
turned up briefly at the same time, the city was able to make a good start on
paying off the accumulated borrowings. But the hopes for a brighter financial
future turned out to be built on the same shifting sands as the 1971–72 budget,
and what might otherwise have been a brilliant feat of improvising turned out
to be merely the first in a string of excesses that culminated in collapse in 1975.

THE BUDGET: 1972–73

1972 opened as though it would be a repetition of the previous year. Lindsay, in the midst of his presidential race, announced a gap of $800 million in the 1972–73 fiscal year, a gap that would have to be closed by state aid. Albany met the proposal with disbelief. Rockefeller was running a current budget deficit and was forced to come to the legislature with a supplemental $450 million tax package. His new budget was actually lower than the previous year's, a jarring return to reality.

Even John Lindsay had to recognize that the state till was firmly shut against cries of doom. Humbled in the primaries, he returned to New York and reduced his gap to $227 million, proposing to make up the difference by borrowing against the hoped-for federal revenue-sharing payments. Typically, Beame claimed that the true deficit was closer to $40 million. An agreement was finally reached with the state on a package that included a string of nuisance taxes, $65 million in new real estate equalization authority, $35 million in increased water rentals, and decisively more optimistic revenue and expenditure assumptions—$162 million, for instance, materialized when the mayor ordered HRA to achieve zero welfare growth.* The legislature provided $100 million more in standby borrowing authority.

The package blew up at the eleventh hour when the City Council and the Board of Estimate staged a tax revolt. The nuisance taxes had been dead from the outset, but the leadership had agreed to the new real estate taxes and water rates. The rank and file, led by Queens Councilman Matthew Troy, refused to produce the votes, and, dramatically, the clock in the council's chambers was stopped for three days while the leadership attempted to piece together another compromise. Finally, Hamilton, who was by now deputy mayor, discovered that the PBA's rejection of a wage settlement permitted $49 million to be carried over into the new year; and further, because the national pay board had not approved another $50 million in raises, that amount could be lagged as well. It was shabby bookkeeping, but it was enough to start the council clock and give the city a legal budget.

Significantly, the revolt staged by the city legislators was a tax revolt, not a spending revolt. Spending estimates were reduced, but not spending programs. To all outward appearances, the city could have its cake, eat it, and bake dozens more in the meantime.

EXPENDITURES: 1970–73

In general, spending rose relatively slowly during Lindsay's second administration. Total city employment dropped under the pressures of the 1971–72 budget and rose by only half a percentage point over the entire four

---

* The cognoscenti didn't question the savings estimate. The local finance law permitted unlimited sale of budget notes to make up welfare deficits. If there had to be a deficit, welfare was a good place to have it.

years. Constant-dollar spending rose by only 2.7 percent in 1971–72, the lowest
increase in four years. The city labor unions, however, were as demanding as
ever, and bargaining often ended in impasse proceedings, leaving the city at
the mercy of imposed settlements that typically took little cognizance of the
state of the city treasury. The round of parity pay settlements substantially
raised the pay base in the uniformed services, and some sort of labor relations
low point was reached in November 1973, when Richard Vizzini, the leader of
the firefighters' union, led his men on a one-day strike. The election supervisors later reported that the men had voted not to strike, but Vizzini lied about
the result to increase the pressure on the city negotiators.

But the union demands were dampened by outside interventions. In 1970
the city quietly negotiated a new pension plan with DC37, the union that had
most consistently supported Lindsay during his first term and his re-election
campaign. The agreement awarded workers half-pay after twenty years and
full pay after forty years, bringing the contract more into line with the generous
retirement concessions won by the teachers in 1969. When the plan hit the
state legislature—right in the middle of the battle over the 1971–72 budget—
they refused to pass it and instead appointed a study commission to review runaway pensions in the city. The union reacted by launching what Gotbaum promised would be "the biggest, sloppiest, strike you've ever seen." Drawbridges
into the city were raised, water was cut off to parts of Manhattan, sewage treatment plants were opened so raw sewage could flow into the rivers, school lunch
supplies were cut off. The strike only angered the legislators even further;
DC37 didn't get its pension improvements,* and the freedom to bargain pensions was effectively removed from the city. It was an embarrassment, but it
was also a relief. There had been rumblings from the police and firemen about
retirement after fifteen years if "the clerks got their twenty years," and a 1972
settlement with the sanitation men was vastly simplified when pensions were
removed from the table. Further restrictions were placed on the city's freedom
of action in August 1971, when President Nixon imposed mandatory wage and
price controls that lasted into 1973. Not only did the controls put a lid on wage
demands, they also turned out to be a useful budget-balancing tool. The complicated bureaucratic process of getting pay awards approved meant that the
city could delay payment on most new contracts—and the local finance law permitted delayed settlements to be funded with five-year bonds.

Open Enrollment

Although liberal enthusiasms were much more restrained during the
second administration, the city was not completely immune to new spending
ventures. The most important was the Open Enrollment program at City University. The decision actually to proceed on Open Enrollment was made at the end
of Lindsay's first term, but implementation did not begin until the fall of 1970.

Open Enrollment has usually been presented as a program designed to satisfy minority groups. The decision itself followed upon demonstrations by black

---

* The city and the union eventually agreed to extend welfare benefits (the union health plan) to retirees at a cost roughly equivalent to the estimated annual cost of the improved pensions.

and Puerto Rican students that closed down City College in 1969. But plans for expansion of the system on the California model to offer some form of higher education to every high school graduate had been going forward for years, and the Board of Higher Education had previously picked 1975 as a tentative start date. Peter Goldmark, the mayor's chief of staff in 1969 and the most forceful advocate in the administration of accelerating the plans for Open Enrollment, insists that, rather than a program for minorities, it was viewed as a major administrative initiative on behalf of whites:

Running the colleges was one of the few things we did comparatively well, and the vast majority of kids just under the qualifying scores for CUNY were white working-class kids. The beauty of the idea was that it was truly colorblind. We could improve access and opportunities for everyone without obviously favoring one group over the other. We saw it as a way of bridging some of the divisions in the city.

The effects of Open Enrollment have still not been fully evaluated—and, of course, ultimate judgments on the program will depend very much on the evaluator's preconceptions of the proper functions of a university system. Certainly, enormous pressures were placed on the faculty and physical plant in accommodating the influx of new students—total enrollment jumped by more than forty-five thousand in just two years. There is considerable evidence that the problems of integrating inadequately prepared students into the higher education system had been underestimated; a very large percentage of the new students performed at the tenth-grade level or below, and a great portion of the system's resources were given over to teaching basic high school material. Goldmark's expectation that the program would significantly benefit whites was borne out in the first two years of the program. Black and Puerto Rican enrollment approximately doubled, but the total enrollment increase among whites—20,000—was greater than the increase among blacks—about 19,000 —and considerably more than the increase among Puerto Ricans. However, by 1975, the last year before the program was cut back under the pressures of the fiscal crisis, total white enrollment had actually decreased (from 143,250 in 1969 to 142,500 in 1975), while black and Puerto Rican enrollment had about quadrupled (from 25,188 to 98,829). In percentage terms, white enrollments dropped from 81.9 percent of the total in 1969 to 52.5 percent. The differential trends in white and black enrollments quite probably reflect both a flight of the abler students from the system—which could have serious long-term consequences—and the fact that blacks as a group seem to value a college education more highly than do some white ethnic groups.

Whatever the long-term advantages or disadvantages of Open Enrollment, the short-term budgetary consequences were significant. Employment in the system jumped 29.3 percent in 1970–71, the first year in which the city's books clearly showed a deficit, and continued to grow 7 percent a year until 1975—that is, during a time when employment in most other city agencies was contracting or being held steady. The city had some success in shifting a progressively higher portion of the increased costs to external funding sources, but the city-financed share of the higher education budget grew at a compound annual rate of 18.5 percent during Lindsay's second four years, increasing from slightly more than $100 million in 1969–70 to just under $200 million in 1973–74.

Daycare

The city had always financed daycare programs for the children of working welfare recipients and for children whose parents had difficulty in caring for them. However, by the 1970s, for reasons probably having most to do with changing attitudes about traditional women's roles, support for expanded daycare programs became one of the litmus tests of liberalism. Eligibility guidelines for public daycare were broadened to include most lower- to middle-income children whose mothers were working or "looking for work," and in New York, state and federal funding programs reimbursed 87.5 percent of local daycare costs. The movement reached its zenith in 1971, when both houses of Congress overwhelmingly passed a sweeping Child Development Act that provided free daycare to every poor child in the country, only to have the bill vetoed by President Nixon.* Lindsay, running for president on a left-of-center platform, could hardly afford to be unforthcoming on daycare. Between 1971 and 1974 the number of children in city daycare grew from eight thousand to thirty-six thousand, the number of daycare centers from 120 to 410, and the daycare budget from $36 million to $120 million.

Daycare had a broad spectrum of supporters. Conservatives like Senator Russell Long backed daycare as a way to increase the employability of welfare mothers. HRA administrator Sugarman promised that expanded daycare could cut the welfare rolls "by 250,000," and comptroller Beame criticized the city for not moving fast enough to increase the number of places. The more radical supporters of the program saw it as a means, variously, to improve social integration at the early childhood level by making tax-supported daycare available across a fairly broad income spectrum; to make up for early childhood learning deficits by adding rich educational components to standard daycare programs; and to equalize the social position of women by removing the burden of child care from mothers who wished to work.

All of the objectives were worthy, but they were conflicting. The enriched programmatic content made daycare so expensive that the city could save money by maintaining a family on welfare†; at the same time, the attempt to

---

* Support for the bill probably overstates the true support for expanded daycare. Nixon's veto was known to be a certainty, and there was no serious attempt at override, even though the bill had won considerably more than a two-thirds majority in each house.

† The cost of keeping a child in a daycare center in 1975 averaged $318 a month and was as high as $525 a month. The average ADC grant was only $404 a month (and supported about three people). If a mother left welfare for a job, the combination of daycare expenses, the earned income disregard, and the allowance for travel and work expenses would total considerably more than the original grant, unless the job paid more than about $9000 per year. If more than one child required care, the arrangement was even more disadvantageous to the taxpayer. Aside from problems of cost, the provision of daycare complicated the employment response to welfare in other ways, because the welfare-rights lawyers soon established that a recipient could avoid employment as long as the government didn't provide suitable daycare. Over the years, of course, the vast majority of women who

achieve income integration in the centers meant that there were fewer places for welfare recipients to begin with. Also, by 1971 there were ample data calling into the question the power of formal educational programs to correct cognitive disabilities rooted in family disadvantage. Possibly the program's greatest service was easing the child care burden on single mothers, but it is doubtful that objective by itself would have drawn much public funding support.

Regardless of the relation between daycare and its stated objectives, the city could arguably afford the programs because of the generous intergovernmental aid available for social services. But as entrepreneurial jurisdictions across the country moved to take advantage of the new open-ended funding, Congress became alarmed and clapped a lid on social services programs in 1972. Instead of the $120 million in aid that the city had expected to receive each year for daycare, there was only $50 million. The state provided a one-time grant of $10 million in 1973 to ease the transition, but from that point the city was on its own. Once again, New York had been out in front with the biggest and most expensive program in the country. Once again, the haste and grandiose scale assured management scandals in the short run. (Among other scandals, the city was systematically bilked by real estate developers who built and leased daycare centers to the city for twenty years, without cancellation clauses, and at sometimes grossly inflated rates.) And once again, the city was left to face the bitter repercussions of its own overreaching.

PRODUCTIVITY

As the year 1972 drew to a close, Lindsay's position was bleak indeed. An object of ridicule at home, anathema to the national administration, harassed by myriad state investigation and audit teams, an almost certain lame duck, he had little to look forward to except the quadriennially massed ranks of potential mayoral contenders, all of them eager to run against his record. His response was to stay at home, keep his head down, and concentrate on running the city. It worked remarkably well.

The problem analyses begun by Frederick Hayes in the budget bureau six years previously were beginning to produce substantive results. The budget bureau analysts were themselves seeded in policymaking or managerial jobs throughout the operating agencies, and the second-term commissioners and administrators were, for the most part, willing to make use of their data. Probably most important, Hayes's successor, Edward Hamilton, had been promoted to deputy mayor in 1971 and was anxious to orchestrate a broadly gauged management improvement program. Andrew Kerr, who headed the budget bureau's project management staff recalls presenting Hamilton with a year's

---

left the welfare rolls to take employment did so without the benefit of public daycare programs, and by the 1970s almost three-quarters of lower-income married women were working—again without the benefit of government daycare. But for welfare recipients, the burden of finding a job and arranging personal affairs to accept employment was shifted almost totally to the government agencies.

research on management improvement opportunities cutting across almost all
the agencies in the city:

Hamilton took it all in almost immediately, but he crossed out the "Operations Improvement" title I had written on the plan and named it "Productivity," and he insisted the
program be announced publicly. My instinct would have been to start working and not
tell anyone what was going on until we had some solid gains to report. Ed wanted to be
out front from the very beginning to increase the pressure on the agency heads.

By the end of the year, the program was fully operating and packaged for
maximum marketing impact. Each quarter, City Hall negotiated a series of
quantitative productivity improvements with the agency heads: so many miles
of sewer pipe laid; so much improvement in housing inspections per worker; a
drop in the cost of issuing a photo ID card for a welfare client. The objectives
were announced publicly, and the results were monitored by a central productivity staff in City Hall. At the end of the quarter, City Hall published each
agency's progress and ranked the agency heads according to their level of
achievement: so many targets made; so many missed.

The publicity attached to the program galvanized even the most ob-
streperous administrators. The productivity concept was catchy and compre-
hensible, and, for once, Lindsay had a slogan he could stand behind without offending anyone. Even the unions had to concede that productivity was a basic
objective of city employment, and they participated in labor-management
councils to seek out productivity savings.

The idea caught on around the country. Other municipalities came to New
York to study the city's program. The federal government organized a National
Commission on Productivity. In 1973 there was a national conference for state
and local governments on productivity, at which the New York City program
was the prime exhibit. And while the publicity from the program was almost all
good, there were solid administrative achievements to back up the marketing.

Sanitation

Sanitation was one of the disaster areas of Lindsay's first term. There were
six different commissioners, and the incompetent response to the great 1969
snowfall exposed a department in serious trouble. The persistent problem was
fleet maintenance—the men couldn't pick up the trash if the trucks weren't
working—but there were serious problems in the scheduling and supervision of
the collection operations as well.

Fleet maintenance was carried out by mechanics scattered among the department's sixty-seven district garages and in two central repair shops—one in
Queens, and a smaller one on Staten Island. Preventive maintenance schedules
were almost never followed; so many trucks were always out of service that district superintendents would refuse to release trucks that were working. There
were no job tickets or time standards, inventory controls were haphazard or
nonexistent (trucks could be out of service for months waiting for parts), the
division of work between the district garages and central shops was hazy, and
supervision was poor. A time study of mechanics at the Queens central repair

shop showed that almost half their time was spent not working; late starts, early quits, and group gatherings were common. Another study showed that most repairs at the shops cost more than outside contractors would have charged—sometimes twice as much more. In some cases, it would have been cheaper simply to buy new parts. In 1970, 38 percent of the collection trucks were out of service on an average day, despite the money spent modernizing the fleet (a year-old truck that has never been maintained is an old truck). Fifty-five percent of the city's mechanical sweepers were out of service throughout 1970, and in some districts more than half of all equipment was inoperable most of the time. The downtimes meant that some seventeen hundred sanitationmen were effectively immobilized every day.

The situation in the cleaning and collection operation itself was only marginally better. The men worked hard while a truck was on its route, but the routes were not carefully designed, so collections totals could vary erratically. The superintendents had considerable flexibility in assigning trucks and manipulating routes but relied almost solely on their own intuition and experience in doing so. A good superintendent could make an enormous difference, but there was no systematic effort to distinguish between good supervisors and poorer ones on the basis of performance criteria.* Although refuse totals varied substantially and consistently, depending on the day of the week—Mondays, for example, were always the heaviest day because of Sunday papers and the weekend backlog—shifts were scheduled evenly through a six-day work week, regardless.

The appointment of Jerome Kretchmer to head the Environmental Protection Administration was in many respects a daring one. Kretchmer was a politician on the make, had no administrative experience, and was being appointed to an agency that was viewed as demanding a fairly high level of technical expertise. However, the politician's style served well: Kretchmer instinctively paid flattering attention to the front-line workers and established good relations with DeLury. For a brief period Kretchmer himself served as sanitation commissioner, then appointed Herbert Elish, a lawyer who had been deputy EPA administrator for about a year. Elish was well-briefed on sanitation problems and had developed good relations with DeLury. He also had the advantage that project management staff had been studying the maintenance operation for more than a year and McKinsey consultants had thoroughly analyzed productivity problems in cleaning and collection.

The first priority was the maintenance problem. The operation was reorganized into a system of borough garages, which were to perform all but the most routine operations. The central shops were closed, and tight controls were placed over the work performed in the district garages. Preventive maintenance schedules were established and adhered to, even though the schedules were strongly resisted by the district superintendents. (Until the maintenance

* A change in superintendents in a Brooklyn district, for instance, converted it from one of the worst districts to the best in the borough. In the year following the new appointment, the district collected on the average 31 percent more refuse per truck shift than the lowest district and 12 percent more than the next highest.

backlog was worked off, pulling trucks out of service for preventive maintenance made the out-of-service percentage even higher than it had been.) A scientific inventory replacement schedule was designed for the borough garages, and downtime dropped almost immediately by a third, simply because
of the greater availability of parts. Industrial time standards were installed for
the mechanics, and disciplinary procedures resuscitated for malingerers.
The mechanics responded with a series of job actions, but without the support
of DeLury's sanitationmen, were forced to yield to the new rules.

Collection problems were more diffuse but susceptible to the same approach. A new standard was developed for comparing route productivity based
on the density of refuse per curb mile (it takes longer to fill a truck in a residential neighborhood where refuse is lightly spaced than it does in a neighborhood of apartment buildings). Productivity teams analyzed all the collection
sections to find ways to increase work output, usually by readjusting routes to
ensure that all the trucks were fully loaded before the end of a shift. The old
"rat patrol" was reinstated—roving inspectors to catch malingerers. A system
was started for rating street cleanliness. An agreement was worked out with the
union to drop the old six-day manning system in favor of a "chart day" schedule
that roughly matched the work force to the pattern of refuse disposal: fifteen
percent more men were on the streets on the heavy days than previously, and
15 percent fewer on the lighter days.

Improved maintenance and better scheduling produced dramatic results.
Collection truck downtime dropped from 38 percent to less than 10 percent,
putting 450 more trucks on the street every day. Average repair times dropped
by factors of 20 to 70 percent. Tons collected per truck shift rose from 8.7 in
1970 to 10.3 in 1973. Missed collections fell from 3,200 in 1970 to virtually none
in 1973, even though 4 percent fewer trucks were officially assigned to regular
collection routes. The increases in productivity released hundreds of men for
special assignments. Streetsweeping miles doubled, and night collections were
virtually eliminated. A hundred men were assigned full-time to clean street
task forces in the main business areas, and another hundred men to community
cleanup days throughout the city. Lot cleaning was increased by almost 75 percent. Task forces were assigned to work with Model Cities groups, arrange
special pickups for rat control programs, or be available for virtually any high-
priority cleanup program.

The department was not above criticism. The productivity increases were
all used to finance high-visibility increases in effective service levels, instead of
reducing city spending, and at its peak, performance was probably still not up to
the standard set by the private cartmen. Elish's armistice with the sanitationmen's union prevented him from pressing the next logical productivity steps—
two-man trucks, instead of three, and experimental contracting-out. But for all
the reservations, Elish's turning around the department was an administrative
achievement of the first order. The methods used were perfectly straight-
forward applications of good management canons and seemed to vindicate—
although sadly late in the administration—Lindsay's original faith in business
methods as one solution to the city's problems.

Health Services

The sanitation department was one of the few city agencies that could be analyzed in classic industrial production terms, but even in the agencies where the fit with business models was not so close, there was considerable room for progress. The appointment of Gordon Chase, who was not a doctor, to head the city's troubled Health Services Administration was probably even more daring than the appointment of Kretchmer to EPA. Chase had originally been recruited to HRA from the federal government and had quickly made a reputation by cleaning up that agency's most serious financial disorders. Lindsay, despite the angry howls of the medical establishment, was convinced that HSA needed management at the top more than it needed medical expertise. Chase was a devotee of project management; his style was to break a program in discrete projects, which were pushed to completion by project managers operating outside the normal bureaucratic chain of command and tightly controlled from Chase's office by means of rigorous reporting systems.

One of the first priority problems when Chase took over the agency was lead poisoning in slum children. About half of all children between the ages of one and six have a constant craving—called "pica"—to ingest or chew solid material. Chips from peeling paint are naturally attractive to a crawling child with pica, and in slum buildings the chips are likely to contain lead. Lead-based paint has been illegal in New York since 1959 and has not been widely used since about 1940, but it still can be found in poorly maintained older buildings—especially where the paint has peeled two or three layers deep. Ingestion of even a small amount of lead-based paint over a relatively short period of time can lead to serious lead poisoning, chronic organ malfunction, retardation, or even death. There were an estimated 121,000 children between the ages of one and six in New York City in 1969 living in housing where they were likely to be exposed to lead-based paint. The health department calculated that 3,750 of the babies born in the slums each year would ingest extensive quantities of lead during the first six years of life, 1,000 would suffer irreparable brain damage, 185 would die of lead poisoning, and an unknown number would suffer from chronic cardiovascular problems, renal malfunction, or other diseases. The problem had long been known to the health department, but despite the pressures of community activists and crusading journalists, nothing had ever been done about it.

Chase set a precedent of sorts by meeting directly with the lead poisoning activists and inviting them to help design a program response. After a series of meetings and reports, he committed himself to examine the entire universe of exposed children; to provide medical treatment where a blood test showed more than 60 micrograms of lead per milliliter of blood; to inspect the living quarters of the positive cases; and if there were lead-paint walls, to ensure that they were covered either by the city's emergency repair program or by the landlord.

Chase delivered substantially as promised. He created a new Bureau of Lead Poisoning, reporting directly to himself, headed by a crusading young doctor and an aggressive project manager. Characteristically, the program was off the ground before Chase received budgetary authorization: Chase counted on high visibility and rapid success to overcome bureaucratic obstacles. A detailed weekly reporting system pinpointed the name of each employee in the project, and performance on lower levels improved remarkably (the rate of apartment inspections per sanitarian, for instance, jumped from about one a week to about four a day almost immediately). The program was not without its problems: Cooperation with the emergency repair program was never totally satisfactory; hospital clinics carried a much smaller share of the testing load than Chase would have preferred; and there were continual budget problems. Lead-painted walls were not extirpated from the city, as the more hopeful activists would have wished, but the universal screening was delivered on schedule, the follow-up was reasonably comprehensive, and the public education implicit in the program had a decided impact. The incidence of lead poisoning found in the clinics dropped from 3 percent positive samples in 1970 to just 1 percent in 1972. The results were considerably short of perfection, but when measured against the years of hand-wringing inactivity that had preceded Chase's arrival at the agency, it was a most impressive performance.

With complaints about his lack of medical background effectively quelled, Chase began to apply the project management style to one program after another. Treatment for drug addicts was an area in which Lindsay's first-term policies had been a decided failure. The city had committed itself to building a network of drug-free residential treatment centers, but the programs proved difficult to organize and either ineffective or fiercely expensive. The few successes seemed to last only so long as the addicts were in residence at the centers; and the city clearly couldn't afford perpetual housing for its armies of addicts.

The solution that appeared most promising was methadone maintenance. Methadone was a synthetic opiate that relieved heroin craving with oral administration. Compared to heroin, it was relatively long-lasting—one dose would be good for three or four days. The concept was pioneered by two doctors associated with Beth Israel Hospital, Vincent Dole and Marie Nyswander, who had been claiming for several years a high rate of success with small groups of carefully programmed addicts. The advantage of the method was that the addict could hold a job and live with his family, gradually adapting to the "straight" world while receiving methadone twice weekly at a treatment center.*

---

* The claims made by the most devoted of methadone's adherents were almost certainly inflated. Methadone, particularly when injected, apparently provides a most satisfactory high. The successes claimed by Dole and Nyswander were reasonably well-documented but were achieved with a stable group of addicts who were strongly motivated toward cure. There was no reason to expect similar results from a broad sample of addicts. The advantage of methadone, in the final analysis, is that once it had achieved "wonder drug" status in the public mind, it allowed the United States to adopt a drug maintenance strategy for large numbers of addicts, which was arguably more sensible—and certainly cheaper—than the other approaches that had been tried and had failed up until that time. The advent of multiple-drug abuse in the 1970s has gradually made methadone a less relevant response to addiction problems.

Once the city had made a decision that methadone seemed the most appropriate approach for large-scale programs, Chase's project managers had a program launched in a matter of weeks—again, long before formal budgetary approval. City and state funding followed action. Four thousand addicts were in treatment by the end of the first year, 11,500 by 1972, and 40,000 in 1973—by far the largest methadone program in the country. The success was far from unqualified. The long lines of addicts queuing up for their methadone often created problems in the neighborhoods where clinics were opened. Some of the immense new amounts of methadone being dispensed in the city found its way onto the black markets. Few of the addicts seemed really to be cured; for many, methadone was simply the path of least resistance: too strung out to work or steal to support their habit, they accepted methadone as the next best alternative. But the criticisms go more to the claims originally made for methadone than to the operation of the program. Chase's virtue was that he didn't lose his way in the endless philosophical debates that had so strangled most other treatment agencies. The city had declared itself in favor of methadone programs on a large scale and, under Chase, the programs were developed, implemented, and administered with dispatch and efficiency.

There seemed to be few health programs to which the project management approach could not be effectively applied. The vital statistics section was completely reorganized and automated. The time to issue a birth certificate was reduced from eight weeks to one. Programs were mounted against sickle cell anemia, hypertension, and alcoholism. The rat control program was made to work more effectively than ever before: Alleys and cellars were cleaned out, an agreement with the sanitation department ensured that refuse was carted away, rat holes were poisoned and sealed. Reported rat bites dropped 40 percent in two years, even with a tighter reporting system. The new abortion program was developed over a short time with no major mishaps. After riots in the city's jails in 1970, HSA took over a scandalously deteriorated prison health program; two years later the program was cited as one of the few prison health bright spots in the country.

The flaws in Chase's approach were the obverse of its virtues. The project management style most naturally lent itself to creating new programs or expanding old ones at a time of considerable budgetary stringency. When an energetic executive mounts programs quickly and efficiently to meet widely perceived public needs, few mayors will resist on monetary grounds. It was also not a style that was easily institutionalized. Chase made an effort in his last year in office to absorb the project management system into the ongoing operations of the various health agencies but had only marginal success. But the criticisms don't detract from Chase's achievement. In four years he converted one of the most consistent non-performers among city agencies into one of the administration bright spots.

Welfare

Despite all the criticisms emanating from the state Welfare Inspector General, by about 1972 the city had begun to get a grip on its runaway welfare system. The application form was redesigned to present a more complete picture of a client's resources, and Ginsberg's declaration system was modified to require documentary evidence of a client's financial claim—rent receipts, bank books, birth certificates for the children. The eligibility decision was removed from the front-line worker, and an overnight waiting period was installed for non-emergency cases to ensure that the case file had been properly reviewed and aid accurately computed before a grant was awarded. Specialized teams were created to handle new applications to allow better scheduling of the work flow, and industrial engineers redesigned the centers to create a more orderly flow of clients. Breaking the centers into clearly defined worker and client areas prevented clients from hovering over the shoulders of workers, rooting through files, or intimidating clerks and supervisors. The entire case closing operation was computerized and reallocated to a central case closing unit. A process that had averaged sixty days when performed manually was reduced to only 21 days, including a mandatory fifteen-day waiting period that allowed a client to request a fair hearing after being notified that his case was being closed.

The addict caseload was assigned to specialized worker groups, and a computerized central registry of addicts prevented duplicate applications at different centers. In most parts of the city, addicts and employable-singles cases— the cases that accounted for a disproportionate share of ineligibility and fraud— were organized into separate welfare centers so closer control could be maintained. By 1973 each addict on welfare was registered in an approved treatment program, and his attendance was regularly monitored. Backlogs were sorted out and aged, and an overtime crew worked off the backlogs over a period of months so new work could be properly scheduled. Output per worker rose by about 12 percent between 1972 and 1973. Disciplinary procedures for employees were revived and decentralized, with particular emphasis on lateness and absenteeism. Between 1972 and 1973 the welfare agency moved from worst lateness and absence record in the City to the second-best.

The most immediate effect of the new procedures was on caseloads. The tighter controls on applications increased rejection rates, and case closings rose sharply, from a low of 1.66 per thousand cases in 1971 to 2.19 in 1973 and 2.45 in 1974. The rise in closings related almost entirely to agency administrative actions, indicating the more stringent standards that were being applied. The year 1973 saw the first year-to-year decline in welfare rolls in more than a decade and the first reduction in total welfare costs in more than twenty years. The caseload drop was partly explicable by demographic and economic trends, but the sharpest declines were in the categories of single employables, where the city had concentrated most of its management attention.

By 1974 a study by the Citizen's Budget Commission noted the enormous amount of work yet to be done but concluded there had been significant progress. The centralized case-closing system was singled out as a "cost-saving process achieved by good system design and speedy implementation," while the agency's new error accounting and management reporting system was praised as an instance where an agency "dared to set up a system which spotlights the problems and failures and thus raises the specter of doing something about them." Politically, the caseload decline was an enormous relief. During the entire 1973 mayoral campaign, welfare was barely mentioned as a major issue.

Police

Patrick Murphy was appointed police commissioner upon the sudden resignation of Howard Leary in 1970. Murphy was a former New York City policeman who had served as commissioner in Syracuse, Washington, D.C., and Detroit. He had a national reputation as a police expert and was known as a martinet. His immediate problem was to restore the force's integrity. A series of articles in *The New York Times* had exposed widespread corruption at all levels in the force, ranging from the acceptance of small favors from shopkeepers to systematic narcotics rackets. Lindsay appointed an investigation panel, the Knapp Commission, in the wake of the exposés. The commission hired policemen as undercover agents and documented a pervasive laxity toward the problem reaching all the way to Lindsay's office.*

To Murphy corruption was merely an aspect of overall management. A department with strong accountability, from first-line supervision right to the top, could not have a major corruption problem. He stressed from the outset that supervisors would be held responsible for their men's wrongdoing. If there was widespread cooping on the third shift, the precinct commanders would be disciplined. Captains would answer for the corruption of their men. Precincts filled out corruption questionnaires: Where was corruption most likely to occur? How much money was probably involved? What were they doing about it? Commanders were furnished with corruption "shopping lists" to jog their imaginations.

There was a 90 percent turnover in the ranks above captain during the first two years of Murphy's tenure, and virtually every top-ranking officer in the force resigned or was forced to retire. The "system," the tradition of lockstep promotions based primarily on seniority, was broken, possibly irrevocably. The impact on corruption cannot be measured precisely, but most observers agree that it was profound. The truly dishonest policeman would still find plenty of opportunities for graft and extortion, but the complacent self-protectiveness of the bureaucracy that made corruption seem part of the normal pattern of business was no longer available as a shield.

Murphy's managerial emphasis reached beyond exposing corruption and complacency. The precinct consolidation plan that the administration had been forced to drop in 1967 was quietly put into effect, and seven of the eight precincts originally scheduled to be closed were shut down with no adverse public reaction. The four-platoon system, which had never been effectively implemented, was installed throughout the city, and by 1972 more than 50 per-

---

* The Knapp exposures were a major political embarrassment for Lindsay, and in some ways an ironic one. He had fought hard to get the Knapp Commission authorization through the Board of Estimate—after the board turned the commission down twice. Corruption had simply not been a priority with Leary. Lindsay's first-term concentration on changing the nature of the police response (see Chapters III and IV) absorbed whatever reforming energies that had gone into the department.

cent of the available patrol force was on duty during the high-crime hours. The city pioneered in experiments with anticrime patrols, plainclothes decoys and team policing, which attempted to combine the best of the old beat system with the increased speed and range available from motorization and technical advances. A civilianization program was pushed, releasing several hundred uniformed men from desk duty. Warrant issuance was automated, saving thousands of hours of clerical and uniformed time. Central booking of prisoners reduced the amount of overtime spent to process arrests.

Murphy's record was always controversial. He was probably cordially hated by the men in the front ranks and detested by the old-line officers, who saw his two-year-long bloodletting among the top brass as needlessly cruel and destructive of the force's morale and reputation. He was worshipped by many of the younger officers, for whom he cleared away the encrustations of decades. Not all of his innovations were successful. A much-publicized new duty chart that was installed in 1972 after fierce resistance by the union had to be retracted three years later—to provide extra training it reduced patrol hours more than the city could afford. (Changing the schedule back also met with the fierce resistance of the union.) He was never able to outface the union on the installation of one-man patrol cars. But he was unquestionably an innovator and a strong manager, and he restored a level of discipline and control in the agency that had been missing for a number of years.

Perhaps significantly, New York City's reported crime rate dropped much faster than the national average during Murphy's tenure—although the city was acknowledged to have one of the best reporting systems in the country. Its place among the major cities dropped from second in 1966 to nineteenth in 1972. Whether crime statistics have anything at all to do with the quality of police work is very much open to question, although neither Murphy nor the mayor was reluctant to cite the figures.

Other Agencies

Under the goad of the productivity program, virtually all city agencies were focusing on quantitative measures of achievement. The parks department began to report on the number of benches replaced, shelters repainted, and playgrounds rehabilitated. Meter readings per man-day rose in the water department. Lateness and absenteeism records improved throughout the city. The fire department reduced its out-of-service rates on motorized equipment, introduced smaller hoses, and began its "adaptive response" system to allow smaller equipment responses to specific types of alarms. In most of the larger agencies, vacation schedules were redrawn to reduce overtime expenditures during the summer months and achieve more level staffing throughout the year. The finance administration computerized its cash-flow management program and began to earn interest on overnight deposits. Andrew Kerr took over the Housing and Development Administration in 1972 and broke through the agency's worst bottlenecks. The Maximum Base Rent notices for landlords were finally produced on time—Kerr scrapped the agency computer system and used teams of clerks with programmable calculators to get out the notices.

The housing construction program broke out of its long stagnation. The combined totals of new public and publicly aided housing completed rose from its low point of 4,231 units in 1970 to an average of 12,705 units in each of the next four years. In 1973 construction was started on more than 19,000 new Mitchell-Lama units, an all-time high.

The productivity program had an ample measure of flimflam. Agency heads would be careful to establish goals that they were sure of meeting, even if that meant understating reports of past performance. The mayor's office was more interested in progress reports than in tracking down inflated claims: If goals turned out to be too ambitious, they could be changed or shifted to targets that could be accomplished more easily; and again, many of the targets measured effectiveness rather than productivity. Painting more park benches was a true productivity increase only if city spending didn't rise. What the city needed most of all was to increase output and reduce staff simultaneously.

While there is no doubt that the city's rhetoric outran its performance, much of the performance improvement was real, and the change in rhetoric itself was enormously important. During Lindsay's first administration, the city seemed to be committing itself to solve overwhelming problems of race and inequality, to bridge social divisions that arose from long-term trends of immigration and suburbanization, and somehow to reverse secular economic tides. Such overarching goals made for round phrases and ringing speeches but were of little use in deciding what to do on any particular day. Hamilton's insight was to focus the administration on the achievable and the mechanical, simply to make the city run better, and to clothe the refocusing with a rhetoric that sounded every bit as grand as any that had gone before.

Respite

Nineteen seventy-three was John Lindsay's last year in office and the first in which events, on the whole, began to break right for the administration. The emphasis on management improvement was paying dividends that the public could see and appreciate. The streets were obviously cleaner. The welfare rolls actually dropped, although few people had placed much credence in the Mayor's "zero-growth" order. Crime rates were dropping; addiction seemed possibly to be coming under control. The federal government took the first step toward assuming a larger share of the welfare burden by undertaking responsibility for payments to the aged, blind, and disabled. The new program meant that—at least temporarily—New York City's troublesome addict caseload would become a federal responsibility. The capital construction program was moving forward strongly, and there was a dramatic upgrading of the city's stock of schools, hospitals, police stations, fire houses, and libraries. New air-conditioned subway cars were coming on line. The innovative theater district zoning techniques pioneered by the City Planning Commission were paying off in a brighter, more varied, and exciting downtown.

The economy turned up again during the 1972–73 fiscal year, seeming to bear out the hopes of the optimists who had prepared the city's spending plans. Business activity in 1973 was at its highest level since 1969, and unemployment in the city dropped from 7 percent to 6 percent, a drop sharper than in the rest of the country or in New York State. Black unemployment in the city was only 7.2 percent—decisively below the national average of 8.9 percent. With the economic upturn, revenues from the various city taxes firmed. State aid remained almost flat with the drop in welfare spending and the restrictive state budget, but federal receipts jumped by 34.1 percent—more than $500 million—as the new revenue-sharing program overlapped with the last year of open-ended social services funding. Budget director David Grossman was able to close the budget books without making use of the $100 million standby borrowing authority granted by the legislature. RANs outstanding were reduced from more than $1.1 billion to less than $900 million, and $152 million in budget notes were paid off, reducing the outstanding balance to $308 million. It was the first time since Lindsay's first year in office that there had been a year-to-year reduction in short-term debt.

Lindsay, Grossman, and Beame began an intensive campaign to make believers out of the financial community—particularly the out-of-town bond buyers. Personalized tours of the city's new computer facilities, visits to the new sanitation maintenance shops, chart presentations detailing construction starts and welfare caseload controls, demonstrations of the overnight cash flow management system, and explanations of the new algorithms for scheduling housing and health inspections—delegations of businessmen were given the full treatment and came away impressed. City managers were as articulate, intelligent, and committed as any in their own companies: The problems were harder to solve, so it took longer to show results. The bond-rating agencies concurred: At the end of 1972 Moody's Investor Service announced it would move the city's rating back up to "A", citing its "amazing resiliency." Standard & Poor's followed in 1973. Interest rates on city borrowings dropped to their lowest point in six years.

As the 1973 mayoral campaign unfolded, criticism of Lindsay's administration was distinctly muted. There was considerable editorial praise for the new financial ratings. The Citizens' Budget Commission cautiously praised the new productivity programs. Democratic candidate Albert Blumenthal drew attention to Kerr's "first-rate work" at HDA. Even Beame conceded that "Lindsay could go anywhere if he'd do the kind of job he's been doing for the last eight months." Welfare was no longer in the headlines. There were no riots. Even union militancy showed some signs of moderating. Magazines began running nostalgic articles on the tone and style of the Lindsay years. John Lindsay could go out on a high note.

VIII. *The Lindsay Balance Sheet — I*

JOHN LINDSAY'S TWO administrations were periods of shattering change for the city. Welfare rolls and public dependency soared, particularly in the first term. Racial divisions became acute. Employee relations were marked by almost unrelieved bitterness, while wages and pensions grew faster than ever before. As the costs of operating the city spiraled out of control, taxes were raised almost continuously, and the city was in a state of permanent fiscal crisis. Despite the brief flowering of good feeling during Lindsay's last year in office, most New Yorkers placed the lion's share of the blame for their increasingly desperate straits squarely on Lindsay and his liberal theorizing. The years before his accession to office, particularly the decade of the 1950s, began to appear as a golden age of calm and stability. The election of Abraham Beame as mayor in 1973, so different from Lindsay in every obvious way—manner, speech, dress, appearance, background—was a patent rejection of the policies that had apparently brought the city to the brink of chaos.

Unquestionably, a mayor is accountable for his administration, and the condition of the city before and after his term of office is the most obvious measure of his performance. But the period of Lindsay's mayoralty was a time of immense change for cities across the nation. To construct a balance sheet for his administration that is both accurate and fair, the events in New York must first be disentangled from the national trends. To the extent that the symptoms of decline outpace those elsewhere, one may reasonably look to the city administration for the source of the trouble; to the extent that the city's problems mirror national trends, one must look for more general causes.

This chapter and the one following will attempt to evaluate the Lindsay record in the key areas of spending control, finance, management, race relations, and government reform. None of the judgments offered is intended to be conclusive. Although there is a fair amount of data available to construct intercity comparisons for growth in employee compensation, welfare rolls, and developments in debt utilization and pension finance, the wide differences from city to city in employment, accounting, and management practice make precise

analysis very difficult. The data are sufficient, however, to be strongly sugges-
tive—particularly, when the emphasis is on identifying the direction and ap-
proximate magnitude of trends rather than on making specific year-to-year,
city-by-city comparisons. In the areas of race relations, management reform,
and government reform, of course, the argument moves quite outside the
realm of data; where opinions rule, the best that can be hoped is that they are
based on a reasonable understanding of the underlying problems.

In some respects the conclusions reached run counter to the conventional
view of the Lindsay administration. For instance, trends in employee compensation during the Lindsay years, although high in comparison to the private sector, were well within the normal range for other large cities, even when reasonable allowances are made for improvements in pensions and fringe benefits.
Similarly, growth in the welfare rolls was very close to the national average, although the growth came earlier in New York City. The heavy burden of local
social welfare costs borne by city taxpayers is more the result of state reimbursement policies than of local profligacy. On the other hand, the Lindsay administration undertook major new spending commitments in health and higher
education that were of considerable consequence in building the continuing
deficits that underlay the eventual fiscal crisis. It was also during Lindsay's second term that the city began the wholesale reliance on short-term debt that ultimately brought it to grief. Finally, in the area of city management, the Lindsay record is probably very much better than he is usually given credit for; but
in the areas of race relations and government reform, the judgment here is
that Lindsay was much less successful than he himself must have hoped upon
taking office.

SPENDING: WAGES, PENSIONS, AND FRINGE BENEFITS

Wages

It is generally conceded that Lindsay was, as *Fortune* magazine put it, "a
pushover" for the city unions. Certainly, city employees made greater relative
gains during the Lindsay years than private sector workers. When the real (constant-dollar) salary increases for a city patrolman are compared to the increases
awarded a selection of seven categories of private-sector employees during the
period 1965–70, the patrolman's increases outpace every private-sector category but one (keypunch operator). More importantly, during the inflationary
period 1970–76, the patrolman's real salary still increased by 10.3 percent,
while five of the seven private-sector titles actually lost ground. Similar comparisons can be drawn from a survey of public and private clerical employees
carried out by the city's Office of Labor Relations. An entry-level clerk improved his real income by 10.4 percent from 1965 to 1973 and continued to
make gains during the high inflationary period in the early 1970s, while private-
sector clerical workers began to suffer real wage losses.

To some extent the disproportionate wage gains by municipal workers were
necessary to make up for years of low wages. In 1965 the average teacher in
New York City earned $5,300 per year and a policeman with three years on the

force earned $8,483, while the average construction worker earned $11,200. But the traditionally lower wage scale in the public sector could be at least partly justified by greater job security and generally richer pensions and fringe benefits available to government workers. In any case, by 1974, in most titles where comparisons are available, city wages had outstripped those in the private sector, while fringe and retirement benefits had, if anything, moved ahead even faster. Clearly, if Lindsay's bargaining performance is compared to that of bargainers in the private sector, he was the pushover his critics claim him to have been.

But it is also reasonable to measure Lindsay's performance by that of mayors in other large cities. Public-employee unionism advanced in giant strides during the Lindsay years, not only in New York City, but all across the country. For example, in 1968, the year of the New York sanitation strike, there were sanitation strikes in at least ten other United States cities. And since governmental activities tend to increase in times of adversity, public-sector union demands were much less constrained by economic recession than those of their private-sector counterparts;* salaries, benefits, and working conditions improved sharply everywhere. If New York City's compensation trends are compared to those of the nation's other large cities, quite a different picture of the city's collective bargaining performance emerges. Changes in employee wages in New York and the rest of the nation's ten largest cities (by 1966 populations)

Change in Average Salaries, 1966–73: Common Municipal Functions[1]

	1966			1973		
RANK	CITY	AVERAGE SALARY	RANK	CITY	AVERAGE SALARY	% CHANGE
1	Los Angeles	$8,836	1	Washington, D.C.	$14,668	95.2
2	New York	8,090	2	Detroit	14,137	91.2
3	Chicago	7,523	3	Los Angeles	13,933	57.7
4	Washington, D.C.	7,511	4	Chicago	13,324	77.1
5	Detroit	7,393	5	New York	13,135	62.3
6	Philadelphia	6,505	6	Philadelphia	12,389	90.5
7	Cleveland	6,123	7	Cleveland	11,535	88.5
8	Houston	5,834	8	Dallas	9,559	73.4
9	Dallas	5,456	9	Houston	9,540	63.5
10	Baltimore	5,453	10	Baltimore	8,892	63.1

[1] Cities vary widely in the tasks that they undertake. To facilitate intercity comparisons, the Bureau of the Census collects data on municipal common functions—police, fire-fighting, sanitation, highways, sewerage, parks and recreation, libraries, and financial administration. The data must be used with caution. Because accounting practices vary so widely from city to city, the census bureau has reconstructed a common set of accounts from the various city financial reports. As a result, it is difficult to tie the census data back to specific developments in a single city. With all their flaws, the data are the best available, and it would seem reasonable to use them to identify longer-term trends. The trends shown are consistent with data compiled by the City Office of Labor Relations or by the municipal unions.

* The insulation of public employees from economic recession is, of course, only relative, although it was the source of much concern to private-sector observers around 1975. In fact, it seems merely to take longer for economic conditions to work their way through to the public sector. City workers, for example, have accepted substantial real cuts in income since the fiscal crisis.

can be seen in the table on page 173.

Clearly, when compared to municipal workers in other large American cities, New York City's workers lost ground. Average salaries slipped from second place to fifth, and the percentage increase during the entire period was ninth lowest of the ten cities.

The figures in the preceding table understate the degree of New York City's slippage. New York City's living costs were the fastest-growing in the country during most of the period; if employee wages are deflated to take account of cost-of-living differences, the wage gap between New York employees and the higher-paying cities on the list grows even wider.

1973 Average Salaries in Effective Dollars*
Common Municipal Functions

RANK	CITY	AVERAGE SALARY	% DIFFERENCE FROM NEW YORK
1	Washington, D.C.	$14,104	+24.6
2	Los Angeles	13,933	+23.0
3	Detroit	13,593	+20.0
4	Chicago	12,812	+13.2
5	Philadelphia	12,028	+6.2
6	New York	11,323	—
7	Cleveland	11,199	-1.1
8	Houston	10,600	-6.4
9	Dallas	10,394	-8.2
10	Baltimore	8,892	-21.5

* Effective salaries are calculated from an index derived from the U.S. Bureau of Labor Statistics Intermediate Budgets for Families of Four in U.S. Metropolitan Areas. The family budgets are probably reasonably reflective of a city worker's actual purchases.

Another way of viewing New York salary progress is to measure the salary gains against the family budget requirements calculated by the U.S. Bureau of Labor Statistics. Labor leaders have long targeted their wage demands against the intermediate budget for a family of four.

1966–73 Average Salaries Compared to
Intermediate Family Budgets: Selected Cities

	EXCESS/ SHORTFALL: INTERMEDIATE BUDGET (percent)	
	1966	1973
New York	-26.9	-11.2
Los Angeles	-6.9	+10.8
Chicago	-26.4	+1.5
Detroit	-21.5	+11.4

Obviously, considering wages alone, New York City employees made substantial salary progress during the Lindsay years, but employees in comparable cities moved ahead even faster, both relatively and absolutely, and in some cases their progress was much faster.*

Pension Benefits

Pension benefits paid to employees increased rapidly during the Lindsay years and by 1973 were high in absolute terms—particularly, when compared to private-industry standards. The city retirement plans, in contrast to private plans, provided for many employees a three-tiered benefit—the pension payment, the social security payment, and, for teachers and uniformed employees, a payment from annuity funds maintained by city contributions, although the amount of the annuity payments typically were small.† The major cost difference between the city's plans and those in the private sector stemmed from the earlier retirements allowed municipal employees. Assuming that the average employee dies by age 75, a pension that starts at 55 will cost about twice as much as one that starts at 65, and the contributions will have to be spread over a shorter earnings period. Secondly, the city's plans are an add-on to social security benefits, while private employers typically take social security benefits into account in planning their pension programs; and finally, private plans normally set a ceiling on total pension benefits, whereas city employees with long service could accumulate annual pension and social security benefits worth more than their final salaries.

Even restricting comparisons to general employees who do not enjoy the extremely liberal early retirement benefits available to uniformed personnel, city pensions tend to be higher than those in the private sector, although the differences narrow when the private allowances are calculated to include the total available retirement package—pension, thrift plan, profit-sharing plans, and so on. The following are illustrative cases drawn from a 1976 survey.

---

* Salary progress can also be measured by changes in workload relative to real wages. Interestingly, educational workloads dropped substantially from 1965 to 1971, while real wages rose. In welfare and sanitation per-employee workloads rose, but not quite as fast as real wages. Police and fire workloads, on the other hand, rose substantially faster than real wages by every available measure. Unfortunately, there are no comparative data for other cities.

† Policemen, firemen, and sanitationmen received an annuity contribution of $261 per year, while an optional plan for teachers included a $400 annuity contribution—that is, the annuity contributions ranged between 1 percent and 2 percent of salary in 1975. Assuming that annuity contributions would be continued over fifteen years, the uniformed annuity accumulations would have a present value of about $2,900, with a 4 percent discount rate. That would be enough to purchase a twenty-year annuity of $213 per year. The teachers' annuity is a variable annuity plan—that is, one invested in common stock. Because of poor stock market performance, the fund's assets were worth less in 1975 than when the plan started. The importance of the uniformed forces' annuity plans has less to do with payments to beneficiaries than with the additional financial power that the funds gave the unions, because the city's contributions were paid to and administered by the respective unions. The total cost of annuity payments was $20 million per year in 1975, or 1.5 percent of pension contributions.

Total Retirement Allowance: Percentage of Final Salary, Including Social Security

ILLUSTRATION	A	B	C	D	E
Years of service	10.69	16.22	20.25	31.42	38.00
Final salary	$8,020	$11,390	$8,280	$12,725	$11,300
Age at retirement	63-0 mo.	58-7 mo.	61-0 mo.	55-9 mo.	63-10 mo.
% final salary paid New York City (city-wide employee)	42.1	58.6	73.6	88.6	106.0
AT&T	21.3	40.9	58.8	54.3	67.1
Con Edison	38.6	40.0	62.2	44.0	73.0
Exxon	25.3	44.9	62.6	57.5	82.9
Citibank	42.1	49.9	72.5	63.0	84.8
General Motors	48.4	53.8	77.8	70.3	93.0
Metropolitan Life Insurance Co.	31.3	35.3	54.1	46.5	64.6
Union Carbide	34.7	38.3	58.5	49.5	70.2

As the table shows, the city benefits are higher than those paid by any of the seven private employers in three of the five cases, while in cases A and C, the General Motors payments exceed the city's and Citibank's are closely comparable.

When New York City's plans are compared to those of other large municipalities, the differences are much less marked than the differences from private plans, as the next table shows. For one thing, the majority of municipal plans also include social security benefits as an add-on,* although rarely for uniformed employees as is the case in New York.

Comparing pension benefits from one city to another is complicated by the variety of provisions for continuance of benefits to survivors of the beneficiary. Many cities simply continue benefits to the surviving spouse as part of the basic plan, while others, such as New York, provide survivors' benefits only if regular benefits are first reduced by a specific factor. The table presents the benefit packages in terms of index numbers (New York = 100) to facilitate comparisons while at the same time accounting for the different survivors' options in the pricing of the plans.

* Public employees were originally excluded from social security. When Federal regulations were changed to admit public employees in 1951, most public pension plans were already of long-standing duration, so the addition of social security was viewed by public employee lobbyists as a method of increasing their benefits. The process in the private sector typically worked in the reverse: Pension plans were created only after employees had been covered by social security, so it was natural to include the federal benefits in targeting the total pension package. New York State and City employees joined the system in 1957. The average benefit payable at that time was about $81 per month. The social security benefit has become a truly significant aspect of the total retirement package, both in terms of cost and benefits, only since 1972, when Congress voted to link benefits payable (and therefore costs) to changes in the consumer price index. It is probably worth noting that inclusion of New York public employees in the system was not the doing of feckless politicians. The change was made by voter referendum after a previous referendum to integrate social security and pension benefits had failed.

Public Pension Benefits, 1975, Including Social Security

| ILLUSTRATION | GENERAL EMPLOYEES | | | TEACHER | SANITATION WORKER | POLICE / FIRE[1] |
	A	B	C	D	E	F
Years of service	16.22	32.93	43.23	31.50	20.77	20.00
Final salary	$8,280	$14,700	$20,150	$20,350	$12,263	$17,582
Age at retirement	61-0 mo.	62-10 mo.	65-0 mo.	55-0 mo.	55-6 mo.	49-0 mo.
New York City	100	100	100	100	100	100
Chicago	53	66	75	52	40	53/29[5]
Los Angeles	67	84	102	82	65	103
Newark	76	65	66	90	67	69
Philadelphia	124	108	100	104	112	111
San Francisco	112	99	100	86	85	—[3]
Baltimore	89	72	78	82	73	69[3]
Boston	55	65	69	51	37	65
Detroit	84	57	64	68	—[3]	—[3]
New Orleans	95	86	93	—[2]	51	92
New York State	99	78	87	80	80	85
Federal civil service	47	56	70	67	—[4]	—[3]

1. Excludes social security. 2. Not applicable. 3. Not eligible at this age. 4. Vested, but not payable until 62. 5. Police, 53; fire, 29.

As the table shows, the city's pensions are high when compared to most other municipalities, ranking either second or third in each category in which comparisons were drawn. On the other hand, New York City is clearly not the most generous granter of pensions in the country. Philadelphia takes that honor, while the pensions payable in San Francisco and New Orleans, and in certain categories in Los Angeles, are more or less comparable to New York's. Overall, the New York City pensions are about 15 percent higher than those paid by the state and from 16 to 33 percent higher than the median benefit package in each of the six categories in the table.

It is important to note, however, that the table tends to overstate the level of the New York City benefit with respect to certain other plans that have escalators built into their retirement programs.* The New York plans make no provision for regular increases—although the state legislature did approve a supplementation for low-pay retirees who retired before 1969. By contrast, Chicago's pensions have a 2 percent annual cost-of-living increase built into the basic plan, so that over the lifetime of a retiree, the payments will be considerably higher then the value of the first-year benefit shown on the table would indicate. The police and fire pensions in Los Angeles increase automatically whenever existing uniformed employees win a salary increase, so there are cases of current retirees earning more than three times their final salary. Federal pensions are linked to the consumer price index in such a way as to guarantee real income increases in times of high inflation: Whenever the consumer price index rises 3 percent, Federal pensions rise 4 percent. Thus, although

* The table understates New York's police and fire pensions to the degree that retirees will be able to collect social security at age 62, a benefit not available in the other cities.

federal pensions appear on the table to be low, with the current high inflation they are probably the most valuable and most expensive in the country.

Evaluating changes in employee pensions during Lindsay's administration also requires reference to the relative generosity of city benefits before he took office. Precise comparisons among a number of cities over time would be extremely difficult to construct, but a comprehensive comparative survey of city pensions was carried out in 1962 and is a useful benchmark—although the illustrative categories are, of course, not precisely the same as in the 1976 survey and methods of pricing necessarily differ in detail. The same index point system is used as on the previous table. Where there is a choice, the more liberal New York City pension option available is chosen.

Public Pension Benefits, 1962, Including Social Security

ILLUSTRATION	GENERAL EMPLOYEES		TEACHER	POLICE/FIRE
	A	B	C	D
Years of service	30–0	30–0	35–0	30–0
Final salary	$8,000	$5,400	$8,500	$8,000
Age at retirement	65–0	65–0	65–0	55–0
New York City	100	100	100	100
Baltimore	76	76	NA	NA
Boston	79	76	NA	105
Chicago	55	50	61	89
Dallas	55	50	NA	52
Detroit	56	57	67	70
Houston	73	67	NA	61
Los Angeles	76	76	NA	82
New Orleans	42	35	NA	NA
Milwaukee	72	72	NA	NA
Philadelphia	76	76	NA	75
San Francisco	76	76	NA	NA
Cleveland	NA	NA	NA	84
Washington, D.C.	NA	NA	NA	100
Illinois	NA	NA	61	NA
Massachusetts	NA	NA	79	NA
Pennsylvania	NA	NA	65	NA
Texas	NA	NA	46	NA
New York State	NA	NA	88	NA

NA: not applicable or not available.

It is clear from the table that New York offered higher benefits than any of the other public plans in three of the four categories surveyed. With respect to police and fire pensions, the Boston plan provided better benefits and Washington, D.C., the same. Strikingly, the difference between the New York benefit and the median benefit of the other plans surveyed ranges from 18 percent to 39 percent, slightly greater but very similar to the 16 to 33 percent difference from the median found in the 1975 survey.

Any comparisons among entities as infinitely variegated as pension plans are necessarily imprecise, but the reasonable conclusion seems to be that although New York's pension plans improved markedly during the Lindsay administration, the rate of improvement was not very much different from that in other cities. Indeed, if there is any tendency at all in the data, it is convergence. Details on private pension plans included in the 1962 survey are sketchy, but the gap between the city's plans and private plans appears likewise to have closed between the two surveys, suggesting the possibility of convergence with the private sector as well.

The fact that trends in the city mirrored those across the country does not necessarily mean that details of the city's new plans were not outrageous; but it does imply that outrageousness was a pandemic condition. Not coincidentally, the same type of action taken by the New York State legislature to cap public employee pensions in 1973 occurred at about the same time in statehouse after statehouse across the country as lawmakers finally took alarm at leapfrogging benefits and ballooning unfunded liabilities. The most important conclusion for the purposes of the present chapter, however, is merely that the slippage of salaries for New York's workers, compared to workers in other cities, was not made up by relative improvements in pension benefits. Relative salaries slipped while relative pension benefits about held their own.

Fringe Benefits

The final piece of an employee's total compensation package is the fringe benefit—time and leave benefits, health insurance, uniform allowances, and the like. By any standard—private industry or other governments—New York City's fringe benefits are very high, although the myriad detailed benefits make comparative pricing even more difficult than in the case of pensions. The next table presents estimates of the costs of various major fringe benefit categories as a percentage of base salary in selected titles.

Fringe Benefits as Percentage of Base Salary, 1975: Selected Titles

	BASE SALARY	% HEALTH AND OTHER*	% TIME AND LEAVE †	% TOTAL RETIREMENT ‡	% TOTAL
Senior clerk	$11,183	9.3	22.4	33.6	65.3
Nurse	15,467	7.5	29.6	31.4	68.5
Social worker	18,909	5.5	21.5	30.3	57.3
Sanitationman	15,731	8.1	27.8	32.4	68.3
Patrolman	17,458	7.8	32.9	49.4	90.1
Teacher	20,350	5.5	6.7	35.2	47.4

*Includes health insurance, welfare fund payments, and miscellaneous benefits.
† Includes vacation, sick leave, personal leave, and so on.
‡ Includes pension, social security, and annuity payments, if any.

Teachers' benefits appear lower than those of other employees because teachers receive no special vacation provision; they are employed on a ten-month basis and accommodate their personal vacations to the school schedule.

It should also be noted that the percentages of salary shown in the "Time and Leave" column do not represent cash payments to the employee, but are the costs that the city would incur if it paid for full coverage during an employee's absence. Presumably, in some positions, such as nurse, the post-coverage system fully accounts for permitted absences, so the time-and-leave percentages shown reflect fairly accurately the additional costs of providing substitute coverage. In other titles increased time-and-leave benefits will simply imply reduced coverage and represent a cost only in the theoretical sense of lost output.

The most comprehensive survey of municipal fringe benefits, using the same pricing system as in the table, shows that in the Northeast in 1975, total benefits for police averaged 50.6 percent of salary; for sanitation workers, 51.8 percent; and for general employees, 42.3 percent. The city benefits, in other words, were 78 percent higher for patrolmen, 32 percent higher for sanitationmen, and about 50 percent higher for general employees. The comparison tends to overstate New York's position, however, because the sample is predominantly one of small cities and towns: The great majority of jurisdictions in the survey have populations of ten thousand or less, and no municipality included in the Northeastern sample has a population of five hundred thousand.

Although comprehensive pricing data are not available to make a comparson of New York's benefits package to those of other large cities, inspection of surveys available in the city Office of Labor Relations shows that New York consistently provides substantially greater benefits in certain areas. Following is a brief item-by-item rundown.

▪ *Time and leave benefits.* New York's position is about average with respect to personal leave, sick leave, and holidays, but the city grants substantially more vacation—four weeks from the very first year of employment, compared to thirteen days for New York State and federal employees and two weeks in most other large cities. Pricing the extra vacation time at the cost of full coverage, it represents probably the most expensive benefit offered to city employees that is not normally found elsewhere. It is also a benefit of long standing; there were only minor changes in time-and-leave benefits during the Lindsay years.

▪ *Health insurance coverage.* The city's health insurance program tends to be more expensive than those in other cities because the city offers a wider choice of plans. The insurance is also noncontributory, a benefit granted in 1966. Elsewhere, a slim majority of other large cities require some employee contribution, commonly 25 percent of the cost of coverage for dependents. A further important difference in health coverage costs between New York and other cities, however, is represented by New York's payments to union welfare funds, amounting to $400 per employee in 1975. As late as 1975 New York's welfare fund programs were unique, although in more recent years they have begun to be adopted by other jurisdictions. The unions use the welfare fund allowances to purchase supplemental health and life insurance coverage (for example, dental and eyeglass coverage). Welfare fund payments were first negotiated by the sanitation union in 1963, were extended to other uniformed employees the following year, and covered virtually all city employees by 1967.

■ *Pension contributions.* Most cities assess employees between 4 percent and 6 percent of salary. New York's contribution rates were nominally higher, but the presence of ITHP (increased take-home pay) brought them down to an effective rate of .3 percent to 2.2 percent on the average. The ITHP was reduced since the fiscal crisis.

■ *Working hours.* The City's thirty-five-hour work week for white-collar employees is common among white-collar employers in the New York area, but work weeks tend to be between 37.5 and 40 hours in the rest of the country (but 33.25 hours in Nassau County). The forty-hour basic week for police is typical of the rest of the country, but the forty-hour week for firemen is not. Large-city firemen elsewhere have work schedules that average forty-two to fifty-six hours per week. Again, the preferred position of New York firemen is of long standing; the work schedule itself is written into the state constitution.

■ *Miscellaneous provisions.* Bizarre fringe benefits can be found in strong-union towns across the country—"hazardous" duty pay, time off for birthdays, intricately protective work rules, and the like—but New York seems to have a bigger and more oddly assorted grab-bag of extra fringes than anywhere else—summer hours, blood days for policemen, time off for civil service tests, uniform allowances for people who don't wear uniforms, a legislative presumption that any heart ailment suffered by a policeman or a firemen is presumed to have been a line-of-duty injury, and the like. (Some of the extra benefits—blood days and summer hours, for example—were modified or eliminated after the fiscal crisis.) With respect to the more commonly found miscellaneous benefits, however—shift differentials, overtime allowances, accumulation of sick leave—New York practice is generally in line with that found elsewhere. Benefits that New York does not provide but which are found in several other jurisdictions include unemployment insurance for laid-off workers and severance pay.

The cost of fringes exclusive of retirement benefits rose rapidly from 1966 to 1975, at an average annual rate of 20.8 percent. Most of the increase, however, was driven by changes in the cost of benefits already awarded: Medical costs rose sharply, and the value of time and leave benefits rose along with average salaries, which increased at the rate of 9.9 percent a year. The major new awards were the shift from 75 percent to 100 percent health insurance coverage and the extension of union welfare funds' coverage. Interestingly, during Wagner's last term, although salaries rose at an average rate of 4.4 percent, average fringe benefit cost rose by 24.2 percent a year—a rate higher than that of the Lindsay years and more than twice as high relative to salaries.

The most important question for the present chapter, however, is whether the total compensation package—fringe benefits, pensions, and salaries—for city employees rose at a rate under the Lindsay administration that outstripped the improvements won by employees in comparable jurisdictions. With all the imprecisions of the data, a fair reading of what is available would seem to indicate that New York employees merely maintained their relative position to large-city employees elsewhere, and it is not inconceivable that they lost ground. Salaries certainly slipped, when compared to the sharp improvements in other cities; pensions seem to have improved at about the same rate as elsewhere; and if fringes were higher in 1973 than probably anywhere else, they were also higher in 1966. Moreover, when due allowances are made for improvements in fringe benefits, they can barely compensate for the loss of position as a leader in basic pay. The most direct comparison that can be made with prevailing municipal wages reinforces this conclusion; by the end of the Lindsay administration, employees in key titles in neighboring communities, especially in Nassau County, were earning substantially more than city employees in basic pay and enjoyed pensions and fringes that in most respects equalled or exceeded those offered by the city.

Changes in Functional Expenditures

Finally, the impression that New York City's labor costs did not change at a significantly different rate from costs in other large cities is strengthened by comparing total cost changes in the census bureau's common municipal functions and public education—that is, the areas where New York's responsibilities most closely parallel those elsewhere and the areas where collective bargaining probably exercised the most influence over total costs.

Change in Per Capita Expenditure* for Common Municipal Functions: 1965–66 to 1973–74

	1965–66			1973–74		
RANK	CITY	AMOUNT	RANK	CITY	AMOUNT	% CHANGE
1	Washington, D.C.	$203	1	Washington, D.C.	$369	81.8
2	New York	138	2	Baltimore	290	150.0
3	Dallas	121	3	New York	233†	68.8
4	Baltimore	116	4	Detroit	228	121.4
5	Los Angeles	116	5	Cleveland	195	101.0
6	Detroit	103	6	Dallas	191	57.8
7	Philadelphia	98	7	Philadelphia	184	87.8
8	Cleveland	97	8	Los Angeles	174	50.0
9	Houston	91	9	Chicago	163	87.4
10	Chicago	87	10	Houston	111	22.0

*Census bureau cost figures do not allocate pensions, fringes, or debt service by function. Pension and fringe benefit costs have already been discussed; debt service is discussed in the next chapter.
†The staff of the Temporary Commission on City Finances suggest that the Census figures may underestimate New York's police and fire expenditures in 1973–74 by not properly including revenue-sharing allocations. If the TCCF staff is correct, police and fire expenditures would be about 20 percent higher and about that amount above the average for other cities. Total city per capita spending would rise from $233 to $253, and the percentage growth would change from 68.8 percent to 83.3 percent. The city would still rank third in per capita spending, but it would move from seventh place to sixth in rate of growth.

New York City's expenditures for common functions were high relative to other cities at the end of Lindsay's administration, but certainly no higher than before he took office, and the growth rate in per capita expenditure was lower than average. Analyzing the common function components, New York City's expenditures in 1973–74 appear about average in police, fire, parks, and financial administration, but from 50 percent to 75 percent higher than average in sanitation, sewerage, and libraries. (New York's average sanitation salaries are higher than almost anywhere else, and collections are scheduled more frequently; its sewage treatment system is far more elaborate than elsewhere; and its library system is much more extensive than in other cities.) New York ranks significantly below average in highway expenditure. Chicago, interestingly enough, manages to maintain its relatively low position in total spending by a very low rate of expenditure on sewerage and parks (sewage finance, like education expenditure, is handled by a special district), while spending on police, fire, sanitation, and highways tends to be about average. Washington, D.C. ranks first in six of the eight categories, often by substantial amounts.

A similar comparison for public education (excluding higher education) follows. Because central cities do not commonly provide education services, the comparisons, where appropriate, are with the expenditure incurred by the county government containing the core city.

Changes in Per Capita Expenditure for Public Education
1966–67 to 1973–74

	1966–67			1973–74		
RANK	CITY (*county*)	AMOUNT	RANK	CITY (*county*)	AMOUNT	% CHANGE
1	Los Angeles (Los Angeles)	$172	1	Washington, D.C.	$298	102.7
2	Detroit (Wayne)	156	2	New York	270	87.5
3	Washington, D.C.	147	3	Los Angeles (Los Angeles)	269	56.4
4	New York	144	4	Chicago (Cook)	267	118.9
5	Houston (Harris)	138	5	Detroit (Wayne)	256	64.1
6	Cleveland (Cuyahoga)	136	6	Cleveland (Cuyahoga)	242	77.9
7	Dallas (Dallas)	125	7	Baltimore	233	86.4
8	Chicago (Cook)	122	8	Philadelphia (Philadelphia)	218	83.2
9	Baltimore	121	9	Dallas (Dallas)	206	64.8
10	Philadelphia (Philadelphia)	119	10	Houston (Harris)	200	44.9

In this comparison, New York moves from fourth to second place on the tables, although in the 1973–74 fiscal year, the second through fourth-place cities are very closely bunched. Spending in New York rose about 10 percent faster than the average increase in the other cities. Per *pupil* expenditures in New York City, however, are considerably higher than elsewhere but are consistent with the spending patterns in New York State, which consistently spends twice the national average per pupil. (In 1975, for example, New York State spent $1 billion more on public education than California but educated a million fewer pupils.) The pattern long predates Lindsay and possibly relates to the longer tradition of generous State aid than elsewhere. Per pupil spending in immediately adjacent counties is typically substantially higher than in New York City.

Summarizing all the data presented in this section, there appears to be little warrant for the belief that the Lindsay administration was the unusual pushover for the municipal unions it is frequently alleged to have been. Real income for city workers rose much faster than for workers in the private sector, but the same phenomenon occurred in most other large cities. Detailed labor department surveys published in 1976 show that the discrepancies between public- and private-sector earnings in New York were about average. Nor is there much warrant for the fear expressed by the 1975 Temporary Commission on City Finances that increases in employee compensation were consuming resources that should properly have gone to finance service improvements. That is true, of course, in the trivial sense that compensation increases used money that could have been spent otherwise; it is not true in the sense that New York disproportionately reduced service levels to finance union wage settlements. As has been shown, changes in total employee compensation over the period were about average, and by 1974 the number of city employees per capita in the common functions was still somewhat above the average for other large cities.

To conclude that changes in employee compensation during the Lindsay administration were not substantially different from those elsewhere, however, is not to say that the city's collective bargaining performance was good. The long waiting lists for entry-level sanitation jobs, for instance, is a sure indication that salaries were higher than necessary to attract qualified candidates. Both Wagner and Lindsay should be seriously faulted for their tendency to allow so much of the compensation package to be pushed toward improvements in pensions and fringe benefits. Changes in pension formulas were made so frequently and so haphazardly as to defy the reconstruction of any coherent improvement plan. The payment of annuity and welfare funds to unions unduly enhanced union financial power and created a highly uneven and inconsistent benefit structure easily subject to abuse and probably inefficient in terms of the cost of the benefits actually delivered. From a management point of view, administration of the benefit programs became needlessly difficult, cost projections uncertain, and the calculation of collective bargaining changes was layered with complexity. Finally, the melange of benefits is confusing to the public and obscures true compensation levels.

But with respect to the narrow issue of Lindsay's success in controlling the labor costs of city government, the conclusions of a team of economists who studied the growth of city spending until 1971 would seem to apply to the entire Lindsay period:

With respect to [non-welfare] expenditure, and with respect to "common municipal functions," expenditures by the New York City government appear relatively "normal" in terms of both per capita level and growth rate. Labor costs, a focus of growing concern in all cities, also do not appear "abnormal" in New York City, as compared with other cities. Both the ratio of city government employees per resident and the average level of wages appear well within the normal limits.

In short, for all the rancor that engulfed municipal labor relations, and despite Lindsay's apparent ineptitude in dealing with the unions, overall changes in employee compensation appear to be not much different from those found anywhere else. The causes of the disproportionate increase in city costs will have to be sought elsewhere.

SPENDING: WELFARE, HIGHER EDUCATION, HOSPITALS

Although New York City's spending for common municipal functions and average employee compensation did not differ significantly from those in other large American cities, its level of spending on welfare (public assistance and Medicaid), higher education, and hospitals was virtually unique, whether measured by total spending or spending per capita. In fiscal year 1973–74 the city spent more than $4 billion—far more than any other city—on these three functions. About a third of the total cost—$1.3 billion—was financed by local taxes ($1.3 billion is roughly equivalent to all the local revenues collected from the sales tax and the personal and business income taxes.) On a per capita basis, only Washington, D.C., which doubles as a state government, exceeds New York City's rate of spending in these areas, and no other government comes close to the New York City level—$584 per capita in New York in 1973–74, compared to $105 in Detroit, $234 in Los Angeles, $89 in Chicago, and $76 in Philadelphia. Again, some analysis of national and state spending trends is required to separate accurately the responsibility of the Lindsay administration from other factors that were operating across the country.

Public Assistance Caseloads

The growth in welfare during Lindsay's administration was staggering, particularly during his first term. Caseloads grew at a rate of 27 percent a year in both 1967 and 1968, and expenditures grew by almost 52 percent in 1968 alone. In his first years as mayor, Lindsay was much criticized for defending rather than deploring the increases, and his first welfare commissioner, Mitchell Ginsberg, made no secret of his sympathies with the system's radical critics who were actively encouraging poor families to join the rolls and deliberately disrupting administrative processes. But defending a situation is different from causing it. Whatever the direction of Lindsay's sympathies, to blame his policies for the rapid increases in the rolls is to give him more credit for controlling events than was actually the case.

As the chart on caseload growth makes clear, for the entire period from 1960 to 1975, Aid to Dependent Children (ADC) cases* roughly quintupled in both New York City and the rest of the nation, although the growth occurred in somewhat different time sequences. The period of greatest divergence between the national and the New York City growth rates occurred between 1960 and 1965—that is, before Lindsay was mayor—when the city rolls grew about twice as fast as those in the rest of the country. The five years from 1965 to 1970 saw the most rapid growth period in the city (an average of 16.4 percent per year) but also an almost equivalent rate of growth (15.8 percent) elsewhere.

* The ADC comparison is used instead of total caseload because it is the largest and most controversial caseload category and the one most directly comparable from state to state.

From that point the national caseload continued to grow rapidly, although the city growth rate slowed down sharply. During Lindsay's entire eight years as mayor, in fact, the city ADC rolls grew an average 13.9 percent per year, a rate that was *slower* than the 14.6 percent average annual growth recorded in the rest of the country. By the end of the period, the percentage of the population on welfare in New York was not notably different from that in most other of the nation's largest cities and was lower than in many.*

ADC Caseload Growth, 1960–75: New York City, and United States
(thousands)

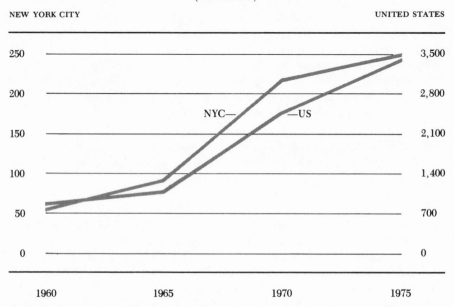

NEW YORK CITY   UNITED STATES

Comparisons between New York City and the rest of the state tell much the same story, for all the moralizing that issued from Albany during Lindsay's second term. From 1961 to 1968 the city's total assistance caseload grew by 275 percent while growth in the rest of the state was only 94 percent. During the next seven years, the situation almost exactly reversed: Rolls in the rest of the state grew by 254 percent, while the city's rolls grew by only 109 percent. The average annual growth for both the city and the state was very similar for the entire period: 15.8 percent for the city and 14.8 percent for the state. The rapid

* Data from early 1976 showed the following welfare dependency figures: St. Louis, 16.8 percent of the population; Baltimore, 15.6 percent; Philadelphia, 14.5 percent; Washington D.C. 14.2 percent; Boston, 14.2 percent; Newark, 13.2 percent; Detroit, 11.5 percent; New Orleans, 11.2 percent; New York 11.0 percent; Chicago, 10.8 percent. Interestingly, New York's unemployment rate was second highest among the cities shown. It should also be noted that the data are drawn from county areas for most of the cities, so extensive suburban areas are covered in most of the calculations. The central city welfare dependency must even be higher than the figures indicate.

growth in the rest of the state is the more interesting because it occurred during a period when the state and federal governments were taking a hard line on welfare growth and placing special emphasis on eligibility controls and case closings. Finally, although the administrative disorder in the city welfare centers was the stuff of legend, when the state carried out the first truly detailed eligibility audits in 1973, it was discovered that the error rates in the city and in the rest of the state were virtually identical—within a tenth of a percentage point of each other. The broad conclusion is inescapable: There were factors operating nationally to push up welfare caseloads from 1960 to 1975. They operated in New York City four or five years earlier than elsewhere, but there was not much difference in the total effects.

The reasons for the sudden national surge in welfare rolls are not well understood, although there seems to be considerable validity to the radical hypothesis that rolls were maintained at artificially low levels throughout the 1950s by arbitrary and unfair administrative practices. The black migration to the northern cities peaked in the 1950s, but there was very little growth in welfare. It was simply much harder to get on the rolls and much easier to be put off. If New York City had maintained the same acceptance and closing rates as were recorded in the 1950s,* the 1975 caseload would have been only about a third as high as it actually was. But maintaining those rates of acceptances and closings would have meant turning away hundreds of thousands of eligible people—the caseload was only about 11 percent ineligible in 1975, and half of the "ineligibility" stemmed from misclassification (for example, people who should have been on ADC were listed as disabled). Absent a drastic change in the underlying eligibility of applicants, it seems clear that much of the rapid growth in the rolls stemmed simply from the system's complying for the first time with its own rules.

There were other factors at work as well. A detailed study by the Rand Corporation identifies the welfare rights movement as a critical factor in inducing increased applications during the period of most rapid growth. Only about half of the eligible families in the city were on the welfare rolls in 1965, but in 1975 about two-thirds—and among Hispanics about three-quarters—of the eligible families were receiving welfare. At least in the poor neighborhoods, the stigma of receiving welfare seems to have been largely removed. Secondly, until 1969 grant levels were regularly increased by the legislature with strong support from the city: From 1964 to 1968 the annual grants increased 8 percent a year faster than the cost of living. Each increase in the standard made more families eligible and made welfare an increasingly attractive alternative to low-wage employment, particularly when the welfare benefits were combined with gen-

---

* Throughout the 1950s the city generally accepted about 50 percent of all applicants and closed four cases per thousand per month. Acceptances rose to 68 percent by 1965 and to 79 percent during the welfare rights drive in 1968. During the same period closings dropped to two per thousand. The drop in closings can be attributed both to the administrative disruption in the centers and the pressures of the rapid growth in applications (applications tended to be accompanied by angry applicants and therefore took first priority) and to a series of court decisions and administrative regulations that made the case-closing process much more time-consuming and complicated.

erous Medicaid entitlements. (A more recent study, in fact, suggests that a surprising number of families go on welfare simply to establish their eligibility for Medicaid). The change in the acceptance rates during Ginsberg's tenure— probably the most accurate measure of the extent of liberalization that took place—turns out to have been among the least important factors accounting for the growth, because acceptance rates had already reached high levels before he took office.

The growth in the rolls, then, resulted primarily from a national change in attitudes toward welfare on the part of legislators, administrators, and recipients.* The earlier impact of the shift in attitudes in New York City, as compared to other places, seems amply explained by the intensity of the New York welfare rights movement and the fact that the city instituted a number of procedures by agreement—for example, fair hearings before case closings— that were implemented only later by court mandate in the rest of the country. Of course, to the extent that Lindsay and Ginsberg were national spokesmen for the most liberalized attitudes, they bear a share of the responsibility for the rise in the caseloads. But except perhaps for the political recriminations that surrounded the issue and the violence of the welfare rights movement, welfare in New York City, like employee compensation, was really not very much different from welfare anywhere else.

Public Assistance Spending

New York State's public assistance expenditures are high, relative to other states, because its grant levels are high. For instance, the average grant paid to ADC recipients in 1975—$351 a month—was the highest in the country. The second-, third-, and fourth-ranked states paid $340, $295, and $289, respectively. But although average grants were high at the end of the decade, they were high at the outset as well. Moreover, although the legislature increased grant levels rapidly between 1965 and 1970, the rate of expenditure increase for ADC in New York City during Lindsay's two administrations was actually *lower* than in the nation as a whole: ADC expenditures grew at an average annual rate of 17.8 percent in New York City from 1966 to 1973, compared to an increase of 21.6 percent a year in the United States. If grant levels were going up fast in New York, they were going up at least as quickly elsewhere.

New York City's welfare spending is higher than any other city's—leaving aside the special case of Washington, D.C.—because no other city has to bear so heavy a share of the local costs. Where welfare is administered locally in the United States, it is usually administered by the county government; therefore, only the few cities that, like New York, combine city and county government have any welfare responsibility to begin with. More important, no other state government mandates so heavy a share of welfare costs on its local governments

---

*The same shift probably accounts for figures cited by Moynihan in his famous 1965 report on the Negro family. For the first time, starting about 1962, ADC caseloads grew at the same time that black male unemployment declined. Moynihan took it as marking a sea change in black family stability. More likely it marked a sea change in welfare availability.

as New York State does. Of the fifty-four states and territories that administer federal welfare programs, forty-three assume all the costs of assistance at the state level. Of the eleven that pass along a portion of costs to local government, none passes along so much as New York State—25 percent of all assistance and administrative costs or half the non-federal share—and eight of the eleven pass along less than 20 percent.

The high level of local financial participation in welfare costs and the apparently universal tendency for welfare recipients to concentrate in central cities significantly disadvantages New York City—and New York City taxpayers—relative to other New York counties. During the period 1961–75 the number of welfare recipients in New York City grew somewhat but not dramatically faster than in the rest of the State. But during the same period the total population of the rest of the state grew, while the population in New York City began to decline. Worse, personal income grew much more slowly in New York City than in the rest of the state as the effects of suburbanization and immigration combined with the sharper bite of economic recession in the city. The result was that by 1975 the city had 41 percent of the state's population, but 68 percent of its welfare recipients, and with 44 percent of the state's personal income, the city had to pay 73 percent of the local welfare costs—Put another way, City taxpayers had to pay almost four times as much as taxpayers in the rest of the state to support local welfare spending. An equitable distribution of local share—either per capita or by income—would have reduced the drain on city tax revenues by $140 million in 1973.*

To sum up the Lindsay contribution to New York City's heavy public assistance burden: He was a strong lobbyist for higher grants—particularly in the first term, when Mitchell Ginsberg was his welfare commissioner—but it was a time of virtual consensus on the need to raise welfare incomes, and the legislature, the governor, and the state welfare authorities were all supporters of increased benefits. Although total caseloads rose dramatically in the city in 1967 and 1968, it was only a harbinger of the sharp increases coming everywhere else. Over Lindsay's entire administration, the rate of spending growth and caseload growth in ADC, the basic welfare program, were actually lower than in the rest of the country. There is no question that New York City taxpayers were shouldering a crushing burden of welfare costs by the end of Lindsay's two terms; however, that was not because of disproportionate welfare growth in New York City, but because of the disproportionate share of welfare costs shifted to the city taxpayers by the state government.

* State budget officials sometimes contend that the state revenue-sharing program, which is skewed toward New York City, makes up for the disproportionate welfare burden. In 1973 New York received $331.8 million in state revenue-sharing funds, or 60.5 percent of the state total. If aid had been distributed on a strict per capita basis, the city would have received about $107 million less. When the extra welfare burden is added to the equally burdensome extra Medicaid share, it can be seen that the favorable revenue-sharing formula goes less than halfway toward covering the social welfare burden. City officials would maintain, in any case, that the skewing of revenue-sharing was intended to cover the generally higher operating costs in older cities, and not to make up for shortchanging in social welfare.

Medicaid

By 1973 the local financial burden for welfare medical assistance was even higher than the local cost of cash assistance. The Medicaid program was passed by Congress in 1965, almost as an afterthought, as part of the same law that created the Medicare program. It was designed to replace the current system of welfare medicine and, its proponents seriously believed, to reduce welfare costs by supplying the medical services recipients needed to become self-sufficient. Because of the higher rate of federal financial participation, Rockefeller and the state legislature viewed the program as something of a windfall. Incredibly, Rockefeller originally proposed to the legislature that the program impose no income limitations at all on participants. When that was too much for the legislature to swallow, a compromise bill setting a limit of $6,000 for a family of four was passed, virtually, without debate. The initial federal share estimate calculated by the state—$145 million, and far too low—was only slightly short of the federal government's original estimate for the entire country. Potentially, 45 percent of the State's population was covered, and in some upstate counties—to the mixed horror and delight of the medical societies—the percentage ran to 70 percent.

Administratively, the program was a mess. Although many states—California, for example—elected to contract with fiscal intermediaries such as Blue Cross and Blue Shield to operate the program, New York delegated the program to local welfare agencies, mandating a startup date that left only a few weeks for planning and administrative development. To complicate matters, there was a confusing division of jurisdiction between the local health and welfare agencies and an equally vague division of authority between local and state health officials. Finally, Medicaid hit the city welfare department just as the welfare rights movement was moving into high gear; the administration was in the period of its most serious disarray, and the program was never able to extricate itself from the initial paperwork tangle. The one bright spot was an aggressive and innovative attempt by the city health department to ferret out fraud and abuse by providers of medical services.

Costs were quickly out of hand. Medicaid caseloads rose in tandem with the welfare rolls, but medical prices and medical utilization went up even faster. The first year's total costs in the state were $461 million (against an estimate of $350 million), and in just two years costs tripled to $1.29 billion. Rockefeller publicly recanted his earlier enthusiasms, and the legislature enacted deep cuts in the program in 1969 and 1971—in the latter year despite a lawsuit by the city that delayed action for several months. The cuts dampened the growth, but by 1973 state expenditures had risen to $2.3 billion, more than total spending on cash assistance: Medical providers collected more welfare payments than the welfare recipients themselves.

The primary cause of the high rate of spending was the extremely high rate of costs for Medicaid services in New York compared to the rest of the country; but it is not entirely clear why that should be so. Even though the pattern of service utilization by recipients was about normal compared to other states, the costs per recipient were the highest in the country—$811, compared to a national average of $432 in 1973 and, strikingly, an average cost of $362 per recipient in California, a state with a program as broadly gauged as New York's and with a much higher proportion of elderly recipients, who tend to use the most expensive services. The cost of a stay in a hospital under the New York program was $2,029; in the next highest state it was only $965. The average New York cost for recipients in skilled nursing homes was $6,654; Alaska was in second place with $4,424, and the national average was only $2,842. Home health care in New York cost $487 per case; in the rest of the country, it cost $224.

It is virtually impossible to sort out responsibility for the runaway costs. Rockefeller was responsible for the program's initial grandiosity, although he had many allies, including Lindsay and the top city welfare officials. The city's administration of the program was chaotic at best, but lack of planning and administrative confusion at the state level contributed mightily to the chaos. The state and the city joined forces to build expensive and unnecessary new hospitals, made possible by Rockefeller's off-balance-sheet financing techniques and his new state construction authorities. Hospital management throughout the state was notoriously poor—particularly in the city's hospitals, which at that time had longer average hospital stays per patient than anywhere else—but the state allowed hospitals almost free rein in setting their reimbursement levels. The state construction authorities built scores of new nursing homes geared to provide the most lavish standards of care, and with per diem operating costs double and triple those in progressive states elsewhere. State health officials fumbled badly in overseeing the rates and service provision of a vulturish private nursing home industry. Medical institutions and medical providers of all kinds distinguished themselves by a degree of rapacity simply not found in other places.

However one assigns the ultimate responsibility for the management debacle, the program bore heavily on the city taxpayer. The state-local cost-sharing formula was the same as for welfare. Early in the program, when Medicaid costs first took off on their wild spiral, New York City was spending one out of every four Medicaid dollars in the country, and thirty cents of that dollar was coming from local tax rolls.

Higher Education and Hospitals

The city's university and hospital systems are the other areas in which New York's spending was far out of line with other municipalities; and in these areas, Lindsay's responsibility was far more direct than in welfare. The growth of both systems was described in some detail in Chapter II. The city's tradition was to provide richer services by far than any other municipality, and the tradition was powerfully reinforced by the Lindsay administration, aided and abetted at every step by the state.

In the hospital program the promise of Medicaid revenues was an incentive to upgrade services; the opportunities presented by the fast-track state construction authorities proved irresistible; and the creation of the quasi-independent Health and Hospitals Corporation in 1970 was a fundamentally expansionary step—it was explicitly designed to expedite hiring, construction, and purchasing. If the city's share of Medicaid dollars allocated to municipal hospitals is included in the hospital budget, city tax spending for hospitals in 1973 amounted to $470 million—34 percent more than the local revenues spent that year on public assistance and an increase of 142 percent since 1966.

Certainly, there are ample justifications and rationalizations to explain the increased commitment to hospitals. Much of the city system was in deplorable condition when Lindsay took office and seemed urgently to require an infusion of cash and new facilities. None of the state planning or regulatory authorities seemed to divine that the advent of much broader third-party payment coverage for lower-income people would mean sharp declines in utilization for the municipal system. Nor was the growing trend toward sharp reductions in the length of patient–stay correctly anticipated. The current skepticism about the relationship between medical services and overall health simply did not exist in the 1960s. Substantial reduction of so well-entrenched and traditional a system as city hospitals is also extremely difficult politically. Even with the spur of a fiscal crisis and the aid of a virtual consensus that the municipal system is too large, Lindsay's successors have been unable to engineer significant shrinkage. Finally, a system reduction would have been alien to everything Lindsay stood for and had campaigned for. But if the currency of the misconceptions helps explain, it does not excuse. Whatever the justifications, the fact remains that the Lindsay administration, on its own motion, undertook an upgrading of the municipal system to a point well beyond what was required to maintain the city's role as residual provider of medical services and did it at a cost substantially greater than the city could afford.

The expansion of the city university system proceeded in similar fashion but on more solidly grounded premises, for higher education doubtless does improve life's chances. Still, leaving aside issues of whether the system could absorb such rapid expansion without long-term damage, the fundamental question was not the worthiness of the goal, but whether the city could afford the enterprise. It was not until the fiscal crisis that New York's leaders began to ask whether mere worthiness necessarily qualified a program as a proper function for the city government. Again, a number of defenses can be marshaled for the city's policy. The California system of universal higher education was widely admired. The State Board of Higher Education enthusiastically endorsed Open Enrollment and announced its intention to follow suit. The new state financing and construction authorities put facility development on a fast track, just as with hospitals. The expansion of the city system proceeded apace with the vast expansion of the state system. The seemingly obvious logic that an expansion of the state commitment to higher education implied the possibility of a reduction in the city commitment, or that the city system might be absorbed into the state network, was somehow unthinkable in the 1960s. But again, explanations are not justifications. City tax spending on higher education was the fastest-growing area in the city budget, jumping from $35 million in 1966 to $200 million in 1973. It was much more than the city could afford.

THE LINDSAY SPENDING RECORD: A SUMMARY

The Lindsay spending record may be summarized as follows.

▪ Overall employee compensation, including wages, pensions, and fringes was not unusually high, compared to other major cities, at the end of Lindsay's two terms. Growth in wages seems to have been below average, in fringe benefits, above average, and in pensions, about average. New York City's compensation package was high when Lindsay left office, but it was high to begin with. City employees made disproportionate compensation gains, compared to private sector workers, but local government employees throughout the country did the same thing. The muscular new maturity of municipal unions, the immense amounts of new money funneled into local government from state and federal treasuries, and the short-lived flowering of interest in programs to redeem the core cities touched off localized public-sector inflation in virtually all major cities. Lindsay's collective bargaining record was neither much worse nor much better than anyone else's.

The fact that compensation gains were commensurate with those elsewhere does not mean that they were justified. By private-sector standards big-city workers throughout the country were substantially overpaid in 1973. Had city pay increases kept pace with private-sector awards, the city could have saved hundreds of millions of dollars over the eight years.

▪ Per capita costs and per capita employees for common municipal functions were approximately normal in New York City when compared to those of other large cities. The areas in which New York City tended to rank higher than other cities—sanitation, sewerage, and libraries—were the areas in which New York had traditionally outspent the rest of the country. Per capita and per pupil expenditures on public education were high, but the change in New York's position compared to other large cities was not dramatic.

▪ Perhaps surprisingly, the growth of public assistance caseloads and expenditures was slightly lower than the national average, although the growth spurt in New York City came earlier than elsewhere. Spending per client was high, a policy that Lindsay favored but did not ultimately control. The burden on city taxpayers was unusually high, but that was the result of the unique share of welfare costs that New York State imposes on its local governments.

▪ Medicaid spending rose more rapidly in both New York City and New York State than anywhere else, and again, the city taxpayers had to bear a disproportionate share of the costs. The causes of the inordinate cost increases are extremely complex, involving the nature of the program itself, the technological revolution in medicine, the fumbling of officials throughout the state and city governments, and the pervasive dishonesty of the professionals. Although Lindsay and his administration clearly played a role in the development of the Medicaid problems, it is difficult to assign a separate weight to the city's contribution or to point to any obvious ways in which another city administration could have made much difference.

▪ The expansion of the commitment to the city's hospital and higher education systems was clearly much more within Lindsay's control. In light of the vast expansion of the state university that was going on at the same time, the city might reasonably have chosen to retrench instead of trying to outstrip the state development. The increased spending for city hospitals reinforced an outdated city role as a major provider of quality medical care. Some replacement of municipal institutions was probably justified, but there was virtually no attempt to rationalize the city's commitment consistent with the wider availability of third-party financing and the declining utilization of inpatient beds. The fact that hospital planning groups generally concurred with the city's actions and that the state was embarked on much the same course is useful context for understanding the city's policies, but it does not relieve the administration of its responsibility.

To summarize, the city could have afforded service expansion had it resisted the nationwide inflation in spending for common functions and public education. Or if the state had absorbed a much larger share of local welfare and Medicaid costs, the new taxes enacted during Lindsay's term in office would have been enough to finance the increased commitments to hospitals and higher education and to pay for the increases in employee compensation. But there was *not* enough money to pay for cost inflation in the common services, support the disproportionate local share for welfare and Medicaid, and increase the commitments to higher education and hospitals all at the same time. It was this mismatch between the city's commitments and its resources that accounted for the persistent deficits that began to appear during Lindsay's second term.

IX. *The Lindsay Balance Sheet—II*

THE RECORD ON FINANCE

Revenue and Taxation

THE MOST IMPORTANT CHANGE in the City's overall revenue structure during the Lindsay administration was the marked shift toward increased dependence on state and federal aid: Intergovernmental aid rose from 35.6 percent of total revenue in 1965–66 to 48.2 percent in 1973–74. The practical implication of the shift was that the city was increasingly vulnerable to changes of heart and policy at higher levels of government. When Rockefeller was forced to cut back on state spending after ten years of aggressive expansion, the formula aid programs on which cities were heavily dependent were always the first to feel the pinch (the notable exception was school aid with its strong suburban constituency). Across-the-board cuts in formula programs generated large savings and shifted the unpleasant details of service reduction to city halls. Similarly, when the federal government shifted its welfare policy from one of advocacy for liberalization and higher grants to cost-consciousness and strict enforcement of eligibility requirements, the city found its own revenues imperiled by the threat of financial penalties for exceeding allowable error levels. The retrenchment in antipoverty spending was less important financially, because the city did not generally replace the lost federal money with its own, but the political pain and unrest associated with the cuts were vastly disproportionate to the amount of money involved. A number of other cities had maintained an arm's-length relation to the antipoverty programs in the first place, leaving the problems to the new nonprofit agencies.

Although the city's dependence on outside aid was greater than elsewhere, the sharpest increases in aid availability were concentrated in the areas where New York tends to carry far greater responsibility than other cities—welfare, Medicaid, social services, education, and hospitals. Federal and state aid for antipoverty programs—the area in which the city could have chosen not to become so heavily involved—amounted to only 2.5 percent of total outside aid in 1973. But even if the city had enjoyed greater policy flexibility, there would have been little justification for the administration to spurn increased outside aid. Nailing down a larger share of the state and federal dollar was a prime municipal objective since early in the Wagner administration and was an important theme of the 1966 report of the Temporary Commission on City Finances. When Lindsay took office, there was a sizeable consensus that a long-term shift of financing responsibility to higher levels of government was not only inevitable, but equitable and sensible. Watchdog groups regularly criticized both Lindsay and Wagner for not moving fast enough to capture additional aid. In fact, the perception that increased federal and state financing was a long-term necessity was undoubtedly right; and there is no question that the trends are in the general direction anticipated in the 1960s. What was not anticipated was the year-to-year unpredictability of the outside funding and the extremely disruptive effects of short-term swings in allocation policies.

In other revenue areas, Lindsay continued the long-standing trend toward multiplying local nuisance taxes and, more importantly, introduced income taxation on both personal and business incomes, which accounted for 19 percent of local revenues in 1973–74. The business income tax replaced the tax on gross business receipts, and shifted the tax burden away from low-margin, high-volume industries toward companies that operated with higher margins and lower volumes. (It heavily favored the garment industry, for example, whose leaders were key Lindsay supporters.) Staff of the 1975 Temporary Commission on City Finances argue that the business income tax was an important factor in hastening the decline of manufacturing in the city—but the loss of jobs after 1970 was just as dramatic in industries that benefited from the tax change, like the garment industry, as in those that were penalized by it.

Revenues from progressive income taxes respond more buoyantly to economic growth than revenues from other kinds of taxes, which was the major argument for their enactment in the city. In 1966–67 the personal income tax performed as its advocates had hoped, with receipts growing much faster than the rate of change in incomes. The shocker was that the elasticities ran both ways. As the distribution of the city's income shifted downward after 1968 (that is, as proportionately more of the city's income was held by people in the lower tax brackets), income tax receipts began to lag income changes: In 1968–69 the increase in personal income tax receipts was only about half as great as the rate of change in incomes. Shortfalls between estimated and actual income tax collections were a major element in the budget deficits that began to appear at the end of Lindsay's first term.

New York City's local taxes were high compared to other cities, but, as with employee compensation, the increases under Lindsay were not exceptional—other cities were experiencing the same pressures and reacting in more or less the same ways. Corrected for inflation, in fact, taxes rose more rapidly during Wagner's third term than during Lindsay's two terms. A 1972 comparative study showed that New York had the third highest tax effort of ten large cities but that the growth rate from 1966 to 1971 was the lowest of the ten, even including Lindsay's 1966 tax increase package.

Pension Financing

New York City's employee pension plans are, with a few unimportant exceptions, actuarially funded. The objective of actuarially funded pension plans is to accumulate assets that will be sufficient for future benefit payments. In technical terms, a plan's assets should have a present value approximately equivalent to the present value of its "accrued liabilities," that is, the future benefits already earned by covered workers. With a properly managed plan, in other words, if a company should go out of business, there would be enough money in the fund to pay out the benefits earned. Obviously, estimating accrued liabilities and funding requirements involves a series of problematic assumptions regarding future pay increases, worker retirement practice, mortality rates, and the earnings on accumulated pension fund assets.

In funding a plan, actuaries customarily distinguish between normal costs—the annual contributions required to maintain the equivalence between the present value of assets and accrued liabilities—and supplemental liabilities—the unfunded liabilities that arise when, for instance, benefits are liberalized or the actuarial assumptions of a plan are revised. Accepted practice calls for amortizing supplemental liabilities by level payments over a period of years (usually 30 to 40 years). Most pension plan contributions, therefore, will include both an actuarially calculated normal cost payment and an amortization payment for supplemental liabilities. In other words, it is a typical condition of the soundest pension plans to have unfunded liabilities. The question is whether the liabilities have been reasonably estimated and provided for in a systematic way.

In view of the publicity concerning alleged serious under-funding of the city's pension plans around the time of the fiscal crisis, it is probably worth stressing that the city's plans were, and still are, probably the most conservatively funded big-city plans in the country. A number of municipalities have, in fact, resisted the concept of actuarial funding of pension plans altogether, and not entirely without logic: Governments presumably do not go out of business, so the elaborate funding precautions used to ensure that private pension assets are available even in the event of bankruptcy may not be appropriate in the public sector; furthermore, it appears inconsistent to make current payments into an inert fund while borrowing for capital improvements—the more so in view of the sorry earnings record of most government pension funds. Nonactuarial funding means that the costs of new pension settlements are deferred into the indefinite future, although, of course, they must eventually be paid. Washington, D.C., for example, uses pay-as-you-go financing for its police and fire pensions (that is, pension payments to retirees are simply appropriated as a normal budgetary item instead of being paid from accumulated pension funds); by 1990 pension costs will equal about 100 percent of salaries and should rise to 130 percent. Los Angeles switched from actuarial to pay-as-you-go financing during the Depression and tried to switch back in the 1950s. Even with a seventy-year amortization period for unfunded liabilities, by 1971–72 the police and fire pensions alone were consuming about a third of the real property tax base; although average pension contributions both per employee and as a percentage of salary were considerably higher than in New York, accrued liabilities were still about five times total assets. At about the same time, Detroit came under a court order to put its plans on an actuarial basis, which promised to increase its rate of contributions sharply. Philadelphia's per employee pension contributions are lower than New York's, but its pension benefits are typically higher, and the city is accumulating a huge overhang of unfunded liabilities. Chicago's plans claim to be funded and generally pay rather low benefits, but the level of fund contributions remained absolutely flat from 1973 to 1977, although salaries rose rapidly—an almost certain indication of under-funding. Boston has militantly retained pay-as-you-go principles for all of its plans. The classic example of an unfunded public plan, of course, is the federal social security system. Trust fund assets have been less than a single year's disbursements since the mid-1970s, and the unfunded accrued liability is in excess of $2 trillion, an amount roughly equivalent to the nation's personal savings for twenty-eight years.

In New York City, by contrast, the major plans were all converted to actuarial principles in the period between the two world wars, and the funding principles were, if anything, excessively conservative, leaving later mayors considerable room for financial maneuver. The retiree life expectancies assumed by the plans were always too short but were offset by extremely conservative projections of interest earnings and retirement patterns. Further, instead of amortizing new unfunded liabilities over a fixed period of years, the city typically funded them over the projected working lives of members currently in the plan—creating a short funding period with payments skewed into the early years. It was apparently also common practice for the city actuary to overestimate future liabilities in order to build up a nest egg against later plan improvements.

In light of the city's perennial fiscal difficulties, some adjustment in pension funding procedures was warranted, and the funding changes introduced by Lindsay, and later Beame, were not sufficient to undermine the basic soundness of the plans,* although some changes were more defensible than others. Introducing fixed-period amortization for certain unfunded liabilities in

---

* By 1975 total pension fund assets equalled 43 percent of accrued liabilities on fully updated actuarial assumptions (or 53 percent, depending on how the city's contribution was valued). Comparable ratios for the New York State retirement systems and the federal civil service system were 61 percent and 21 percent, respectively, and for five private plans were 21 percent, 51 percent, 100 percent, 61 percent, and 24 percent. Total income of the city's funds will exceed disbursements for the foreseeable future, an important sign of financial health. On new actuarial assumptions and with level amortization of all unfunded liabilities, it was calculated in 1976 that the city needed to increase its annual pension contribution by $200 million, or about 16 percent, to fund the plans fully, an amount that is being phased in as part of the city's post-crisis financial plan. Finally, the city's total contribution will remain relatively level after approaching a peak about 1981—in marked contrast to most other large cities, who face years of steadily escalating costs to make up for past funding practices. The firemen's plan is an exception to the general rule. Because of a long-standing dispute between the city and the union over respective contribution shares, the plan will be in serious trouble in the 1980s.

1968 was in accordance with good practice. Lengthening projected service periods, also in 1968, was justified, but the new funding periods were too long for safety. Lagging payments by two years to the teachers' system was barely defensible, because the other plans had been similarly lagged since their inception. Appropriation of excess interest earnings for the general fund was not actuarially justifiable, and the valuations of plan assets seem to have been inflated. Most seriously, the changes were introduced haphazardly, as year-to-year fiscal expedients, rather than as part of an integrated funding reform plan, and the overall drift was in a dangerous direction. Without the check on benefit enrichment by the state legislature in 1971 and the overhaul of funding assumptions introduced after the fiscal crisis, the plans would have soon been in a precarious condition.

Debt

The city's outstanding debt grew substantially during the Lindsay administration, although there was only minimal change in the ratio of debt to the city's real estate tax base, and the ratio of debt service to local revenue actually declined somewhat, despite steadily rising interest rates. The most important changes related to the city's utilization of debt rather than to overall totals, but an analysis of changes in the city requires first an understanding of the evolution of debt practice in New York State.

Like most states, New York State's capacity to borrow is severely limited by its constitution. Revenue bonds can be issued whenever the project being financed promises to be sufficiently profitable to attract private lenders on its own merits; but since few state projects are self-financing, most bond issues require a pledge of general tax revenues to ensure payment of debt service (that is, they are "general obligation" or "full faith and credit" bonds)—and tax revenues can be assigned to repay borrowing only with the approval of the state's voters in a general referendum. Early in Nelson Rockefeller's administration, his plans for expansion of state transportation, housing, higher education, and health programs were set back by an increasing reluctance of voters to approve bond issues, and the funds required for capital investment were far too large to be provided from general budget appropriations. Toll roads and similar projects were often suitable for revenue bond financing, but the returns from housing and human service programs were considered too risky to attract investors at reasonable interest rates. The governor and his advisers—notably John Mitchell—hit upon the device of the "moral obligation" bond to provide the requisite security. The moral obligation bond is essentially a revenue bond, but carries the additional proviso that if the issuing agency's reserves for debt service fall below a specified level, the agency must present the shortfall to the governor and the legislature, who must then consider whether to supply the deficiency through a special appropriation. The authorizing statute strongly implied that the legislature would feel compelled to make up moral obligation reserve deficiencies but stopped short of unconditionally pledging the state's credit. The necessity for referenda was thereby avoided, but the intimation of legislative support was enough to secure a market at only a small premium above the interest on general obligation issues; and as time went on, the distinction between state general obligation and moral obligation bonds became increasingly blurred in the eyes of most investors.*

Not only did the moral obligation concept permit enormous expansion of state and state-labelled debt but, even more important, it opened broad new vistas of debt financing possibilities for entrepreneurially minded administrators and legislators throughout state and local government. The rigid constitutional canons that so strictly limited capital undertakings in the past could obviously be easily circumvented, and quite legally so, with only a modicum of creativity. The new technical sophistication in conceiving debt instruments and the increased familiarity with debt financing for all purposes was a prerequisite to the intricate budget-balancing techniques that became such a fixture of the state and city budgets by the late 1960s. Frederick Hayes recalls:

When I first met with the legislative leadership in 1967, I remember trying to explain to them that the city didn't really need money; we just needed a commitment so we could borrow. But just a couple of years later, those guys were full of new financing ideas to avoid an appropriation. The whole attitude toward using debt had changed.

Rockefeller's financing of the Albany Mall complex of state office buildings was the most spectacular new gimmick of all. Construction bonds were sold by Albany *County* on the security of future state leases on the buildings. The amortization of the construction debt was scattered throughout the real estate budgets of the various state agencies using the buildings. Not only was voter approval bypassed, but the total cost of the project never appeared in a state budget, even though expenditures were well in excess of a billion dollars. In effect, the state had discovered how to tap seemingly limitless amounts of money without any public scrutiny whatsoever.

City budget technicians were no less creative. If the Albany Mall financing was the most spectacular of the new financing ploys, the city's Transit Construction Fund, authorized by the legislature in 1973, was probably the most intricate.† A complex series of borrowings and leasebacks between the Metropolitan Transportation Authority, the Transit Construction Fund, and the city would permit funds to be borrowed for subway improvements with the debt service secured by annual payments from the city. The gimmick was that the bonds would not encumber the city's debt limit, so as not to restrict borrowing for other purposes. Better yet, the city would be allowed to borrow to meet the annual debt service payments.

The new financing techniques led to sharp increases in debt at all levels of government in New York State. State debt from all sources, including the

_____

*The moral obligation ploy also hewed an ingenious path between the state constitution and federal banking statutes. Commerical banks are permitted by federal law to underwrite only general obligation bonds. The moral obligation device was not a general obligation bond under the state constitution but squeezed within the general obligation definition for federal purposes—making the underwriting resources of the commercial banks available to the state, and, of course, opening up the underwriting profits to the banks.

†The Fund was in fact never used, due at least in part to the criticism generated by its facile gimmickry.

public authorities, rose from $3.9 billion outstanding in 1964 to $13.4 billion in 1974, while New York City's outstanding debt—again from all sources—rose from $7.1 billion to $13.5 billion during the same period, and that of other local governments in the state from $4.5 billion to $10.6 billion. The debt outstanding was equivalent to 34 percent of the state's personal income in 1974, or $2,070 per capita—considerably more than double the per capita average in the rest of the country.

As the figures suggest, the growth of debt in the city was not so rapid as elsewhere in the state. During most of Lindsay's first term, in fact—until the capital construction program was put on track—the amount of funded (long-term) debt redeemed each year tended to exceed the amount issued. From 1966 to 1974 funded debt outstanding grew from $5.0 billion to $7.7 billion, a 54 percent increase, while the real property tax base grew by 88 percent. About $800 million, or 30 percent of the increase, could be attributed to the shift of operating expenses to capital financing late in the administration.

The significant change was the use of short-term debt. The city had always issued relatively small numbers of notes to smooth cash flow problems between cyclical receipts of taxes and outside aid and had almost always resorted to budget notes to meet deficits at the end of the fiscal year. During Lindsay's second administration, however, short-term borrowing grew very rapidly, and revenue anticipation notes, in particular, began to be used to mask operating deficits. The rapid run-up of short-term debt was virtually unique. State and local governments elsewhere in the country—with only a few exceptions, like Boston—borrow sparingly short-term, and by the early 1970s, the city regularly accounted for about 25 percent of all outstanding short-term state and local paper in the country.

As can be seen from the next table, Lindsay reduced the volume of short-term debt during his first year in office, and debt outstanding grew only slowly throughout his first term. But there was a virtual explosion of debt, particularly in RANs, during the difficult budget years from 1970 through 1972. The brief economic upturn in 1973 allowed some stabilization and substantial reduction in the volume of RANs. The resumption of the whole-sale reliance on RANs during the fiscal year that overlapped into Beame's first administration will be discussed in the next chapter. The rapid expansion in BANs resulted from technical financing decisions—and wholly misguided ones—by the comptroller's office and will also be discussed in the next chapter.

The use of short-term borrowing on such a scale is objectionable on a number of grounds. First of all, financing deficits by borrowing other than through budget notes is illegal—although the city's books were sufficiently vague that it would have been difficult to pinpoint any particular issue of RANs as deficit financing. Secondly, borrowing diverts city resources to pay interest costs—$101 million in 1973–74—although a certain amount of short-term borrowing is unavoidable. But the most serious consequence of borrowing short in such quantity, and a problem that seems not to have been at all understood by the city leadership at the time, was that the city became dangerously dependent on the willingness of the financial community to supply cash to keep the

Short-term Debt Outstanding as of June 30: New York City
(millions)

YEAR	TOTAL	TANS[1]	RANS[2]	BANS[3]	URNS[4] AND OTHER	BUDGET NOTES
1965	$ 525.6	$ 88.8	$ 118.6	$225.5	$ 24.0	$ 68.7
1966	466.7	100.3	45.0	274.5	25.8	21.0
1967	634.9	136.5	93.8	374.7	29.9	—
1968	693.2	147.5	93.8	403.6	48.3	—
1969	747.3	155.5	128.8	404.6	58.4	—
1970	1288.2	170.0	536.7	467.6	113.9	—
1971	2319.4	206.0	1096.3	586.6	147.4	360.8
1972	2650.2	232.0	1180.0	687.7	89.7	460.8
1973	2517.5	265.0	887.1	957.1	100.0	308.3
1974	3415.9	317.0	1798.3	908.7	83.6	308.3

1. Tax anticipation notes.   2. Revenue anticipation notes.   3. Bond anticipation notes.   4. Urban revewal notes and capital notes.
Source: Annual Report of the Comptroller, 1965–74.

city's paper turning over. Because the average maturity of city paper was about six months in 1973–74, for instance, the city had to go to the markets for $7.3 billion throughout the year to finance the $3.4 billion outstanding on June 30. When the financial community turned out to be a fragile reed in 1975, the whole complicated fiscal edifice tottered and collapsed, leaving the city in ransom.

To summarize the Lindsay record on finance: Growth in local taxes was high but not significantly different from that elsewhere, while the growth in funded debt and debt service was consistent with growth in tax base and revenues. The drift in pension financing policy was in a dangerous direction, but the actual harm to the plans was not great. The ominous discontinuities were the increased use of short-term borrowing and the new dependence on outside aid, both of which made the city suddenly vulnerable to policy shifts and economic decisions outside its control.

In the final analysis, the true missing ingredient in the Lindsay financial policy and the root cause of the new vulnerability was the failure to recognize that the precipitate economic recession that set in after 1969 would prove to be more or less permanent. Throughout the 1960s New York's world prestige and booming downtown and financial districts had allowed it to maintain healthy growth and low unemployment, despite all the forces—immigration, rising crime, suburbanization, aging of the infrastructure—that were generating only decay and decline in most other older cities. But the 1970s were a new era and called for wholly new financial policies. In previous years, when the city had been overextended, business and watchdog groups had wrung their hands and raised alarums, but economic growth and mild retrenchment were always enough to restore the city to basic health. Indeed, a not seriously painful slow-down in the rate of real spending increase after 1972, combined with the brief economic upturn in 1973, were enough to allow the city to reduce its RANs and budget notes outstanding by $400 million. If the 1973 trends had continued for two or three more years, it is entirely likely that the city would have been able to wriggle out of its dependence on the bankers. But the new semipermanent character of the recession called for nothing less than real cuts in city commitments: Palliative slowdowns and fiscal expedients could defer the reckoning but would ultimately make the problems much worse than they needed to be. Lindsay failed to recognize this—or, recognizing it, failed to act on it—which meant he was about as prescient as most other local politicians or, for that matter, most academic economists, bond-rating agencies, and editorial writers of the time.*

THE MANAGEMENT RECORD

Lindsay's first- and second-term management records can be sharply differentiated. The first term was a period of painful flailing at ill-defined problems, a disorderly rallying of slogans. In contrast, there were solid management accomplishments in the second term, particularly after Lindsay dropped his presidential ambitions. To an important degree, however, it was a mass of first-term analytic work, carried out almost independently of the tumultuous face that the administration presented to the public, that made the second-term achievements possible. And the managers who finally achieved a measure of success in the second term were to a large extent the youthful administrators who had been so ill-prepared for the harsh realities of city government in 1966.

The Management Task

It is a vastly more difficult task in government than in the private sector, and commensurately more important, to define precisely the expected outcome of an enterprise. With only minor qualifications, the success of a business can be deduced fairly directly from its rate of profit. But in most government undertakings, the final objectives—safer streets, healthier citizens, sounder housing—do not so readily lend themselves to measurement, and so the administrator must instead fall back on controlling variables that stand as surrogates for the result to be accomplished: cases cleared, children examined, violations inspected. The choice of the output surrogates is often crucial to management outcomes. If the buildings department measures units inspected, inspectors will tend to concentrate on sound buildings that perhaps need little attention; if the measurement is violations reported, the emphasis may shift to buildings beyond hope of redemption. Similarly, concentrating on ineligibility statistics in welfare will cause more intensive scrutiny of applications, more rejections of marginal cases, and longer waiting lines in the centers. Stress on courtesy, flexibility, and promptness of service, on the other hand, will often lead, disappointingly enough, to a deterioration of the underlying eligibility

*An academic awareness of the possibly long-term nature of the city's economic problems was emerging only about 1973, and the contrary view still had a robust set of supporters.

base.* Obviously, without the final, unarguable measuring rod provided by the profit line, good public-sector management requires artful choice and continued refinement of measurements, coupled with a sound understanding of front-line worker behavior, so the stated and actual tasks can be brought into ever-closer consonance with each other and workers can proceed with a fairly clear and consistent comprehension of what is expected of them.

The soaring rhetoric of Lindsay's first administration did not lend itself to easy translation into day-to-day measuring rods of performance and seems to have generated only confusion and hostility among front-line workers. Not just Lindsay, but liberals generally began to expect very much more from government in the 1960s, particularly, local government. When Walter Lippmann announced that the War on Poverty would have to be won in New York City, he was sounding a theme that Lindsay, his young aides, and probably most of the electorate and the media that supported him took very much to heart. The entire battalion of city agencies—parks, welfare, police, housing, the new antipoverty programs, hospitals, even sanitation—were to be part of a massive effort at uplift, a final breaking-through of the barriers of oppression and discrimination that prolonged the abject misery of blacks and Hispanics and imposed such heavy costs upon the city.

It was a splendid vision, but one that was seriously flawed and, from a management perspective, positively damaging. City government is for the most part a fairly dull and mundane business, a grab-bag collection of routine housekeeping and regulatory functions. Its major contribution to the assimilation of immigrant groups in the past—except for the education system—had been the offer of low-skill, secure employment. The sudden call to lofty achievement was, for most agencies, simply muddling. How much of sanitation's resources was to be devoted to cleaning the slums? Should playgrounds be rebuilt if they'd been repeatedly vandalized? Was it more important to build more housing units or to integrate neighborhoods? Most workers seemed to find the conceptual complications profoundly alienating. And even where the relationship between city services and the plight of the poor was less attenuated—in the schools, in social and health services, and in higher education—and the new policies argued for rapid expansion, there was still no very clear notion of the sort of outcomes that should be looked for. The expectations that smaller class sizes would lead to better reading levels in the public schools, more medical services to better health, or manpower training to productive employment were based ultimately on faith, not data. It was never possible to tell—at least on a scale that mattered—whether any of the social intervention programs made a difference. In almost every case, the changes in clients that might be traceable to a program input were of about the same magnitude as the random variations that occurred in the absence of any programs at all: Individual program participants might be gaining enormous personal benefit, but that was

*There is an interesting current example of the problem in the effort to control hospital costs. The emphasis has been on limiting costs per patient-day. However, the simplest way to lower average patient costs is to increase the hospital census, so fixed costs are spread over a larger base. The net result may well be an increase in overall spending.

always very difficult to prove. With outcomes only vaguely defined—or, to make matters worse, defined only over the long term—there was no way to hold program managements genuinely accountable or to avoid dissipating resources and time on the merely silly.

To an important degree, of course, the charge of mismanagement or non-management in the antipoverty programs is beside the point. From the federal level on down, the programs had a strong tendency to emphasize symbol over content, to value structure and participation over program results. Even the federal evaluation forms emphasized that employment of poor people in a program was as important as the program's outcomes. Black leaders stated forthrightly that antipoverty money and the expansion of human services was their first real opportunity for sizable amounts of political patronage. The very structure of the city's Community Development Agency, with its cascading tiers of interlocking community boards and directorates, is ample evidence that the program's designers had something other than tight management on their minds. But however justified, the concentration on the purely emblematic was an antimanagement position; and it was hardly conducive to an atmosphere of tight discipline or control in the more traditional agencies. Whatever the measures, on the narrow issue of management achievement, Lindsay's first term must be deemed a resounding failure.

Things were very much better in the second term. Changes of heart are difficult to demonstrate, much less pinpoint, but it seems clear enough that after the debacles of 1968, Lindsay realized that the city government was going to have much less short-run impact on the personal attainments of city slumdwellers than he may have once hoped and that his responsibility for delivering basic services to the rest of the city's residents were perhaps greater than he had been willing to accept. In fact, work had been going forward since the very beginning of the administration on improving basic service delivery (expediting capital construction was one of the earliest successful examples), but it was not until about 1969, with the election at stake, that Lindsay seems to have identified his own personal goals with micromanagement of the city's mechanics and accepted that incremental change might still be a good result—a far more humble vision of his job than the sweeping renaissance that he seemed to be promising in 1966.

Deputy Mayor Hamilton's creation of the productivity program in 1972 fixed the final direction of the administration. As suggested in Chapter VII, the productivity effort and the graceful scaling-down of rhetoric that it entailed was a key step in restoring most agencies to a sound management track and achieving the practical definitions of short-term outputs and long-range goals necessary to make sense of public sector enterprises.

Management and Technology

The rationalist strain that produced the more arrogant overreachings of the first administration had an important positive side as well. Because the rationalist believes that the most intractable problems will yield to the application of superior intelligence, he places a premium on quality analytic work. Under

Lindsay's first budget director, Frederick Hayes, who combined one of the best analytic minds in government with a somewhat healthier skepticism toward nostrums and short-term solutions than many other top officials, the city produced some of the best analyses of local government management problems in decades.

Some of the best early results from filtering city problems through a scientific bias came in the fire department, particularly in calculating deployment and response patterns that were faster and more economical than previously. Fire equipment was traditionally dispatched to calls on a district system. Each fire house served a defined area of the city and responded to all calls within its area. When all the equipment in a fire house was occupied, further alarms were allocated to the next contiguous district. Because each fire house was located as far as possible in the center of the district it served, the own-district response rule would generally ensure the shortest response time to an alarm, usually the most critical factor in keeping a fire under control. The system worked more or less as designed so long as there was sufficient equipment available in a district to respond to its own alarms. But when the incidence of ghetto fires and false alarms began to rise exponentially in the 1960s, fire companies in some parts of the city were overwhelmed (alarms ran from thirteen to thirty times the city average) and were increasingly relying on assistance from other districts to handle their calls. With coverage in the home districts stripped during high-alarm periods, response times became increasingly unpredictable as outside companies undertook long routes in unfamiliar neighborhoods.

There was no way to solve the problem in any final sense, but analysts from the Rand Corporation considerably eased its effects by redesigning response policy around probability equations, derived from a painstaking historical analysis of fire patterns in the city, that predicted approximately when and where fires would occur. Although the new dispatching algorithms often called for a longer, out-of-district response when closer in-district coverage was available, the mathematics showed that average response time was still significantly reduced. A simplified example demonstrates the logic of the process. Assume only two districts, A and B, with a greater frequency of alarms in district A, and that A's manning complement can cover two fires at a time. If one of A's two companies is already engaged and another alarm is called in close to the border of B, it may well make sense to dispatch a B company, even though its response time will be longer than that of A's second company. If the probabilities are strong that the next alarm will also be in A and at a point even farther from B, use of the B company relatively close to its district will leave an A company in reserve to handle the later call, and the average response time to all three calls will be lower than if A had taken the second call itself. The most efficient response, therefore, can vary considerably, depending on the district, the time of day, the coverage still available in the home district and contiguous districts, and other factors. With a department management that understood the Rand approach and were eager to make use of their findings, the analysts, over a period of several years, perfected a computer model that accounted for the various response contingencies, provided easy-to-use response rules throughout the city, and significantly smoothed workloads and improved response efficiencies. Later, the same reasoning was applied to fire equipment. The city instituted its "adaptive response" system in 1972, when the analysts demonstrated that a reduction in the initial equipment response to an alarm could cause a higher average equipment availability to all alarms.

Even in agencies with less of a hardware orientation than the fire department, the city was badly in need of the technological thrust provided by Hayes and his two successors at the budget bureau, Edward Hamilton and David Grossman. Most agencies still relied heavily on old manual operating systems, many of which—like those in welfare, in purchasing, or in fire dispatching— had been overwhelmed by the sudden spurts in volume that began about 1960. For the most part, the manual systems were not documented, and it could take weeks for even a diligent newcomer to track back through fundamental processes like the budget modification system to find out who had to do what to keep the paper moving. The computerized systems were, if anything, in even worse shape: The manual systems were slow, but at least they could usually be made to work. Computerized systems had been developed piecemeal and haphazardly, were almost always poorly documented, and often operated only with the assistance of numerous manual overrides—that is, interventions by the operator to change what the computer was programmed to do. The welfare computer system was a particularly horrendous example. There were no less than a dozen different machines, from a range of manufacturers, operating in a polyglot of computer languages, and with the entire system so lacking in documentation that its continued functioning quite literally depended on the delayed retirement of a handful of key staff members who had been with the system since its inception.

No fundamental improvements were possible until the basic systems were documented in a standardized way, but the city bureaucracies were so sprawling, and the dearth of information so pervasive, that it took at least two years to compile just the beginnings of a rigorous knowledge base. It was not until 1968, for example, that the capital construction process was fully understood; that police and fire department deployment problems were beginning to be cast in a quantitative form; that a useable data set was being developed to measure sanitation productivity; or that the city began to acquire a solid understanding of the dynamics of welfare housing and the economy of rent control. It was tedious work and, for the most part, productive of little in the way of short-term results; but the longer-term outcomes can fairly be termed impressive. Almost all of the productivity improvements during the second administration were based on the analytic work begun during the first term. Even where work had less direct practical impact, it often contributed to a deeper understanding of urban problems: A very large share of the detailed quantitative data available nationally on welfare caseloads and urban housing derives directly from the analytic work in New York City.

Finally, the large numbers of new younger people Lindsay attracted into the government by his promise of scope and challenge was an accomplishment in itself. The learning periods were often painful, and many merely passed

through, taking a taste of adventure before going on to more conventional occupations; but a large number stayed, and they have made significant contributions to government. In 1979 the commissioners of two major departments in
New York State, three major New York City departments, and the director of
the Port Authority were all Lindsay recruits, and former Lindsay staffers were
scattered throughout key government positions, not only on the state and local
levels in New York, but in the federal government and in other local governments throughout the country.

Evaluating the Management Record

In the final analysis, evaluations of Lindsay's relative success or failure as a
manager must turn on a judgment about how deeply the city was in management difficulty when he took office. If things were operating reasonably well
before 1965, then the accomplishments of the second term did nothing except
repair the damage of the first. If the city was in the serious trouble that some
commentators supposed at the end of the Wagner administration, then Lindsay's first term—for all the rhetorical aberrations—could be viewed as a period
of building capacity for the management improvements that came later. Unfortunately, of course, there is no precise way of making comparative evaluations
because of the changing nature of city problems and the general unavailability
of good historical data. Some judgments can be offered, but they are nothing
more than the author's reasonably informed opinions.

One key question is how much truth is contained in the widespread belief
that the city's management ranks were seriously depleted by the retirements of
the 1930s recruits, the "Depression geniuses." A top management corps departing en masse clearly put the city on its mettle to try out new approaches
and to begin some unconventional recruitment and promotion policies. Probably the best answer is that there is considerable truth to the myth of the
Depression genius, and considerable exaggeration as well. City government
was not the place where people with energy looked for work in the 1950s, but
on the other hand, the talent gap between the top layers of the civil servants
and the next several layers down was probably never so wide as sometimes supposed. Cynics have observed that the veterans themselves were anxious to
vouch for their own irreplaceability. But however irreplaceable the old-timers,
Lindsay and his new managers made poor use of the civil service talent that was
available. The whole tone of the new administration was almost calculated to
alienate the veterans, with the inevitable result that learning curves were
longer and more costly than necessary and there were more retirements of key
personnel than otherwise might have been the case. In those instances where
the best professionals of the old school were drawn into the administration, the
results were often extremely fruitful. Martin Lang seized upon the capital construction management information system and improved output sharply in the
Bureau of Water Pollution Control. John O'Hagan was an admirable bridge between the new technology and the veteran firefighters in the fire department.
James Cavanagh, the prototypical insider, was practically an alter ego to Hayes
at the budget bureau. But the relatively few cases where there was a sensible

integration of talents merely underscore the numerous instances where the links were not made, to the city's detriment. There was better melding and more mutual respect during the second term, but the losses in premature retirees were permanent. In general, Lindsay gets poor marks on this count.

On the issue of agency performance, there were numerous instances in which Lindsay was outperformed by his predecessor. Wagner's housing construction record, for example, could not be touched until the very end of Lindsay's two terms, and then only with the help of the state's new Urban Development Corporation. For all of Lindsay's success in untracking the capital construction program, it is not at all clear that on a constant construction dollar basis, he came up the mark of Wagner's best years. Wagner and Screvane's success in clearing away a monster snowfall in 1961 showed Lindsay up badly in 1969. But Wagner's high points tended to occur in his first two terms, and there really does seem to have been a pervasive breakdown of internal discipline and control in the years immediately before Lindsay took office—a fact usually conceded by civil servants and administration insiders of the time. The city's crippling inability to carry out the most basic tasks of paying its employees, making payments to vendors, changing a job specification, buying minimum supplies for its institutions, repairing its garbage trucks, balancing its books, was too patent to be ignored. There are a number of theories to explain the falloff in capacities. One is that Wagner himself was losing energy and interest and simply wasn't paying enough attention to his job. Another is that there *was* no falloff—that the city had always been in deep management trouble, but the fact had been sporadically publicized and forgotten for years.

While there is almost certainly no exclusive explanation, one that fits well with a number of other developments is that there were important changes in the management problem, starting about 1960. The work performed by most of the basic city departments is not intrinsically complicated, and so long as the city had the benefit of a self-disciplined and reliable work force, the management task was greatly simplified. The complicated paperwork systems seemed to work, as long as everyone in an organization could be relied upon. When work attitudes became slovenly, the paperwork systems turned into an endlessly complicated nightmare. The streets were cleaner when sanitationmen swept between truck loads, even without on-the-spot supervision; management was much more difficult when the work force dogged it at every opportunity, sabotaged their own equipment, bought and sold sick leave certificates, and even attacked their supervisors. Police management was simpler when the average foot patrolman had a dozen or more years' experience and was fully tested under pressure; the problem was radically more difficult when policemen became just another angry mob. The evidence, in short, is that there was a sharp falloff in the quality of personnel. The same phenomenon must also have affected private industry, but the city was one of the few labor-intensive industries that could not either shift its production overseas or, like the telephone company, automate virtually all of its operations. A reliable, self-motivated work force performing mostly repetitive task needs only the lightest management touch: There was plenty of room in city departments for patronage jobs and no-shows and not much need for complex command-and-control systems. But when the stance of the work force shifted toward non-cooperation—or, more accurately, toward the kind of legalistic cooperation that exists in an intensely unionized industry (see, for instance, the plight of the construction industry)—the management task was wholly changed; management information systems, accounting and control procedures, and all the trappings of modern large-scale enterprise became vastly more important. This was a basic change, and Lindsay took office just as the change was most precipitate and most destructive, coinciding with the period of rapid increases in workload and the greatest pressure on established institutions.

The new management problem did not necessarily mean that the old ways would no longer work. When Martin Lang took over the sanitation department after a sharp falloff in departmental morale and street cleanliness early in the Beame administration, he restored production to the same level that had been achieved by Elish in 1973, but with fifteen hundred fewer men,* and with no industrial engineering assistance: all of the new technicians had been let go at the orders of a mayor anxious to restore the traditional ways. Lang simply overwhelmed the department with his own energy and personal forcefulness and bullied and cajoled the men and their supervisors into pushing production back up to its highest levels. But Lang's was a virtuoso performance, built around seven-day weeks, fifteen-hour days, and a rare dedication to the city. Something is clearly wrong when routine management requires heroic effort. The more scientific style of management introduced under Elish was probably more expensive than Lang's methods, but it was much more replicable and sustainable.

The final judgment here, then, is that the Lindsay administrations put city management on a much firmer technical base than had previously been the case, a proper and much-needed response to the suddenly novel management problem. The technical contribution to city management has turned out to be a more or less permanent one—in principle, if not in every detail—and it probably considerably outweighs the false starts and false rhetoric of the first term.

LINDSAY AS REFORMER

One of the most persistent criticisms of the Wagner administration was its apparently casual attitude toward graft and corruption. It was a campaign theme that Lindsay hit hard and repeatedly: With no ties to the traditional "interest groups" and "power brokers," his would be a reform administration, a new era of clean government. It was a promise on which he conspicuously failed to deliver, and his administration was dogged by scandals and corruption from the very start. The first-term Marcus scandal was probably the most notorious. James Marcus, a campaign aide of apparently independent means, was

---

* Productivity was about the same. Elish had about fifteen hundred men handling special details—Model City cleanups and the like—which Lang no longer had the capacity to deliver; but the cut in manpower had been used by department supervisors to justify deep cuts in basic services, particularly in the poorer neighborhoods.

appointed water commissioner with no background checks whatever. He was soon enmeshed with organized crime in the sale of contracts and regulatory favors in an effort to redeem his own tangled personal finances. The widespread stealing and corruption in the Human Resources Administration has already been discussed. The corruption in the police department was—according to Patrick Murphy, at least—possibly the worst anywhere, and the Knapp Commission disclosed evidence that top officials in the administration ignored the corruption when it was brought to their attention.

The Marcus scandal or the theft of HRA pay checks by an inventive computer operator could be charged to inexperience—a new administration was being victimized—but by the time of the presidential race, the administration was playing the game of politics as usual and with a vengeance. Four of the five county JVL associations, the fund-raising arm of the Lindsay campaign, were headed by city commissioners or assistant commissioners, at least two of whom (in the purchase and highways departments) were in a position to award substantial favors for contributions. The solicitation of donations from city contractors and vendors for advertisements in fundraising programs was, if anything, more organized than ever. One official was even found offering to fix parking tickets for contributions. Certainly, Lindsay was not above making deals with the unions in the finest machine tradition: The police parity deal was only the most costly example. Furthermore, although the administration was ostensibly committed to the principle of merit hiring, an elaborate paperwork procedure ensured that every provisional hiring in the city paying more than $7,500 per year—thousands of jobs annually—was funnelled through a political aide at City Hall. The political clearance even had its own set of forms, and separate clerical operations were established in the major city agencies just to handle the processing.

The original commitment to the antipoverty programs sprang from conviction, but few opportunities were lost to use the flow of funds into black and Hispanic neighborhoods to build a new political base—one that was crucial in the 1969 re-election victory. Illustrative of the possibilities was the case of a black church in Brownsville that, quite legally, was able to skim hundreds of thousands of dollars off its sponsorship of city Mitchell-Lama housing, use the proceeds to buy automobiles and more buildings, and later expand its operations to city-financed day care centers. Unless one is willing to insist that black churches are more worthy of the city's largesse than white real estate operators, there is little to distinguish the Brownsville operation from the highly publicized renewal scandals of the Wagner administration.

On other reform issues Lindsay's record was better. The organization of the "Big Six" mayors as a concerted interest group was a counterweight to the growing suburban dominance in the state legislature. Lindsay lobbied for years, single-mindedly, almost single-handedly, and finally with some success, to reform the state aid structure so that it would treat its major cities more equitably. Finally, despite the false starts on "Little City Halls," Lindsay made an important contribution to the concept of neighborhood government by creating a system of district managers to coordinate interagency services in local areas.

In 1973 Columbia University researchers found the projects "surprisingly" successful, and the concept was carried forward into the 1975 charter revisions.

THE RECORD ON RACE

An evaluation of Lindsay's record on race relations depends again very much on how the problem is defined. Certainly, relations between the administration and minorities were for the most part excellent, better even than Wagner's generally good record. The city Human Rights Commission, under Eleanor Holmes Norton, was probably the best of its kind in the country. The new antipoverty and Model Cities programs provided greatly increased middle-management opportunities for minorities. The administration worked hard on minority recruitment in the police department and showed both courage and tenacity in halting the city construction program for a year until the craft unions improved their minority employment record. Blacks were appointed to top posts throughout the administration, including a number outside of the antipoverty structure: At various times there were black commissioners of the fire, traffic, correction, and mental health departments.

If race relations is defined as improving relations *between* the races, however, the record looks very much different. There is more than a grain of truth to Albert Shanker's accusation that Lindsay tended to polarize whites and blacks by his penchant for accusing his opposition of being against poor people or blacks. The problem stemmed directly from his early tendency to view problems through a moralistic lens, the hallmark of the puritan approach to government. The school strike is, of course, the outstanding example. Had Lindsay chosen to insist that the problem was primarily an administrative issue, one that concerned whites as well as blacks, and appointed a board with that point of view, it is likely that the Ocean Hill-Brownsville problem would never have escalated so uncontrollably. By defining the issue as one of community control for minorities—or by allowing it to be so defined—Lindsay made it a problem central to the evolving struggle for civil rights, which had much to do with the violent emotions that surrounded the strike and the extraordinary bitterness it elicited. Lindsay's second-term attitude was considerably modified. Aides report, for example, that he was most anxious to find a solution to the Forest Hills public housing project dispute that would save face on all sides— although by that time, his bargaining position was made much more difficult by the profound distrust in which he was held by whites and the impracticality of executing a total reversal of his previous public position on the importance of the project for blacks.

It was argued earlier that Lindsay's tendency to view all problems of race through the civil rights prism may have been his greatest failing. Discrimination and racism had very much to do with the fact that blacks were still in the economic and social position of recent immigrants in the 1960s. But although warring on the residual discriminatory barriers was still important, from that point it had only the most marginal impact on black status. The view that the low socio-economic status of blacks demonstrated not only past discrimination but continued oppression was, for the most part, simply wrong. Even with the discriminatory barriers largely down, blacks would still have to undertake the generational processes of economic and educational self-improvement and were in fact doing so. By apparently taking the position that socio-economic uplift for blacks required, rather than self-improvement, more rights and more services—that is, placing the problem squarely on whites and the government—Lindsay succeeded only in angering whites, misleading blacks, and confusing the government.

Lindsay's point of view, of course, was one that was widely shared by important sectors of the government, the media, and the public at the time. He was simply one of the few national spokesmen for the position who happened to become mayor of a large city when the struggle for civil rights and economic equality was at its most emotional and most intense. Given his personality and the times, it would have been surprising indeed if his stance had been other than what it was. But however sincere and explicable his positions, the racial polarization that resulted was seriously damaging and detracted substantially from the good that was done by competent equal rights enforcement and the increased opening of opportunities in the government to minorities.

SUMMARIZING THE RECORD

Lindsay's successes and failures were probably not in the areas he himself might have predicted when he took office. His most obvious failures were in reform and in improving relations between racial groups; his most obvious success was in putting city management on a sounder technical base than when he found it.

His contribution to the eventual fiscal crisis lay in not cutting back on city services after the economy turned downward during his second term and, in particular, not cutting back on spending in health and higher education, where he enjoyed greater policy flexibility than elsewhere. The increased reliance on short-term debt began a pattern that eventually brought the city to the brink of bankruptcy.

The style and rhetoric of his first administration contributed to the rancorous character of the city's labor relations, and his leadership in the national movement for welfare reform reinforced New York's image as the nation's welfare capital; but overall employee compensation seems to have risen at about the same rate as elsewhere, and there was nothing unusual about the growth in city welfare rolls. In both of these areas, national trends seem to have been far more influential than local administration.

How to scale the successes and the failures? The first-term Lindsay was very much a man of his time, reflecting—magnifying—the intensity and stridency of political dialogue in the late 1960s. He attempted, and almost accomplished, a painful readjustment when the inevitable reaction set in about 1970, but he squandered valuable time and political credits on a dreadfully miscalculated presidential race. Although there was considerable solid work carried out from the beginning of the administration, it was not until 1972 that the management leadership came from the top, and by then the time remaining to the administration was really too short to carry out the thorough redirection of city policies and practices that was needed. In many ways, then, the failures of the first term were the failures of a position, of an ideology; the failures of the second term—and the substantial successes—were much more his own. The final question is not whether the successes outweighed the failures, but whether, making reasonable allowance for the times and the trends, the Lindsay administrations fell short of what they might reasonably have accomplished. My own judgment is that they did, and by substantial margins.

X. *The Clubhouse Returns*

ABRAHAM BEAME

THERE IS a prevailing myth that traditional political machines bring cities wiser, more competent, more practical government than reform administrations. It is the failures of the reform movements—from those lamented by Lincoln Steffens in 1913 to the excesses of the first Lindsay administration—that make the myth plausible. Sadly, there is little truth to the rest of the story. Traditional politics, in the person of Abraham Beame, came back to control in 1973 at a critical stage in the city's history and demonstrated resoundingly that it was unequal to the task.

An accountant by training, Beame's reputation was grounded on a fifteen-year career in the city budget bureau and two stints as city comptroller—the first, when Wagner raided the ranks of the civil service to fill out his 1961 antiboss campaign ticket, and the second, beginning in 1969, when he was returned to his comptroller's post—almost by acclamation—after losing to Lindsay in the 1965 mayoral election. Beame's 1973 campaign slogan, "He Knows the Buck," was pitched to the public's slowly growing awareness of the primacy of fiscal policy for the city's future, and his public projection—the reassuring Brooklyn rasp, the colorless syntax, his wholly orthodox ties to the Democratic organization, his presumed mastery of the mechanical details of city administration, the image of quiet and grey-visaged competence—all promised the return to normalcy and stolid civic virtue so ardently desired by middle-class New Yorkers. Although Beame fretted publicly about the overconfidence of his campaign workers, the outcome of the election was never really in doubt. An attempt by Rockefeller to enlist Robert Wagner as the Republican candidate resulted only in painful embarrassment for all concerned. Beame overwhelmed Herman Badillo in the Democratic primary runoff, and the November election was no contest. Beame collected almost 60 percent of the total vote and enjoyed a 3:1 advantage over the closest contender, Republican John Marchi.

Despite the sudden wave of nostalgia at Lindsay's departure and the adroitly publicized improvements in the city's financial and management standing during his last year in office, the city's problems in 1973 were deep-seated indeed. The combination of steadily rising municipal costs, a weakened economic base, a dangerous overhang of short-term debt, and one of the worst of the post–World War II recessions called for fiscal management of the highest order if the city was to avert disaster. But for all his vaunted reputation as a fiscal expert, there was nothing in Beame's record to indicate that he was capable of rising to the challenge. The unparalleled master of the purely expedient, he had devoted whatever wizardry he possessed to devising, year after year, new financial gimmicks to avoid politically unpalatable tax increases or cuts in spending. In 1963, for instance, it was Beame who beat back Wagner's proposed tax increases in the Board of Estimate by tinkering with the city's spending and revenue projections, and then, a year later, it was Beame who enjoyed the luxury of excoriating Wagner when the books closed on an operating deficit. Beame may well have been the first to propose the systematic use of the state-city "magic window" fiscal year overlap as a budget-balancing device, and after returning to the comptroller's office in 1970, he proved never able to resist the short-term political advantage of underestimating city spending requirements and overestimating the return from taxes and aid. It was Beame who found the $267 million in pension funds, deferred obligations, and wistful revenues to help balance the 1971–72 budget without spending cutbacks and who, even after his proposals had been adopted, insisted there was still $330 million worth of room for maneuver in an obviously unsound budget. The following year was a repeat performance as Beame undercut Lindsay's plea for more state assistance by conjuring away a budget gap of more than $200 million.

Although Lindsay must bear the ultimate responsibility for the city's increasingly unsound budget practices, it was Beame who sold the bonds and notes that financed the city's growing operating deficits, who certified the inflated figures for tax and aid receivables, who maintained the muddled books that defeated the most diligent inquiry into the city's true situation, who insisted on the "surpluses" in the city's pension funds, and who supervised the subtle shifts between cash and accrual accounting methods that masked spending overruns and revenue shortfalls. Characteristically, in 1971, when the city administration seemed finally prepared to dig in its heels against persistent overspending at the Board of Education, it was Beame who, probably illegally, shifted teachers' salaries into the next budget year to relieve the board of the consequences of its own irresponsibility.

The one solid achievement in the Beame financial record was his success during his first term as comptroller in shortening the city's excessively long-term debt structure. But from that point he made something of a fetish of short-term debt and seemed never to appreciate that, particularly in times of high inflation and favorable interest rates, judiciously lengthened debt had significant advantages from the point of view of cash flows and present value calculations of future payments. Just before the fiscal crisis, for example, Beame boasted that half the city's debt would mature within five years—precisely the point that so worried the bankers. His mismanagement of housing debt contributed substantially to the city's financing problems. The city sub-sidized middle-income housing construction by financing mortgages for quali-fied sponsors with city bonds, relying on the lower interest costs of city debt and tax abatements to keep monthly rentals within a reasonable range. Because short-term debt usually carries lower interest charges than longer-term debt, Beame made a practice of issuing bond anticipation notes (BANs) to finance housing debt and rolling over the notes as they matured, instead of putting the projects on a permanent financial footing. Inevitably, as the program expanded, the volume of housing notes grew to alarming proportions; but in 1973 Beame publicly attacked a suggestion by Lindsay housing officials that he take advan-tage of the sharply favorable break in interest rates to fund the notes. Two years later, with almost $1 billion in BANs outstanding, short-term rates were hover-ing between 7 and 9 percent, compared to the 5 to 6 percent that had been available on long-term debt in 1973. The necessity for continued refinancing of the BANs was an important contributor to the city's eventual week-to-week dependence on the financial markets to meet its obligations.

The commencement of Beame's mayoralty was no less inauspicious than his career as a financial manager. Three of his top appointments had to withdraw before being sworn in because of ethics problems—one because he circulated a letter to business customers that his new position in the administration should be of great benefit to his clients. With the exception of a few quality appoint-ments—such as Roger Starr at Housing and Lowell Bellin at Health—and the civil service holdovers like Lang at Water Resources and O'Hagan at Fire, the first round of selections for key positions was decidedly lackluster. The chief qualification of Melvin Lechner for the critical post of budget director seemed to be that he was the nephew of one of Beame's closest friends. Robert Groh at Sanitation set about dismantling Elish's industrial engineering and productivity teams and presided over a sharp falloff in departmental morale and output until Lang took over the department in 1975. James Cavanagh would have been a good choice for budget director but was visibly uncomfortable as first deputy mayor. James Dumpson, Wagner's last commissioner of welfare, was selected to head HRA and, by staff accounts, never attempted to come to grips with that agency. Jerome Hornblass had no apparent qualifications for the post of addic-tion services commissioner except a relatively unperceptive audit report on the agency he had written while on the staff of the comptroller's office. Michael Codd's chief virtue at the police department was that he maintained a lower public profile than Donald Cawley, Patrick Murphy's handpicked successor.

Beame's perception that the public wanted a return to the solidities of the 1950s was undoubtedly correct, but he exhibited a deplorable lack of discrimi-nation in rooting out the vestiges of the Lindsay administration. Lindsay's most substantial achievement—improved analytic and technical management capa-city—depended heavily on the ranks of middle- and upper-level industrial en-gineers and other management technicians who had been recruited into the city's service. But most of the technicians were summarily dismissed by the new administration, and the remainder were simply not used until they left of their own accord. When the city's productivity effort was revived after the fiscal crisis, the city's management ranks had to be painfully rebuilt. Similarly, hopeful steps that had been taken during Lindsay's last two years in office to decentralize the budget transactional process, to improve accounting controls over city agencies, and to modify civil service rules for increased management flexibility were scrapped. The budget bureau reverted to the old system of line-item transactional controls, and the civil service rules were made more rigid than ever: Instead of a manager's being allowed to choose from the top three finalists on a civil service list, his choice was restricted solely to the person with the highest score on a written test, regardless of what other qualifications might be relevant to an applicant's capacity to perform.

But Beame's initial management steps were not, in the final analysis, of very much consequence, because all thought of management issues was quickly swept away by the city's growing financial crisis. When the crisis reached its first uneasy resolution, responsibility for financial and managerial policymaking had been effectively removed from Beame's hands and key decisions became the responsibility of newly-created agencies outside the control of the city's voters.

THE BUDGET: 1973–75

Both Lindsay and Beame subsequently disclaimed credit for the 1973–74 budget—the budget that was formulated during Lindsay's last year in office and overlapped into Beame's first term. Although the budget was prepared in the midst of a mild economic upturn and generally good revenue reports for the 1973–74 fiscal year, it underscored the city's continued fiscal stringency. Lindsay's original proposal, at $10.6 billion, was moderately restrictive, essentially providing only for mandated expenditure increases. But available city revenues still fell some $200 million short of the funds required, even after deferring rainy day fund payments, assuming a sharp increase in real estate taxes, and scheduling a sizable increase in capital budget financing of operating expenses (primarily by shifting vocational education expenses to the capital budget).

Although the city insisted that the state "had cash hidden all over the place" after two restrictive budgets in a row, neither Rockefeller nor the legislature was in a mood to increase levels of assistance, and Lindsay, visibly exhausted after eight years of continuous strife, had no stomach for the kind of all-out assault on the Albany treasury that had characterized most previous budget years. The legislature finally authorized an aid package nominally valued at $90 million, but more than half of the total consisted merely of further borrowing authorizations, while the remainder was of dubious financing value, because the new aid was earmarked for social services and required matching expenditures by the city.

Into the breach stepped Beame, as he had in virtually every previous budget crisis, with his own estimates of revenues and spending and $144 million in proposed new borrowings, although he had ritualistically denounced the level of city borrowing just a few weeks earlier. His total package reduced spending estimates to just under $10.2 billion, eliminated the need for new operating tax revenues, and still left a sufficient "surplus" to hire three thousand additional policemen—a key promise in Beame's race for the mayoralty. This time Lindsay yielded without a struggle. It was an election year, so there was no sympathy for tax increases or budget cuts in the City Council or the Board of Estimate. Beame seemed almost certain to be the next mayor, and there was little doubt that he could carry the council and board in a showdown. At a closed-door Gracie Mansion meeting, in what the *Times* called an "exercise in political hero-making," Lindsay accepted the entire package of Beame changes, allowing the budget to zip through the local legislative processes the following week virtually without dissent. It was a display of the precise qualities that Beame was attempting to project in his campaign—technical mastery over the arcana of budgets and finance, a shift of spending priorities back toward basic services, and the ability to engineer consensus on tough issues—a welcome relief after the shrill divisiveness of Lindsay's budget battles.

The budget may have been good politics, but it was a financial disaster. Shortly after the election the Beame budget transition team announced almost in panic that the current year's budget deficit was running at a rate of $200 million to $300 million and the next year's budget gap might be as high as $1.5 billion. Nonsense, scoffed *The New York Times:* Standard & Poor's had just upgraded the city's bond rating to A, an action that would hardly be consistent with the transition team's gloomy forecasts. Surely, Beame was not going to resort to the tiresome histrionics of the Lindsay years?

Beame continued to preach doom, but in the most muted tones, and his actions belied his predictions. He talked about a relentless attrition program, but total city employment was allowed to rise about 2 percent, and, after some hesitation, he substantially delivered on his promise to increase the police force. The crisis, however, was real. Inflation—driven now by the 1973 Arab oil price increase—jumped 9 percent, putting cruel pressure on city expenses, while collective bargaining agreements kept wages moving up faster than ever. Private-sector job losses accelerated again, and the per capita personal income of city residents flattened out, dropping sharply in real terms. Unemployment, after having been reduced to 6 percent in 1973—still almost double the 1969 rate—crept up to 7.3 percent by the end of the year. With the economy slipping into deep recession, receipts from every major city tax dropped in constant-dollar terms.

The situation was in every way comparable to the fiscal crises that wracked the Lindsay administration from 1970 to 1972, except that the city was now dealing from a weaker economic base. Like Lindsay, Beame undercut his own arguments that the city was in serious financial trouble by concealing the deficits through borrowing—this time in amounts unprecedented even in New York City. The nominal deficit at the end of the fiscal year was only $200 million—about half the nominal deficit at the end of the 1970–71 fiscal year, when Lindsay had resorted to budget notes for the first time. But the true deficit was probably closer to $1 billion. Capital budget financing of operating expenses increased from $274 million to $564 million; borrowing against uncollected real estate taxes rose to $317 million (although with a rising rate of delinquencies, there was little hope of collecting even half that amount); the $300 million in budget notes from 1970–71 were left unpaid; and, most serious of all, RANs outstanding jumped $900 million—for a total of $1.8 billion by the end of the year. By this point the issuance of RANs had lost any but a purely fictional connection with anticipated federal and state aid. The $900 million increase—presumably anticipating aid due in the last quarter of the year*—measured against a total increase in outside aid during the entire year of only $226 million, while the RANs outstanding at the end of the year equalled about 46 percent of the total aid received. Making even the most liberal assumptions about delays in federal and state aid payments,† possibly $1 billion of the RANs was simply a permanently floating short-term debt that the city would have to redeem, if at all, from its general operating revenues.

As the 1974–75 budget—the first that was indisputably Beame's own—was being formulated, it was obvious that the city was in serious financial trouble. The world-wide recession that had set in after the oil price increases was showing signs of becoming permanent; "double-digit" inflation had entered the political vocabulary; and with the wholesale economic decline of the Northeast now an established fact, there was little reason to expect buoyancy in the city tax base. The increase in total property values had slowed to a crawl, increasing at less than half the rate of inflation; the index of business activity was dropping to its lowest point in ten years; and unemployment was moving up rapidly toward a depression-level high of 11 percent later in the year, almost quadruple the rate just five years before. There were built-in spending problems. Welfare rolls had begun to expand again, after two years of decline, and the legislature had approved a grant increase, which promised to push up costs even faster. The time limit on repaying the $300 million in budget notes from 1970–71 had expired. Debt service costs were up by $600 million over the previous year, a 50 percent increase. Pension costs had increased $500 million in just two years, an increase of 86 percent.

Beame certainly understood the gravity of the problems but seemed confident of his ability to ride out the storm. More important, he seemed unwilling to jeopardize his carefully constructed reputation for quiet competence. His approach to the state for assistance was decidedly low-key, as though an all-out campaign for more aid would be too reminiscent of Lindsay's annual clamors.

If Beame made a forceful presentation of the city's problems to the state leadership, he did so privately, and got nowhere. Stanley Steingut, a long-time Beame crony and the key figure in the Democratic assembly, was straining to gain control of the legislature and was reluctant to exhaust his credit on an expensive city aid package. Malcolm Wilson—who after many years as lieutenant governor, succeeded Rockefeller when the latter was chosen to be the vice-president—was anxious to win the gubernatorial election in his own right the following fall and feared the political repercussions of a state tax increase to help

---

* A small and relatively constant portion of the RANs—less than 10 percent—was issued against the sales tax and other general fund receipts.

† The largest single block of outside aid—the payments for welfare and Medicaid—was paid 80 percent in advance each quarter on the basis of city-prepared spending estimates.

the city. According to Cavanagh, he told Beame, "Why don't you just borrow?" By docilely taking that advice, Beame committed a major political blunder—even leaving aside the financial dangers of more borrowing. For at least the previous decade and a half, the only truly substantial aid increases won from the state had come during gubernatorial election years, when elected state leaders needed the support of the powerful downstate voting blocs. The tax increases to finance new assistance could always be deferred until the following year, when the votes had already been nailed down and counted. Of course, Wilson was a fiscal conservative and might have resisted aid requests, no matter how aggressive a campaign the city waged. But by giving up without a fight, Beame passed by the quadriennial opportunity for shifting more of the city's costs to the state's broader tax base and left himself only the alternatives of deep cuts in ongoing operations or resort to fiscal gimmicks on a scale not matched by anything that had gone before.

The major piece in the package finally stitched together with Wilson was the Stabilization Reserve Corporation, another off–balance sheet debt mechanism with the purpose of stretching out payments on city notes. The SRC was authorized to issue $520 million of ten-year notes, guaranteed by debt service payments from the city. Three hundred million dollars would pay off the 1970–71 budget notes, $150 million would finance part of the deficit from the 1973–74 fiscal year, and the remainder would contribute toward funding the deficit anticipated for 1974–75. The rest of the nominal gap was made up by a variety of new revenues and gimmicks. There were two new taxes—a 1 percent addition to the city sales tax, worth about $200 million, and a 5 percent surcharge on the Off-Track Betting winners' pool, worth about $25 million. New state aid totaled $87 million. (The figure was an overestimate, but when the new comptroller, Harrison Goldin, challenged the number, Beame simply asked if he had any better ideas.) Needless to say, all reserve fund payments were skipped. The amount of operating expenses assigned to the capital budget was raised from $564 million to $722 million. A rollback of state aid scheduled for the following year produced $114 million, presumably leaving the next year's problems to be solved when they arose. One hundred ninety-nine million dollars was materialized by tinkering with the city's contributions to its pension funds. The pension funds assumed that assets would earn 4 percent interest; and in recent years the city had counted earnings in excess of 4 percent as a surplus to offset required contributions.* But because the city lagged its pension contributions two years, declarations of surpluses were likewise lagged two years. Beame's new wrinkle was to deduct not only the surplus earned in 1972–73, the contribution year paid in the 1974–75 budget, but the estimated surpluses for the next two fiscal years as well, aggravating again his budget problems in the years immediately to come. Finally, even though the borrowings and gimmicks that can be pinpointed with precision

---

* The practice, of course, made no actuarial sense, for the principle of actuarial funding is that a plan will achieve its earnings assumptions only as an average: good years offset bad ones. But the practice was not altogether unreasonable, because the city had for many years supplemented its contributions when earnings fell below 4 percent.

were in excess of $1.5 billion, there was still a substantial gap that was covered simply by underestimating expenses and overestimating revenues. The exact amount of the problem that was wished away by juggled estimates is difficult to price with any accuracy, but by September Beame was admitting to a deficit of $200 million, and by winter he conceded $450 million, while Goldin estimated that the city was running $630 million in the red.

Passing the budget through the City Council and the Board of Estimate was a *tour de force*, probably Beame's last, and certainly most Pyrrhic, political success. The city's legislators—although by this point beyond shock when it came to budget gimmicks—were completely opposed to any increases in taxes and served notice that the revenue proposals were in for heavy weather. Beame, working almost entirely behind the scenes, pulled out all the political stops. Queens Councilman Matthew Troy, the chairman of the Finance Committee, who had made a reputation cutting taxes at the end of the Lindsay administration, opened his mouth in fierce protest but ended up swallowing the budget whole. By promises and threats, and by calling in the debts he had accumulated over the years, Beame rammed the budget and taxes through the council and the board, virtually without dissent and without debate, while Troy stood sputtering on the sidelines. It was a most impressive performance, a "smashing political victory," wrote *The New York Times*, and to most onlookers an immense relief after the consecutive budget cliffhangers that had rattled the nerves of New Yorkers for at least the previous ten years.

But it was finally too much. Cutting through the legerdemain and the technical sophistication of the various budget-balancing devices, they mostly amounted to the same thing: the city would borrow, predominantly short-term, to cover current operating expenses and would keep on borrowing to pay off the accumulated borrowings. The strategy was sustainable so long as the banks made money by handling and investing in the city's paper. But by 1975 the city was overwhelming the financial markets, and at a time when the bankers had found more profitable uses for their funds. When the city's access to the financial markets was cut off, the result of the accumulated gimmicks was exposed in a way that anyone could understand: the city's commitments were massively greater than its income; unless the city could keep on borrowing, there was no way it could pay its bills.

FINANCIAL COLLAPSE

By the fall of 1974, awareness of the city's deep trouble was beginning to spread among financial analysts. Fitch Investors' Service published a report downgrading the city's bonds from A to BBB or BB, depending on their maturity dates, and highlighting the city's persistent current deficit—cash disbursements had exceeded cash receipts for a number of years, and in 1973–74 the cash gap reached $2 billion, a 152 percent increase over the previous year. Fitch feared that with multiplying signs of a debilitated financial base—rising real estate tax delinquencies, continuing revenue shortfalls, depleted reserves, growing pension obligations, and extensive capitalization of operating expenses—investors might lose confidence in the city and stop supplying its cash requirements.

In the comptroller's office two of Goldin's aides, Jon Weiner and Steven Clifford, wrote a series of memoranda detailing the city's mounting difficulties, and some of the numbers were filtering into the financial community. In one memo Clifford speculated that perhaps $2.7 billion of the city's receivables would have to be written off if the city were to apply normal accounting principles in balancing its books. The $2.7 billion write-off figure appeared the following week in an internal memorandum at the Morgan Guaranty Bank; Morgan's analyst was worried whether the write-off required might already be too large for the banking community to finance. The banks' own analyses were generating increased concern. Karen Gerard, a Chase Manhattan Bank economist, prepared a series of studies showing that the city's announced budgetary problems were not just political ploys to attract more aid. This time, she wrote, "the budget gap is real." In another analysis Gerard compared the increases in RANs over the previous several years with the actual increases in aid receivables and wondered whether the rapid runup in RANs could be fully accounted for by slow aid payment cycles. "The large volume of new issues," she speculated, "could conceal a serious problem of whether there is in fact anticipated aid behind the debt. If the latter were true, the consequences would be grave for both the short term and long-term municipal market."

The banks' steadily increasing skepticism came at a time when the city was resorting to the capital market as never before. To keep the steadily mounting short-term debt rolling over, the city had to borrow $2.5 billion in one two-month stretch ending in November, 1974, and it borrowed another $600 million in December. Total borrowing in the calendar year 1974 was in excess of $8 billion, and in November short-term debt outstanding was $5.3 billion—$1.9 billion up over the amount outstanding in June and a fourfold increase in four years. The sheer volume of debt began to overshadow all the city's other problems. In late 1974 New York City accounted for over 40 percent of short-term tax-exempt borrowing in the United States, and with redemption dates looming inexorably throughout the months ahead, it was clear that the city would have to resort to the markets continuously and without regard to borrowing conditions to keep from default. Under the circumstances, the highly touted "first lien on revenues" that supposedly protected city investors began to look like an increasingly flimsy shield. The Fitch report speculated on whether the city's "police power" obligations might operate as a superior lien on revenues: In other words, if it came to a choice between paying lenders and paying firemen and sanitationmen, was there any doubt whom the city would choose to pay? In December Morgan advised a substantial client to reduce her holdings of city securities; in January Citibank decided not to purchase city securities for its fiduciary accounts; and in the same month, an internal First Boston memorandum said:

Despite the possibility of some temporary improvement, it was felt the longer-term prospects for the City's finances were not encouraging. Therefore, it was voted to discontinue approval for the purchase of general trust investment of all obligations of the

City of New York, and sale should be considered on all issues maturing after August, 1975.

With investor confidence waning rapidly, interest rates on city notes and bonds soared, even though Standard & Poor's and Moody's—after strenuous pressure from Beame—reconfirmed the city's A rating. Through the fall the rate on notes jumped to 7.3 percent, then 8.3 percent, and by January interest rates on RANs were at a record high of 9.4 percent, even higher than the rate on comparable taxable U.S. Treasury bills and twice as high as the rate on similarly graded tax-exempts elsewhere in the country.

To make matters worse, New York City debt was falling under a shadow at a time when the market for tax-exempt securities was weakening everywhere, both because of the large volume of new issues and shifts in business investment patterns. The increase in tax-exempt debt in the rest of New York State more than kept pace with the upsurge in the city, and with the increased popularity of special-district financing, outstanding state and local debt elsewhere in the country had risen by almost $100 billion since 1964. Moreover by 1975 the market was swelled another 10 to 15 percent by newly authorized private industry tax-exempt issues for pollution control. At the same time tax-exempt issues were becoming increasingly less attractive to their traditional purchasers—insurance companies and commercial banks. Insurance companies suffered their most spectacular underwriting losses ever in 1974 and 1975 and had little need for income tax shelters, while commercial banks were shifting their investments overseas and enjoyed large foreign tax credits. In 1970 commercial banks took up 95 percent of the net increase in municipal debt, but in 1975, only about 20 percent. From about 1973 the only sustaining force in the tax-exempt market was private households, as inflation moved more and more people into tax brackets where tax-exempt income began to be an attractive investment. By 1975 individuals bought about 60 percent of the net new municipal issues. The increased penetration of private individuals into the tax-exempt market made debt offerings much more subject to what underwriters called "confidence factors." As newspaper stories spread gloom about the city's problems, the city's huge overhang of short-term debt was increasingly vulnerable to a sudden flight from the market.

Beame showed little indication that he appreciated the perilousness of the city's circumstances, even in the face of the first definite signs, in October 1974, that the market for city paper was drying up. An underwriting syndicate failed to resell, even at a substantial discount, almost half of a $500 million bond issue, and by December paper losses on the underwriting were calculated to approach $50 million. But as the bankers became increasingly nervous about the future of city debt issues, Beame steadfastly insisted on ignoring their fears. In a series of meeting requested by the bankers to discuss the impending fiscal crisis, Beame berated the financial community—"beat us over the head," as one banker put it—for their failure to sell city bonds and notes. The mayor insisted that the city was borrowing against "firm receivables" as it always had, and if the institutional and out-of-state markets were closing to city issues, it was the bankers' fault. When interest rates hit 9.4 percent on notes in January, the mayor called a meeting of the bankers at Gracie Mansion and accused them of "bad mouthing" the city. The banks were taking advantage of the city's problems, he insisted. The 9.4 percent rate had resulted from a single bid, and the underwriters were reselling the notes so briskly that interest rates were dropping as low as 8.5 percent. All the city's debt carried a first lien on its revenues. Beame contended, and the high interest rates were not reflective of the city's underlying financial strength. In February Beame wrote to a leading banker about reports that some institutions were advising clients against purchases of city paper. It was "destructive advice," he said, "malicious," "nonsense," and

I think it is up to the financial community to turn this topsy-turvy situation right-side up again. As I said at our meetings, I believe the financial community has a selling job to do to make the investing public see the financial strengths of our obligations.

We in the City government are going everything in our power to deal with the budget problems which the national recession-inflation created, and I believe the general public supports what the City administration is doing.

Although Comptroller Goldin often split with Beame at the most awkward moments, he generally backed Beame against the financial community. When the bankers demanded that the city put its financial house in order and traced the contracting market for city issues to chronic overspending, Goldin joined Beame in insisting that budget balancing and access to the credit markets were unrelated problems. In Goldin's words, "New York's budget problems should be of only marginal interest to investors, who are protected by the State Constitutional guarantees making New York City bonds and notes a first lien on all revenues." A joint press release in January said that budget-balancing problems "have nothing to do with a city's ability, willingness and legal mandate to repay its debt."

Beame's administration of the city budget did little to allay the financial community's concerns. An ongoing spat with Goldin over the actual size of the city's deficit was disquieting—their respective figures were consistently about $200 million apart. Beame repeatedly announced austere fiscal measures that had a way of dissolving upon close examination. Several months after the mayor imposed a "rigid hiring freeze," *The New York Times* reported that city payrolls had grown by 13,000 in a single quarter. *The New Yorker* traced back a "massive layoff" of 7,935 workers and found that only 436 people had actually lost their jobs. When the mayor's capital budget for 1975–76 was announced in January, it was disclosed that almost $1 billion of the city's borrowing authority was consumed by operating expenses, payments of past judgments and claims, and fare subsidies to the transit system. Although the collapse of the West Side Highway had underlined the badly deteriorated condition of the city's capital plant, there was, for all practical purposes, no money left for maintaining the city's infrastructure. When Beame's 1975–76 expense budget plans were announced the following month, according to the *Times*, they "left knowledgeable observers gasping with disbelief." Beame estimated that he could close about $800 million of a projected $1.68 billion gap through a variety of financial maneuvers, leaving almost $900 million to be supplied by hypothetical new state and federal aid. In the words of the *Times* editorialist:

[The City is facing] a fiscal crisis from which there can be no escape without drastic cuts in personnel and services and substantial increases in taxes . . . Incredibly, there is little indication in the Mayor's budget presentation so far that Mr. Beame, once widely hailed as a tough fiscal expert, is prepared at last to grapple with these hard realities.

February 1975 was the month when the city's tangled fiscal web began finally to unravel. First, the tax-exempt markets were badly shaken by the default of the state Urban Development Corporation on $100 million of BANs. The corporation had depended heavily on the availability of federal subsidies to maintain the rents of its projects at marketable levels, and when the subsidy program was sharply curtailed, it found itself badly overextended. The bankers demanded that the state replace UDC revenue bonds with its own credit as a precondition to further rollovers of the corporation's paper. When the new governor, Hugh Carey, offered only better-secured revenue bonds, the banks refused to refinance the BANs and the corporation defaulted. And it was lost on no-one that the legislature came up with the cash to pay contractors and suppliers while the notes went unredeemed. Although the UDC's problems were theoretically distinct from the city's, the distinction was a fine one in the eyes of most investors, and the experience was a pointed object lesson in political payment priorities.

Then, in the same month, the city's cash flow projections were violently dislocated by a taxpayer's suit that blocked the projected sale of the $520 million in Stabilization Reserve Corporation notes that had been authorized to balance the 1974–75 budget and redeem maturing budget notes. The suit's contention that the SRC was an unconstitutional evasion of the city's debt limit was of dubious merit, because the city still had sufficient unencumbered debt margin to accommodate the SRC borrowing in any case, but the pendency of a legal action made SRC notes unmarketable. The city's problem was that it had already redeemed the budget notes that the SRC borrowings were intended to finance. Without the SRC proceeds there wasn't enough cash left in the treasury to meet the February payrolls.

The failure of the SRC notes set in train a pattern of frantic improvisation by Beame and Goldin, a day-to-day scrambling, often near the edges of the law, to raise the cash to keep the city operating. The banks agreed to put up a $170 million, three-day "bridge loan" in RANs to get the city over a payroll period, while a plan was devised to replace the SRC proceeds by issuing $260 million in TANs and arranging for the pension funds to purchase another $249 million in BANs. The pension funds agreed to the purchase but were $200 million short of the necessary cash. That problem was resolved by arranging for the sinking funds, which Goldin controlled, to buy city securities already held by the pension funds in order to free sufficient pension assets. The transaction required a change in the city charter and an emergency amendment of the local finance law to permit the sinking funds to buy city notes at par when comparable notes were available in the market below par. The required legislation, the purchase of pension assets by the sinking funds, and the purchase of the new BANs by the pension funds were all accomplished in time to redeem the bridge-loan RANs with a day to spare—even though a last-minute hitch threatened the entire transaction. The provision restricting sinking fund purchases of securities at par was written into the contract between one of the sinking funds and its bondholders and was not affected by the legislative amendments; Goldin received legal advice that the transaction should not proceed. Working against the clock, he conducted an impromptu market survey and concluded that there was enough cash in the fund to buy any readily available below-par notes and still participate in the BAN transaction. Armed with this information, he secured a revised legal opinion, and the deal went through.

Just as the pension fund BAN purchase was worked out, the $260 million issue of TANs—the other half of the arrangement to replace the SRC proceeds—ran into trouble. The TANs had been sold on February 19 to two syndicates—one headed by Bankers Trust and the other by Chase—at an average 7.1 percent interest, the best that the city had enjoyed in several months. On February 26, however—two days before the sale was to have been closed— Bankers Trust informed the city that its counsel, White and Case, who were acting as counsel on a city issue for the first time, were having trouble certifying that the notes were being validly issued. Without a "clean" legal opinion the bankers could not resell the notes. The problem related to the city's certification that there were sufficient uncollected taxes on its books that had not yet been borrowed against to back up the sale of such a volume of tax anticipation notes. As was its custom, the city had certified its tax collectibles as of the close of the previous month—January 31 in this instance, when the books showed $409 million in uncollected taxes available for borrowing purposes, more than enough to support the issue. White and Case was concerned, however, that a strict reading of the local finance law required a certification as of the day of the issue. Goldin's position was that bond counsel had never required such a certification before and that assembling current information from the city's manual accounts simply wasn't possible in the time available. He offered a compromise certification as of February 6 but could do no better than that. Wood, Dawson, Chase's counsel, who had been involved in most city issues for the previous thirty years, were willing to stick with long-standing practice and give a clean opinion. The Wood, Dawson partner in charge of the underwriting felt that there was no point in reading the statutes strictly in municipal financings because there was "generally plenty of fat all over the place." A series of hastily called meetings throughout February 27 and 28 and a somewhat hopeless attempt by White and Case associates to decipher collection receipts failed to produce a compromise. On the afternoon of February 28, Bankers Trust withdrew from the purchase, and Chase, unwilling to go it alone, followed suit. An angry Goldin announced the cancellation of the TANs, saying it had come about because of "a sudden demand by the underwriters, unprecedented in the history of the City, for data that could not physically be compiled, checked and verified in the short time available" and that it was "completely inaccurate to report or imply that there's any question concerning the sufficiency of tax revenues to meet all obligations, including the notes which were subject to today's [cancellation]."

But White and Case's insistence on a literal reading of the statute was well grounded. January 31 was the last day of the grace period for making semiannual tax payments, and a large volume of late collections flowed into the city throughout February. It was perfectly reasonable to question whether the city still had enough uncollected taxes to cover $260 million in TANs; and in fact, when all the collections were finally tabulated, the city was shown to be $112 million short of the required borrowing authority. The issuance and sale of the notes would have been illegal.

The TANs cancellation, on top of the SRC suit and the UDC default, heightened the market's suspicion of city issues, but the city's cash requirements were now more pressing than ever. The city had to redeem approximately $500 million in bonds and notes throughout March, and a massive $600 million TAN redemption was scheduled for April 14. Overall, budget officials were quietly calculating, the city's total cash needs through the end of the fiscal year to finance regular operating expenditures, note and bond redemptions, and the anticipated deficit would be more than $2 billion in excess of anticipated cash receipts, requiring borrowing in at least that amount. The city's legal borrowing authority, it appeared, fell about $900 million short of the amount required, assuming that the SRC notes had no market regardless of the outcome of the pending litigation.

Beame and Goldin slogged steadfastly on. By the end of the first week in March, in the wake of the TANs cancellation, there was only $176 million in the city treasury, but $427 million was required by March 14 for payrolls and note redemptions. Goldin had already announced a $537 million BANs sale, then arranged a $140 million bridge loan, placed privately with the banks, and on March 7 announced a $375 million RANs offering. The BANs and RANs offerings, if they sold, would be enough to get the city through March and defer the next crisis until the April 14 TANs redemption.

By this time the banks were thoroughly frightened. About 20 percent of their equity was tied up in city paper, so if they refused to underwrite continued note offerings, their own financial stability would be threatened. But at the same time, they could no longer pretend ignorance of the city's financial situation. In a skittish market drowning in city paper, there were grave doubts that the city could accomplish the immense amount of borrowing it had scheduled through the end of the fiscal year and equally grave doubts about its legal capacity to borrow that much even if the markets were available. At the gloomy meetings of the underwriters, discussion began to turn to their own possible criminal liability if they sold notes they knew the city would have difficulty redeeming. Only a delicately hair-splitting series of legal rationalizations kept them in the market. When the March BANs were offered to the public, a press release from Goldin's office that alluded to the city's fiscal problems was called a "disclosure statement" in the underwriters' internal memoranda. Wood, Dawson soothed the bankers' fears that the March RANs were beyond the city's borrowing capacity by suggesting that if the city said that it had the authority, the banks were not required to look behind the city's figures unless there were some evidence of "hanky-panky." White and Case were not so sure. Knowing what the bankers knew, they reasoned, a failure to examine the city's claims of borrowing authority could be construed as a failure of their duty to potential notebuyers. The problem was resolved by providing buyers with a "Statement of Essential Facts" about city finances that, in the words of one banker, "substituted for a very damaging disclosure statement," and managed to avoid any discussion of the imminence of the city's financing problems. The underwriters reassured themselves that they were representing to notebuyers only that they had no reason to believe that city financial data were incorrect. They were only "providing information," not "verifying" it.

The bankers began putting out feelers to the federal government. Even after the March BANs and RANs sales, revised estimates showed that the city still needed to borrow another $2.6 billion to get through to the end of the fiscal year. With $6.1 billion of short-term city paper already in the market, one banker estimated that the public markets could supply only $100 million to $200 million of that amount. And by the end of March, almost half of the BANs—some $249 million, which represented virtually the entire part of the offering with more than a six-month maturity date—were still unsold, while the RANs had been almost a total bomb—only $57 million of the $375 million offering sold during the first two weeks after the offering to the public. With public markets closing, only the Federal Reserve system or the national treasury could come up with the volumes of cash that the city needed in order to keep operating. Federal officials seemed interested and sympathetic but had little to offer. The Federal Reserve was reluctant to undertake large-scale lending to the city, and the Treasury could not act to make or guarantee loans without a congressional mandate. With a Midwestern conservative president, Gerald Ford, in office, there was little hope of passing the required legislation.

The bankers were floating other ideas. Some kind of borrowing authority, similar to the aborted SRC, that could stretch out the city's short-term obligations and get it off the borrowing treadmill seemed to be one of the few feasible ways to avert a disaster. Longer-term obligations that were part of a comprehensive program of city fiscal reform might be salable, they calculated, but only if there were clear evidence that the city was putting its house in order. There was an emerging consensus in the financial community about what kind of evidence was needed: At the very least there would have to be a return to sound accounting principles, an admission to operating deficits, and a systematic writing-off of bad receivables and other phony budget ploys, coupled with sharp cuts in city employment to bring operating expenses gradually in line with income.

Beame would have none of it. The more the bankers pressed for tangible demonstrations of reform, the more he stonewalled. When Walter Wriston, the head of Citibank, warned about the difficulties of finding a market for the March BANs, Beame replied that he "expected the banks to take the BANs into their portfolio, so the issue of marketability was moot." When the bankers tried to impress upon the mayor in a March meeting the dangers of a vanishing market and the necessity for action to restore confidence, the mayor retorted that the city had already suffered hundreds of millions in austerities. The $900 million budget gap in 1975–76 would not be a problem, Beame insisted, and because all city borrowings were backed by revenues, it was wrong even to speak of an increase in short-term debt. The market could be calmed if only the underwriters would start stressing the city's financial strongpoints. Each of the major firms present at the March meeting presented its view of the perils facing the city, but Beame stuck resolutely to his position. Later a quiet meeting between Beame and the heads of New York's major banks—quiet because of fears that knowledge of the meeting could "trigger a real panic in the market"—seemed likewise to get nowhere. A few days afterward, Beame issued a press release that said:

The "scare" talk by some persons in the banking community does the City a severe disservice, since it does make it more difficult for the City to market its new short-term obligations.

I want to reassure the general public, City employees and the investing public that the City will meet its payrolls and debt service if the banks cooperate and stop casting unwarranted suspicion on the City's ability and willingness to pay all of its obligations on time.

Beame made a television speech on March 23 dealing with the city's financial problems, but in the eyes of the bankers, it was "a disaster." Essentially, it reviewed the actions that the city had already taken and included no new measures. Even the announcement of an ostensibly reduced borrowing schedule was, according to another Clifford memorandum, essentially phony: More gimmicks would contrive merely to make overall borrowings appear lower, but the deficits would increase. Beame seemed to believe that he could bully the banks into compliance. As Cavanagh put it, "The banks and us are in a community of interest; if we go down, they go down." When the banks laid their vision of apocalypse before Cavanagh in late March, he observed merely that the banks had a "real problem" and he hoped that they would resolve it.

It was in some ways a brave display, but the real problem was now the city's, for the banks could be pushed no further. Perhaps the last straw was the financial community's realization, in April, that the highly touted "first lien" on revenues that protected purchasers of city paper was probably a myth.* *Bonds* had a clear first lien on revenues, but notes did not. The state constitution and local finance law appeared to give BANs no first lien at all, and the principal amounts of RANs and TANs were protected only five years after their issuance. But because of legal sloppiness all note issues carried the apparently unequivocal assurance that the noteholders had a "first lien." As a partner from Wood, Dawson—the firm most intimately involved with city debt issues over the

* It eventually turned out that there *was* a first lien, or at least something very much like it. In 1976, the state court of appeals, construing the constitutional provisions governing payment of city debt broadly, overturned two lower court decisions and threw out a state law declaring a moratorium on the payment of city notes. City officials later defended themselves against the accusation that they had misled investors about the first lien by citing the court's decision. The defense was, to say the least, disingenuous, because the city had supported the Moratorium Act.

years—explained, the language had been allowed to remain in the offerings "because it was sort of historically considered to be true and characteristic of City obligations." It was the point of no return. When the city proposed the sale of $550 million of various notes to meet the massive TAN redemption scheduled on April 14, White and Case stated flatly:

[Although] we understand from the Banks that the adverse information required in a [disclosure] report would in all likelihood render the City securities unsalable . . . we re-emphasize our advice that public sales of New York City securities, in the absence of what may be agreed upon as full and meaningful written disclosure, would be contrary to the best interests of both the City and the Banks and could result in substantial exposure to liability both to the primary and secondary purchasers of the securities.

In other words, if the banks sold the notes, they might very well have to make up any losses incurred by purchasers if and when the City defaulted—which looked increasingly likely. White and Case also suggested that the banks consult their own counsels about whatever other difficulties they might be in. The banks had no choices left: When the city ran out of money on April 14, the banks were no longer there to lend it to them. The markets were closed, and the city was broke. Abraham Beame, who had wanted only to return to the old ways when the city was a comfortable place to be, found that he had completely lost control.

Epilogue

F OR FOUR YEARS after the credit markets closed to the city in the spring of 1975, the city careened from crisis to crisis, repeatedly escaping default by the narrowest of margins, and then only by dint of a series of state and federal rescue efforts that bound together the fates of the city and the much-protesting union pension funds and banks in progressively more intricate mutual dependence. The loss of control by local elected officials was enshrined in statute as the new governor, Hugh Carey, steadily asserted control over the city's internal affairs.

At first it took some months for the full extent of the city's fiscal difficulties to sink in. The immediate problem of finding funds to get through the April cash squeeze was resolved when the state agreed to advance $400 million in revenue-sharing funds due in June. But when the city attempted to re-enter the credit markets in May, they were told by the banks that there was no market for city paper—at all—and the banks weren't interested in buying any for themselves.

With another note and bond refunding date scheduled for June, Beame turned to the state for more aid. Carey, by now alarmed for the state's own credit, appointed an advisory panel to look into the city's affairs comprising Simon Rifkind, one of New York's pre-eminent lawyers, Richard Shinn and Donald Smiley, heads of Metropolitan Life Insurance and Macy's, respectively, and Felix Rohatyn of the investment bankers Lazard Frères, who had played a prominent role in a recent restructuring of the New York Stock Exchange and rescue attempts for the financially troubled Lockheed Corporation.

The advisory panel proposed the creation of the Municipal Assistance Corporation (MAC) to restructure the city's debt in return for compliance by the city with detailed stipulations on spending and accounting practices. Beame at first refused to go along with the idea, considering it a humiliating intrusion into local affairs, but finally—only days away from default—he was forced to embrace it as his own. MAC—or "Big Mac" in local argot—was empowered to issue long-term bonds and purchase city notes with the proceeds in order to get the city off the short-term debt treadmill. The city sales tax was repealed and replaced by a special state sales tax in the same amount, which, together with the stock transfer tax, was paid directly to MAC to secure its debt issuances. The state advanced $800 million in local assistance funds due the following year to close the city's operating deficit, and the banks bought enough MAC bonds to get the city through the June refunding. The hope was that with $3 billion in borrowing authority, MAC could buy out the city notes throughout the summer and, armed with a newly manageable debt structure and reformed accounting systems, the city would be back in the credit markets by October.

But when the bankers tried to resell their MAC paper, it bombed on the market, dropping almost immediately to 88 or 89 against a par value of 100. The bankers blamed it on Beame. His fulminations against an alleged "cash boycott" by the bankers indicated that he still hadn't conceded the basic problem of city overspending. Throughout the month of June he jockeyed with the legislature in traditional style for more taxes and aid to minimize cutbacks, and his submission of a two-option budget—an "austerity" budget and a "crisis" budget—was depressingly reminiscent of Lindsay's 1971 option-budget ploy. Rohatyn and the MAC board decided that the market still didn't believe the city was serious about reform.

Summer was a time for reality testing. MAC demanded a wage freeze, layoffs, an increase in the subway fare, and tuition at City University. The unions retaliated with threats and a wildcat sanitation strike ("the best organized wildcat strike in the City's history," one official called it). The firemen started a work slowdown, the police assailed visitors with lurid warnings about "Fear City," and in the fall the teachers struck the opening of school. It didn't make any difference. The unions swallowed the wage freeze, the transit fare went up, university funding was cut sharply, and there were staffing cutbacks across all city agencies.

But it still wasn't enough. MAC completed a billion-dollar refinancing operation in August—our "monthly miracle," Rohatyn called it—but there was another billion to be refinanced in September. The public markets, alarmed by the disarray in the city, were closing to MAC, the pension funds could not absorb that much debt on their own, the federal government refused to help, and the banks announced that they would not roll over any more notes.

In September Carey took control. Calling a special session of the legislature, he created the Emergency Financial Control Board, with a voting majority securely controlled by the state, which effectively removed financial management from Beame's hands. From that point all the revenue received by the city or the "covered agencies"—for example, the Transit Authority, the Board of Education, the Board of Higher Education, and the Health and Hospitals Corporation—were to be deposited with the control board and disbursed only upon its approval of detailed spending plans. The board was given approval power over most city contracts, including those with labor unions. A special deputy state comptroller was appointed to audit the city's books and oversee financial reporting on a continuing basis. With these safeguards the banks agreed to roll over their notes, the pension funds agreed to buy MAC debt, and the September crisis was passed.

It still wasn't enough. In October MAC 9¼ percent bonds plummeted toward 70, and on October 17 the city came literally within minutes of default when Albert Shanker's union pension fund trustees refused a purchase of MAC bonds as a pressure tactic for a favorable wage contract. At the last minute Shanker relented, and the participating banks extended their business hours to consummate the transaction. Even so, by the end of the month, the situation looked increasingly hopeless. The city had eliminated twenty thousand employees and cut heavily into essential services. The state had taken decisive action to eliminate the possibility of further fiscal shenanigans and had put its own shaky credit on the line. The pension funds had committed $500 million and were legitimately worried whether their fiduciary responsibilities would permit them to go further. Timely federal intervention seemed the only escape route, but when Carey spearheaded an aggressive lobbying campaign for federal loan guarantees, President Gerald Ford, sensing an anti–New York mood in the country, answered with an unequivocal "no"—or as the *Daily News* headline put it, "Ford to City: Drop Dead."

Ford's rejection was the low point. Surprisingly, his sense of the nation's animosity toward New York may have been wrong—at least, once the city was a decided underdog. Reaction to his speech ruling out federal assistance was at best mixed; he was assailed by mayors of both parties; and financial experts became genuinely worried about the credit consequences of a chain-reaction city and state default. Carey redoubled his lobbying efforts and in November was rewarded with a signal from Treasury Secretary William Simon that there might be conditions under which the president would reconsider his position.

In November, after three weeks of intense bargaining, the complex deal was struck. Another special session of the legislature declared a three-year moratorium* on the principal payments of $2.4 billion in city notes in order to force noteholders to exchange them for MAC bonds. The pension funds agreed to purchase $2.7 billion worth of city debt. The banks turned in $819 million in notes for MAC bonds and restructured the maturities and interest of the MAC bonds they already held. The city sinking funds traded $200 million in city notes for long-term city bonds. Congress passed (by only ten votes in the House), and Ford signed, a Seasonal Financing Act to provide up to $2.3 billion in short-term cash-flow loans during each of the next three years at 1 percent above the federal cost of money. Beame's closest fiscal aides—one of whom, James Cavanagh, was a long-time friend—were replaced by men the bankers felt more comfortable with. The city's financial survival seemed assured —largely due to Carey's tenacity and the ingenuity of Rohatyn and state budget director Peter Goldmark.

But the city wasn't home yet. In November 1976 the state court of appeals overturned two lower-court decisions and declared the legislature's Moratorium Act unconstitutional, making the city suddenly liable to pay $1 billion

---

* The word "default" was sedulously avoided throughout the episode, but default it was.

worth of notes. The banks announced that if some noteholders were going to be paid they wanted to be paid, too. The unions said that if the banks dropped out of the rescue plan, the pension funds would stop buying city paper. The new federal administration said that they would withhold seasonal loans until the problem was resolved. By early 1977 the city was again staring at the specter of default.

This time there was an odd lack of alarm. The "monthly miracles" had become routine. When the banks refused to participate in a rescue deal without the assurance of stronger long-term controls on city spending, the city snubbed them and worked out a package anyway, with a series of financial gymnastics reminiscent of the old razzle-dazzle ("hocking the stove, the bed, and the family jewels," Goldin said). A sale of Mitchell-Lama mortgages raised $400 million; $100 million was scraped out of city reserve accounts; the unions agreed to defer another $100 million in MAC principal payments; an advance repayment from a quasi-independent construction agency and a small cash flow windfall generated another $100 million. A slightly more attractive MAC bond/city note exchange offer mopped up the rest of the debt. It looked almost easy.

Nineteen seventy-eight brought more hurdles. Everyone had known that the three-year recovery plan had been too optimistic. Although the city had a nominal surplus by the end of the 1977–78 fiscal year, there was still a $700 million deficit under generally accepted accounting principles. When a new mayor, Edward Koch, took office in 1978 (Beame, with Carey's opposition, had been defeated in a re-election bid), the federal seasonal loan program was in its final year, and the city was clearly still unable to stand on its own.

Working out a new plan was not without its cliff-hanging moments, but by now Carey and Rohatyn had their moves memorized, and a new four-year arrangement even more complex than the 1975 three-year plan was structured in late summer. The city made a commitment to have its budget balanced in accord with generally accepted accounting principles by 1982—most particularly, by eliminating the last vestiges of capital-budget financing of operating expenses and by fully funding its pension plans. The state, the city, the banks, and the unions, after much haggling, agreed to a semipermanent control board. The board's powers were extended for thirty years, or until the city has paid off all the MAC and federally guaranteed debt, balanced its budget for three consecutive years, and re-entered the credit markets on its own. The federal government passed loan guarantee legislation to enable the city to re-enter the long-term capital markets and begin reconstruction of its decaying physical plant. The pension funds agreed to buy up to $1.65 billion in federally guaranteed city debt if it should become necessary. The pension funds, the banks, and other financial institutions agreed to buy $1.8 billion in MAC debt and provide seasonal financing for the city's 1978–79 fiscal year. The legislature indemnified the pension fund trustees for any liabilities arising from their purchases.

As of mid-1979, the city still has a long and difficult road to traverse before it achieves financial independence. The four-year financial plan, applying generally accepted accounting principles, projects substantial deficits that will have to be closed by further service cutbacks or by state and federal aid—$431 million in fiscal year 1979–80, $877 million in 1980–81, and $1.16 billion in 1981–82. Worse, the projected deficits do not take account of future wage increases and quite possibly underestimate the impact of a national recession on tax receipts and the demand for transfer payments. The market value of the city's real estate tax base has grown only about 2.8 percent a year from 1975 through 1979, much slower than the increase in inflation; assessed values have actually dropped, although some of the decrease resulted from cleaning out un-collectibles from the tax base estimate. Unemployment has improved since the peak year in 1976, but it still remains higher than in the rest of the country, and is one of the highest of the big-city rates. Most ominously, New York City and the eastern seaboard is heavily dependent on oil-fired electricity and could be harder hit than the rest of the country by successive rounds of oil price hikes. Continued deterioration in the economic base can spell only continued financial difficulties, continued degradation of services, and continued decline in the quality of city life.

On the other hand, a great deal has been accomplished since the fiscal crisis. The city's books are in the best shape they have been for at least forty years, and the accounting and budgeting systems are now probably the most conservative and careful of any major city. The deficits projected in the financial plan, it can easily be forgotten, would have appeared as healthy surpluses by the accounting standards of only a few years ago. Among the major achievements:

• Overall municipal employment has been reduced by more than 20 percent, the most indefensible of the work-avoidance practices have been eliminated, and wage increases have been held below the level of price inflation—which, over the long run, is the best hope for restoring parity between private- and public-sector pay levels.

• The staggering $4.5 billion burden of short-term debt that was on the city's books at the end of the 1974–75 fiscal year has been completely discharged or refinanced. The laws governing tax and revenue anticipation borrowing have been rewritten to preclude a recurrence of deficit financing through income anticipation. The City closed the 1977–78 fiscal year with *no* short-term debt at all, and the $800 million loan from the state—originally advanced in 1975 and renewed each of the following three years—was paid off in 1979.

• In 1979 the city was able to enter the seasonal financing market on its own for the first time since 1975 and again was able to close its fiscal year with all of its short-term seasonal debt discharged. With the new acceptability of city notes, MAC bonds have not only stabilized, but by 1979 were priced at a premium, permitting the pension funds to sell off a substantial amount of their MAC paper at a profit.

• The city's budget and accounting systems have been synchronized for the first time ever. Actual expenditures against budget can now be tracked at the lowest level of detail, making possible cost center management and executive control without endlessly detailed paper processing. Outside aid accounts are tracked by grant number, and the city's books tie to the detailed appropriations in the federal and state budgets. Aid receipts are not recognized until the cash is actually paid, or, in some cases, is accrued when a claim is actually made. Reserve accounts have been created against uncollectible aid and taxes, and inflated assessments have been eliminated from the city tax base. The cash and accrual accounting inconsistencies have all been rectified, and a consortium of outside accountants regularly audits the city's books. Rigorous control is maintained over the assignment of revenues and expenditures between fiscal years: for example, cash received in 1979 that is properly assignable to an activity in 1978 cannot be spent except to reduce debt or other liabilities from 1978.

▪ Pension plans for new employees have been standardized and modified to bring them more in line with accepted practice. The actuarial bases of existing plans have been recalculated, and the plan for full funding by 1982 appears well on its way toward achievement. The definition of capital projects has been considerably tightened, and the elimination of capital funding of operating deficits should also be completed by the 1982 target date.

And the economic outlook is not completely bleak, for the city's economic collapse started in train the classic corrective mechanisms. Price inflation in the city, after leading the nation throughout the 1960s, has now fallen below the national average and will gradually help make New York more competitive with other parts of the country. Pay levels in New York have increased more slowly since 1974 than in other large cities, and the price of New York office space is now roughly comparable to that in other major metropolitan areas. Although oil price escalation imposes heavy energy costs on city businesses, continued tightening of gasoline supplies will increase the relative attractiveness of the city's unique access to bulk transportation. The recovery of the downtown Manhattan office economy seems to be real, and although there has not been equivalent progress in the other boroughs, there are at least hopeful straws in the wind. Decreased population density should make industrial land assemblage economically and physically feasible again. Within the last year, for instance, several furniture manufacturers have begun to move their assembly operations from the South to New York to save on transportation and to take advantage of the low land costs and the ready availability of unskilled labor in the city.

Much will depend on the continued assimilation of the city's black and Hispanic minorities into the stable working classes, and—probably above all—on a reduction in the crime rate, particularly among black young people. (Businessmen in a Bronx survey cite crime as their single biggest problem— one that is much more important economically than differential land and energy costs; crime means theft losses, additional security guards, interior loading bays to protect shipments, curtailed shift work, and so on.) But again, the demographics give at least some cause for hope. The youthful minority population should be relatively stable for the next decade or so, and then should actually decline somewhat. The solid middle-class black neighborhoods in areas like Brooklyn's Crown Heights, troubled as they still are, hold the promise of a new social equilibrium. Even in the most disturbed city neighborhoods—like those of the South Bronx—an observer is struck by the energy of the local population, the intense desire to halt the blight, and the commitment to rehabilitation and reconstruction.

The demographics, however, are at least as unpredictable as the economy. Deterioration and destruction is still sweeping northward in the Bronx, consuming stable neighborhoods. And there are still hundreds of millions of impoverished peasants south of the United States border. Whether, or how, they decide to come to New York City to seek their fortunes, and how they assimilate when they get here, may finally be of more importance to the city's future than any other development.

Of course, New York City will remain a world capital, but with a difference. The arrogant swagger is gone, the confidence with which New Yorkers once viewed the rest of the world has been perhaps permanently shaken. As talent and wealth are spread more evenly across the country, the fiscal crisis has exposed the city as one more aging Northeast metropolis—bigger than the others, louder certainly, a little faster and more glittering, not "dead" by any means, despite some of the despairing rhetoric, but with fundamental problems of a fragile economy, an inadequate financial base, severe pressures of race and immigration, and few pretensions to grandeur—a more constrained vision than that of the Empire City of a decade or so ago, but one much better grounded in gritty reality.

A postscript to the debacle: Did city officials—Beame and Cavanagh, Lindsay and his three budget directors, Hayes, Hamilton, and Grossman, know what they were doing when they led the city down the path to financial collapse? Or if they didn't know, does that demonstrate monumental incompetence or stupidity?

My own opinion is that neither supposition is true. The imputation of stupidity is absurd on its face: For sheer intellectual ability, Hayes, Hamilton, Grossman, and Cavanagh would rank high anywhere. But for all their intelligence, they probably did not understand where the city's financial policies were so inevitably leading. Certainly, they were aware that they were running deficits—although they had no way of knowing with any precision how big their deficits were. Certainly, they were responsible for creating the individual gimmicks that accumulated to disaster, and they must have understood how indefensible some of the gimmicks were. But they seem never to have grasped how all the borrowings, all the deficits, all the gimmicks linked into an overall pattern of debt and deception. It was the inability to grasp the totality that permitted officials to walk straight ahead, eyes wide open, and plunge directly off the financial cliffs.

The dreadful inadequacy of the city accounting systems was an important contributor to the problem. The comptroller's accounts and the city budget did not tie to each other, so it was almost impossible to track specific examples of overbudgeting to specific agency deficits. Revenue information was extremely poor. Federal and state aid payments, when they finally arrived, were usually not designated to an agency activity, so there was no practicable way of knowing how collections were faring against individual aid estimates. Agency record-keeping compounded the problem: With all of their accounting resources devoted to the process requirements of line-item budgeting, agency records of aid earned, drawdowns claimed, disallowances charged, and payments received were disorderly and inconsistent at best and nonexistent at worst. Budget officials would phone around the agencies each quarter to try to discover how revenues were holding up; not surprisingly, the estimates were often wildly misleading. That accounts were allowed to deteriorate to such a degree is, of course, a grave sin of omission, but the problem of accounting for a variety of outside aid sources was still a new one, even in the 1970s. There were never sufficient resources to bring the problem really under control; and although inattention to line-item budget processing would bring the city machinery to a halt, there seemed to be no comparable penalty for letting the accounting problems slip.

The deep gulf that existed between the comptroller's office and the mayor's office—which seems to be a permanent hallmark of the city institutional arrangement—grievously aggravated the problem. Mechanical questions of accounting or vendor payments readily became hostage to political enmities. More important, budget administration was, for the most part, divorced from budget financing. As Frederick Hayes states it, for example, he knew the city was running a deficit if he had to sell budget notes or borrow from reserves. Cash-flow financing through RANs and TANs was the comptroller's business and seemed to have little to do with overall spending control. Even later, the explosive growth of RANs was not clearly related to the possibility of deficit financing, although there was considerable concern about short-term interest costs. In 1972 a team of management consultants was called in to review the city's growing short-term debt burden, but their report focused almost entirely on aid timing. The notion that aid to support the borrowing might not exist seems not to have occurred to people on either the mayor's or the comptroller's side of the fence.

Framing the problem was of critical importance. This book is replete with examples of the policy consequences of imperfect problem definitions. City officials, for the most part, were looking at the wrong ball. David Grossman maintained: "I knew we were overextended, of course, and I expected the other shoe to drop. But I thought that would mean we would finally have to face up to service cuts if the economy or the aid picture didn't improve sharply. I never expected the crisis would be a *financing* crisis." Cavanagh expressed similar sentiments: "Maybe we were dumb, but nobody else seems to have understood what was happening either."

Cavanagh seems to be right. Even the bankers—presumably the real fiscal experts—did not understand until very late in the day the consequences that flowed from the steady increase in short-term financing; and it is not clear that the bankers would have perceived the problem when they did without a change in the external market for tax-exempt debt issuances. Understanding was difficult, because, for all the apparent artifice underlying the most complex and elegant gimmicks, they were for the most part not the product of conscious design. The delicately balanced financial superstructure was a kind of evolutionary extrusion that had emerged from hundreds of piecemeal decisions. Even after the fiscal crisis, for example, there was no immediately clear understanding of the processes by which short-term debt shifted annually between the books of the state and its local governments—the "pendulum" described in Chapter VI. Peter Goldmark, who became state budget director in 1975, described the process of state and city officials gradually and painfully comprehending the intricate interconnections between state deficits and local borrowings, of tracing the laocöon coils of gimmicks and deferrals, advances and accruals, floating debt and seasonal anticipations—the entire compound of expediencies that created such dangerous credit interdependence. "Remember the fourteenth century and the advent of the plague," says Goldmark. "Was it possible for those people to stand on the docks in Genoa or Venice, watch the rats pouring off the ships, and *not* understand?"

Yes, it was possible.

Notes

I N THE NOTES FOLLOWING I have attempted to indicate fully the sources I used in compiling the book, but I have not followed rigorously all the rules of citation that apply to an academic work. For instance, when a chronological account is drawn from several sources, I simply indicate the sources instead of tracing each statement to the specific source; in particular, when a chronology is drawn from *The New York Times*, I indicate that fact instead of citing each and every article to which I made reference. Finally, because of the nature of the research, a fair amount of the material used is unpublished. Where I used unpublished material, I cite that fact and indicate where I found it. If anyone doing detailed research on any of the matters covered in the book would like additional information on unpublished source material, I should be more than happy to be of assistance.

INTRODUCTION

p. 12 Moynihan quotation: Daniel P. Moynihan, "The Politics and Economics of Regional Growth," *Public Interest* (Spring 1978):18.

I. WAGNER AND LINDSAY

p. 15 The account of Wagner's political career is developed from Warren Moscow, *What Have You Done For Me Lately?: The Ins and Outs of New York City Politics* (Englewood Cliffs, N.J.: Prentice-Hall, 1967), and *The Last of the Big-Time Bosses: The Life and Times of Carmine deSapio and the Rise and Fall of Tammany Hall* (New York, Stein and Day, 1971); Robert A. Caro, *The Power Broker: Robert Moses and the Fall of New York* (New York, Vintage Books, 1975); Barbara Carter, *The Road to City Hall* (Englewood Cliffs, N.J.: Prentice-Hall, 1967). These sources were supplemented by various accounts in *The New York Times* and interviews with Warren Moscow (August 27, 1978) and Julius C. C. Edelstein (January 31, 1979) two of Wagner's former aides. The "little schnook" phrase is from Warren Moscow, *What Have You Done . . . ,* p. 40.

pp. 16–17 Quotations from *The New York Times:* October 19, 1961. Information on scandals comes from New York State Commission on Investigation, Final Report of the Special Unit, *Government for Sale: a Glimpse of Waste and Corruption in the City of New York*, July 1961, and Third Annual Report, February 1961. The "delicate sense of self-protection" quotation is from Moscow, *What Have You Done*, p. 80; Wagner's "secret corruption" quote is from *The New York Times*, August 6, 1961. Sharkey is quoted in *The New York Times*, September 1, 1961. Wagner's new machine is described in Theodore Lowi, "Machine Politics: Old and New," *Public Interest* 9 (Fall 1967):83–92. Wagner on "slumless city" is from Carter, *The Road to City Hall*, p. 34.

p. 18 Housing accomplishment developed from data in Frank S. Kristof, "Housing: Economic Facets of New York City's Problems," in Lyle C. Fitch and Annemarie Hauk Walsh, *Agenda for a City: Issues Confronting New York* (New York: Institute of Public Administration, 1970): pp. 297–345. Roger Starr, "Housing: Prospects for New Construction," ibid., 349–76; and Temporary Commission on City Finances, Fifteenth Interim Report to the Mayor, *The Effects of Rent Control and Rent Stabilization in New York City*, June 1977. The construction record is from New York City Office of the Mayor: *The Administrations of Robert*

F. Wagner 1961, and from tables in *1976–77 Fact Book on the New York Metropolitan Region* (New York: New York City Council on Economic Education 1978), pp. 119–23. ". . . he will always be the Mayor," is quoted in a letter to the author from Warren Moscow. The ". . . how much he wanted it" quote appears in Carter, *The Road to City Hall,* p. 32.

p. 19   Wagner's relation with Moses is documented in Caro, *The Power Broker.* His relation with Kennedy is documented in Susan Tolchin, "The Police Policy Area as a Subsystem of New York City Politics" (Ph.D dissertation, New York University, 1968), pp. 98–110.

pp. 20–22   For racial strife, see, generally, the accounts in *The New York Times.* For antipoverty program, see Diana T. Murray, "Experiment in Federalism: The Community Action Program in Washington, New York City and East Harlem (Master's thesis, Columbia University, 1971), pp. 62–96. Javits on "travesty" in *The New York Times,* May 9, 1965. CORE attacks reported in *The New York Times,* April 8, 1965. All other quotes are from the *New York Herald-Tribune's* "City in Crisis" series, January 24, 1965 through February 18, 1965. Dick Schaap, *New York Herald-Tribune,* January 31, 1965, and Richard A. Whalen, "A City Destroying Itself," *Fortune* (September 1964):114. Wagner's "A bad loan" comes from an interview with Edelstein; "human needs" comes from *The New York Times,* May 14, 1965; "Incredible fiscal mismanagement," ibid.; Wagner's slip in polls, ibid, April 26, 1965.

p. 23   "Big men . . . for common good" quotation appears in *The Power Broker,* p. 784.

pp. 24–25   The account of Lindsay's early political career is developed from Carter, *The Road to City Hall;* Nat Hentoff, *A Political Life: The Education of John V. Lindsay* (New York: Alfred A. Knopf, 1969); and Oliver Pilat, *Lindsay's Campaign* (Boston, Beacon Press, 1968). These sources were supplemented by accounts in *The New York Times.* Quotation about "one of the bright hopes," is in Hentoff, *A Political Life,* p. 67. Moynihan is quoted in Carter, *The Road to City Hall,* p. 64; Lippmann's opinion in ibid., p. 21; Lindsay was "troubled" in *The New York Times,* May 12, 1965.

pp. 26–27   Ginsberg is quoted from an interview with the author (November 30, 1978). "I never had any trouble . . ." is quoted from the author's interview with Herbert Elish (November 29, 1978). Lindsay's inaugural quotes are from *The New York Times,* January 2, 1966; "a lone figure . . . ," ibid., April 10, 1966; "Riding Shotgun . . ." appears in Hentoff, *A Political Life,* p. 101; Lindsay's "fight without compromise," *The New York Times,* March 25, 1966; "power brokers," ibid., January 11, 1966. Lindsay's administrative style was culled from various accounts in *The New York Times* and Hentoff, *A Political Life.* "There are a lot of lonely people," is from ibid, p. 85.

p. 28   Lindsay's ". . . stands supreme . . ." quoted, *The New York Times,* January 21, 1966; Kriegel quote is from Hentoff, *A Political Life,* p. 157. Screvane is quoted in *The New York Times,* April 10, 1966. "He just doesn't know . . ." quotation appears in Hentoff, *A Political Life,* p. 109. "If they would only give us time," Woody Klein quoted in ibid., p. 118; Quill is quoted in *The New York Times,* January 1, 1966.

p. 29   Moses is quoted in Caro, *The Power Broker,* p. 1118. Lindsay's "receiver in bankruptcy" remark is from *The New York Times,* November 11, 1965; Chamber of Commerce "in chaos" quote is in ibid., July 6, 1964.

p. 30   Lindsay's remarks are quoted in ibid., March 25, April 18, and May 23, 1966.

pp. 32–33   Citizens' Budget Commission "amazing reversal" quote is in ibid., July 21 and 25, 1966; Procaccino quote, ibid., November 1, 1966; quotations from *Better Financing for New York City,* Final Report of the Temporary Commission on City Finances, August 1966, p. 1.

II. THE PUBLIC SECTOR EXPANDS

pp. 34–35   Trends in federal spending priorities and federal-local relations developed from Barry M. Blechman, Edward M. Gramlich, and Robert W. Hartman, *Setting National Priorities: The 1975 Budget* (Washington: Brookings, 1974); Alan K. Campbell, "National-State-Local Systems of Government and Intergovernmental Aid" *Annals of the American Academy of Political and Social Sciences* (May 1965):94–106; and George C. Benson, "Trends in Intergovernmental Relations," ibid., pp. 1–7. "Vertical autocracies," in Benson, "Trends in Intergovernmental Relations," p. 6.

pp. 36–37   Rockefeller background and accomplishments generally from Michael Kramer and Sam Roberts, *I Never Wanted to be Vice-President of Anything: An Investigative Biography of Nelson Rockefeller* (New York: Basic Books, 1976). The quote about Rockefeller's "nineteenth century optimism" appears in Kramer, *I Never Wanted,* p. 10. The "a few small, scattered colleges" quote is from New York State, Office of the Governor. "Higher Education in New York State," *Report of the Task Force on Financing Higher Education,* March, 1973, p. 3.

p. 38   The account of the history of the City hospital system is developed from: New York City Department of Hospitals, *The History of the Development of the Department of Hospitals* (New York: Macmillan Co., 1943); Herbert E. Klarman, *Hospital Care in New York City* (New York: Columbia, 1963); and Eli Ginzberg et al., *Urban Health Services: the Case of New York City* (New York: Columbia, 1971). Report about "deplorable condition" of hospitals in Ginzberg, *Urban Health Services,* p. 99.

pp. 39–41   Affiliation contract background and abuses developed from Miriam Ostow, "Affiliation Contracts," in Ginzberg, *Urban Health Services,* pp. 96–119; Robb K. Burlage, *New York City's Municipal Hospitals: A Policy Review* (Washington: Institute of Policy Studies, 1967), 2 vols.; and New York State Commission on Investigation, *An Investigation Concerning New York City's Municipal Hospitals and the Affiliation Program,* March 1969. "not private patient" quotation, p. 62, from ibid. p. 186. Heyman quotations are from Burlage, *New York City's Muncipal Hospitals,* Vol. 1, p. 56; Catholic Charities quotations, ibid., Vol. 1, pp. 93, 125. "few millions" Ostow, "Affiliation Contracts" p. 106.

p. 42   Hospital cost trends from Charles Brecher, *Where Have All The Dollars Gone?: Public Expenditures for Human Resource Development in New York City 1961–71* (New York: Praeger, 1974), and additional mimeo materials assembled by Mr. Brecher at the Conservation of Human Resources Project, Columbia University; Joan M. Leiman, *Federal Financing and Local Control* (PhD. dissertation, Columbia University, 1977); and Temporary Commission on City Finances, *Sixteenth Interim Report to the Mayor, The Medicaid Program in New York City: Some Proposals for Reform,* June 1977.

p. 43 History of CUNY from Duncan Pardue and Suzanne Ryder, *A Forty-six Year Summary of the Board of Higher Education of the City of New York* (New York: New York City Board of Higher Education, 1973); and Pearl Max, *Step-by-Step Toward the Ph.D. 1920–60* (New York: New York City Board of Higher Education, 1961).

p. 44 Heald Report quote in New York State, Office of the Governor, "A Report to the Hon. Nelson A. Rockefeller," *Meeting the Increasing Demand for Higher Education in New York State,* 1960, p. 8.

p. 45 City College study group quotations in *Minutes, New York City Board of Higher Education,* December 13, 1960, p. 11. Decline of high school placements in 1950s is from New York City Board of Higher Education: *A Long-range Plan for CUNY, 1961–1975,* 1962, p. 3. Costs and enrollment changes recorded in Temporary Commission on City Finances, Tenth Interim Report to the Mayor, *The City University of New York: Proposals for the Future,* January 1977.

p. 46 "High efficiency" quote is from *The New York Times,* January 3, 1966. Lindsay quote is from Hentoff, *A Political Life,* p. 82.

p. 48 Hayes quotes are from *Creative Budgeting in New York City* (Washington: the Urban Institute, 1972), p. 2.

p. 75 Air pollution control is detailed in *New York City Housing Authority Air Pollution Abatement Project,* Intercollegiate Case Clearing House (ICCH) 9-372-127, November 1973. Capital construction program is described in *Improving New York City's Capital Construction Process: A Report to the Board of Estimate,* New York City Bureau of the Budget, June 1970.

p. 49 Project management approach: *New York City Project Management Staff,* ICCH 6-470-005, 1969. ". . . no generation to follow them" quotation is from James A. Reichley, "A Nightmare for Urban Management," *Fortune* (March 1969):170.

p. 50 Series on hospital conditions printed in *The New York Times,* June 26, 1966, and subsequent issues; Brown quoted in *The New York Times,* July 7, 1966. Conditions in hospitals: New York State Commission on Investigation, *An Investigation Concerning New York City's Municipal Hospitals . . . ;* New York State Senate, *New York City's Municipal Hospitals: Interim Report to the Hon. Nelson A. Rockefeller,* 1966, and *The New York Times* series; Hayes is quoted from an interview with the author (November 26, 1978).

p. 53 "Once you start learning . . ." comes from the author's interview with Jon Weiner (August 1978). Lindsay is quoted in Hentoff, *A Political Life,* p. 180. Health center sequel is recounted in author's interview with Hayes. For an account of the City's addiction program, see Diana R. Gordon, *City Limits: Barriers to Change in Urban Government* (New York: Charterhouse 1973), pp. 63–106.

pp. 54–55 Hayes is quoted from the author's interview with him.

III. BLACKS AND PUERTO RICANS

p. 57 The account of American racism is developed from, among a number of other works, Gunnar Myrdal, *An American Dilemma* (New York: McGraw-Hill, 1964) 2 vols.; Thomas Sowell, *Race and Economics* (New York: McKay, 1975); and Charles E. Silberman, *Criminal Violence, Criminal Justice* (New York: Random House, 1978), pp. 117–68. For the early black experience in the North, see Sowell, *Race and Economics* and Gilbert Osofsky, *Harlem: The Making of a Ghetto: Negro New York 1890–1930* (New York: Harper Torchbooks, 1968). The quotation, p. 57, ". . . harshest intergroup hatreds . . ." is from Osofsky, p. 45. The account of racial violence is from, among other sources, Allen D. Grimshaw (ed.), *Racial Violence in the United States* (Chicago: Aldine, 1969).

p. 58 Black migration data is from U.S. Bureau of the Census, *A Statistical History of the United States: From Colonial Times to the Present.* The data on Puerto Rican migration and poverty are from United States Bureau of Labor Statistics, Middle Atlantic Regional Report No. 46, *A Socio-economic Profile of Puerto Rican New Yorkers,* July 1975. See also Nathan Glazer and Daniel P. Moynihan, *Beyond the Melting Pot* (Cambridge, Mass.: MIT and Harvard, 1963). Note on influx of other Hispanic groups from temporary Commission on City Finances, Thirteenth Interim Report to the Mayor, *Economic and Demographic Trends in New York City: The Outlook for the Future,* May 1977.

p. 59 Quotations from Lyndon B. Johnson come from "To Fulfill These Rights," speech at Howard University, June 4, 1965, reprinted in Lee Rainwater and William L. Yancey, *The Moynihan Report and the Politics of Controversy* (Cambridge, Mass: MIT, 1967), pp. 125–32. Ginsberg quotation from an interview. Aide quotation from an interview with Steven Isenberg (November 1978). For an account of civil rights radicalization after Watts, see Rainwater and Yancey, *The Moynihan Report,* pp. 194–203, and also therein the collection of commentary by civil rights leaders and intellectuals, pp. 395–467. Silberman quotes in Charles E. Silberman, *Crisis in Black and White* (New York: Random House, 1964), pp. 331, 358. Hubert Humphrey was quoted in *The New York Times,* July 19, 1966.

p. 60 Kerner Commission quotation from *Report of the National Advisory Commission on Civil Disorders* (New York: Bantam, 1968), pp. 1–2.

p. 61 The early history of the war on poverty is drawn from Daniel P. Moynihan, *Maximum Feasible Misunderstanding: Community Action in the War on Poverty* (New York: Free Press, 1969); and Robert A. Levine, *The Poor Ye Need Not Have Always With You* (Cambridge, Mass.: MIT, 1970). Note derives from Kenneth B. Clark, *Dark Ghetto: Dilemmas of Social Power* (New York: Harper & Row, 1965).

pp. 62–63 The account of the early antipoverty program in New York relies primarily on Murray, *Experiment in*

Federalism, 62–96; Henry Cohen, "Coping with Poverty," in Fitch and Walsh, *Agenda for a City,* pp. 131–37; and reports in *The New York Times.*

pp. 63–65 The account of the Lindsay antipoverty program is developed from Murray, *Experiment in Federalism,* pp. 105–23, 142–54, and 201–16; Stephen M. David, "The Community Action Program Controversy," in Stephen M. David and Jewel Bellush, *Race and Politics in New York City: Five Studies in Policy-making* (New York: Praeger, 1971), pp. 25–58; reports in *The New York Times;* and interviews with Jay Kriegel (November 20, 1978) and Mitchell Sviridoff (December 4, 1978). The quotations from Sviridoff are from the interview. The quotations on p. 64 are from *Developing New York City's Human Resources: Report of a Study Group of the Institute to Mayor John V. Lindsay* (New York: Institute of Public Administration, 1966), pp. 8, 22, 34, 7.

p. 66 The note is from Charles V. Hamilton, "The Patron-Recipient Relationship and Minority Politics in New York City," a paper delivered at the 1978 annual meeting of the American Political Science Association.

pp. 67–71 The account of the welfare protest movement relies primarily on Larry R. Jackson and William A. Johnson, *Protest by the Poor: The Welfare Rights Movement in New York City* (New York: The Rand Institute, 1973), pp. 75–207 and an interview with Mitchell Ginsberg, supplemented by reports in *The New York Times.* The Ginsberg quotations are from the interview. The radical welfare strategy is outlined in Frances Fox Piven and Richard Cloward, *Regulating the Poor: the Functions of Public Welfare* (New York: Vintage, 1971). Data on caseload and expenditures is from Temporary Commission on City Finances, Twelfth Interim Report to the Mayor, *Public Assistance Programs in New York City: Some Proposals for Reform,* February, 1977. Banfield citation on p. 71 is from Edward C. Banfield, "Welfare—a Crisis without Solutions," *Public Interest* 16 (Summer 1969):89–101.

p. 72 Chronology of the riots comes from *National Advisory Commission,* pp. 35–108, supplemented by reports in *The New York Times.*

pp. 73–74 For the analysis of the riots, see Edward C. Banfield, *The Unheavenly City Revisited* (Boston: Little, Brown, 1974), pp. 211–33. The sources cited therein were also helpful. "these crazy kids . . ." comes from Bennett Kremen, "Night Walk in Harlem," *The Nation,* April 22, 1968, p. 532. For "Within a one-hour time period . . . ," see Anthony Oberschall, "The Los Angeles Race Riot of August 1965," *Social Problems* 15 (Winter 1968):339. Remaining riot descriptions are from *Time,* March 19, 1968. "Rumors were coming in . . ." Mayor Patricia Sheehan, quoted in National Advisory Commission, p. 69. Information in the note on p. 74 derives from Banfield, *The Unheavenly City,* p. 319. "whatever the outcome" quote is from *The New York Times,* April 24, 1968.

pp. 74–78 The account of the New York riot response is developed from Barry Gottehrer, *The Mayor's Man* (New York: Garden City, 1975) and from interviews with Jay Kriegel, Sanford Garelik and Sidney Cooper (both of the latter on January 11, 1978), supplemented by reports in *The New York Times.* Lewis Feldstein is the aide, quoted from author's interview (December 15, 1978). Kenyatta quotation on p. 75 is from Larry L. King, "Lindsay of New York," *Harpers,* August 1968, 38.

pp. 78–79 The most persuasive statement of the "immigration" hypothesis is Thomas Sowell's *Race and Economics.* See also Irving Kristol, "The Negro of Today Is Like the Immigrant of Yesterday," *The New York Times Magazine,* September 11, 1966. The comparative ethnic data are from Sowell, *Race and Economics.* For Irish slum conditions, see Pauline Goldmark, ed., *West Side Studies* (New York: Russell Sage, 1914). Description of Irish riots as "massive, recurrent, and violent" is from Sowell, *Race and Economics,* p. 73. Note on black violence is derived from Silberman, *Criminal Violence,* pp. 117–23.

p. 80 The data on black economic progress is developed from mimeo materials compiled from U.S. Government sources by the staff of the Ford Foundation. Black home ownership information is from Henry J. Aaron, *Politics and the Professors: The Great Society in Perspective* (Washington, D.C. Brookings 1978) p. 52. Statistics on black teenage unemployment are compiled from various tables, U.S. Bureau of Labor Statistics, *Handbook of Labor Statistics,* 1977.

p. 81 "In each generation . . ." comes from Pauline Goldmark, *West Side Studies,* p. iv. Riot Commission data calculations are reported in Abraham H. Miller, Louis H. Bolce, and Mark R. Halligan, "The New Urban Blacks" *Ethnicity* 3 (December, 1976):338–67.

IV. EMPLOYEES

p. 83 The account of the transit strike relies primarily on A. H. Raskin, "Politics Upends the Bargaining Table," in Sam Zagoria, ed., *Public Workers and Public Unions* (Englewood Cliffs, N.J.: Prentice-Hall, 1972), pp. 125–30. See also Carter, *The Road to City Hall,* pp. 156–66, and the reports in *The New York Times.* Quill's "not demands . . ." quote is from *The New York Times,* November 5, 1965.

pp. 84–85 Jimmy Breslin is quoted in Carter, *Road to City Hall,* p. 163. Quill's quotes come from *The New York Times,* December 2, 31, 1965, and January 1, 2, 1966. "The judge can drop dead. . . ," from Raskin, "Politics Upends the Bargaining Table," p. 130; Lindsay's "The government of the city . . . ," in *The New York Times,* January 11, 1966.

p. 86 Characterization of the strike as an "insult," by A. M. Rosenthal, ibid., January 13, 1966; DeLury quote in ibid., January 21, 1966. "First, the strikers proved . . ." is found in ibid., January 25, 1966. Information about the $500 pension bonus comes from Ken Auletta, *The Streets Were Paved with Gold* (New York: Random House, 1979), p. 61. Anthony Russo is quoted from an interview with the author (November 8, 1978) A. H. Raskin's quote from "Politics Upends the Bargaining Table," p. 129; "Lindsay has walked into . . ." Victor Gotbaum, quoted in *The New York Times,* January 25, 1966.

p. 87 The account of the history of municipal unions relies primarily on Raymond D. Horton, *Municipal Labor Relations in New York City: Lessons of the Lindsay-Wagner Years* (New York: Praeger, 1973). See also H. H. Wellington and Ralph K. Smith, *The Unions and the Cities* (Washington, D.C.: Brookings, 1971). The account is supplemented by various reports in *The New York Times* and interviews with Anthony Russo, Herbert Haber (December 7, 1978), Alan Viani (November 22, 1978), and Harold Melnick (February 1, 1979). Meany is quoted in Jack Stieber, *Public Employee Unions: Structure, Growth, Policies* (Washington, D.C.: Brookings, 1973), p. 116. DeLury quote is from Raskin, "Politics Upends the Bargaining Table," p. 133. Note on grievance procedures is derived from an interview with Hilda Hollyer (October 23, 1978). Russo is quoted from an interview. "palmanship" is found in Raskin, "Why New York is Strike City" *The New York Times Magazine*, December 22, 1968, p. 8. Quotations on transit bugging come from Raskin, "Politics Upends the Bargaining Table," p. 127.

p. 90   Schottland panel result is quoted in Horton, *Municipal Labor Relations*, p. 69. The chronology of Lindsay's relations with employees is reconstructed, for the most part, from accounts in *The New York Times* and Horton, *Municipal Labor Relations*.

p. 91   Quote about "simple ultimatum" is from Frederick O'R. Hayes, "Collective Bargaining and the Budget Director," in Zagoria, *Public Workers*, p. 97; "We resented the Chinese error . . ." remark comes from an interview with Hilda Hollyer; "It might not have been so bad . . ." derives from an interview with Edward Kiernan. (January 6, 1979) DeLury's complaint ("these young and immature . . .") is in *The New York Times*, December 21, 1966; Gotbaum's "Lindsay is an upper-middle class . . . ," ibid., December 25, 1966. The note on fire manning deals with what is at best a murky story, and there are different versions. The account in the note is reconstructed from interviews with officials of the fire department, the Office of Labor Relations, and the Office of Management and Budget.

p. 92   Quote about "freighted with all the fears . . ." comes from Raskin, "Why New York is Strike City," p. 7. Kriegel quotation comes from an interview. The account of the civilian review board is drawn from Tolchin, *The Police Policy Area . . .*, pp. 57–96, and E. T. Rogowsky, L. H. Gold, and D. W. Abbott, "The Civilian Review Board Controversy," in David and Bellush, *Race and Politics*, pp. 59–97; "swiftly, cruelly . . ." and "to deplore brutality . . ." are in Tolchin, *The Police Policy Area*, p. 63.

p. 93   "I'm sick and tired . . ." quote comes from *The New York Times*, September 11, 1966. Kriegel is quoted from an interview. Kiernan is quoted from an interview; "hippies . . . I think today . . ." statement by Norman Frank, quoted in ICCH case 9-378-551, *Police Guidelines*, 1975, p. 7.

p. 94   The "fourth platoon" comes from ICCH case C14-75-013, *The Fourth Platoon: Police Deployment— General Considerations and Particular Problems in New York City*, 1975. Cassesse is quoted in David Stanley, *Managing Local Governments under Union Pressure* (Washington, D.C.: Brookings, 1972), p. 103. Police standards information comes from the New York City Police Department, *Police Training and Performance Study*, 1969, p. 36; "These new guys . . ." is quoted in *The Fourth Platoon*, p. 23. Melnick quotation is from an interview.

p. 95   The quotations from Russo, Kiernan, Hayes, and Lang are from interviews.

pp. 96–97   The "career civil servant" quotations are from an interview with Hilda Hollyer. The ". . . woefully inadequate" is from ibid.; "utter disdain" comes from a Cohen interview. (November 6, 1978)

p. 98   Details of city contracts on this and the following pages are reconstructed from *The New York Times* and from contracts on file with the city's Office of Labor Relations. Staff of the OLR were particularly helpful in organizing material on the various settlements to facilitate its analysis. "The police were panicked . . ." comes from an interview with Herbert Haber. Note on former pensions is derived from New York City Commission on Pensions, *Report on the Pension Funds of the City of New York*, 1916, 2 vols.

p. 99   Information on later pension changes comes from Economic Development Council of New York City, *Pension Changes in New York City: 1962–72*, August 1972.

p. 100   Russo is quoted from an interview. Note on sanitation department settlement comes from Hayes and Haber interviews. Haber claims that the extra settlement was in fact taken into account in the following year.

pp. 101–102   Shanker quotations are from an interview. (December 28, 1978) Kheel is quoted in *The New York Times*, January 2, 1968. The Russo quotation is from an interview.

p. 103   The chronology of the sanitation strike is drawn from Raskin, "Politics Upends the Bargaining Table," pp. 132–34; ICCH cases 9-475-606 and 9-475-607, *The New York Sanitation Strike*, 1969; Hentoff, *A Political Life*, pp. 201–8; and reports in *The New York Times*.

pp. 104–106   Rockefeller quoted in *The New York Sanitation Strike*, p. 16; quote about "union-busting of the worst sort . . . ," ibid., p. 24; Lindsay quotation ibid., p. 27. Rockefeller on "the crassest kind of political move . . ." is in Raskin, "How to Avoid Strikes by Garbagemen, Nurses, Teachers, Welfare Workers, etc.," *The New York Times Magazine*, February 25, 1968, p. 94. Other quotations are from Raskin, ibid., 34, 94.

V. THE END OF THE LIBERAL EXPERIMENT

pp. 106–107   "Why Not Lindsay?" *Nation*, April 22, 1968, p. 3; Larry L. King, "Lindsay of New York," *Harpers*, August 1968, p. 36. aide quotation: Lewis Feldstein interview. The chronology of the teachers' strikes is drawn primarily from Martin Mayer, *The Teachers' Strikes: New York 1968* (New York: Harper & Row, 1969), supplemented by the accounts in Diane Ravitch, *The Great School Wars: New York City 1805–1973* (New York: Basic Books, 1974), and Marilyn Gittell, "Education: the Decentralization—Community Control Controversy," in David and Bellush, *Race and Politics*, 134–63. Melvin Urofsky, *Why Teachers Strike: Teachers' Rights and Community Control* (New York: Doubleday, 1970), provides extended interviews with virtually all the major actors in the strikes. The author also confirmed details of the chronology with Albert Shanker and Lewis Feldstein, Lindsay's education aide.

p. 113   Lindsay's "more or less" remark is reported in Mayer, *The Teachers' Strikes*, p. 73. Mayer quotation is in ibid., p. 99.

pp. 114–115 The account of labor divisions comes from Raskin, "Politics Upends the Bargaining Table," p. 135. "If one accepts the rules . . ." comes from Urofsky, *Why Teachers Strike*, p. 20; "from meaning well to . . ." is in Mayer, *The Teachers' Strikes*, p. 118; "reconnection" of parents was mentioned in the Fantini interview in Urofsky, *Why Teachers Strike*, p. 85. The Fantini report was entitled *Reconnection for Learning*. "Community control . . ." Urofsky, *Why Teachers Strike*, p. 18. Feldstein is quoted from an interview.

p. 116 "The callous disinterest . . ." appeared in the final draft of the city's proposed master plan released in the fall of 1967. It was stricken from the printed version. Shanker is quoted from an interview.

pp. 117–120 The account of HRA's difficulties is drawn generally from a series in *The New York Times* beginning January 12, 1966, supplemented by New York City Council, *Final Report of the Special Committee to Make an In-depth Study of the Human Resources Administration*, July 1969, and an interview with Mitchell Ginsberg. "It's so bad it will take ten years . . ." comes from *The New York Times*, January 12, 1969; "monstrosity" quote, ibid., February 7, 1969; "unqualified" remark, ibid., January 12, 1969; "last blow," ibid., Janaury 13, 1969; "six-month last chance," ibid., January 23, 1969. The account of the snow emergency is drawn from ICCH 9-378-528, *Snow Emergency in New York City*, and reports in *The New York Times*; Troy is quoted in *The New York Times*, February 13, 1969; DeLury is quoted in ibid., February 14, 1969. For Lindsay housing policies, see Jewel Bellush, "Housing: the Scattered-site Controversy," in David and Bellush, *Race and Politics*, pp. 98–133. Housing statistics appear in the *New York Fact Book*, p. 121, and Kristof, "Housing: Economic Facets of New York City's Problems," in Fitch and Walsh, *Agenda for the City*. Lang's and Edelstein's quotes are taken from interviews. (February 1 and January 31, 1979, respectively)

pp. 120–124 The account of the police parity pay negotiations is drawn primarily from interviews with Harold Melnick, Herbert Haber, Anthony Russo, and Edward Kiernan. The 1966 arbitration award by the Cole panel, which is on file with the city Office of Labor Relations, includes a useful history of the parity relations. Details of various contracts come from material on file at the city Office of Labor Relations; the chronology was developed from *The New York Times*. Raymond Horton's interpretation of the episode is in Horton, *Municipal Labor Relations*, pp. 89–90. The account of the re-election campaign is developed from reports in *The New York Times*. DeLury is quoted in *The New York Times*, October 18, 1969. Lindsay's remark about "pressures on working whites . . ." appears in *The New York Times*, November 30, 1969.

VI. FINANCE

In general, information about the background and legal constraints on city finance is drawn from the New York City Charter and the New York State Local Finance Law. Spending information is from the city Expense Budget and Annual Report of the Comptroller for various years. A useful compilation of revenue and expenditure data is in The Temporary Commission on City Finances, *The City in Transition* (New York: Arno, 1978), pp. 274–94. Historical compilations are available in The Temporary Commission on City Finances, *Better Financing for New York City*. For the most part, the calculations of summary data and tables are by the author. An historical perspective on city finance is in Wallace S. Sayre and Herbert Kaufman, *Governing New York City: Politics in the Metropolis* (New York: Norton, 1965).

p. 131 For operation of budget gimmicks, I am particularly indebted to Jon Weiner and Peter Goldmark.

p. 132 Details of the pension funding change came from an interview with James Beirne, assistant to the city actuary.

p. 134 The calculation of pendulum debt is from Donald Haider, "New York State Finances: The End of an Era," *The City Almanac*, April, 1976, p. 10.

p. 135 Information in the note on dropped account comes from an interview with James Cavanagh. The "self-taxation" remark was made by Steven Clifford and is quoted in United States Securities and Exchange Commission, *Staff Report on Transactions in Securities of the City of New York*, August 1977, Vol. 3, p. 27.

p. 139 *The New York Fact Book*, pp. 10–62, is a useful compilation of economic and employment statistical data on New York City. Roy W. Bahl, Alan K. Campbell, and David Greytak, *Taxes, Expenditures, and the Economic Base: Case Study of New York City* (New York: Praeger, 1974), pp. 1–63, is an excellent source on the taxing and economic capacity of the city.

p. 141 The tax equivalence calculations are derived from tables in Bahl, Campbell, and Greytak, *Taxes, Expenditures, and the Economic Base*, pp. 145–48. The account of the decline in the city's real estate tax base is drawn primarily from Kristof, "Housing: Economic Facets of New York City's Problem" in Fitch and Walsh, *Agenda for a City* and Temporary Commission on New York City Finances, *The Effects of Rent Control . . .* , supplemented by Bahl, Campbell, and Greytak, *Taxes, Expenditures and the Economic Base*, pp. 79–102.

p. 143 The housing expert cited is Louis Winnick, who advanced these views in an interview. (May 16, 1979)

pp. 144–145 The Hayes quotations come from an interview. Detailed interpretative data is also to be found in Hayes, "Money," an unpublished paper.

VII. THE SECOND LINDSAY ADMINISTRATION

In general, the chronological account is developed from reports in *The New York Times*.

p. 147 The inaugural quotations came from *The New York Times*, January 2, 1970.

p. 148 Lindsay's aide quotation in ibid., February 1, 1970. Aurelio's "to take national soundings," ibid., December 6, 1971; "Come back . . . ," Meade Esposito, quoted in ibid., March 29, 1972.

p. 149 "Don't give this man . . . ," ibid. January 12, 1971; Rockefeller's accusation of "incompetence," ibid.,

December 6, 1971. Rockefeller's "inept and extravagant . . . corrective action" is from ibid., June 6, 1971; "where housing can't be found . . . ," ibid., December 6, 1971.

p. 150 Quote about "40 percent of caseload" is in ibid.; "was crumbling," ibid., April 25, 1972. A useful account of the 1971–72 budget struggle appears in Harvard Business School Case 4-372-096, *The 1971–72 New York City Tax Program*, revised in March 1972. The option budgets and supporting detail are in the untitled submission to Governor Nelson A. Rockefeller et al. by John V. Lindsay, April 19, 1971.

pp. 152–153 Rockefeller's "exercise a comparable discipline . . ." appeared in *The New York Times*, April 20, 1971. Lindsay complained about "arrogance and contempt" in ibid., June 30, 1971. Lindsay's "more chillingly anti-City . . ." assessment of the legislature is quoted in *The 1971–72 New York City Tax Program*, p. 22. The note on the value of gimmicks was calculated by the author from the *Annual Report of the Comptroller: Fiscal Year 1971–72*.

pp. 156–157 Gotbaum's prediction of the "biggest, sloppiest strike . . ." is quoted in Raskin, "Politics Upends the Bargaining Table," p. 141. The background on the Open Enrollment decision relies partially on an interview with Peter Goldmark (November 30, 1978). See also Martin Mayer, "Higher Education for All," *Commentary*, (May 1973) 37–47. Goldmark is quoted from an interview. Financial and other statistical data was drawn from The Temporary Commission on City Finances, *The City University of New York*.

pp. 158–159 Background data on the city daycare program is from ICCH 9-378-905, *Agency for Child Development*, revised December 1977. Sugarman's promise of a cut in the welfare rolls "by 250,000" was reported in *The New York Times*, June 25, 1972.

pp. 160–162 Andrew Kerr's story about Hamilton is taken from an interview (November 28, 1978). The account of the productivity effort in the sanitation department is developed from ICCH 9-673-098, *Sanitation Case B: Maintenance Operations*, September 1973; ICCH 9-673-099, *Sanitation Case C: Cleaning and Collection Productivity*, November 1973; McKinsey and Co., *Improving Cleaning and Collection Productivity*, 1970; Citizens' Budget Commission, *The New York City Productivity Program: The Dept. of Sanitation*, March 1974; and interviews with Herbert Elish, Martin Lang and Andrew Kerr.

pp. 163–165 The account of the productivity effort in the Health Services Administration is developed from ICCH 9-378-554, and 9-378-555 *Lead Poisoning*, 1975; ICCH 9-372-146 and 9-372-147, *Addiction Control in New York City*; and interview of Gordon Chase (November 27, 1978) and an analysis by Frederick O'R. Hayes in *Profiles in Change and Innovation* (unpublished). The statistics are reported in Office of the Deputy Mayor, *The New York City Productivity Program*, various reports, 1971–73, and an interview of Gordon Chase by the author.

p. 166 The account of the welfare productivity effort is developed primarily from the author's own experience. See also Citizens' Budget Commission, *The New York City Productivity Program: the Dept. of Social Services*, January 1974. Caseload and transaction data are from: The Temporary Commission on City Finances, Twelfth Interim Report to the Mayor, *Public Assistance Programs in New York City: Some Proposals for Reform*, February 1977. Quotations from the Citizens' Budget Commission report appear on pp. 19–20.

p. 167 The account of the productivity effort in the police department relies primarly on the analysis in Hayes *Profiles in Change*.

pp. 168–169 The detail on other agencies is from The Office of the Deputy Mayor, *The New York City Productivity Program* and from an Andrew Kerr interview.

p. 170 Blumenthal quote comes from *The New York Times*, October 20, 1973; Beame is quoted in ibid., September 7, 1973.

VIII. THE LINDSAY BALANCE SHEET—I

pp. 172–174 "Pushover" quotation from Wyndham Robertson, "Going Broke the New York Way," *Fortune*, August 1975, 146. The data on employee wages is developed from Data in The Temporary Commission on City Finances, various reports, and surveys and other comparative material on file with the city's Office of Labor Relations. Additional survey material was furnished by the research staff of District Council 37. The comparative city analyses are from data published by the U.S. Bureau of the Census, *Local Government Finances* for the respective years. Data on comparative living costs are from the U.S. Bureau of the Census, *Statistical Abstract of the United States* for the respective years.

p. 175 For the analysis of city pensions, James Beirne, Office of the City Actuary, supplied various internal reports. The most careful recent survey of city pension benefits is The Mayor's Management Advisory Board, *Pensions* (April 1976). I also consulted The New York State Commission to Make a Study of the Municipal Government Operations of New York City, *New York City Pensions* January, 1973; New York State Permanent Commission on Public Employee Pension and Retirement Systems, *Recommendations for a New Pension Plan for Public Employees*, March 1976; Program Planners, Inc., *A Survey of Municipal Employee Pension Benefits*, December 1975. The most complete analysis (by now somewhat dated) is Martin E. Segal and Associates, Inc., *The Retirement Systems of the City of New York*, 9 vols., 1962–64. For the development of public pension benefits in New York and elsewhere in the country, see William C. Greenough and Francis P. King, *Pension Plans and Public Policy* (New York: Columbia, 1976); Robert Tilove, *Public Employee Pension Funding* (New York: Columbia, 1976); and Barbara P. Patocka, "Public Funds: The Herculean Task is Under Way," *Pensions* 2 (May/June 1973):33–48.

pp. 176–177 These tables are derived from data in The Mayor's Management Advisory Committee, *Pensions*.

p. 178 The table is derived from Segal, vol. 2, *The City Systems Compared with the Retirement Plans of Other Employees, Public and Private*.

pp. 179–181 The table on fringe benefits is from Temporary Commission On City Finances, Seventh Interim

Report to the Mayor, *The Fiscal Impact of Fringe Benefits and Leave Benefits: Some Proposals for Reform,* June 1976, p. 48. The "comprehensive survey of municipal fringe benefits" is Labor-Management Relations Service, *National Survey of Employee Benefits for Full-time Personnel of United States Municipalities* (Washington, D.C.) various, 1971–75. The comparative analysis is drawn from various surveys on file with the city's Office of Labor Relations.

p. 182 This table was developed from U.S. Bureau of the Census, *Local Government Finances* for the respective years.

p. 183 This table developed from ibid. Per pupil data is from mimeo materials furnished by the New York State Division of the Budget; comparative educational costs also may be found in *The Report of the New York State Commission on the Quality, Cost, and Financing of Elementary and Secondary Education,* 3 vols., 1972.

p. 184 The labor department surveys come from "How Salaries of Large Cities Compare with Industry and Federal Pay," *Monthly Labor Review,* November 1976, pp. 23–28. The quotation beginning "With respect to [non-welfare] expenditure . . ." is from Bahl, Campbell, and Greytak, *Taxes, Expenditures,* p. 173.

pp. 185–189 The discussion of welfare costs and caseloads is drawn from The Temporary Commission on City Finances, *Public Assistance Programs;* Jackson and Johnson, *Protest by the Poor;* C. Peter Rydell, *Welfare Caseload Dynamics in New York City* (New York: The Rand Institute, 1974); David deFerranti et al., *The Welfare and Non-welfare Poor in New York City* (New York: The Rand Institute, 1974); David W. Lyon et al., *Multiple Welfare Benefits in New York City* (Santa Monica, Calif.: The Rand Corporation, 1976). National data are from The U.S. Social and Rehabilitation Service, *Public Assistance Statistics.*

pp. 190–191 The Medicaid data is drawn primarily from: The Temporary Commission on City Finances, *The Medicaid Program in New York City.* The administrative and legislative background is from: Robert Stevens and Rosemary Stevens, *Welfare Medicine in America: A Case Study of Medicaid* (New York: The Free Press, 1974.)

p. 192 For higher education and hospitals, see the sources cited in Chapter II.

IX. THE LINDSAY BALANCE SHEET—II

pp. 195–196 For changes in the revenue structure, see the data assembled by the Temporary Commission on City Finances, *The City in Transition,* pp. 274–94. The discussion of local taxes draws from The Temporary Commission on City Finances, Ninth Interim Report to the Mayor, *The Effects of Taxation on Manufacturing in New York City,* December 1976, and Bahl, Campbell, and Greytak, *Taxes, Expenditures,* pp. 85–93 (for shifts in the real estate tax) and p. 129 (for the calculation of income tax elasticities).

pp. 197–199 In general, for pension financing see the sources cited for the previous chapter, pp. 333–40. In addition, see George E. Peterson, "Finance," in Nathan Glazer and William Gorham, eds., *The Urban Predicament* (Washington: the Urban Institute, 1976), p. 46; and David Stanley, *Cities in Trouble* (Columbus, Ohio: Academy for Contemporary Problems, 1976). With respect to the mention in the note on p. 198 on alternative methods of valuing city contribution to pensions: Since the City lags its contribution to the actuarial funds by two years but then pays with interest, it can be plausibly argued that the deferred city obligation is a note—that is, an asset of the funds. Under reformed funding assumptions, the city obligation is not credited, however, until it is actually paid.

pp. 199–203 The discussion of state and local debt relies primarily on New York State Moreland Act Commission on the Urban Development Corporation and Other State Financing Agencies, *Restoring Credit and Confidence: A Reform Program for New York State and its Public Authorities,* 1976 (particularly the tables on pp. 78–82). The Hayes quotation on p. 200 is from an interview. The table on city short-term debt is developed from *Annual Reports of the Comptroller.* The note on academic awareness of the impending fiscal crisis: Bahl, Campbell, and Greytak, *Taxes, Expenditures,* points clearly to the growing problem but is too technical an analysis to be readily accessible. The contrary view is represented by Eli Ginzberg et al., *New York Is Very Much Alive: A Manpower View* (New York: McGraw-Hill, 1973).

pp. 206–207 The discussion of fire dispatching policy is from Edward H. Blum, *Deployment Response of the New York City Fire Project* (New York: The Rand Institute, 1972).

pp. 211–212 The material on the scandals in Lindsay's administration was drawn from accounts in *The New York Times.* The Brownsville church episode is documented in *Urban Renewal in Brownsville,* pp. 49–55. The Columbia University researchers were quoted in *The New York Times,* November 25, 1973.

X. THE CLUBHOUSE RETURNS

pp. 215–218 The chronology of Beame's campaign and Beame's accession to office is drawn primarily from *The New York Times,* supplemented by interviews with various city officials. Essential background was provided by James Cavanagh in an interview.

p. 218 The chronology of the 1973–74 and 1974–75 budgets on this and the following pages is reconstructed from *The New York Times.* Financial data is drawn from the *Annual Report of the Comptroller* and the *Expense Budget* for the years in question, supplemented by the compilations in the various reports of the Temporary Commission on City Finances. Economic and employment data is drawn primarily from the compilations in *The New York Fact Book.* "had cash hidden . . ." David Grossman, quoted in *The New York Times* May 16, 1973.

p. 219 "exercise in political . . ." ibid. June 20, 1973; "scoffed" Ibid. December 20, 1973.

p. 221 Wilson's "Why don't you just borrow?" was cited by Cavanagh in an interview. The explanation of the use of surplus pension contributions is from Bernard Jump, Occasional Paper No. 16, *Financing Public*

Employee Retirement Programs in New York City: Trends Since 1965 and Projections to 1980 (Maxwell School of Citizenship and Public Affairs, Syracuse University, 1975).

p. 222 "Smashing political victory" comes from *The New York Times*, June 22, 1979. "Financial Collapse." For the events leading up to the fiscal crisis itself, a useful chronology can be found in vol. 1 of S.E.C., *Staff Report on Transactions in Securities of the City of New York*, August 1977, but the report must be read in conjunction with Special Counsel to the City of New York, *Response of the City of New York to the Report of the Staff of the S.E.C. on Transactions in Securities of the City of New York*, 1977. In several instances, key events, which seem to be well documented but tend to exculpate city officials, are omitted from the S.E.C. staff chronology. A chronology is also given in Fred Ferretti, *The Year the Big Apple Went Bust* (New York: Putnam, 1976). The data on finance and the economy are drawn from the same sources as those used in the previous chapters.

p. 223 The Gerard quotations are from S.E.C., *Staff Report*, Vol. 4, pp. 14, 18. The First Boston memorandum is quoted in ibid., Vol. 1, 63a.

p. 224 Data on the tax-exempt market factors come from Peterson, "Finance," in Glazer and Gorham, *The Urban Predicament*, p. 69–70. The "beat us over the head" remark is quoted in S.E.C., *Staff Report*, Vol. 1, p. 201.

p. 225 The quotations from Beame came from ibid., p. 84. Goldin is quoted in ibid., p. 49; joint press release, in ibid., p. 59; hiring increases cited in *The New York Times* November 18, 1974; *New Yorker* article cited in S.E.C. *Staff Report*, Vol. 2, p. 60.

p. 226 The *Times* editorial mentioned appeared in *The New York Times*, Febru, 1975.

p. 227 The "generally plenty of fat . . ." quote is cited in S.E.C., *Staff Report*, Vol. 1, p. 111; Goldin is quoted in *ibid.*, p. 118.

p. 229 The "hanky-panky" quote appears in ibid., p. 147. The ". . . very damaging disclosure statement" is mentioned in *ibid.*, p. 182; "providing information . . ." in ibid., p. 172. Beame's ". . . take the BANs into their portfolio . . ." quote appears in ibid., p. 140.

pp. 230–231 The "trigger a real panic . . ." quote is from ibid., p. 187. "The 'scare' talk . . ." press release is quoted in ibid., p. 208; "disaster," ibid., p. 30. Cavanagh's "The banks and us are in a community . . ." comes from ibid., p. 209; his remark that the banks had a "real problem," from ibid., p. 247. The "because it was sort of historically . . ." quote is in ibid., vol. 4, p. 69. The White and Case letter appears in ibid., pp. 252–53.

EPILOGUE

The chronology is drawn, in general, from *The New York Times*, supplemented by Ferretti, *The Year the Big Apple Went Bust.* A good summary of the mechanics of the various financial arrangements appears in recent prospectuses prepared by the city for the issuance of debt. One good example is *Official Statement of the City of New York Relating to the Issuance of General Obligation Revenue Anticipation Notes*, February 1979. An analysis of the interlaced debt and spending problems appears in Charles Brecher and Miriam Cukier, "New York City's Financial Plans: Lessons in Fiscal Reality," *City Almanac*, June 1978. See also various issues of the *Fiscal Observer*. Details of the city's current financial problems are in Staff Report, Emergency Financial Control Board, *A Review of the New York City Four-Year Financial Plan: FY 1979–82*, June 1978, and other reports of the board.

p. 233 Beame's complaint about a cash boycott" is cited in Ferretti, *The Year the Big Apple Went Bust*, p. 199; "the best organized wildcat strike . . . ," ibid., p. 233. Rohatyn's "monthly miracle" quote comes from *The New York Times*, August, 1975.

p. 234 Ford's "Drop Dead" message is reported in Ferretti, *The Year the Big Apple Went Bust*, p. 358.

p. 235 The "hocking the stove . . ." remark is cited in *The New York Times*, March 12, 1977.

p. 237 The Bronx survey is on file with the South Bronx Development Office of the City of New York.

p. 239 The Grossman and Cavanaugh quotations come from interviews.

p. 240 The quotation from Goldmark is in a letter to the author.

Index